Did Dōgen Go to China?

What He Wrote and When He Wrote It

STEVEN HEINE

OXFORD
UNIVERSITY PRESS

2006

OXFORD
UNIVERSITY PRESS

Oxford University Press, Inc., publishes works that further
Oxford University's objective of excellence
in research, scholarship, and education.

Oxford   New York
Auckland   Cape Town   Dar es Salaam   Hong Kong   Karachi
Kuala Lumpur   Madrid   Melbourne   Mexico City   Nairobi
New Delhi   Shanghai   Taipei   Toronto

With offices in
Argentina   Austria   Brazil   Chile   Czech Republic   France   Greece
Guatemala   Hungary   Italy   Japan   Poland   Portugal   Singapore
South Korea   Switzerland   Thailand   Turkey   Ukraine   Vietnam

Copyright © 2006 by Oxford University Press, Inc.

Published by Oxford University Press, Inc.
198 Madison Avenue, New York, New York 10016

www.oup.com

Oxford is a registered trademark of Oxford University Press

Library of Congress Cataloging-in-Publication Data

Heine, Steven, 1950–
Did Dōgen go to China? : what he wrote and when he wrote it / Steven Heine
  p. cm.
Includes bibliographical references.
ISBN-13 978-0-19-530570-8; 978-0-19-530592-0 (pbk.)
ISBN 0-19-530570-1; 0-19-530592-2 (pbk.)
 1. Dōgen, 1200–1253. 2. Rujingchanshi, 1163–1228. I. Title.
BQ9449.D657H43 2006
294.3'927'092—dc22   2005044915

9 8 7 6 5 4 3 2
Printed in the United States of America
on acid-free paper

Preface: A Fisherman's Dream

Book Title and Subtitle

The title and subtitle of this book both seek to reopen an investigation of key elements in understanding Dōgen's life and works and to reexamine some of the most basic issues in Dōgen studies. The main title indicates that the book challenges the very heart of the "Ur-myth" of Dōgen's relation to Ju-ching, including the records of his experiences with and citations from the Chinese mentor. The book will reconstruct the context of Dōgen's travels and his reflections on China by taking a critical look at traditional sources, both by and about Dōgen. This exploration is carried out in light of recent Japanese scholarship, which has been questioning just about every angle and nuance of the largely pseudo-historical traditional account, in the constructive sense of reconsidering and reevaluating fundamental ideas that have been taken for granted as representing set answers to complex questions. Remaining fixed on apparently tried and true approaches may well impede our efforts for a big catch, to use the fisherman's metaphor that introduces this preface and that will be explained below.

There is a reciprocal relation between the issues indicated in the book's title and subtitle. The significance of Dōgen's relation to Ju-ching is crucial for understanding the way he appropriated Chinese influences in creating a distinctive Japanese brand of Zen. As the subtitle of the book indicates, the question of what transpired in China leads to considerable dialogue and debate regarding an analysis of the sequence of Dōgen's writings, since some of the basic facts and features of his collected works have been obscured or misunderstood because of a variety of historical or hermeneutic factors. These range from lost or possibly apocryphal manuscripts to sectarian orthodoxy and other examples of methodological bias or limitations in interpretive perspectives. As a corrective, this book critically evaluates recent Japanese scholarship about the history of Dōgen's works, some of which helps clarify and some of which, in my analysis, tends to obscure further the sequence of his writings.

In following the lead of scholarly trends in Japan, which are not without their own flaws and lacunae, this book assesses assumptions and stereotypes, fills in gaps of knowledge, and overturns some misleading notions that have been accepted as commonplace in Western scholarship since the boom in Dōgen studies began three decades ago. The aim is not to tarnish the images of the great figures by denying the possibility of their meeting, but rather to illuminate connections from a comprehensive historiographic and bibliographic standpoint in order to understand more clearly what and when Dōgen wrote as well as why he wrote it.

The first question of the subtitle, What did Dōgen write? appears rather straightforward, since he is known for the *Shōbōgenzō* and—more recently in what is available in English—the *Eihei kōroku*. Both are collections of sermons dealing with kōan records and other examples of classical Chinese Ch'an literature, particularly rules and regulations regarding monastic life. However, this deceptively simple query is problematic when one considers that there are several versions of the *Shōbōgenzō*, most of which were edited and perhaps altered centuries after his death, as well as the *Eihei kōroku* and other main texts such as the *Shōbōgenzō zuimonki* and *Eihei shingi*.

The complexity of interpretive issues raised by the multiple editions of the *Shōbōgenzō* and other texts is compounded when one considers the second question: When did Dōgen write his works? For example, many accounts, in viewing the *Shōbōgenzō* as an autonomous, unified text, do not acknowledge that it is constituted of discrete segments that often reflect the specific context of the periods in which they were composed, recorded, or edited rather than a grand unity of design or purpose. Furthermore, it is important to recognize that Dōgen's writings are very much interrelated with key issues in his biography. These include the travel and return from China, the establishment of monastic centers at Kōshōji in Kyoto during the mid-1230s and at Eiheiji in the Echizen mountains during the mid-1240s, as well as his visit to the temporary capital at Kamakura in the late-1240s and final return to Kyoto near the end of his life.

The two hermeneutic issues indicated in the book's subtitle converge with the question in the main title in that the issue of when Dōgen developed a focus on Chinese influences can best be seen through an analysis of why sources about the trip to China were generated during later phases of his career. This issue is examined in light of a new theory I propose that divides Dōgen's career into three main phases (early, middle, late) rather than the conventional two-period or early and late phase approach. The crucial middle period that I highlight was marked not only by the physical or geographical move from Kyoto to Echizen, but also by a turn toward a Sinitic style of monasticism. This is evidenced in the transition from the informal, vernacular (*kana*) *jishu*-style sermons of the *Shōbōgenzō* to the formal, Sino-Japanese (*kanbun*) *jōdō*-style sermons of the *Eihei kōroku*.

These changes were accompanied by a shift from a universal stance to sectarian divisiveness, which has been criticized by some commentators as a diminishing of Dōgen's religious vision and talents. Yet an interesting feature is that the writings of the middle period demonstrate the heights of Dōgen's Japanese literary skills in both *Shōbōgenzō* fascicles and *waka* poetry, in addition to the beginning of an enhancement of the *kanbun*-style compositions. Citations of Ju-ching particularly flourish during this phase, which lasted for about three years, from 1241, when Dōgen's monastic community was joined by a number of former members of the Daruma school (following Ejō's conversion seven years before), to 1244 and the establishment of Daibutsuji temple in Echizen.

To appreciate the significance of linking Chinese influences to a theory of the stages of Dōgen's literary productivity, it is also necessary to consider the issues of textual formation by evaluating recent developments and diverse theories that have emerged in Dōgen studies in both Japan and the West. Although scholars have often pointed out the importance of particular events for understanding some of the writings, most studies have been vague or misleading about the sequential development of the compositions, because of false assumptions or simplistic notions about early versus late periods in Dōgen's career.

How is Ju-ching's influence related to the surge of creative impulses of this challenging yet dynamic phase? In considering this issue, I will explore some of the important differences between Mount T'ien-t'ung, where Dōgen trained in China under Ju-ching, and Eiheiji temple, established by Dōgen in Japan. In contrast to a common view, I argue that Eiheiji should not be considered "Mount T'ien-t'ung East" but that it reflects different styles of construction and religious practice. It is important to analyze the differences between Dōgen and other Chinese Ch'an (Ju-ching) and Japanese Zen (Eisai and Enni) religious leaders.

Of Fishing and Dreaming

The title of this preface suggests the need for an ongoing, open-ended interpretive process for an understanding of Dōgen's life and writings. The image of a fisherman's dream alludes to a foundation legend (*engi*) about the establishment of Kōshōji temple and evokes a complex nexus of elements revolving around the image of dreams. Kōshōji was Dōgen's first main temple and was established in 1233 in the village of Fukakusa, at the time a relatively out-of-the-way countryside location (the name literally means "deep grass"). Fukakusa was a favorite retreat site for both courtiers and recluses seeking to escape the somewhat corrupted and troubled urban center, though today it is a congested lower middle-class suburb in the outskirts of Kyoto. In 1236 Kōshōji featured perhaps the first examples of Sung dynasty Ch'an Monks Hall and Dharma Hall buildings created in Japan, which were no doubt a sign that Dōgen was already becoming somewhat successful in attracting many followers. It is possible that at this stage he was considered too popular by the Tendai mainstream, which sought to squelch upstart movements. Just a few years later, in 1241, a much larger and grander Rinzai Zen temple, Tōfukuji, modeled after the Ch'an Five Mountains monastic system, was being constructed just to the north of Kōshōji. This construction had the support of the Tendai establishment at Enryakuji temple on Mount Hiei and of the Fujiwara family. Enni Ben'en, a monk who first visited China in 1235, a decade after Dōgen's travels, and returned in 1241, was named head of Tōfukuji in 1243, the year Dōgen left the Kyoto area for Echizen. The various reasons for the move in relation to influences from Ch'an as well as pressures from Japanese Buddhist institutions will be discussed in detail in Chapter 5.

The original Kōshōji built in Fukakusa was first left to the disciple Gijun, a former member of the proscribed Daruma school, but it quickly fell into a state of disrepair shortly after Dōgen's move, initiating a long process whereby the Sōtō sect spread mainly in the northern countryside while Rinzai Zen came to dominate the Kyoto area. In 1649, as part of Tokugawa era sectarian reforms, which also led to the formation of the comprehensive 90-plus fascicle edition *Shōbōgenzō* and related developments in the appropriation of Dōgen's writings, the temple was relocated and rebuilt by Bannan Eishu in the town of Uji, south of Kyoto and midway to Nara. Long known for the presence of the Fujiwara clan's Heian-era temple, Byōdōin, with its utopian gardens, Uji was also the setting for many of the events in the final episodes of the *Tale of Genji*, which have been featured in a recent tourism campaign. Ten years after the move of Kōshōji, the town of Uji would also become home to the head temple of the new Ōbaku Zen sect, Manpukuji temple, established in 1659. The Ōbaku sect, an anomalous development in isolationist Tokugawa Japan, was based on a migration of Ming Chinese masters led by Ingen Ryūki, who were able to gain a foothold as the third Zen movement, known for an emphasis on the precepts and for combining meditation with *nembutsu* practice. The dozens of other small temples and shrines around the town make it a rich area for historical and cultural studies of religion.

Uji is situated in a magnificent river valley that is a kind of fisherman's paradise. An elegant, classical vermillion-painted wood bridge has recently been constructed near the fishing area, since the main bridge spanning the Uji River, which was for years left in the traditional style, was rebuilt to serve as a concrete automobile thoroughfare. According to legend, when the temple was to be moved to Uji, a monk was sent in advance to select the appropriate location and Kōshōji was eventually placed on a hillside on the west bank of the river, opposite Byōdōin. There are small rushing streams on both sides of the pathway leading from the temple at the top of the hill down to a road by the riverside that now heads in the direction of the train station. Since the flow of these waters makes a beautiful musical sound, the path is known as the *kotozaka*, or "hill of the koto strings," and is particularly attractive when surrounded by *momiji* or crimson leaves in autumn.

In one version of the legend, the ideal temple site was disclosed by a local deity disguised as a fisherman who appeared to the emissary in a dream. In another version, which echoes similar legends for other temples throughout Japan, the god was away fishing when the monk came to make an inquiry. Apologizing for being a deficient host, the god granted the monk a wish by offering a premier location, and in a variation of this version of the legend their delayed encounter took place in a dream state, either the monk's or the god's. Dream is also an important metaphor in Dōgen's writings, where, as in other forms of Buddhist thought, it functions either as a symbol of illusion that is a lesser state than ordinary reality or as representative of an ultimate

Fisherman's paradise in the heart of Uji town

standpoint beyond the mundane realm. The Rinzai master Musō Soseki called his dialogues with an inquirer "Muchū mondō" (Dialogues in a Dream). Dōgen's fascicle "Muchū setsumu," which can be translated as "Unraveling (or Disclosing) a Dream Within a Dream," extends the conventional meaning of the term to suggest the extremes of delusion compounding delusion or of realization surpassing realization.

The image of a fisherman's dream, whether of human or divine origin, also evokes the spectacular location of the temple by the Uji River and becomes a rhetorical device for interpreting the stream of Dōgen's work. Dōgen's writing is like a mighty river flowing from the mountains in which we—Zen scholars, students, practitioners, and other more casual and merely curious readers and observers—are fishing for big and small catches by using our impressions and opinion as edible bait. Yet we must also realize that while we are valiantly trying to reel in the best of the prey as the stream rushes by, there are so many more fish going uncaught or undetected (representing ideas that are neglected, overlooked, or suppressed) that it may not be clear what the real goal is.

Contents

The first chapter in Part I, on Methodological Issues, " 'A Dharma-Transmitter Who Went to Sung China,' " examines the impact of Chinese Ch'an on Dōgen's overall career development and critically assesses some of the traditional and modern sources that often conflate hagiography with historiography. Chapter 2, "Gone Fishin': Sources and Re-Sources," discusses the multiple editions of Dōgen's main writings, including the Shōbōgenzō (95-, 75-, 60-, 28-, and 12-fascicle versions), Eihei kōroku, Shōbōgenzō zuimonki, and Eihei shingi. It also evaluates recent Japanese and Western scholarship by analyzing several main theories of Dōgen's career trajectory characterized as the Decline and Renewal Theories and laying out a theory of three main periods in Dōgen's life subdivided into seven stages.

In Part II, on Theory of Periodization, Chapter 3, "The Early Period: Dōgen Went to China," examines the formation of Dōgen's canon of writings by discussing the materials he studied both before and during his travels to China in the mid-1220s. It evaluates and deconstructs the pseudo-historical quality of sources dealing with the trip, and it assesses the role of his earliest writings after his return to Japan, especially Bendōwa. The next two chapters cover the crucial middle period. Chapter 4, "The Middle Period, Part I: The Kyoto Cycle," discusses Dōgen's earliest approaches both to using kōans and to developing monastic rules in the texts produced in the 1230s. Chapter 5, "The Middle Period, Part II: The Echizen Cycle," explores the complex reasons for his move from Kyoto to Echizen in 1243. It shows how this move affects the formation of the Shōbōgenzō and renewed interest in Ju-ching, as well as the transition in the early days at Eiheiji from the *jishu* or informal style of sermons of the *Shōbōgenzō* to the *jōdō* or formal style of the *Eihei kōroku*.

The final chapter, Chapter 6, "The Late Period: Outpost Administrator or Brilliant Innovator?" explores a variety of developments in Dōgen's later career at Eiheiji both before and after his trip to Kamakura in 1247–1248, including a reliance on yet criticism of the records of Hung-chih and Ju-ching, a turn toward an emphasis on karmic causality in the later portions of the *Eihei kōroku*, 12-fascicle *Shōbōgenzō*, and *Hōkyōki*, as well as the integration of supernatural elements and ritual repentance in the evangelical efforts at Eiheiji to disseminate the teachings to lay followers. In addition, the chapter presents concluding remarks on the relative merit and weight of various theories.

Acknowledgments

Some of the material in this book has been reworked from a series of my publications on Dōgen, including the following:

"Critical Buddhism and Dōgen's *Shōbōgenzō*: The Debate over the 75-fascicle and 12-fascicle Texts," *Japanese Journal of Religious Studies* 21/1 (1994): 37–72

"The Dōgen Canon: Dōgen's Pre-*Shōbōgenzō* Writings and the Question of Change in His Later Works," *Japanese Journal of Religious Studies* 24/1–2 (1997): 39–85

"After the Storm: Matsumoto Shirō's Transition from 'Critical Buddhism' to 'Critical Theology,' " *Japanese Journal of Religious Studies* 28/1–2 (2001): 133–146

"Why (Not) Dōgen?" *Buddhadharma* (Fall 2002): 71–74

"Abbreviation or Aberration: The Role of the *Shushōgi* in Modern Sōtō Zen Buddhism," in Steven Heine and Charles S. Prebish, eds., *Buddhism in the Modern World: Adaptations of an Ancient Tradition*. New York: Oxford University Press, 2003, pp. 169–192

"Did Dōgen Go to China? Problematizing Dōgen's Relation to Ju-ching and Chinese Ch'an," *Japanese Journal of Religious Studies* 30/1–2 (2003): 27–59

"The *Eihei kōroku:* The Record of Dōgen's Later Period at Eihei-ji Temple," in Steven Heine and Dale S. Wright, eds., *The Zen Canon: Understanding the Classic Texts*. New York: Oxford University Press, 2004, pp. 245–273

"Dōgen and the Precepts, Revisited," in Damien Keown and

Mavis Fenn, eds., *From Ancient India to Modern America: Buddhist Studies in Honor of Charles Prebish*. New York: Routledge Curzon, 2005, pp. 11–31

"An Analysis of Dōgen's *Eihei goroku*: Distillation or Distortion?" in Steven Heine and Dale S. Wright, eds., *Zen Classics: Formative Texts in the History of Zen Buddhism*. New York: Oxford University Press, 2005, pp. 113–136

"Is Eiheiji Temple 'Mount T'ien-t'ung East'? Geo-Ritual Perspectives on the Transition from Chinese Ch'an to Japanese Zen," in Steven Heine and Dale S. Wright, eds., *Zen Ritual*. New York: Oxford University Press, forthcoming

I thank several faculty members at Komazawa University who, over the years, have extended themselves to help enable my research on Dōgen, including Ishii Seijun, Ishii Shūdō, Ishikawa Rikizan, Kawamura Kōdō, Matsumoto Shirō, and Yoshizu Yoshihide, in addition to other professors in Japan, He Yansheng, Masao Abe, and Sueki Fumihiko. Numerous Western scholars from whom I have benefited include David Barnhill, Carl Bielefeldt, William Bodiford, Bernard Faure, Griffith Foulk, Chris Ives, Tom Kasulis, Hee-Jin Kim, James Kodera, Gereon Kopf, Dan Leighton, John Daido Loori, Shohaku Okumura, Mario Poceski, Morten Schlutter, Pamela Winfield, and Dale Wright, among many others. Maria Cubau, Aviva Menashe, and Cristina Sasso helped prepare and proofread the manuscript.

I also appreciate the following illuminative, quasi-apocryphal comment: "We go to bed with the beautiful vixen of philosophy and wake up in the morning with the hag of history" (Carl Bielefeldt, circa 1992).

Abbreviations

The reader may note the use of abbreviations in citing the following works:

DZZ	*Dōgen zenji zenshū*, 7 vols., ed. Kagamishima Genryū, et al.
EK	*Eihei kōroku*, 10 vols., in DZZ III–IV.
SH	*Shōbōgenzō*, 95 vols., in DZZ I–II.
SZ	*Shōbōgenzō zuimonki*, 6 vols., ed. Ikeda Rōsan.
Taishō	*Taishō shinshū daizōkyō*, 100 vols.

In addition, the following abbreviations are used: C. Chinese, J. Japanese, Rpt. Reprint, Skt. Sanskrit.

Contents

Author at memorial for Dōgen's entry to harbor at Ning-po

PART I

Historical and Methodological Issues

Dōgen's Literary Productivity

TABLE I.

Year	Jishu	Jōdō	Other Writings and Biographical Notes
1223			Departs for China 2.22 with Myōzen and two other monks, and arrives 4.2
1224			Itinerancy among Five Mountains temples, meeting abbots and monks, viewing *shisho*
1225			Meets Ju-ching 5.1; Myōzen dies 5.27; *shinjin datsuraku* and receives precepts in 7 mo.
1226			*Kanbun* verses (in EK 10), hears Ju-ching sermons in various parts of compound
1227			Returns to Kenninji in 8 mo.; *Shari sōdenki* (on Myōzen relics); Ju-ching dies 7.17
1228			*Kanbun* verses; receives Jakuen from China
1229			First visit of Ejō at Kenninji
1230			Moves to temporary hermitage in Fukakusa
1231			Settles at An'yōin; first *hōgo* (Dharma-talk) for nun; *Bendōwa* (doctrinal essay) 8.15
1232			Holds first summer retreat (*ango*) at An'yōin
1233	2		*Fukanzazengi*[a] (meditation manual); Kannondōri or Kōshō-hōrinji (Kōshōji) opened
1234	0		*Gakudōyōjinshū* (doctrinal essay); Ejō becomes disciple, begins *Shōbōgenzō zuimonki*
1235	0		*Mana sanbyakusoku* (collection of 300 kōans)
1236	0		*Juko* (verse comments on 90 kōans in EK 9); Kōshōji Monks Hall opened 10.15
1237	0		*Tenzokyōkun* (instructions to cook)[b]
1238	1		*Shōbōgenzō zuimonki* (recorded sayings) completed
1239	3		*Kannon dōri-in sōdō konryūkanshinsho* (monastic rules); *Jūundōshiki* (rules)
1240	6	31[c]	*Kōshōji goroku* (EK 1); *hōgo* (in EK 8)[d]; 12-SH "Kesa kudoku"
A 1241	9	48	Daruma school disciples Ekan, Gikai, Giin, Gien, Gijun join Kōshōji
1242	16	26	Receives *Ju-ching yü-lu* from China
1243	22	21	Enni Ben'en, returned from China in 1241, becomes abbot at Tōfukuji
to c. 7/16	(4)		Moves to Echizen at Kippōji and Yamashibudera temples—key to Decline Theory
after	(18)		
1244	10	0	*Taidaiko* (rules)[b]; 12-SH "Hotsubodaishin"; *waka* on first snow in Echizen
B to 3/9	(10)		Construction begun on Daibutsuji—key to Three Periods Theory
after	(0)		Daibutsuji opened 7.18
1245	5	15	First summer retreat at Daibutsuji
1246	1	74	*Bendōhō* (zazen)[b]; *Chiji shingi* (rules)[b]; *Fushukuhampō* (rules)[b]; Eiheiji named 6.15
1247	0	35	Departs for Kamakura 8.3; presents 12 *waka* to Hōjō Tokiyori
C 1248	0	52	Returns from Kamakura 3.13, delivers EK 3.251—key to Renewal Theory

Year	Jishu	Jōdō	Other Writings and Biographical Notes
after 3/14		(52)	
1249	0	58	*Eiheiji shuryō shingi* (rules for library)[b]; *Jūroku rakan genzuiki* (ritual)
1250	0	52	Eiheiji receives Tripitaka from Hatano Yoshishige; "Senmen" preached
1251	0	68	
1252	0	51	"Genjōkōan" edited; becomes ill in autumn
1253	0	0	"Hachidainingaku," and editing of 12-SH texts; *Hōkyōki*[c]; dies in Kyoto 8.28
Total	75	531	

A—Conversion of Daruma school monks—key to the **Decline Theory** of sectarian pressures

B—Transition from *jishu* to *jōdō* lectures, key to the **Three Periods Theory** of diverse literary styles with emphasis on creative productivity of the overlooked Middle Period

C—Return from Kamakura—key to the **Renewal Theory** view spiritual rebirth

[a] The main edition (Tempuku) of this text was completed in 1233.

[b] Contained in *Eihei shingi*.

[c] These 31 *jōdō* are undated and may have been presented any year beginning 1236.

[d] The *hōgo* are undated and may have been delivered any time from 1231 to 1243.

[e] This text, which contains Dōgen's dialogues with Ju-ching in China between 1225 and 1227, is undated and may have been recorded at any time after Dōgen's return to Japan.

I

"A Dharma-Transmitter Who Traveled to Sung China"

From Sung Ch'an to Kamakura Zen

This book provides a comprehensive examination of the diverse writings of Dōgen (1200–1253), the founder of Sōtō (C. Ts'ao-tung) Zen Buddhism in Japan. (These writings are outlined in Table 1.) It clarifies how and when the works were composed and compiled in relation to central elements of his overall career, especially his travels and complex associations with China and Chinese Ch'an Buddhism. The formative period of Zen encompassing the origins of the various streams of the enduring Sōtō and Rinzai (C. Lin-chi) sects, as well as the short-lived yet historically significant Daruma school, which influenced Dōgen's movement, was very much dependent on Sung dynasty Chinese religion and society. Dōgen's reputation is based largely on his role as one of the first and most important vehicles contributing to the transmission and transition of Ch'an in China to Zen in Japan. According to the colophon (*okugaki*) of Dōgen's earliest major composition, the didactic essay *Bendōwa* was composed in 1231 by "a *sramanera* [J. *shamon*] who transmitted the Dharma by traveling to [lit., entering into] Sung China," and who used Ch'an as a prototype for Japan.[1] The "Shisho" fascicle, composed a decade later, which discusses how Dōgen was shown five authentic Ch'an transmission certificates when he visited temples of the prestigious, government-supported Five Mountains (C. Wu-shan, J. Gozan) system, including Mount T'ien-t'ung (J. Tendōzan), is similarly signed by a "*sramanera* who transmitted the Dharma from Sung China."[2]

In analyzing his major texts, particularly the *Shōbōgenzō* in its multiple editions and the *Eihei kōroku* in addition to the *Shōbōgenzō zuimonki* and *Eihei shingi*, I seek to illumine how Dōgen's literary production expresses a distinctive vision for constructing a new monastery and a style of training appropriate for diverse sectors of monks and lay followers. Dōgen's writings, which are generally collections of various kinds of sermons or instructions on clerical behavior, show that he appropriated and assimilated Chinese approaches to the Japanese socioreligious environment. The Ch'an sources he consulted include the records of dialogues and sayings about the accomplishments of inspirational masters of the golden age in the T'ang dynasty, as well as Sung monastic rites such as oral discourses and administrative functions that he is said to have observed firsthand. Dōgen at times quotes verbatim or nearly reproduces the Ch'an originals. His primary contribution and innovation are a remarkable knowledge and skill in citing creatively while often criticizing or revising Chinese sources through an inventive fusion of a Sino-Japanese "proetic" (prose-poetic) style of writing replete with ingenious punning and wordplay between languages as well as philosophical nuances embedded in lyrical imagery.[3]

The main thesis of this book is that the impact of the "China factor," initiated at the outset of Dōgen's career with studies of Chinese texts and travels to the mainland lasting a little over four years (from spring 1223 to fall 1227), became increasingly important. Dōgen continually turned to Ch'an models for developing an innovative approach to the formation of the Japanese Zen monastic institution in later stages of his career. However, the full significance of the ever-expanding role of Chinese influences on Dōgen's Zen has generally been overlooked or misinterpreted in Western scholarship. An indicator of this lacuna is the relative lack of translations and studies—until recently, when an excellent new rendering was released—of the *Eihei kōroku*, a collection of sermons, verses, and kōan commentaries written in *kanbun* (hybrid Chinese or Sino-Japanese) and based on Sung ritual precedent, which ranks in importance with the *kana* (vernacular) *Shōbōgenzō*.[4] The *Shōbōgenzō* has received a vast amount of attention, deservedly so although many basic issues about this complex text are still much misunderstood, but the focus has been out of proportion to its role in the general Dōgen canon.

The misconceptions about the *Shōbōgenzō* and the *Eihei kōroku*, as well as a sense of imbalance about the relative weight of key texts, are due in large part to the complicated quality of Dōgen's attitudes. Dōgen highlighted Ch'an influences including his training under mentor Ju-ching (J. Nyojō), a Ts'ao-tung monk who served as abbot at Mount T'ien-t'ung for two years beginning in 1225, not as might be expected shortly after returning to Japan, although there are a few exceptions. For the most part, there was a significant delay before Dōgen began to feature citations and remarks about Ju-ching during subsequent periods of his career, particularly at crucial junctures when he was undergoing challenges and struggling to lead followers or contest with rivals.

Two major stages of transition that occurred two decades or more after the outset of the trip to China are crucial for clarifying the development of Dōgen's attitudes toward Chinese Ch'an and the role of Ju-ching. The first was his move in 1243 from Kōshōji temple originally located in Fukakusa in the Kyoto area (and rebuilt in the town of Uji in 1649, some time after the original temple had disappeared) to the remote mountains of Echizen province (currently Fukui prefecture in the Hokuriku district), where Eiheiji temple was established. Carl Bielefeldt points out in *Dōgen's Manuals of Zen Meditation* (which overturns conventional theories about the dating of the *Fukanzazengi*) an important meditation manual long considered one of Dōgen's earliest writings composed in the year of his return:

> Not until the 1240s, well over a decade after his return from China and at the midpoint of his career as a teacher and author, does Dōgen begin to emphasize the uniqueness of Ju-ching and to attribute to him the attitudes and doctrines that set him apart from his contemporaries. Prior to this time, during the period when one would expect Dōgen to have been most under the influence of his Chinese mentor, we see but little of Ju-ching or, indeed, of some of those teachings now thought most characteristic of Dōgen's Zen.[5]

At the time of the move, Dōgen began citing Ju-ching with great frequency, but some of the passages are not found in the Chinese master's recorded sayings. Dōgen placed an even greater emphasis on following a strict Chinese-style monasticism in his writings in a way that appears to depart from earlier attitudes.

The China factor was further accentuated at the time of another important transition marked by a geographical move and concomitant change in attitude: Dōgen's trip from Eiheiji to the temporary capital of Kamakura, apparently at the request of shogun Hōjō Tokiyori, which lasted for eight months from the end of the summer of 1247 to the third month of 1248. Dōgen was invited by the Hōjō and offered the opportunity to lead a new temple, which would have been Kenchōji. However, Dōgen was turned off by the shogun's assimilation of Zen training with the way of the samurai. After his return to the mountain temple, he began preaching a new message emphasizing the inexorability of karmic causality and retribution for evil deeds as well as the need for repentance.

This message is evident in the *jōdō* sermons of the *Eihei kōroku*, beginning with the first sermon after the return, no. 3.251, in addition to the *jishu* sermons of the 12-fascicle *Shōbōgenzō*, a lesser-known but important version of the *Shōbōgenzō* produced mainly late in Dōgen's career after the return from Kamakura. This material also has a resonance with essays contained in the *Eihei shingi*, which were composed in the middle and late 1240s and focus on the precepts and monastic behavior. Ishii Shūdō has pointed out that there seems to be a difference between the *jōdō* sermons collected in the first four volumes of the *Eihei kōroku* and those in volumes 5 through 7, which had a different editor (Gien rather than Senne for vol. 1 and Ejō for vols. 2–4) and an even greater emphasis on causality.[6]

Because the fundamental historical gap between the early trip to China and the evocation of its meaning in later stages has generally gone unrecognized, other elements have overshadowed some key aspects of Dōgen's productivity, to the detriment of developing a balanced and comprehensive over-

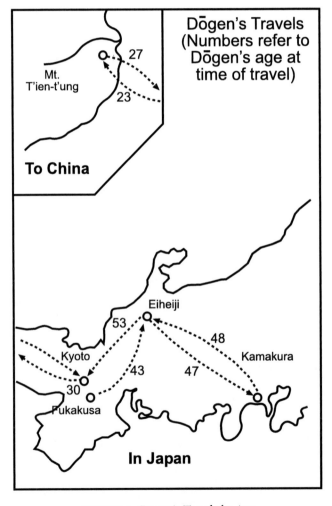

FIGURE I. Dōgen's Travels by Age

view. Historians, many of whom have not extricated themselves from sectarian or methodological biases, are prone either to neglect or to exaggerate crucial factors in his career development by seeking one-sided explanations and evaluations of changes in his approach as a matter of either digression or progression. For example, one school of thought, which I refer to as the Decline Theory, assumes that Dōgen's focus on Ju-ching during the move to Echizen was rooted entirely in partisan concerns, while another view, referred to as the Renewal Theory, maintains that Dōgen's true outlook was not apparent until after his return from Kamakura. To correct the imbalance by exploring Dōgen's diverse styles of religious teaching and writing from a neutral perspective without a value judgment, the approach taken here highlights the rich variety of factors that reflected Chinese influences, rather than trying to pinpoint a particular cause for Dōgen's shifts in attitudes.

My methodological perspective derives in part from Clifford Geertz's theory expressed in his renowned essay on cultural interpretation, "Thick Description: Toward an Interpretive Theory of Culture." According to Geertz, who borrows terms coined by philosopher Gilbert Ryle, a thin description is limited to a one-dimensional manner of depicting apparent facts, whereas a thick description offers an open-ended view of the multiplicity of elements affecting any given situation. For example, if two boys are contracting the eyelids of their right eyes, one may be twitching involuntarily while the other is winking to a friend as a conspiratorial sign. Geertz maintains that a thick-descriptive cultural interpretation investigates "a stratified hierarchy of meaningful structures in terms of which twitches, winks, fake-winks, parodies, rehearsals of parodies are produced, perceived, and interpreted, and without which they would not . . . in fact exist, no matter what anyone did or didn't do with his eyelids."[7] Therefore, the goal is to explore a variety of implications in an open-ended way even if doing so leads to inconclusiveness, rather than to explain an issue according to one perspective for the sake of endorsing a simple, single conclusion.

Travelers to and from Ch'an Temples

The decisions and changes that affected the texts Dōgen produced were a central component in the formation of Zen as a new religious movement in the early Kamakura era, especially at the end of the twelfth and first half of the thirteenth century. Japanese Buddhism in general was undergoing a dramatic transition away from the Heian era's establishment of religious authority in the syncretic Tendai church based at Enryakuji temple on Mount Hiei, which was closely linked to the Fujiwara regency though often at odds with the Tendai faction housed at Onjōji temple (also known as Miidera). As new centers of economic, political, and military power appeared beyond the control of the Tendai (and Fujiwara) hegemony, which also managed to expand for a time, diverse new Buddhist schools arose and came to be dominant in the medieval period, which until the 1330s was ruled by the Hōjō shogunate that strongly supported Rinzai Zen. The initial Rinzai faction to be imported was the Huang-lung (J. Ōryū) school transmitted by Eisai and his disciple Myōzen, who was Dōgen's first Zen teacher and guide to China; however, eventually this stream died out and the main faction was the Yang-ch'i (J. Yōgi) stream that was imported by two crucial figures from Mount Ching, the head temple of the Chinese Five Mountains system. One was the Japanese monk Enni Ben'en, who became founding abbot of Tōfukuji temple in Kyoto a couple of years after his return from China in 1241. The other was the Chinese monk Lan-hsi Tao-lung (J. Rankei Dōryū), who came to Japan in 1246 and was appointed found-ing abbot of Kenchōji temple in Kamakura a few years later with the support of Hōjō Tokiyori, whose offer to Dōgen apparently was rejected by the Sōtō founder.

Dōgen was one of numerous eminent Kamakura-era monks, including Eisai—who in 1202 founded Kenninji, the first major Zen temple in Kyoto— along with Hōnen, Shinran, Ippen, Eizon, and Nichiren, who all broke away from the Tendai church and formed new movements by developing a "selectionist" outlook (senjaku-shugi). According to this approach, the respective Buddhist leaders advocated a specific form of religious practice, be it meditation, chanting, precepts, recitation of scripture, or veneration of a deity or shrine, as well as a single lineal transmission, to the exclusion of all other methods and avenues to enlightenment, which were considered deficient in the quest for religious fulfillment.

For Dōgen, the selected practice was zazen, or sitting meditation, and the lineage was derived from Ju-ching and Hung-chih (J. Wanshi), the latter being another Ts'ao-tung predecessor who served as abbot at Mount T'ien-t'ung two generations before Ju-ching. Hung-chih was compiler of the kōans used in the Ts'ung-jung lu (J. Shōyōroku); he advocated the practice of silent-illumination Zen (C. mo-chao ch'an, J. mokushō zen) in contrast to Ta-hui, the main Lin-chi school exponent of kōan-introspection Zen (C. kan-hua ch'an, J. kanna zen) and critic of Hung-chih's approach, although the two masters were apparently personal friends and respectful of each other. They enjoyed a mutual admiration that led Hung-chih to recommend Ta-hui for the T'ien-t'ung abbacy.

On the one hand, Dōgen steadfastly refused to endorse a view of Zen as a separate, autonomous sect. In the Shōbōgenzō "Butsudō" fascicle, he refers to those who would devise the name of the "Ch'an school" with epithets such as "demons and devils," and he criticizes the designations of the Ts'ao-tung and Lin-chi schools, in addition to other branches and sub-branches of Ch'an.[8] This attitude is echoed in passages in the "Gyōji" fascicle and the Hōkyōki. However, despite universal tendencies in writings that emphasize a pansectar-ian view and seem to discard exclusivism, Dōgen also made clear his dedication to religiosity inherited from Ju-ching and the value of identifying with a specific stream, even if this stance meant in some cases exaggerating or distorting the words and image of his mentor. The basis of the distortion is that the Chinese Ch'an lineages were for the most part not exclusivistic or self-conscious of sectarian identity. As is noted by William Bodiford, who refers to a "dialectical synthesis" in the tailoring of Chinese influences to the Japanese religious context, "Dōgen's emphasis on the Chinese origins of his teachings not only defended his community against charges of illegitimacy but also cloaked his teachings in the prestige of an exclusive transmission of true Buddhism (*shōbō genzō*)."[9] Dōgen uses both nonsectarian rhetoric (appropriate for describing the way the Ch'an school functions in a Chinese context) and sectarian language (which would apply to a Japanese context).

Therefore, to see Dōgen's Zen as being derived from a single method or lineage may be simplistic. His view of religious life is multifaceted and it incorporates yet at the same time alters a number of elements borrowed from Ch'an and related sources. These include adhering to monastic regulations and behavioral codes (C. *ch'ing-kuei*, J. *shingi*), administering the precepts (C. *ch'an-kuai*, J. *zenkai*), interpreting traditional kōan cases that were first expressed as encounter dialogues (C. *chi-yüan wen-ta*, J. *kien-mondō*) in the voluminous body of transmission of the lamp records, delivering various styles of sermons in both *kana* and *kanbun* to the assembly of monks, and preaching to different sorts of lay followers and patrons. It is important to highlight the complexity and diversity of Dōgen's approach, which emerged in an environment characterized by intense competition between traditional and emerging Buddhist sects, as well as by striking changes in the relations between religious institutions and Japanese society and politics.

What was so attractive about the Chinese model of religion for Dōgen and other early Zen leaders? According to accounts in Sung records, Ch'an is usually understood as an iconoclastic, anti-establishment movement characterized by the irreverent, blasphemous, antistructural actions of its leading representatives—slapping, striking, kicking over water pitchers, ripping up sutras, cutting off appendages, jumping off cliffs—that flourished in the middle of the T'ang dynasty, especially the eighth and first half of the ninth century. Like other Buddhist and non-Buddhist cults in China, the Ch'an school was a victim of the devastating suppression of all foreign religions in the mid-840s, including Buddhism, which was considered antinomian and corrupt by the Confucian mainstream. For a few years during that decade thousands of temples were shuttered, tens of thousands of books were destroyed, and hundreds of thousands of monks and nuns were returned to lay life. Although its momentum was stymied for a time, by the end of the tenth century or about 150 years after the suppression, Ch'an had become the most prestigious Buddhist school of the Northern Sung dynasty. It continued to gain great popularity among the literati of Confucian society, who often patronized Ch'an temples, in addition to Taoists and other spiritual seekers, and its dominance would soon spread to Japan as well as Korea.

According to the assessment of Martin Collcutt, whose book *Five Mountains: The Rinzai Zen Monastic Institution in Medieval Japan* examines the transfer from China to Japan:

> Ch'an had survived persecution better [than the declining older schools including T'ien-t'ai], adapting itself to Chinese intellectual and social values to become the most vital school of Chinese monastic Buddhism. By the Northern Sung dynasty (960–1127), Ch'an had established its own history and traditions, compiled distinctive monastic codes, introduced new religious practices, and developed new monastic and architectural forms. Ch'an monasteries—some of them taken over from other Buddhist sects and including monks of very diverse doctrinal interests—were integrated into the Chinese local economy, acted as centers of culture and learning, and enjoyed the patronage of the Chinese gentry class.[10]

When Dōgen arrived in China, the spread of the Ch'an monastic network and the quality of a remarkably rich variety of textual materials was at a developmental peak. Although Ch'an writings clung to a literary style celebrating T'ang masters for their supposedly spontaneous displays of antistructural behavior and disdain for convention by challenging one another and demanding outrageous antics in responses to encounter dialogues, Ch'an became a successful mainstream, highly disciplined institution. It prided itself on developing a self-governing, self-sustaining, effectively organized monastic system suitable to Chinese society, even if this claim—like that of T'ang irreverence—proves, given the volume of government and patronage support, to be more of a rhetorical concoction than a matter of historical substance.

Dōgen was the second in a series of Japanese monks who went to China in pursuit of true Buddhism and returned to found Zen temples. Like Eisai before him, as well as Enni and Shinchi Kakushin among later Kamakura-era pilgrims, Dōgen was first trained as a Tendai novice but forsook this path to study at the Five Mountains temples located near Ming-chou (presently Ningpo, which can refer either to a larger provincial area or to the port traditionally known as Ching-yüan).[11] Ching-yüan was a port city in Chekiang province just east of the Southern Sung capital of Hang-chou (with another important city, Shao-hsing, located in between) on the eastern seaboard of China. Hang-chou, with its multistory houses, was chosen as the capital after the previous site at Kaifeng, the Northern Sung capital, more for its charm and culture as a site for the imperial court to perform ritual sacrifices and also for some geographical advantages than because it was politically or militarily significant. Nevertheless, it was the biggest urban center in the world at the time, with one million residents, and it earned a reputation for grandeur, according to Patricia Buckley Ebrey and the thirteenth-century traveler from the West whom she cites:

> After the north was lost, the new capital at Hangzhou quickly grew to match or even surpass Kaifeng in population and economic development. Marco Polo described it as without doubt the finest and most splendid city in the world: "Anyone seeing such a multitude would believe it impossible that food could be found to feed them all, and yet on every market day all the market squares are filled with people and with merchants who bring food on carts and boats."[12]

From Dōgen's own writings, we find that monks and pilgrims from all over China and from Korea and Japan were thronging to the Hang-Ming area, which in turn was connected to the northwest and southeast of China by canals, waterways, and overland trade routes.

The ancient history of Ming-chou dates back to Hemudu settlements and fishing villages in the fifth millennium B.C.E., making it one of the oldest continuous cultural locations in China. Marked by a confluence of three rivers merging into a bay near the ocean, Ning-po has been a seaport for 2,000 years, although full-fledged urbanization came hundreds of years later, and it remains one of the largest in the world, although it is now overshadowed by the megalopolis of Shanghai across the bay. By the early centuries C.E., Ming-chou was the primary entry to the "Silk Road of the Sea" (Marco Polo embarked from there on his return journey to Italy via the Indian Ocean just about seventy years after Dōgen's visit); it was also a place where several early Buddhist temples had been established with styles of practice perhaps imported directly from India or at least greatly influenced by Indian Buddhism, including Wu-lei temple.

In the late twelfth and early thirteenth centuries, Ming-chou was a cosmopolitan and dynamic port of call with a rich history of diverse cultural and religious development as well as connections with Japan and Japanese Buddhism in addition to countries throughout the Asia-Pacific region.[13] Because of its close proximity to Japan, there were early interactions during the T'ang dynasty, including with Chinese monks who persisted in making the difficult journey to bring geomancy and other elements of Chinese society and to absorb cultural affinities with the Japanese. The two main temples Dōgen visited, Mount T'ien-t'ung and Mount A-yü-wang, located in the foothills of the subtropical T'ai-pai mountains with evergreen foliage, were established by the end of the third century, in 300 and 283, respectively. The latter, named for King Asoka, is said to house one of three main relics of Sakyamuni Buddha found in China, a *sarira* (crystalline relic) maintained on the second floor of the Relics Hall. Neither temple was considered a Public monastery and assigned to the

Ch'an Five Mountains network until the eleventh century (in 1007 and 1008, respectively), the same decade that produced the seminal transmission of the lamp text, the *Ching-te chuan-teng lu* (J. *Keitoku dentōroku*), after over 700 years of being affiliated with various other schools and lineages.[14]

Although ranked one notch higher in the Five Mountains system than Mount T'ien-t'ung, Mount A-yü-wang—supposedly it appeared out of the ground when a monk looking for a harmonious place discovered the miracle—has been better known for its relic and Indian style of practice than its dedication to Ch'an practice. This evaluation, which can imply a deficiency in Ch'an practice, is suggested in a key passage in the "Busshō" fascicle, where Dōgen is quite critical of the temple's leading monks, who do not seem to exhibit typical Ch'an insight.[15] Furthermore, Mount T'ien-t'ung was not known primarily as a Ts'ao-tung temple; abbacies of Ch'an Public monasteries had a rotation of abbots assigned by a central government agency and were not distinguished by subsect, such as Ts'ao-tung or Lin-chi. Therefore, while a prominent monk might have an exclusive affiliation or loyalty to a particular school, the temples never did, so that even when Hung-chih put great effort into refurbishing Mount T'ien-t'ung in the twelfth century, the institution itself did not remain in Ts'ao-tung hands. Its sectarian reputation is directed primarily from a retrospective outlook based on Dōgen's status in Japan and recent shrines and memorials to him established at the temple and elsewhere in Ning-po largely to accommodate the Japanese tourist trade and pilgrimages.

The spread of Buddhism in the Hang-Ming area was not based on official government dissemination policies (unlike the T'ang emperor's sending Hsüan-tsang to India, for example). Yet, by the time of the Sung, this area had become the center of the Chinese Buddhist world, encompassing such venerable institutions as the Five Mountains temples, another important Ch'an center at Mount Hsüeh-t'ou, the sacred island of Mount P'u-t'o considered the earthly abode of Küan-yin, and the massif of Mount T'ien-t'ai along with dozens or even hundreds of temples of the T'ien-t'ai school.

In addition to the five main temples, the Five Mountains system also included ten highly ranked and thirty-five regular temples. Furthermore, there were literally dozens or even hundreds of temples located in the proximity of Ming-chou. When Dōgen got off the ship, even though Mount A-yü-wang is located only about a dozen miles from the port and Mount T'ien-t'ung about two dozen miles, it may have taken him several weeks to reach Mount T'ien-t'ung because he probably would have stopped at some of the temples along the way; they had a custom of hosting itinerant monks or "clouds." Still, the port was not a considerable distance from the temple. In fact, the cook from nearby Mount A-yü-wang (admittedly closer to the harbor than Mount T'ien-t'ung), whom Dōgen met on ship as was cited in *Tenzokyōkun*, planned to return to the temple the evening of their conversation, a fact suggesting that it was within a modest walking distance (for a well-trained yet elderly monk).

FIVE MOUNTAINS
(Wu-shan, J. Gozan)
Temples in China

HAKATA

HANG-CHOU

MING-CHOU

Mt. Ta-mei

Mt. T'ien-t'ai

CHEKIANG

▲ Five Mountain Temples
△ Other temples

1. Mt. Ching-shan Wan-shou Ch'an ssu, of Hang-chou
2. Mt. A-yü-wang-shan Kuang li Ch'an ssu, of Ming-chou
3. Mt. T'ai-pai-shan T'ien-t'ung Ching-te Ch'an ssu, of Ming-chou
4. Mt. Pei-shan Ch'ing-te ling-yin Ch'an ssu, of Hang-chou
5. Mt. Nan-shan Ch'ing tz'u pao en kuang hsiao Ch'an ssu, of Hang-chou

These are the five main temples in the Zen monastic system of Sung China, but there were dozens of additional temples that constituted the entire network.

FIGURE 2. Locations of Ch'an Five Mountains Temples

Mount T'ien-t'ung is said to have housed a community of over a thousand monks at its peak, all fed from a single wok supervised by the temple's chief cook.

Although located on what seems to have been a significant trade route between Fujien and the Hang-Ming area, Mount T'ien-t'ai today remains an isolated, sprawling mountain region marked by hundreds of peaks and valleys with numerous monasteries strewn all over its slopes. Unlike Mount T'ien-t'ung, which was located in the hills close to an urban environment, Mount T'ien-t'ai, several hours' drive to the south, was genuinely remote and pastoral. By the Southern Sung, it had lost prominence and its place as the center of the school except as a site of pilgrimage and history. One of the main temples of the massif, Wan-nien ssu, had officially become a major Ch'an temple and was considered a part of the Five Mountains system.

At this stage of their development, the two schools, the T'ien-t'ai (also known as the Teaching or Doctrinal school) and Ch'an (also known as the Meditation school), both supervised by the government and with priests regulated by official ordinations, were quite similar in terms of religious rituals, doctrinal study, and meditation practices. For the elite clergy within these state institutions, the study of T'ien-t'ai doctrine generally required the practice of Ch'an meditation, and in order to practice Ch'an one needed to have studied T'ien-t'ai. Nevertheless, from the end of the eleventh century on, the Ch'an monasteries, which were also referred to as Public monasteries, superseded those of T'ien-t'ai and other schools in terms of prestige and the vigor of institutional growth based on government support and donations.

Dōgen's travels were sandwiched between the two trips taken by Eisai at the end of the twelfth century, the first in 1168 and the next from 1187 to 1191, and Enni's pilgrimage, which began in the mid-1230s.[16] Whereas Eisai and Enni became leaders of the Rinzai school based in Kyoto, Dōgen at the height of his career departed from the capital in the mid-1240s to form a movement in the mountains of northwest Japan that eventually became known as the Sōtō school through the evangelical efforts of fourth patriarch Keizan and his long list of followers.

Eisai journeyed to China to learn about original Tendai school teaching, having studied Taimitsu (esoteric Tendai) rites at the head temples of the sect's two main factions: Onjōji temple of the Jimon school, located near Lake Biwa due east of Kyoto, and Enryakuji temple of the Sanmon school, located on Mount Hiei northeast of the capital where Eisai was ordained in 1154. According to the *Kōzen gokokuron*, while he was waiting to depart in the port at Hakata, Eisai heard about Ch'an during a conversation with a Chinese monk who was an interpreter. Because over a hundred years had passed since there was significant contact between Japanese Buddhists and China, there was probably an assumption in Japan that nothing special was developing on the mainland. Therefore, news that the Ch'an school had emerged as a dominant force would have likely made a big impression on Eisai. Furthermore, once in China, Eisai no doubt quickly came to realize that T'ien-t'ai religiosity was quite different from what he expected to find. This school, which never embraced the forms of esotericism associated with Japanese Tendai, had fallen into a state of decline and was no longer the main meditative tradition in Chinese Buddhism. Accompanied by a Japanese Shingon school monk he happened to meet, Shunjōbō Chōgen, Eisai traveled to Wan-nien ssu, where he was first formally introduced to Ch'an. Eisai learned that Mount T'ien-t'ai had absorbed key elements of Ch'an training, including *zazen*, and was linked to the Five Mountains system.

During the final segment of the summer journey, as he was about to embark for Japan, Eisai visited Mount A-yü-wang, very near the port of Ming-chou, and must have sensed that Ch'an monasteries had a vibrancy lacking in the religious practice at Mount T'ien-t'ai. Apparently he put questions to the abbot but did not engage in formal Ch'an training. Eisai returned with many T'ien-t'ai scriptures, but once back, he decided that he would dedicate himself to reviving the practice of *zazen* that had long existed, rather obscurely, within the Japanese Tendai school. This was a tradition that had been transmitted by Saichō, Enchin, and Annen several centuries before. By the late Heian era, the practice of Zen meditation was still considered a branch of Tendai training, and little was known of Chinese Ch'an aside from a handful of early texts that were not representative of dynamic developments of the Sung dynasty schools.

Eisai set out in the third month of 1187 on a second and ultimately much more significant trip that lasted four years, with the original intention of traveling all the way to India in order to follow in the footsteps of Hsüan-tsang and other prominent Chinese pilgrims. Stymied in the process because of customs and various restrictions, however, he spent most of his time further exploring prominent Five Mountains temples. He was converted to the Huang-lung stream of the Lin-chi/Rinzai Ch'an school after studying with Hsü-an Huai-ch'ang at Mount T'ien-t'ai, which had mixed (T'ien-t'ai and Ch'an) practices. He then transferred to Mount T'ien-t'ung in 1189 to accompany Hsü-an's new abbacy there. Eisai soon received an explicit Ch'an seal of transmission, and a year later he returned to Mount T'ien-t'ai and remained there for the duration of the trip. It is said that he donated personal funds for the restoration of temples at both Mount T'ien-t'ai and Mount T'ien-t'ung. Under Hsü-an, Eisai was able to maintain his interest in esotericism while also receiving the instruction that strict adherence to *vinaya* discipline was a basic requirement for Ch'an and in no way were the elements of esoteric practices, monastic discipline, and meditation to be considered contradictory.

On returning to Japan in the seventh month of 1191, Eisai at first endured several years of persecution, but eventually this obstacle was removed and he was successful in establishing new monasteries. These included Hōonji in the 1190s in Chikuzen province in Kyushu in the domain of Taira Yorimori; Jufukuji in 1200 in Kamakura with the support of Hōjō Masako, widow of Mina-moto Yoritomo; and Kenninji in 1202 in Kyoto with land granted by Minamoto Yoriie. At Kenninji, Eisai transmitted the Huang-lung lineage to Myōzen, who in turn passed the transmission to Dōgen. Kenninji had a communal Zen meditation hall, or Monks Hall (lit., Samgha Hall, sōdō), which was the first of its kind in Japan, but it also held shrines for Tendai rituals and esoteric (mikkyō) Shingon practices. These and other temples founded by both Eisai and Enni remained affiliated with Tendai esotericism in a system known as Enmitsu-zenkai (the mixture of the complete [and sudden] precepts or en[don] of Tendai with esoteric or mitsu rites and the Zen approach to meditation and the pre-cepts or zenkai). However, this kind of eclecticism was also common in Chinese Ch'an temples, especially those, like Mount T'ien-t'ung and Mount A-yü-wang, that incorporated holdovers of practices from times prior to their Ch'an affili-ation and that were influenced by their masters who rotated back and forth between Ch'an and other, particularly T'ien-t'ai monasteries.

Enni, who was initially trained by Eisai's disciples Eichō and Gyōyū after being ordained at Onjōji, followed the pattern of Eisai and Dōgen in abandon-ing his Tendai background in order to make a trip to the Five Mountains temples in search of genuine Ch'an Buddhism. During a journey that lasted nearly seven years from 1235 to 1241, Enni trained at Wan-shou ch'an-ssu mon-astery on Mount Ching, a temple Dōgen also visited, located west of Hang-chou, when it was in full flower as the institutional flagship. He received trans-mission from the abbot, Wu-chun Shih-fan of the Yang-ch'i stream of the Lin-chi school, who presented Enni with a precious portrait of himself and samples of his calligraphy. On returning to Japan in the early 1240s, Enni became founding abbot of Tōfukuji, which was built in Kyoto and based on the seven-hall monastery (shichidō garan) style of Sung temples, with the con-siderable financial backing of regent Kujō Michiie despite Tendai institutional objections.[17] Michiie was a relative of one of Dōgen's backers in Kyoto, Kujō Noriie. Another Zen innovator of this period was Shinchi Kakushin, who stud-ied under Eichō and Gyōyū as well as Dōgen and who was encouraged by Enni to travel to China in 1249, where he gained transmission under Wu-men Hui-kai, a Yang-ch'i school monk. On his return in 1254, he introduced the Wu-men-kuan (J. Mumonkan) kōan collection originally produced in 1228, the year after Dōgen's departure from China, which had a monumental impact on the development of Japanese Zen literature.

In addition to Japanese monks who traveled to China,[18] the early Kamakura period was marked by numerous Chinese monks coming to Japan, beginning in 1246 with Lan-hsi, who like Enni, was a disciple of Wu-chun at Mount Ching. With the support of Hōjō Tokiyori, who was perhaps the strongest proponent of Zen among Japanese rulers of the era, Lan-hsi in 1253 founded Kenchōji temple in Kamakura, where he used a strict system of regulations that resembled Dōgen's emphasis on rules governing the spirituality of daily chores and other monastic activities.[19] Ironically, Lan-hsi headed the temple that was apparently originally offered by Tokiyori to Dōgen during the latter's visit to Kamakura in 1247–1248. Whereas Kenninji and the temples founded by Eisai and Enni remained affiliated with Tendai esotericism, Lan-hsi and several successors from China who were of the same lineage as Enni attempted to bring "pure, unadulterated Zen" to Japan unencumbered by syncretism with local beliefs.[20] In that sense they were closer to Dōgen's aims. Lan-hsi also helped originate the Japanese version of the Five Mountains system, which was based at temples in Kamakura and Kyoto and was associated primarily with the Rinzai school. Eiheiji and other Sōtō temples were rarely included among the Five Mountains monasteries, although many of the Sōtō along with some of the Rinzai temples formed part of an alternative loose-knit institutional network known as the Rinka temples. Another important visitor was Wu-hsüeh Tsu-yüan, a high-ranking monk from Mount T'ien-t'ung who arrived in Japan at the invitation of Hōjō Tokimune, the son of Hōjō Tokiyori, in 1279, the year after the Mongols under Kublai Khan overtook the Sung dynasty; in 1282 Wu-hsüeh became founding abbot of Kenchōji temple in Kamakura.

As shown in Table 2, the main exception to the pattern of transnational clerical exchange as a necessary component of the transmission of Zen from China to Japan was Daruma school founder Dainichi Nōnin. Nōnin was perhaps the earliest proponent of Zen, starting in the 1180s and 1190s, a few years before Eisai's second journey. However, Nōnin, who apparently had died by 1196, never visited China himself. Instead he sent two of his first-generation disciples, Renchū and Shōben, to the mainland to gain certification from the Five Mountains master Te-kuang, an abbot of the Ta-hui lineage of the Lin-chi school at Mount A-yü-wang. According to a passage cited in "Gyōji" not found in recorded sayings, Ju-ching was harshly critical of Te-kuang as an inferior, inauthentic monk; this citation may be an example of Dōgen using Ju-ching as a voice for partisan concerns in the Japanese context.

Nōnin was severely criticized by both the Tendai establishment and rival Zen masters for lacking authenticity and legitimacy in not having gained a

TABLE 2. Early Ch'an and Zen Travelers

Japanese Monks to China	Chinese Monks to Japan
Eisai, 1168, 1187–1191	Lan-hsi, arrived 1246
Kakua, 1171	Wu-an, arrived 1260
Dōgen, 1223–1227	Wu-hsüeh, arrived 1279
Enni, 1235–1241	Did Not Travel
Shinchi, 1249–1254	
	Nōnin, did not go to China but sent disciples in 1190s

firsthand experience on the mainland, and he was also refuted for advocating a path of antinomianism by denigrating the role of the precepts. The number and meaning of the precepts was a key element of debate between various parties in the formative period of Zen, as Eisai, Dōgen, and Nōnin each had a distinct view that differed from that of the Tendai establishment.[21] Indirect criticism of deficient tendencies in the Daruma school played a major role in the writings of Eisai, particularly the *Kōzen gokokuron* of 1198, and those of Dōgen, especially in works such as *Bendōwa* and *Shōbōgenzō* "Sokushinze-butsu" from the early 1230s, several years after his return to Japan. As Bernard Faure has shown, the Daruma school is crucial for understanding Dōgen because Ejō, who became his head monk in 1234, and numerous other former members who converted in 1241 played key roles at Eiheiji during and after Dōgen's life.[22] Therefore Dōgen's early doctrines must be seen not in isolation but as part of a dialogue—or perhaps even a "quadrilogue"—with the views of Nōnin, Eisai, and the Tendai school in accommodating the transition of Ch'an to Japan and winning followers.

Dōgen's Journeys

Dōgen studied at Kenninji for six years (1217–1223) before accompanying Myōzen and a couple of other Japanese monks to China, and eventually he would gain a dual lineage, including the Ts'ao-tung/Sōtō line received from Ju-ching in addition to the Huang-lung line.[23] Dōgen can be considered to have had a triple lineage if the bodhisattva precepts he received in the Tendai school in 1213 are reckoned in. A major issue to be discussed in Chapter 3 concerns how the 58-article bodhisattva (or Mahayana) precepts (containing 10 major and 48 minor articles) that Dōgen received in Japan from Tendai abbot Kōen and also from Myōzen failed to prepare him for the trip. Ch'an, like other Chinese Buddhist schools, maintained that the primary requirement for one to be considered a genuine monk was the reception of the combined 250-article *Pratimoksha* (or so-called Hinayana) and bodhisattva precepts, preferably taken in sequence. Dōgen's failure to meet that requirement before landing in China greatly affected the course of his trip.

The route for the travels of Dōgen and Myōzen to Ch'an temples was patterned after the journeys of Eisai, as is shown on the map in Figure 3, which traces the three trips (two by Eisai near the end of the twelfth century juxta-posed with Dōgen's travels in the 1220s). On their arrival in the spring of 1223, Myōzen who had received both the *Pratimoksha* and bodhisattva precepts in Japan, was quickly accepted into Mount T'ien-t'ung, where Eisai had received transmission, and instantly joined the summer retreat. He continued training there until his premature death in the fifth month of 1225. Dōgen, lacking these credentials, was at first not accepted and ended up traveling to various Five Mountains temples in search of legitimate status. After struggling to find

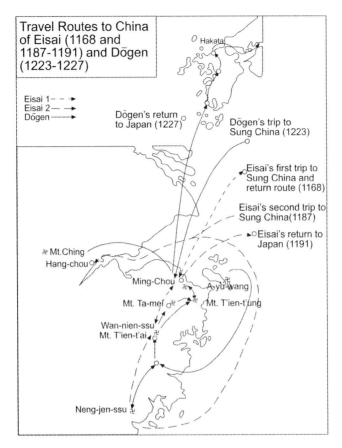

Travel Routes to China of Eisai (1168 and 1187-1191) and Dōgen (1223-1227)

Eisai 1 – – →
Eisai 2 — →
Dōgen ——→

Dōgen's return to Japan (1227)

Hakata

Dōgen's trip to Sung China (1223)

Eisai's first trip to Sung China and return route (1168)

Eisai's second trip to Sung China(1187)

Eisai's return to Japan (1191)

Mt.Ching
Hang-chou

Ming-Chou

A-yü-wang

Mt. Ta-mei

Mt. T'ien-t'ung

Wan-nien-ssu
Mt. T'ien-t'ai

Neng-jen-ssu

FIGURE 3. Map Comparing Two Routes of Eisai with Dōgen's Journey

acceptance, seeking an authentic master during two years of itinerancy, including visits to Mount T'ien-t'ai, where Ch'an meditation was practiced in addition to Mount Ching and Mount A-yü-wang, and almost giving up his quest in despondency, Dōgen finally settled at Mount T'ien-t'ung at around the time of Myōzen's death.

During that year's retreat he began training under the tutelage of Ju-ching, who had recently become abbot, and as a foreign novice he received far better treatment than what was accorded to him by the previous Mount T'ien-t'ung patriarch, Wu-chi Liao-p'ai, a disciple of Te-kuang in the Ta-hui lineage. Dōgen was allowed to enter Ju-ching's private quarters beginning in the fifth month of 1225, a few weeks before Myōzen died, for discussions of doctrine and training methods that were supposedly recorded in the *Hōkyōki*. He quickly reached the climax of the pilgrimage by undergoing the enlightenment experience of *shinjin datsuraku* (casting off body-mind) that was confirmed by Ju-ching in the seventh month. Ju-ching administered the precepts on the eighteenth day of the ninth month (or 9.18.1225), although there is considerable controversy about which set of instructions these represented. Sōtō tradition claims that Dōgen received a set of 16-article precepts from his mentor, and while this has become the standard for the Japanese sect, it would have been a tremendous anomaly given that Chinese Ch'an generally required the sequentially administered combined precepts. The traditional claim that Ju-ching made such an exception for Dōgen is dubious, and in any case this is clearly an area in which the Japanese monk's approach is most at variance with the Ch'an model.

Dōgen continued practicing at Mount T'ien-t'ung, holding numerous conversations with his mentor for two more years. He received the document of transmssion (*shisho*) shortly before returning to Japan in the fall of 1227, a couple of months after Ju-ching's death.[24] Dōgen then stayed for a few years at Kenninji before opening Kōshōji in 1233 as the first Zen temple after Eisai's temple to have a Sung-style Monks Hall for *zazen* training.[25] There he began delivering sermons and indoctrinating disciples in Chinese discipline. He preached a message of the universality of enlightenment for all those who practice "just sitting" (*shikan taza*), including women and laypersons. His early approval of lay practitioners probably stemmed from the way Ch'an interacted with the general community. Of fifty *kanbun* poems (or *kanshi*) Dōgen wrote during the last two years in China, the only written record from this period, over forty verses were dedicated to civil officials who patronized or were served by Ch'an temples. Interestingly enough, not one of these verses makes a direct reference or allusion either to Ju-ching or to specific practice styles at Mount T'ien-t'ung.

Dōgen was positively influenced by Eisai, whom he regarded as a lineal predecessor although they embraced somewhat conflicting views of Zen practice. Both stressed the role of *zazen* and monastic regulations, but Eisai made the combined precepts a centerpiece of his practice even while assimilating Tendai esotericism, whereas Dōgen simplified the precepts while incorporating kōan-based sermons and commentaries as the primary monastic ritual. Dōgen spoke frequently of his great admiration for Eisai in the records of oral discourses collected in the *Shōbōgenzō zuimonki* in the mid-1230s. Indeed, praise for Eisai's leadership at Kenninji is mentioned with much greater frequency in this text than for Ju-ching and Mount T'ien-t'ung.

There is also a prominent passage about Myōzen's making the difficult decision to go to China despite being asked by his dying Tendai mentor, Myōyū, to delay the journey. Dōgen was among those who tried to discourage him, but he was inspired by Myōzen's insistence that the value of pursuing the Dharma and the need to not waste precious time takes precedence over worldly obligations and even over human life.[26] Yet it is unclear how much practice Dōgen may have learned from Myōzen that can be associated with later developments in the Japanese Rinzai style of training, such as the study of kōan cases.

Myōzen's day, which was prior to the importation of Sung Ch'an literary sources to Japan (a development for which Dōgen himself was largely responsible), was simply too early for Rinzai Zen to have fashioned a well-formed sectarian identity. It is also noteworthy that Dōgen gave memorial sermons for his Japanese predecessors, as recorded in the *Eihei kōroku*, only in the last two years of his preaching (1251 and 1252), two and a half decades after his journey.[27]

Dōgen's approach was also greatly affected by a sense of rivalry with Enni, who rose to prominence with his abbacy at Tōfukuji built just up the road from Kōshōji, which was dwarfed by the magnificent new construction. According to Collcutt, "Tōfukuji took more than ten years to complete and remained for centuries one of the most impressive monastic compounds in Kyoto."[28] This may well have caused jealousy or pressure that was one of numerous factors influencing Dōgen's decision to leave the capital in 1243 in order to establish Eiheiji in Echizen. Despite areas of conflict, Dōgen at Kōshōji and Eiheiji and Enni at Tōfukuji along with Lan-hsi at Kenchōji all emulated the basic design of the seven-hall monastery compound. This design, often attributed to the Sung dynasty, was probably one of many aspects of Zen that was categorized and retrospectively applied during the Tokugawa era.

The Zen version was somewhat different from the earlier seven-hall style dating back to the period of Nara Buddhism, because of a new emphasis on the role of several key facilities. These included the Monks Hall, where the assembly of monks was required to sleep, eat, and meditate in common quarters; the Dharma Hall (*hattō*), or the site for *jōdō* sermons and other large, public, or formal convocations; and the Abbot's Quarters (*hōjō*), where monks received private instruction (although this was not considered one of the seven main halls). Like the Chinese model, Zen temples also had numerous embellishments, so most temple compounds encompassed a dozen or more main buildings.[29] However, the scale of the Chinese temples was considerably larger and more grand, with the monastery becoming a large administrative unit with many divisions and departments, whereas Japanese temples such as Kenchōji in Kamakura functioned on a more minimal and simplified scale.

A main factor influenced by the style of Sung China was that Zen temples had a vertical axis emphasizing the gateway to meeting halls as well as a horizontal axis emphasizing the everyday functions of monks. This layout closely resembled Taoist temples of the period, which reflected geomantic principles for channeling energy and warding off demonic spirits and were in turn often based on imperial models of construction.[30] Although, according to Ch'an rules, this model theoretically eliminated the need for a Buddha Hall (*butsudō* or *butsuden*), in actual practice most Zen temples did include this chamber.[31]

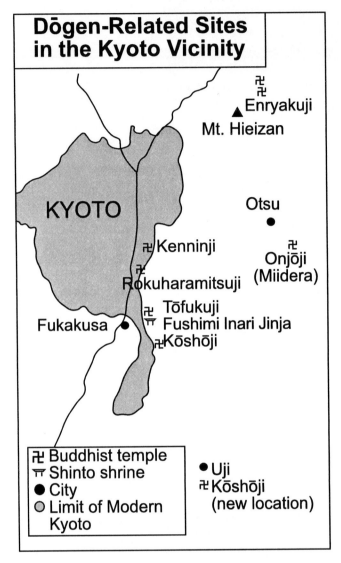

FIGURE 4. Dōgen-Related Sites in Kyoto

Coming Home "Empty-Handed"

According to a frequently cited passage in the *Eihei kōroku*, Dōgen returned to Japan in the fall of 1227 "empty-handed" (*kūshu genkyō*), that is, without having collected the material artifacts of Buddhism—such as icons, scriptures, relics, and regalia—that preoccupied so many of the other Japanese monks who visited China.[32] He brought back only his experience of awakening and under-

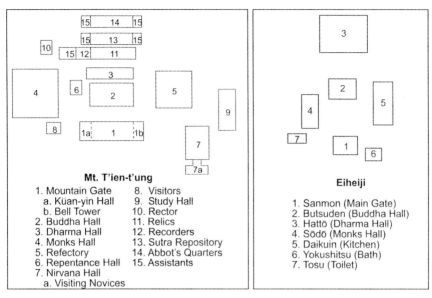

Mt. T'ien-t'ung

1. Mountain Gate
   a. Küan-yin Hall
   b. Bell Tower
2. Buddha Hall
3. Dharma Hall
4. Monks Hall
5. Refectory
6. Repentance Hall
7. Nirvana Hall
   a. Visiting Novices
8. Visitors
9. Study Hall
10. Rector
11. Relics
12. Recorders
13. Sutra Repository
14. Abbot's Quarters
15. Assistants

Eiheiji

1. Sanmon (Main Gate)
2. Butsuden (Buddha Hall)
3. Hattō (Dharma Hall)
4. Sōdō (Monks Hall)
5. Daikuin (Kitchen)
6. Yokushitsu (Bath)
7. Tosu (Toilet)

This diagram shows the key buildings in the temple compound of Mt. T'ien-t'ung juxtaposed with a diagram of Eiheiji, where the compound layout has probably been altered from the Tokugawa era. There are additional buildings on both compounds that are not listed.

FIGURE 5. Diagram of Compounds at Mount T'ien-t'ung and Eiheiji

standing of the Dharma. As Hee-Jin Kim writes, "Unlike other Buddhists who had previously studied in China, Dōgen brought home with him no sutras, no images, and no documents. His sole 'souvenir' presented to his countrymen was his own body and mind, his total existence, which was now completely liberated and transformed. He himself was the surest evidence of Dharma."[33]

Yet Dōgen's literary records show that on his return he was by no means empty-headed (although he may have had a head "full of emptiness"!). Indeed, Dōgen came back to Japan exhibiting a remarkable facility with diverse genres of Zen writings, which he used critically and creatively in his sermons and other works. Dōgen's profound knowledge of Chinese Ch'an literature, especially kōan records, is symbolized by the legend of the "One Night *Blue Cliff Record*" (*ichiya Hekiganroku*). This is a version of the *Pi-yen lu* (J. *Hekiganroku*) collection of 100 kōan cases with extensive prose and verse commentary representing the pinnacle of the Ch'an tradition's literary quality. The legend, which appears in numerous traditional biographies along with other supernatural tales and embellishments, forms a central part of the traditional portrayal of the founder's journey and its impact on Japanese Zen.[34] Dōgen supposedly made a copy of the text in a single night, guided and assisted by

Hakusan Gongen Myōri, the deity of Mount Hakusan, which was the sacred peak near Eiheiji that played a crucial role in the spread of the Sōtō sect. Many of the early temples were located in the vicinity of this or other sacred mountains in the network of Mount Hakusan.

Perhaps the most significant feature of Dōgen's appropriation of Ch'an is the way he absorbed various genres of the voluminous writings produced during the rapid expansion of the Ch'an school in the eleventh and twelfth centuries. The four main genres of Sung Ch'an writings apparently studied by Dōgen and other Japanese monks include: (1) transmission of the lamp records (C. ch'uan-teng lu, J. dentōroku) containing pseudo-historical biographies, or hagiographies, of the multiple branches of Zen lineages; (2) recorded sayings (C. yü-lu, J. goroku) of the sermons and other compositions of eminent individual masters; (3) kōan (C. kung-an) collections with prose and verse commentaries on traditional cases; and (4) regulations (C. ch'ing-kuei, J. shingi) for monastic discipline and rules for behavior.

The first three genres contain overlapping materials that feature the role of encounter dialogues, which are presented with different kinds of emphasis. These genres use dialogues to highlight, respectively, the multibranched process of lineal transmission, the doctrines and pedagogical styles of particular teachers, or the philosophical and literary significance of kōan case records.[35] Much of this content also appeared in the pan-Buddhist genre of monk biography records, especially the Sung kao-seng chuan of 988. The fourth genre is represented primarily by the Ch'an-yüan ch'ing-kuei (J. Zen'en shingi, in Taishō vol. 80, no. 2543) composed in 1103 by Tsung-tse. The genre of monastic rules is traditionally attributed to an earlier passage first published in 1004 in the recorded sayings of T'ang master Pai-chang, known for his communal work ethic summed up by the phrase, "A day without labor is a day without eating," or more succinctly, "No work, no food."[36] The 1103 text, also consulted by non-Ch'an temples, established the quality of monastic life practiced in the Five Mountains system ranging from the role of temple leaders to rites, ceremonies, and codes of etiquette.

Dōgen's Sermon Styles

Intimate familiarity with a vast array of Sung sources is amply demonstrated in Dōgen's two major collections of sermons, the Shōbōgenzō and the Eihei kōroku, both of which exist in multiple editions with varying contents. These texts present two distinct styles of discourse with the samgha that are based largely on precedents and rules set in the Ch'an-yüan ch'ing-kuei. As shown in Table 3, the Shōbōgenzō contains examples of informal jishu sermons delivered in kana mainly while Dōgen was at Kōshōji temple or in the midst of making the transition to Echizen, but for the most part these were not composed at Eiheiji. The jishu style was often presented in an impromptu fashion in the

一夜二碧巖
ヲ寫シ王フ
トキ
白山權現
來テ助筆
シテ畢ル

FIGURE 6. Illustration from *Teiho Kenzeiki zue* of the Hakusan Deity Assisting in Copying the "One Night *Blue Cliff Record*"

Abbot's Quarters or anywhere else in the temple compound other than the main hall (or Dharma Hall), usually in the evening or even late at night for a select audience requiring special instruction, because they sought either advanced or remedial pedagogy.

The *Eihei kōroku* contains in the first seven of its ten volumes a collection of formal or *jōdō* sermons (lit., "ascending the [high seat] in the [Dharma] Hall" to address the congregation) delivered in *kanbun*. The *jōdō* style was presented

TABLE 3. Comparison of Dōgen's Two Main Lecture Styles

	Jishu (Shōbōgenzō)	Jōdō (Eihei kōroku)
Where	*hōjō*	*hattō*
When	evening	day
Language	*kana*	*kanbun*
Style	informal	formal
Schedule	3, 8, 13, 18, 23 of month	1, 5, 10, 15, 20, 25 of month
Expression	rhetorical	demonstrative
Discourse	prolix	laconic
Length	extended with citations	brief and allusive
Audience	diverse (those needing instruction)	monks (general guests)
Atmosphere	private, individual	public, communal
Temple	Kōshōji	Eiheiji
Years	1233–1246	1236–1252

exclusively in the Dharma Hall, usually before the midday meal, for a full assembly of rank-and-file monks as well as outside guests, patrons, and supporters, who stood in rows while the teacher sat on the high seat on the dais. Begun at Kōshōji, the *jōdō* sermons were the primary form of expression at Eiheiji, especially after the decline in the delivery of *jishu*. They were delivered more frequently after Dōgen's return from Kamakura.

According to the *Ch'an-yüan ch'ing-kuei*, both styles were to be delivered on a fixed schedule six times a month or every five days. The *jōdō* style occurred beginning the first of the month (1, 5, 10, 15, 20, 25).[37] The *jishu* style was prescribed for a complementary set of five-day intervals beginning the third day (3, 8, 13, 18, 23). However, for Dōgen—apparently partly on the basis of what he saw Ju-ching doing—the *jishu* was often performed on a spontaneous, unplanned basis that does not seem to have adhered to a regular schedule. Furthermore, the *jōdō* were delivered by Dōgen on various ceremonial and other occasions that were often repeated annually following key textual models, particularly Hung-chih's recorded sayings, but without necessarily adhering to the *Ch'an-yüan ch'ing-kuei* calendrical instructions.

Dōgen's sermons played a crucial role in introducing and disseminating the ideas and sayings of the golden age of Sung Ch'an literature and in transforming these sources into a distinctively eloquent and effective Japanese form of discourse. Both the *Shōbōgenzō* and *Eihei kōroku* show that Dōgen was the first Japanese master to cite and comment on the teachings of Chinese masters—especially encounter dialogues, which form the basis of many kōan case records—extensively, evocatively, and more important, critically, by offering revisions and expansive explanations of source materials.[38] It is clear from the vast number of citations in Dōgen's writings that he was well versed in many of the primary as well as some of the more obscure examples of these genres and was able to refer at will to specific passages found therein. However, since a number of these texts have been lost or conflated over time, there are instances in Dōgen's writings in which it is difficult to track the source of his citation or allusion.

As is evidenced in the comprehensive listing of his references to Chinese masters and the sources for their sayings analyzed by a team of leading Japanese scholars led by Kagamishima Genryū (as summarized in Table 5 later in this chapter), Dōgen's writings are replete with many hundreds of citations from dozens of Ch'an figures, especially from the eighth and ninth centuries.[39] The teachings of these masters are not contained in texts from the period, which either were never collected or were lost following the Wu-tsung suppression of Buddhism in the 840s, but are found in dozens of Sung dynasty chronicles about their thoughts and accomplishments. Dōgen uses these references in an original fashion by placing the citation in a creative context and making insightful remarks or even altering the wording to draw out subtle doctrinal implications and discursive nuances. Dōgen was fully steeped in the styles of commentary on kōan cases (C. *ku-tse kung-an*, J. *kosoku-kōan*) typical of Chinese collections, including verse (C. *sung-ku*, J. *juko*) and prose (C. *nien-ku*, J. *nenko*) commentary. However, he devised his own method of exposition using wordplay and adaptations of grammatical style that has no real precedent in Chinese literature or successor in Japanese Zen.[40]

Generally, the records of Ch'an discourse do not include collections of *jishu* lectures, although these were commonly delivered in Chinese temples. Thus the *Shōbōgenzō* is unique and significant for the picture it offers of a Zen master at the peak of philosophical inventiveness and rhetorical improvisation that plays off the traditional canon. Another important text, the *Shōbōgenzō zuimonki*, consists mainly of a different kind of informal sermon composed in *kana* and known as *shōsan* (lit., "small assembly") or *yōsan* (lit. "evening assembly"), which also features novel interpretations of encounter dialogues. Note in Table 1 that the sermons contained in the *Shōbōgenzō zuimonki* were delivered during the years 1234–1238, when there was a hiatus between the initial delivery of *jishu* sermons in 1233 and the resumption of this style at the end of the decade. Some examples of the *shōsan* style, along with another *kana* lecture style known as *hōgo* collected from different phases of Dōgen's career, are included in the eighth volume of the *Eihei kōroku*.

Modeling and Critiquing the Patriarchs

Aside from the relatively short section of *hōgo*, the *Eihei kōroku*, which has been overlooked in Western scholarship until recently, is particularly important for expressing the Chinese model of instruction. While on one level this means it is a more conservative text in terms of stylistic innovation, the *Eihei kōroku* is distinctive in being the first example of the genre of *jōdō* sermons created in

Japan. This text is crucial for understanding the period of the Eiheiji abbacy and reveals how Dōgen often cites, yet at the same time revises and critiques, the recorded sayings of Ju-ching and Hung-chih (see Table 4 for lineage chart). The sermons were often patterned on those of his predecessors, although Dō-gen took license to modify their words and ideas.

For example, in *Eihei kōroku* 4.296 delivered on the occasion of the winter solstice in 1248 Dōgen cites Hung-chih, as he had on several of these seasonal occasions, including nos. 135 and 206. Dōgen says, " 'My measuring cup is full and the balance scale is level,' but in the marketplace I buy what is precious and sell it for a low price," thereby reversing the statement in Hung-chih's sermon, "Even if your measuring cup is full and the balance scale is level, in

TABLE 4 Ts'ao-tung/Sōtō School Lineage

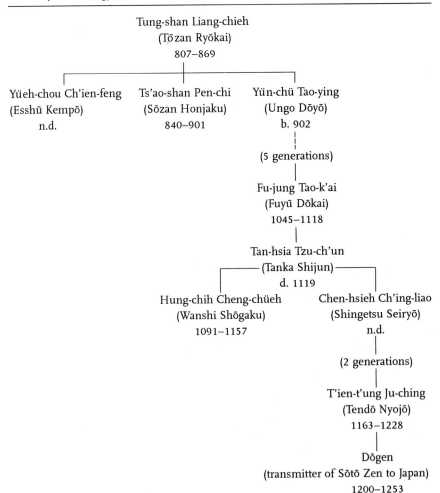

Tung-shan Liang-chieh
(Tōzan Ryōkai)
807–869

Yüeh-chou Ch'ien-feng
(Esshū Kempō)
n.d.

Ts'ao-shan Pen-chi
(Sōzan Honjaku)
840–901

Yün-chü Tao-ying
(Ungo Dōyō)
b. 902

(5 generations)

Fu-jung Tao-k'ai
(Fuyū Dōkai)
1045–1118

Tan-hsia Tzu-ch'un
(Tanka Shijun)
d. 1119

Hung-chih Cheng-chüeh
(Wanshi Shōgaku)
1091–1157

Chen-hsieh Ch'ing-liao
(Shingetsu Seiryō)
n.d.

(2 generations)

T'ien-t'ung Ju-ching
(Tendō Nyojō)
1163–1228

Dōgen
(transmitter of Sōtō Zen to Japan)
1200–1253

transactions I sell at a high price and buy when the price is low."[41] Perhaps
Dōgen is demonstrating a bodhisattva-like generosity or showing the nondual
nature of all phenomena that only appear to have different values. Dōgen's
mentor Ju-ching is not immune to this revisionist treatment, as in no. 3.194:

> [Dōgen] said, I remember a monk asked an ancient worthy, "Is there
> Buddha Dharma or not on a steep cliff in the deep mountains?" The
> worthy responded, "A large rock is large; a small one is small."
>
> My late teacher T'ien-t'ung [Ju-ching] said, "The question about
> the steep cliff in the deep mountains was answered in terms of large
> and small rocks. The cliff collapsed, the rocks split, and the empty
> sky filled with a noisy clamor." The teacher [Dōgen] said, Although
> these two venerable masters said it this way, I [Eihei] have another
> utterance to convey. If someone were to ask, "Is there Buddha
> Dharma or not on a steep cliff in the deep mountains?" I would
> simply say to him, "The lifeless rocks nod their heads again and
> again. The empty sky vanishes completely. This is something that
> exists within the realm of the buddhas and patriarchs. What is this
> thing on a steep cliff in the deep mountains?" [Dōgen] pounded his
> staff one time, and descended from his seat.[42]

The phrase, "The lifeless rocks nod their heads again and again," is a reference
to Tao-sheng, Kumarajiva's great disciple and early Chinese Buddhist scholar,
who, on the basis of a passage in the *Mahaparinirvana Sutra* that all beings
can become buddha, went to the mountain and preached the Dharma to the
rocks, which nodded in response.[43]

In addition to the focus on reinterpreting the words of the patriarchs,
Dōgen's writings emphasize the importance of monastic rules. The *Eihei
shingi*, a collection of six essays written over a dozen-year period beginning in
1237 but mostly during the Echizen period, provides an appropriation or re-
casting in the Japanese setting of the *Ch'an-yüan ch'ing-kuei*'s detailing of every
aspect of monastic discipline and etiquette. For Dōgen, the two sets of Ch'an
records—the three genres highlighting encounter dialogues and the fourth on
regulations—are by no means separate conceptual realms. He liberally uses
kōans to illumine his discussion of behavioral codes, especially in the *Chiji
shingi* from 1249, which cites nearly two dozen cases featuring the stories of
irreverent T'ang-era masters who frequently bent and broke the rules. Dōgen
also, in at least several of his sermons in the *Shōbōgenzō* and *Shōbōgenzō zuimonki,* focuses on issues of monastic organization and conduct.

Collcutt points out how important monastic rules were for the composition
of the *Shōbōgenzō*, which not only is a theoretical work but frequently deals
with the details of daily life. "Of the 90 or more chapters of the *Shōbō genzō*,"
Collcutt notes, "nearly a third are devoted wholly or in part to the detailed
regulation of such everyday monastic activities as meditation, prayer, study,

sleep, dress, the preparation and taking of meals, and bathing and purification."[44] The remaining two-thirds of this text treats doctrinal themes regarding
selfhood, nature, impermanence, and enlightenment based largely on Ch'an
sources.

The model of religious life followed at Kōshōji and Eiheiji integrates the
totality of modalities of Ch'an texts, rather than a particular sector, with Japanese Buddhist perspectives. As Griffith Foulk argues:

> Dōgen was not and never claimed to be an author of monastic rules.
> He presented himself, rather, as a transmitter and authoritative in-
> terpreter of sacred principles and procedures that he had read, been
> instructed about, and/or witnessed in actual practice in the great
> monasteries of Sung China. As exemplified in his *Tenzokyōkun*, Dō-
> gen's real genius consists in his brilliant juxtaposition and elucida-
> tion of Chinese Buddhist monastic rules and Ch'an teachings, two
> types of literature that had usually been treated quite separately in
> China.[45]

Ishii Seijun further argues that Dōgen's writings should be interpreted
neither as strictly philosophical tracts nor as monastic regulations, but rather
in terms of an institutional focus on establishing a Sung Ch'an-oriented way
of life in the social setting of Kamakura Japan.[46] According to Ishii, despite
superficial similarities between the structures of Eiheiji and the two Five Mountains systems—the one in China (Wu-shan) and the one that developed in
Japan (Gozan)—one of Dōgen's primary concerns was to go beyond the Ch'an
model. He sought to develop a distinctive approach regarding relations between the abbot and the regulatory agencies of government and patrons in
addition to administrators and lay followers who supported temple activities.
Central to Dōgen's method was the democratic appointment and rotation of
the monastery administrative council members (*chiji*), who each served a one-
year term, and the enhanced participation of lay believers in regular repentance
rituals and offerings. These initiatives were aimed to free the temple from ties
to political authority by creating a wide base of popular support that buttressed
patronage provided by the Hatano clan led by the samurai warrior, Hatano
Yoshishige, who first connected with Dōgen at Kōshōji, as well as other donors
from the Echizen region.

Eiheiji was thus successful in gaining an air of independence and autonomy from regulation enforced by both the government and the Tendai church,
according to Ishii. However, Dōgen's death after less than a decade of abbacy
at Eiheiji meant that his grand experiment with the institutionalization of Zen,
which greatly depended on his own charisma and connections with the Court,
did not have time to come to fruition during his lifetime. Therefore, it is difficult to evaluate this dimension of Dōgen's career separately from subsequent
developments in the Sōtō sect. Yet, as Bodiford suggests, the legacy continued

to expand, for it can be seen that "Sōtō independence [initiated by Dōgen] contrasted favorably with the constraints suffered by [the Japanese] *Gozan* Zen in the capital,"[47] since the latter temples were continually subject to oversight of their rituals and regulation of their institutional growth.

Dōgen's Relation to Ju-ching: A Delayed Reaction

Among the dozens of Ch'an patriarchs and compositions that exerted an influence on the style of sermons in his major texts, Dōgen was clearly affected most by the words and deeds of his mentor Ju-ching, whose sayings he cites in the *Hōkyōki* as well as in numerous passages in the *Shōbōgenzō* and the *Eihei kōroku*. Dōgen frequently refers to both Ju-ching and Hung-chih as "old buddha" or "ancient worthy" (*kobutsu*) as a sign of admiration and affection, as well as a way of establishing lineal affiliation, but Ju-ching is by far the dominant figure on Dōgen's citation list.[48] The next main figure frequently cited by Dōgen is master Chao-chou, a figure from the T'ang dynasty, like all the others on the list (except for Sakyamuni and Bodhidharma), who plays a prominent role in many kōan cases.

Dōgen's writings and traditional biographies show that the powerful experiences he had while training under Ju-ching represented the crucible of his spiritual awakening by resolving uncertainties and doubts about the meaning of the universality of Buddha-nature in a way that continued to resonate for years to come. According to the opening and closing passages of the "Menju" fascicle written in 1243, on 5.1.1225, just a couple of weeks after the opening of the summer retreat, Dōgen entered the inner sanctum of Ju-ching's quarters, the Miao-kao-t'ai (J. Myōkōdai), and "received *face-to-face transmission* (*menju*) for the first time."[49] Two months later, on 7.2.1225, Ju-ching confirmed

TABLE 5. Dōgen's Most Frequently Cited Chinese Ch'an Masters

Master	No. Citations	Master	No. Citations	Master	No. Citations
Ju-ching	[a]74	Hsüan-sha	12	Yüeh-shan	10
Hung-chih	45	Tung-shan	12	Fa-yen	9
Chao-chou	33	Yüan-wu	12	Huang-lung	9
Sakyamuni[b]	17	Ma-tsu	11	Huang-po	9
Pai-chang	13	Hsüeh-feng	10	Yüeh-shan	9
Yün-men	13	Kuei-shan	10	Bodhidharma	8
Hui-neng	12	Nan-ch'üan	10	Lin-chi	8

[a] Excludes allusions only, memorials, references in Table 28 in Ch. 5, and *Hōkyōki*
[b] Indian Buddha

Kagamishima, *Dōgen in'yō goroku no kenkyū* (Tokyo: Sōtō shūgaku kenkyūjō, 1955).

the authenticity of Dōgen's experience of casting off body-mind, attained earlier that day during a prolonged session of intensive meditation.[50]

Dōgen later asserted that the attainment of *menju* through unwavering training with a mentor based on the practice of single-minded sitting meditation (*zazen* or *shikan taza*) is the linchpin of the religious path and constitutes the necessary ingredient for receiving and transmitting Zen realization. The face-to-face quality stands in sharp contrast to Nōnin's case of sending disciples to China to gain his transmission certification. In *Bendōwa*, Dōgen further suggests the importance of his experiences in China and indirectly criticizes the Daruma school's antinomian tendencies in disregarding the precepts. According to this passage, "I have recollected and written about *what I saw with my own eyes and heard with my own ears* of the style of practice in the Zen monasteries of Sung China, and what I received and upheld as the profound teaching of my master."[51] In *Shōbōgenzō zuimonki* 3.30, Dōgen uses a similar phrase, "I saw with my own eyes," in referring to Ju-ching's way of admonishing those monks who failed to practice meditation diligently enough.[52]

As was indicated, a problematic aspect of this model of the master–disciple relationship is that, although Dōgen mentioned Ju-ching briefly in his early works, historical studies reveal that Dōgen's writings did not place an emphasis on his mentor as a premier teacher or on the exclusive nature of the transmission rite for more than a decade after his return. An emphasis on China first became apparent in the mid-1230s at Kōshōji. *Shōbōgenzō zuimonki* sermons from this phase, which was around the time Dōgen initiated the presentation of *jōdō* sermons collected in the first volume of the *Eihei kōroku*, included just a couple of passages praising Ju-ching.

As Bielefeldt's previously-cited comment shows, the emphasis on Ju-ching became intensified and reached fruition fully fifteen years after the trip to China, at the time of Dōgen's move to Echizen. In numerous *Shōbōgenzō* fascicles from the first several months after the move, when Dōgen and a small band of dedicated followers were holed up over the long first winter in a couple of temporary hermitages, Kippōji and Yoshiminedera, before settling into permanent quarters, Dōgen provided his followers with a strong sense of lineal affiliation by identifying with Ju-ching's branch. He claimed this was the only authentic Ch'an school. The high estimation of Ju-ching expressed during the "midpoint of his career" was not apparent in Dōgen's writings before this juncture. While praising and elevating the status of his mentor, Dōgen also embarked on a devastating critique of rival schools, which he referred to as "filthy rags" and "dirty dogs" that defame the Buddha Dharma. The only Sung figure besides the Ts'ao-tung patriarchs that plays a key role is Ta-hui, whom Dōgen praised and emulated in earlier writings such as *Shōbōgenzō zuimonki* 6.19 for his dedication to *zazen* while having hemorrhoids (the same scatological passage in which Dōgen notes that diarrhea prevented him from entering China when the ship first docked) and 6.21. Yet he harshly criticized the Sung master, particularly in the "Jishō zanmai" fascicle, in part because his lineage was associated with the monks who legitimated Nōnin's status at the time of the conversion of Daruma school monks.

Dōgen notes receiving Ju-ching's recorded sayings on 8.6.1242 in *Eihei kōroku* 1.105,[53] although the first indication of renewed interest was in *Shōbōgenzō* "Gyōji" (part 2), which was written several months earlier and contains four citations as part of a lengthy discussion of Ju-ching, and which comes at the end of a survey of monk biographies as representative of the pinnacle of Ch'an practice.[54] The citation of Ju-ching's attack on Te-kuang indicates that a main factor contributing to the appropriation of the Chinese mentor may have been the arrival at Kōshōji of the erstwhile Daruma school followers. Furthermore, it was when moving to Echizen that Dōgen began citing Ju-ching extensively and in some cases exclusively. Table 6 shows that, apart from "Gyōji" (part 2) covering the main patriarchs in his lineage, all the *Shōbōgenzō* fascicles containing multiple citations of Ju-ching stem from the period of the move (the asterisk indicates that the passages are not found in the *Ju-ching yü-lu* (J. *Nyojō goroku*).

The abundance of citations of Ju-ching at certain periods—and their lack at other times—suggests a delayed reaction and retrospective quality. As is demonstrated by recent Japanese scholarship, Dōgen's citations and evocations of Ju-ching are at times at variance with the recorded sayings, the *Ju-ching yü-lu*, even though Tokugawa-era Sōtō scholar/monks heavily edited this text precisely in order to prove such a consistency.[55] This fact raises basic questions about Dōgen's portrayal of his mentor and use of Ch'an sources, as well as about why his approach seemed to have changed despite claims of unwavering continuity by the sectarian tradition.

The image of Ju-ching presented by Dōgen—that of an idealistic, charismatic religious leader—is somewhat contradicted by the fact that he is generally not regarded as one of the luminaries of the Sung Ch'an school and was in fact given rather short shrift according to annals of the period. It appears that the biggest and perhaps only real supporter of his illustrious status was

TABLE 6. *Shōbōgenzō* Fascicles Citing Ju-ching Multiple Times

Date	Fascicle	Place	No. Citations
1243.9.16	Butsudō	Kippōji	2
1243.9	Bukkyō	Kippōji	2*
1243.9	Shohō jissō	Kippōji	2*
1243.11.6	Baika	Kippōji	8
1243.12.17	Ganzei	Yamashibudera	7
1243.12.17	Kajō	Yamashibudera	5
1244.2.12	Udonge	Kippōji	2

Dōgen, and ironically, Mount T'ien-t'ung is best known today not so much for Ju-ching but for Dōgen's admiration of him.[56] Yet there are also passages in which Dōgen depicts his mentor as a divisive and partisan figure who was hypercritical of representatives of other branches of Ch'an. It is interesting to note that quotations cited by Dōgen that are not included in Ju-ching's recorded sayings reveal the mentor to be more polemical in vehemently attacking opponents than any of the passages found in the recorded sayings.[57] The implication is that he evoked the authority of Ju-ching as a vehicle for self-expression and the advocacy of sectarian identity. Since nearly a dozen of his citations cannot be tracked to the *Ju-ching yü-lu*, itself an unreliable source, it is possible that Dōgen exaggerated or invented at least some aspects of his mentor and his teachings in a way that was exacerbated by subsequent editors.

Questionability of Historical Sources

Investigating multiple elements central to the formation of Dōgen's image of Ch'an is complicated by the questionable dating and authenticity of some of the sources that have served as the mainstay of studies of Dōgen's journey. The fact is that there are no writings attributed to the China period other than the *kanshi* collection. Furthermore, the primary work supposedly stemming from China has been subject to textual criticism in recent Japanese scholarship.

The Case of the Hōkyōki

The *Hōkyōki*, which is ordinarily considered the most likely source for learning about the travels, purports to be a record of about fifty dialogues (the exact number depends on the edition) between Dōgen and Ju-ching in the Abbot's Quarters over a two-year period, from the summer retreat of 1225 until the 1227 departure from China, or the first through third year of the Pao-ch'ing era (J. Hōkyō). Dōgen was apparently given the rare privilege, especially for a novice from a foreign country, of having repeated private audiences with the abbot. The *Hōkyōki* has been translated numerous times and is one of the best-known examples of Dōgen's works in English.[58] The only other available Japanese sources for this phase of the trip are secondary materials that dwell extensively on supernatural occurrences.[59]

However, it turns out that the *Hōkyōki* is not particularly useful or reliable as a historical source, for several reasons. First, the text simply does not deal with the two-year period before the meetings, which led Dōgen to become Ju-ching's most intimate disciple. More important, the *Hōkyōki* was long believed to have been a journal compiled by Dōgen while he was still in China or transcribed from notes very shortly after his return, but it may well be a much later construction or at least it is of highly uncertain provenance. As is indicated by the first of two colophons, the text was discovered posthumously and copied by Ejō, Dōgen's main disciple and recorder/editor (*jisha*) several months after Dōgen's death on the tenth day of the twelfth month of 1253:

> [*Hōkyōki*] is among the manuscripts left behind by the late master. As I began drafting this, I wondered whether there might be still others that have not been discovered. I am concerned that [the record of] his unlimited achievements may be incomplete, and in my sadness fall 100,000 tears.[60]

According to the second colophon, the text was not noticed again until Giun rediscovered it in 1299 at Hōkyōji temple, a branch of Eiheiji founded by Dōgen's disciple Jakuen, who came from Mount T'ien-t'ung in China to study with him in 1228.

The assumption that the *Hōkyōki* was written at the time of Dōgen's return would reinforce a view that he valued Ju-ching highly all along. However, the *Hōkyōki* is of dubious value, even for the period of Dōgen's training under Ju-ching during his last two years in China. Based in part on the posthumous discovery of the text, the main theory that has been put forth by Mizuno Yaoko and is generally accepted by scholars in Japan is that the *Hōkyōki* was actually a late product that reflects the priorities of the the post-Kamakura period.[61] Mizuno argues that the text's focus on the topics of karmic causality (*inga*), the inevitability of moral retribution covering past, present, and future (*sanjigo*), and a refutation of the unity of the three teachings (of Buddhism, Confucianism and Taoism) (*sankyō itchi*) is consistent with other writings from the late 1240s and early 1250s. Although these teachings are attributed to Ju-ching through the question-answer format, when examined carefully, they stand in contrast to the teachings in the recorded sayings of Ju-ching.

Another possibility is that the *Hōkyōki* was composed in the early 1240s, after Dōgen first received a copy of the *Ju-ching yü-lu* in 1242, which was edited by I-yüan and then transported from China. This was when Dōgen developed a new, or at least renewed interest in Ju-ching as reflected in the onset of numerous citations and allusions, especially in the sermons of the *Shōbōgenzō* and *Eihei kōroku* from this and subsequent periods. According to this theory, Dōgen may have been disappointed that the recorded sayings text was not truly representative of his mentor's teachings and he felt the need to amplify the record according to his own personal conversations.

Whichever of these theories is followed, the redating of the *Hōkyōki* highlights the fact that Dōgen had relatively little to say about Ju-ching until a key turning point in his own career and consequent desire to emphasize a distinctive lineage and pedigree, so that the text might be more revealing of his *own* attitudes than of an accurate portrayal of his mentor's doctrines. This possibility indicates the need for a detailed analysis of the main stages of Dōgen's career in order to highlight an evolution in his thinking and style of writing.

Once again, particularly important are the two transitional phases that are likely candidates for the time of composition: the move to Echizen at the middle of Dōgen's career when he needed to solidify sectarian identity, and his return from Kamakura near the end of his career when he developed a new focus on karmic causality and retribution.

Other Quasi-Biographical Sources

A crucial element in interpreting Dōgen's literary production are the questions surrounding the historicity of his pilgrimage to China and the implications for assessing the impact of Ch'an and Ju-ching on his later works. Once the Hō-kyōki is removed from consideration as an authoritative text covering the China journey, it becomes clear that there are not many reliable sources. The limitation in historical records is compounded by the fact that very few sources were written by Dōgen while he was visiting China. In addition to the kanshi collection, Dōgen wrote a short remembrance for Myōzen, which may have been composed upon his return, explaining the extraordinary number of relics (sarira) that Myōzen's remains emitted.[62]

A host of references to the trip are found scattered among a couple of dozen sources by or about Dōgen, which do not have a coherent structure. Any sense of order in the sequence of events was no doubt superimposed retrospectively. Autobiographical observations or reminiscences are contained in sermons, journals, lineage records, or sectarian biographical works, in which there is some mention, however brief or ambiguous, of conversations Dōgen had in China or transmission documents he viewed or received there. These records include many blatantly hagiographical elements, such as apocryphal dialogues, supernatural encounters, mysterious dreams, and the intercession of magical animals and deities.

There is nothing that resembles a single sustained narrative prior to the production of the primary traditional sectarian biography of Dōgen, the Kenzeiki, composed over 200 years after the master's death in 1472 by Kenzei, the fourteenth abbot of Eiheiji. The Kenzeiki is filled with hagiographical elements further filtered and distorted by subsequent annotated editions, particularly Menzan Zuihō's Teiho Kenzeiki, produced four centuries later in 1753. Menzan was one of the giants in the Tokugawa revival of studies of Dōgen's life and thought; his contributions were monumental, although by modern standards they are subject to cricticism. Menzan made significant additions and emendations that seem misleading or inaccurate when compared with earlier manuscripts of the Kenzeiki, as is shown in a seminal textual study by Kawamura Kōdō.[63] The Teiho Kenzeiki has Dōgen encountering various gods during his pilgrimage to China, in addition to other embellishments.

Furthermore, a series of about 60 ukiyoe-style illustrations known as the Dōgen zenji go-eden (or the Teiho Kenzeiki zue) that covers important events in

江西ニテ
猛虎ヲ
伏シ玉フ
圖

FIGURE 7. Dōgen Frightening a Tiger in *Teiho Kenzeiki zue*

Dōgen's life has enhanced (or aggravated) the romanticized elements of the account. Created in 1806, the *Teiho Kenzeki zue* makes for a fascinating record of Dōgen's career but in numerous instances compounds the gap between history and hagiography. As in the depicted legend of Dōgen fending off a ferocious tiger through the power of his meditation (*zenjōriki*), in this collection the blatantly mythical incidents, such as interaction with deities or miraculous occurrences, are presented in a way that does not distinguish them from historical events. The *Teiho Kenzeiki zue* illustration in Figure 7 is part of a series that shows Dōgen being assisted by the Japanese folk deity Inari, who cures his illness; the Hakusan avatar, who helps copy the *Blue Cliff Record* (Figure 6); and the bodhisattva Küan-yin (J. Kannon), who saves him while he is traveling back to Japan during a typhoon. According to David Riggs, Menzan's reputation for impeccable scholarship has served to exacerbate the problem:

> [T]he popular illustrated text highlighted events that are absent or unclear in the original *Kenzeiki*, and makes it all that much easier to ignore the distinction, already blurry at any rate, between Menzan's additions and the original *Kenzeiki*. These problems have caused some diminution of Menzan's reputation as a careful scholar, but it should be pointed out that this was a text explicitly written for a popular audience and crafted to paint a portrait of the founder whom Menzan was promoting as an inspiration to all. He makes this hagiographic purpose clear in the preface, yet such was Menzan's reputation that his story was taken as the definitive biography for many years.[64]

With back-to-back celebrations in 2000 of the 800th anniversary of Dōgen's birth and in 2003 of the 750th anniversary of his death, there have been two colorized versions of the *Teiho Kenzeiki zue* released in recent years, one produced by Eiheiji and the other by a nonsectarian publisher.[65] In addition, a variety of popular cultural expressions of Dōgen's biography have been appearing, including representations on Internet sites, Manga or comics-style publications (often for adults), and television shows. All of these tend to accentuate mythological features, such as an episode in which Dōgen met or saw an apparition of an arhat on Mount Ching who advised him to return to Mount T'ien-t'ung, where Ju-ching would soon be taking over duties as the new abbot. Figure 9 shows that one of the favored themes in popular cultural approaches is to glorify the inspirational "moment" of the experience of *shinjin datsuraku* attained by Dōgen during his interaction with Ju-ching. In addition, a Kabuki play recently commissioned by the Sōtō sect and performed in Tokyo, titled *Dōgen no tsuki*, focused on the visit to Kamakura and the rejection of the Hōjō's offer to lead a temple there as well as subsequent developments near the end of his life.[66]

Each successive edition of the *Kenzeiki* and its popularization, whether specifically a sectarian product or not, have increased the emphasis on hagiographical material and the crossing of the line between fact and legend/myth/fantasy. Until very recently, modern studies have been overly reliant on the *Teiho Kenzeiki* and *Teiho Kenzeiki zue*, and by accepting uncritically traditional accounts of Dōgen's travels, Western approaches have not necessarily kept pace with more recent revisionism in Japanese scholarship. The main work in English on the topic of China, Takeshi James Kodera's *Dogen's Formative Years in*

FIGURE 8. Dōgen Visiting Mount Ching (Web site view)

China, now a quarter of a century old, remains a useful resource but only for the trip itself and not its impact on later events.

A Tale of Two Travelers

In our analyzing what took place in China and why it is of such great significance for later developments, a question arises: How much do we really know about the journey on the basis of scanty traditional sources, many of which have been shaped by sectarian commentators, especially the Tokugawa-era editing of the recorded sayings and biographies of Ju-ching and Dōgen? What are the problems in examining the records?[67] Accounts of Dōgen's travels are

FIGURE 9. Dōgen and Ju-ching on Shinjin Datsuraku (Manga View)

Nakano Tōzen, *Dōgen nyūmon: Makoto no Buppō o motometa tamashii no kiseki* (Tokyo: Sanmāku shuppan, 2001), p. 185.

unverifiable or contradictory and can easily be questioned, just as the "Travels" of another even more famous thirteenth-century adventurer and observer of the religions of Sung China are not verified by objective historical sources and are subjected to revisionist historiographical inquiry.

Given the spurious, hagiographical, and at times contradictory or conflictive quality of materials that have been relied on for historiographical purposes, the whole question of whether Dōgen even went to China may be brought under consideration, as is suggested in the deliberately playful title of this book, which emulates Frances Wood's controversial revisionist tract, *Did Marco Polo Go to China?*[68] My aim in raising this issue, as I earlier indicated, is not necessarily to debunk the trip or refute the legitimacy of Dōgen's experiences in China, but to point out significant discrepancies in accounts of the dates and locations of his travels and to underscore that little should be taken at face value.

Dōgen's relation to Ch'an and to Ju-ching is problematized in order to probe more deeply into the underlying connections and disconnections between the historical record and Dōgen's literary productivity, which is perhaps the main evidence for his inheriting the legacy of Chinese Ch'an. On the one hand, the title of this book mocks those who would take historical deconstruction to its extreme by denying just about any religious truth claim. At the same time, it is important to recognize that even when the blatantly hagiographic references in the narrative are eliminated—such as to the Hakusan deity, Inari, and Kūan-yin—significant discrepancies remain in accounts of the dates and locations of Dōgen's travels.[69]

To explore the parallels, Dōgen and Marco Polo were foreign travelers whose records are still heavily relied on for an understanding of the condition of religious practice in the Sung era. Polo traveled a great distance from the West and stayed in China for a long period. His entire journey lasted 25 years (1271–1295), with 17 years spent in various parts of China during the Mongol hegemony. His journey was made possible by the *pax Mongolica* initiated by Genghis Khan, who died in 1227, the year Dōgen left China. Although Polo was an adventurer who was not a religious practitioner or someone concerned primarily with this realm, he recognized the crucial role that diverse religious traditions played in Chinese society and was able to offer some insightful and generally unbiased comments, at least for his time. His travelogue provided Europeans with one of their first insider glimpses of Buddhism (which he referred to as "idolatry," suggesting some degree of bias) as well as other foreign traditions in China, including Nestorian Christianity, Islam, Zoroastrianism, and Manicheism, which had preceded his pathways on the Silk Road.

Half a century earlier, Dōgen traveled a short, though at the time arduous distance from Japan, primarily in search of a purer form of Buddhism than he experienced in his native country. He stayed four and a half years and returned to Japan tremendously impressed and influenced by the style of practice he found in the Five Mountains monasteries. But he was also eager to leave us with a severe and at times harsh critique of some features of Buddhist practice that did not live up to his expectations or ideals. Not surprisingly, both visitors spent a good deal of their time near Hang-chou, the cosmopolitan capital city located close to the port of Ming-chou and the central Buddhist temples of the period.

The records of these journeys have long been admired and studied and are still today considered reliably informative sources for this period of Chinese history, especially since other kinds of materials and documents are so sparse or unreliable. Frances Wood questions the idea that the Italian adventurer's travel record is a historical fact and values it primarily as an incomparable literary feat and cultural phenomenon. Nevertheless she remarks, "Marco Polo's description of places in China and beyond form, perhaps, his most lasting contribution to our knowledge of the East in the thirteenth century. The first, traditionally 'eyewitness,' account of the great cities of China is of special significance because many of the places he describes have either vanished . . . or been transformed beyond recognition."[70] Similarly, Dōgen's depictions—as well as criticisms of the lack of discipline in some cases—of the Five Mountains monastic system are among the key historical sources for examining that period.[71] His literary citations and allusions to Sung texts remain a major vehicle for interpreting Chinese Ch'an materials that became increasingly popular in Japan as their use diminished in China.

One of the main common features in the narratives about Marco Polo and Dōgen is that an inexperienced, uninformed foreigner finds himself plucked from obscurity and placed in a position of great respect and responsibility by a mainstream institution, whether secular/political or religious/monastic. This situation gives their observations of the Chinese religious and social orders great weight and authority. Both narratives are driven by the high status of the foreign visitors awarded by the Chinese system, and this element is also what makes them rather questionable. Could it really have happened in this way? In Dōgen's case, is it plausible that a young monk from Japan at first not allowed to enter the summer retreat because he lacked the prerequisite precepts was, shortly after Myōzen's untimely death in 1225, which left him in an even more vulnerable position, invited to come to the abbot's private quarters to receive special teachings and offered the chance to become a head monk (which he turned down)?

It also seems that in both cases some of the claims that are most basic and central to the narrative of their journeys have become suspect when examined in light of modern historiography. For example, Marco Polo's descriptions contain some misleading or inaccurate passages and exaggerations as well as glaring oversights such as not mentioning the Great Wall or calligraphy. He was said to be governor of Yang-chou, but no mention of this fact is found in any Chinese records. He also probably did not bring back noodles and ice cream to Italy, despite the widespread legends that are still frequently told to school-children. Wood concludes, "Beginning with the negative, *the Descriptions of the World* [or *Travels*] is not an itinerary or a straightforward account of travels."[72] Wood speculates that the book was a fiction woven together in 1298 by Polo's prison mate Rustichello with an eye toward commercial success, based on stories Polo had heard and the writings of other thirteenth-century adventurers to the East.[73]

As for Dōgen, the most famous saying that he attributes to his mentor as the epitome of Ch'an teaching, *shinjin datsuraku*, was almost certainly not something Ju-ching or Sung Ch'an masters ever uttered. The use of this phrase in sectarian biographies such as various manuscripts of the *Kenzeiki* and the *Teiho Kenzeiki*, which contain several different versions of the event, must have developed over the years.[74] Many other aspects of Dōgen's citations of Ju-ching and related Ch'an sources are questionable. For example, he probably did not bring back to Japan the "One Night *Blue Cliff Record*," or at least did not copy it in a single night, although there is evidence that supports the existence of a version of the collection in Dōgen's hand that is at variance with the main edition of the text.

Contradictory Elements in the Traditional Account

Traditional sources are rife with contradictions and inconsistencies concerning the question of whether Dōgen traveled among the Five Mountains Ch'an temples by land or sea. They are unclear whether this trip took place in the fall of 1223, the first year of the journey, or the following year. For example, as is illustrated in Figures 10 and 11, there are two theories about Dōgen's sup-posed lengthy period of itinerant travels (*tangaryō*)[75] to various temples in pur-suit of an authentic master before he settled on studying with Ju-ching, who had been recently appointed abbot, at Mount T'ien-t'ung during the summer retreat of 1225. One is a "land route" theory, which suggests that Dōgen traveled in circular fashion from Mount T'ien-t'ung westward to Mount Ching, the leading Five Mountains temple, and then to the nether reaches of Mount T'ien-t'ai (Neng-ren ssu) in the south and back to the first temple.[76] The other is a "sea route" theory, which suggests that Dōgen actually made two trips, one to Mount Ching and back by land and another to the Mount T'ien-t'ai region by sea.

Kagamishima Genryū has proposed the sea route theory, in part because of the forbidding mountainous terrain located between Mount Ching and Mount T'ien-t'ai, although other scholars suggest that itinerant monks crossed this area by foot (whereas the military or civil official would have traveled by horse or in a small caravan).[77] Would Dōgen have traveled by himself or with a group? The sea route theory rests on the idea that Dōgen visited the island of Mount P'u-t'a (or P'u-t'o-loka, J. Mount Fudaraku), considered in popular

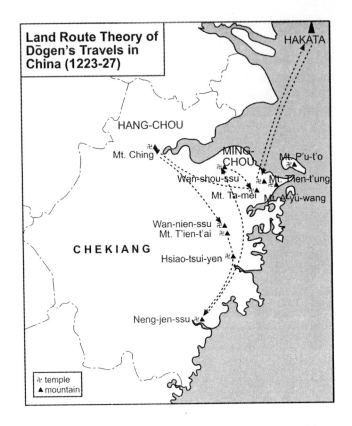

FIGURES 10 and 11. Land Route and Sea Route Theories

Buddhism the earthly abode of Küan-yin (J. Kannon) in 1224; it was one of several mountains in a sacred network in China considered to be the dwelling places of bodhisattvas.[78] According to the theory, the Küan-yin mountain, on an island just east of mainland China not far from Mount T'ien-t'ung, was Dōgen's stop to find a port of embarkation to the south.

Although it is likely the island was used in this way for seafarers, the only evidence for Dōgen's side trip to the island is an undated *kanbun* poem (*Eihei kōroku* 10.45), "Written on the Occasion of Visiting Mount P'u-t'a in Ch'ang-kuo District":

> Hearing, thinking, practicing alone
> Actualize the mind of original enlightenment;
> Whoever seeks a vision of a god in a cave—
> Ye seekers must come to understand,
> Küan-yin does not abide on Mount P'u-t'a.[79]

Dōgen's comment in the final line suggests that he rejects the otherworldly implications of the veneration of Küan-yin by emphasizing the self-power approach of Zen. However, this verse could well have been written at some other time, such as on the way to or on the way back from China. Alternatively, it could even refer to an island just off the coast of Shimane prefecture in Japan that perhaps borrowed the name and goddess worship from China. Also the antisupernatural message of the poem makes an interesting contrast to reports in traditional sources such as *Teiho Kenzeiki zue* that Dōgen was guided through a typhoon by a manifestation of Küan-yin when he was traveling by boat in the Japan Sea on his return home, an event that resulted in another notable verse in Dōgen's collected writings.[80]

In addition to the issue of how and where he traveled, there is also a dispute about when Dōgen journeyed to various temple locations. Did the itinerancy begin in the fall of 1223 during Dōgen's first year in China, or in the following year? Perhaps, as the sea route theory may suggest, there were two trips that may have occurred in different years. What are the sources for the respective theories, and how are they documented and argued by scholars today? There are numerous other problematic aspects of Dōgen's journey to China. Examples include a controversy concerning his qualifications for receiving admission to the summer retreat and challenges to the Ch'an monastic system; his viewing a variety of *shisho* documents; conversations with a number of masters and monks; a series of prophetic dreams that steered his path in finding Ju-ching; apparitions of the moon that he saw at Mount A-yü-wang on two separate occasions; and the conditions of his departure from China relative to the death of Ju-ching, in addition to tales of supernatural occurrences during the return trip.

A careful examination must acknowledge that the conventional chronology of Dōgen's trip to China has been derived by modern scholarship through piecing together snippets of clues amid scattered references in a wide variety of writings. These include *Hōkyōki*, *Tenzokyōkun*, *Shōbōgenzō zuimonki*, and *Shōbōgenzō* fascicles "Shisho" and "Busshō," as well as the traditional biographies *Denkōroku* by fourth Sōtō patriarch Keizan (in *Taishō* vol. 82, no. 2585) and the *Kenzeiki*. This process has created a fascinating, if not necessarily accurate, mosaic of Dōgen's quest for the true Dharma. The narrative encompasses a series of dialogues, visions, and dreams that led him to connect with Ju-ching, who had taken over as abbot of Mount T'ien-t'ung in the fall of 1224 upon the death of Wu-chi after serving at several Five Mountains temples in the early 1220s.

All of the sources used to reconstruct the journey either are attributed to Dōgen but were probably edited later or are sectarian biographies written generations or even centuries after his death and then further revised, and there are simply no objective third-party accounts to verify traditional claims and no independent property or travel records to consult. Because no particular source of evidence is strongly supported, once some of the main factors of the account are effectively challenged, such as the visit to Mount P'u-t'a in the sea route theory, much of the rest of the narrative begins to unravel, at least in terms of the standards of historiographic verification.

To what extent is the trip to China an "invention of tradition"?[81] Bielefeldt points out the following about the journey:

> Perhaps this is what happened [in China], but the account I have summarized here depends heavily on the hagiographic literature of early Sōtō. This literature includes considerable material not confirmed by earlier sources and introduces many fanciful elements into its story of Dōgen's life. Though modern biographers now reject at least the most obvious of these latter [fanciful elements in the story], they have yet to question seriously the basic account of Dōgen's itinerary in China.[82]

Looking at the issue from another angle, for the sake of upholding Sōtō religious claims and basic sectarian concerns, did Dōgen have to have gone to China, or can this belief be maintained despite historiographical objections? It is at least possible to question whether the whole idea of itinerancy was invented by the Sōtō tradition in order to link Dōgen with the most prestigious of the Five Mountains temples and leading patriarchs of the day.

The controversy surrounding the historicity of Dōgen's travels is directly linked to an examination of his attitudes toward Chinese Buddhism.[83] These range from high praise to a devastating critique of doctrines and practices he apparently found there, especially in the laxity of monks regarding the trimming of nails and hair, washing of face and hands, and wearing of the robe.[84] The controversy also sheds light on the influence on Dōgen from Hung-chih, Ju-ching, and other sources, as well as the impact of the Chinese legacy on his

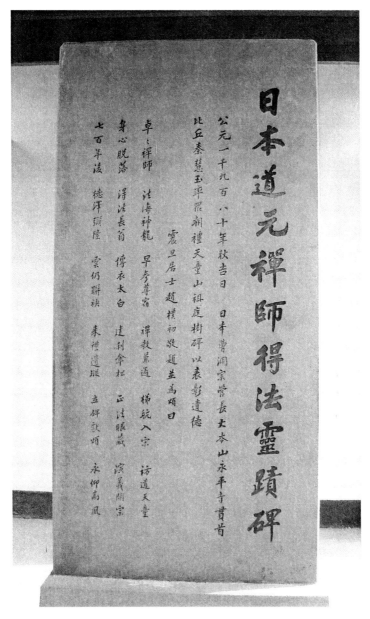

日本道元禪師得法靈蹟碑

公元一千九百八十年秋吉日　日本曹洞宗管長大本山永平寺貫首

比丘秦慧玉率罷朝禮天童山祖庭樹碑以表彰遺德

震旦居士趙樸初敬題並為頌曰

卓卓禪師　　法海神龍　　早參尊宿　　禪教兼通　　梯航入宗　　訪道天童

身心脫落　　浮法長翁　　傳衣太白　　建利傘松　　正法眼藏　　濱義開宗

七百年後　　德洋彌隆　　雲仍聯袂　　來禮遺蹤　　立碑歌頌　　永仰高風

FIGURE 12. Modern Stele at Mount T'ien-t'ung Commemorating Dōgen's
Visit

handling of sectarian disputes in Japan. These issues, which include Dōgen's views on such topics as Buddha-nature and mind (vs. form), language and the sutras, the precepts and monastic routine, and the various Ch'an lineages in relation to the notion of the unity of the three teachings, are important for understanding the period when Dōgen was evangelizing the group of followers who converted to Sōtō Zen from the proscribed Daruma school.

Evidence supporting the trip includes a couple of artifacts, such as stele at Mount T'ien-t'ung (though these are clearly of more recent vintage, including a marker installed in the 1990s to commemorate the 750th anniversary of Dōgen's death), a poem written on Dōgen's return trip supposedly inscribed on a boat, Dōgen's *shisho* (transmission) document, and a portrait of Ju-ching held at Hōkyōji temple.[85] Additional supporting evidence includes the exchange of visitors, such as the monk Jakuen, Dōgen's Dharma-brother in China who joined his community at Kōshōji, and the disciple Giin, who traveled to China after Dōgen's death to show his collected sayings to the Mount T'ien-t'ung monks who remembered him.

Yet it is Dōgen's accomplishments as a sermonizer, essayist, and poet with a remarkably extensive reliance on Sung texts that makes the most compelling argument for his intimate familiarity with Chinese Ch'an. As Bodiford states, "Today Dōgen stands out because of his prodigious and prestigious literary productions."[86] In this context, the tale of the "One Night *Blue Cliff Record*" becomes a significant reminder rather than a quaint legend. Therefore, understanding what Dōgen wrote and when he wrote it requires critical reconstruction of the chronology of Dōgen's life and works to clarify the shifting nature of his attitudes toward establishing Ch'an-style religiosity in the Japanese context.

2

Gone Fishin'

Sources and Re-Sources

Various Theories about Diverse Texts and Their
Multiple Versions

A fundamental irony of Dōgen's career path, or at least our appropriation of it, is that as a writer, he is known primarily for producing
the literary flourishes of the *Shōbōgenzō* influenced by his poetic
background gained while residing in the capital, as well as for his
ability to create a hybrid Sino-Japanese phantasmagoria. As a religious leader, however, he is most famous for the establishment of
highly disciplined monastic life at Eiheiji temple in the secluded
provincial mountains where the *Eihei kōroku,* based largely on ceremonial occasions, was produced. However, it is not always recognized that these accomplishments represent two very different time
frames and models of religious theory and practice that in some
ways seem to contradict as much as complement one another. The
Shōbōgenzō was almost entirely composed prior to the Eiheiji abbacy
and therefore does not reflect the religiosity of that period, with the
prominent exception of the 12-fascicle *Shōbōgenzō*, which will be analyzed later here in relation to other versions of the text and which
was composed primarily near the end of Dōgen's life.

A key feature of the move to Echizen is that Dōgen's composition of vernacular *Shōbōgenzō* fascicles reached a peak during the
year of the transition, or a stretch of about nine months from the
time of the arrival in the seventh month of 1243 until construction
of Daibutsuji began in the third month of the following year. During
this phase, over a third of the fascicles were composed, in addition

to many of the 31-syllable Japanese poems contained in the *waka* collection (*waka-shū*) traditionally known as *Sanshōdōei*.[1] In the throes of moving from Kyoto to the mountains, Dōgen turned increasingly to his Chinese master as a source of inspiration and a sectarian image for his struggling community. He began celebrating Ju-ching as a stellar figure among Sung Ch'an masters by devoting several *Shōbōgenzō* fascicles to a discussion of the mentor's sayings, especially "Baika" and "Ganzei," both delivered at Kippōji temple in the fall of 1243. The increasing importance of Chinese influences also became apparent in that the *jōdō* sermons, first delivered during the Kōshōji abbacy, flourished at Eiheiji just at the point that the level of *Shōbōgenzō* production began to subside shortly after reaching its peak. After a two-year hiatus in the delivery of these sermons during the move until a new Dharma Hall was established, the only other lapse was the eight-month period of the visit to Kamakura. Otherwise, the *Eihei kōroku* was clearly the main work of Dōgen's Echizen period.

The irony that pervades Dōgen's reputation is further seen in that many of the writings that highlight the pristine purity of nature as a necessary back-drop for meditation, such as the *Shōbōgenzō* "Sansuikyō" and "Keisei san-shoku" fascicles on mountain asceticism, were written in 1240 while Dōgen was still in Kyoto. Moreover, writings emphasizing the importance of *kanbun* literature came from the time he was living in a remote province, far removed from elite society that was well versed in Chinese.

What is the relation between the period in which the *Shōbōgenzō* was com-posed and that of the *Eihei kōroku* sermons? Is there an underlying continuity or discontinuity? Some recent commentators have evaluated the extent of con-nectedness or disconnectedness as a matter of a dramatic, fixed, and irrevers-ible change—understood as either a progression or a digression—in Dōgen's rhetorical skills and depth of thought. For example, the phasing out of *jishu* lectures is seen as a sign of continuing decline in Dōgen's later period by some scholars who generally disregard the *Eihei kōroku*, whereas for others the com-position of the 12-fascicle version of the *Shōbōgenzō* is understood as indicative of a late-developing spiritual renewal and rejection of misguided tendencies in his earlier thought. Either way, the importance of the *Eihei kōroku* is neglected.

However, these theories, while useful and stimulating in some regards, are, in the final analysis, unconvincing because they fail to deal with the full complexity of the phases of Dōgen's life. Studies of Dōgen have been so dom-inated by an emphasis on the *Shōbōgenzō*, a text often misrepresented in terms of its formation and content, that there has been an inability to stay open to the remarkable diversity yet consistency in the flow of Dōgen's career path. *Correcting this imbalance must begin by emphasizing the role of the Eihei kōroku and the continuity underlying the transition in writings from the jishu- to jōdō-style sermons.* Continuity in Dōgen's approach is further evidenced in his ongoing composition of monastic rules texts. It is true that of the six essays eventually collected in the *Eihei shingi*, five were composed in Echizen, giving the impression that a concern with monasticism was entirely a later development. However, several *Shōbōgenzō* fascicles dealing with the topic of rules, along with the most prominent essay, *Tenzokyōkun*, were written at Kōshōji. Dōgen's interest in monasticism was not limited to a particular period but reflected the need to organize his community as opportunity and demand required. The fact that the contents of the *Eihei shingi* were disparate until a unified text was constructed by Tokugawa-era editors tends to cloud our understanding of what was really going on in Dōgen's time regarding his concern with monastic regulations.

Therefore it is important to avoid reductionist notions of "early" and "late" periods—or of "early Dōgen" and "late Dōgen"—supposedly marked by sudden, abrupt changes that were discontinuous with previous or subsequent stages. My argument is that periodization is a very useful methodological tool for examining the impact of China on Dōgen's writings, but it is preferable to distinguish between three periods rather than two in order to capture the full range of Dōgen's oeuvre. Each of the three periods lasts about a decade. The early period covers the trip to China and return to Japan up to the establishment of Kōshōji; the crucial yet generally overlooked or misunderstood middle period spans the formation of the *Shōbōgenzō* and the move to Echizen; and the late period covers the Eiheiji abbacy, including the *Eihei kōroku* and other texts that have also been neglected. I will further break down the three main periods into seven subperiods as outlined in Table 14 near the end of the chapter and Table 15 at the beginning of Part II.

95- *and* 75-*Fascicle Editions of the* Shōbōgenzō

Very little is simple or uniform in Dōgen's collected works, and claims to the contrary based on taking things at face value must be distrusted and reexamined. The text that is generally known as the "Shōbōgenzō," for example, is by no means a single independent or autonomous scriptural entity.[2] Rather, it consists of multiple versions of sometimes common and sometimes disparate collections of textual units or fascicles (C. *chuan*, J. *kan* or *maki*, lit., scrolls or volumes), most of which were originally presented orally as *jishu* sermons at certain phases of Dōgen's career and later compiled and collected in different ways by various recorders and editors during the medieval and early modern periods.[3] In some cases the oral delivery was subsequent to a written record, but in most instances the sermon was recorded by a disciple and then edited, mainly by Ejō but sometimes with Dōgen's input, before being collated with other fascicles.

Many different manuscripts with alternative versions of the fascicles have been stored at temples throughout regions where the Sōtō sect was strong and, because of complications now apparent, recent Japanese scholarship has called into question traditional assumptions about the status of these editions. As Riggs points out, "[Dōgen's] writings, especially the collection of essays which is now called the *Shōbō genzō* . . . were treated as secret treasures, but there was no commonly accepted version and no commentaries were written from about 1300 until the seventeenth century."[4] According to Ishii Shūdō, the *Shōbōgenzō* must be seen as a "provisional text," that is, as fluid textual entities undergoing a continuing formative process up to and well beyond Dōgen's demise.[5]

The contents of the *Shōbōgenzō* need to be analyzed from a variety of perspectives, including where and/or when the fascicles were written and recorded and the ways in which they were collected and organized into various editions. It is necessary, for example, to distinguish between fascicles composed in Kyoto and those in Echizen, as well as to understand how recorders/editors and compilers have dealt with organizing and sequencing the pieces. Since there is no definitive edition that captures clearly and unequivocally the author's intentionality, no one version of the text or single approach to historical examination is sufficient for grasping the significance of the work or its relation to Dōgen's other writings.

Given the discrepancies and debates, it is important to specify that the main version being dealt with here is the collection of 75 fascicles that will be referred to as the 75-*Shōbōgenzō* and distinguished from the 95-fascicle text, in addition to several other versions that are also identified and labeled according to numbers of fascicles (see Appendix V). The 95-*Shōbōgenzō* is no doubt the best known and has often been considered authoritative, but at the same time it is perhaps the least representative of the main *Shōbōgenzō* versions because it was not created until 1690, well over four centuries after Dōgen's death. During the Tokugawa era, when all Buddhist sects were required to define their basic teachings and institutional structure by government supervisors who generally favored other forms of religion, including Neo-Confucian and *Kokugaku* (Nativist Learning) ideologies, the Sōtō monk Kōzen sought to compile in a single edition, sequenced by chronology, all of the vernacular materials included in various versions then available.

Kōzen used as a foundation the 89-fascicle edition created a few years earlier by Manzan Dōhaku, which sequenced the fascicles in the chronological order of when they were composed, beginning with the recently discovered *Bendōwa* (not included in any previous compilations). He also included a couple of additional writings that had been left out of the other main versions (there are 96 fascicles if the spurious *Chinzō* is included). This attempt at inclusiveness is distorting, however, just as is Menzan's attempt in the *Teiho Kenzeiki* to cover all of the available materials regarding Dōgen's biography. At the same time as these efforts were going on, the Sōtō sect continued years of prohibiting outsiders from studying the *Shōbōgenzō* because the teachings were regarded as too powerful and secret for the casual reader, instigating the government to impose a ban in 1722.

The 95-*Shōbōgenzō*, known as the Kōzen-bon and considered the official publication of the sect, gained prestige when Gentō reissued it in 1811 as the "Honzan" or Head Temple edition, although five of the fascicles ("Den'e," "Busso," "Shisho," "Jishō zanmai," and "Jukai" were still not made available to the public because their contents were considered inappropriate). From 1938 to 1943 the publisher Iwanami bunko produced this version in a famous paperback edition edited by Etō Sokuō, a leading modern Sōtō scholar known for his book that argued against secular appropriations of Dōgen by Kyoto School philosophers such as Watsuji Tetsurō, Tanabe Hajime, Nishida Kitarō, and Nishitani Keiji.[6] Ōkubo Dōshū included the 95-fascicle version in the first modern edition of the collected works published in 1970, although another prominent edition from that time issued by the Iwanami shoten imprint and edited by Terada Tōru and Mizuno Yaoko contained 92 fascicles (75 plus 12, and 5 irregular ones, or fascicles that cannot be properly identified as authentic).[7] The 95-*Shōbōgenzō* is not altogether unreliable and it should be studied for historical purposes, but reading or referring to this edition alone may create a misleading impression of the order and relative significance of the fascicles. If taken as authoritative, this version tends to suppress the fact that in Dōgen's era and subsequent generations there were multiple versions that had their respective advocates and competed for attention.

One of the misconceptions about the *Shōbōgenzō* has to do with the dates of composition. Dōgen's interest in the formation of the *Shōbōgenzō* extended from the time of the first composition (excluding *Bendōwa*), the "Genjōkōan" fascicle in 1233, to 1252 when he composed "Hachidainingaku" and apparently reedited "Genjōkōan" (according to some versions of this fascicle's colophon). These dates create an impression for many readers that the *Shōbōgenzō* was constructed during a twenty-year period and was the main concern over the course of Dōgen's entire career. However, such a view is undermined by a careful analysis of the dates of composition, which reveals that the 75-*Shōbōgenzō* reflects a much more compressed period and is indicative of a particular phase of his career. The great majority of 75-*Shōbōgenzō* fascicles were composed prior to the Echizen period and as is shown in Table 1 in Chapter 1, a plurality was from the nine-month 1243–1244 transitional period.

The 75-*Shōbōgenzō* has been generally highlighted in part because it was the first complete version of the text that was published with extensive commentary by Dōgen's direct disciple, Senne, and his main follower, Kyōgō; their combined commentaries, known as the *Go-Kikigakishō* or *Goshō* (or *Shōbōgenzō-shō*), consist of Kyōgō's commentary (ca. 1308) on Senne's original comments (ca. 1263) on the *Shōbōgenzō*. Senne's own remarks are lost, although his views are discernible through the filter of his disciple's appropriation and presentation of them. The 75-fascicle text contains many of the fascicles often associated with Dōgen's most inspiring philosophical reflections on such topics as Buddha-nature, time, nature, and language in "Busshō," "Uji," and "Genjōkōan," among other noteworthy examples. However, several noted texts such as *Bendōwa* and *Shōji* are not contained therein, although these are included in the expanded 95-*Shōbōgenzō*. It is important to recognize that these writings often thought of as constituting the *Shōbōgenzō* are not part of the 75-*Shōbōgenzō* and are thus of questionable status, so these are referred to here not as fascicles but rather as separate texts.

The *Goshō* commentary produced by two disciples who returned from Echizen to establish their own temple, Yōkōji, in Kyoto—according to one theory, they may never have left the capital for the mountains—puts forward an interpretation of the 75-*Shōbōgenzō* heavily flavored by the dominant ideology of Japanese Buddhism, the Tendai sect's doctrine of original enlightenment (*hongaku shisō*). According to this pantheistic teaching, which Dōgen in part rejected because of his emphasis on personal effort to renew the experience of enlightenment, each and every phenomenon is a manifestation of ultimate reality. Understanding or fully penetrating a single phenomenon results in an awareness of the totality, or the experience of a single instant of time leads to the attainment of eternity. The *Goshō* commentary on "Genjōkōan" refers to this as the doctrine of *ippō gūjin* (total penetration of a single phenomenon), but this term is not used by Dōgen himself. It also supports a strong critique of Dōgen's ideological and sectarian rivals among Ch'an masters, such as proponents of certain styles of interpreting kōans. In other words, the *Goshō* commentary has a certain agenda and bias regarding Chinese sources in relation to Japanese Buddhism that must be recognized in an evaluation of its significance as representative of the thought of Dōgen himself.

Nevertheless, for followers of Sōtō Zen the *Goshō* commentary has been considered the epitome of sectarian orthodoxy and, because of its provenance, the 75-fascicle text was thought of as "the" *Shōbōgenzō* well before the construction and ascendancy of the 95-fascicle edition, though never without some degree of disputation. Yet it remains a subject of debate as to whether the 75-*Shōbōgenzō* should have priority as the major edition or whether there may be another version that better represents Dōgen's thought. From the early days of the Sōtō sect there were additional versions in circulation that have enjoyed prestige in some quarters, including versions ranging from 12, 28, and 60 to 84 fascicles.

12-*Fascicle* Shōbōgenzō

Many of the fascicles of the 12-*Shōbōgenzō* were used as the basis for the Meiji-era abbreviated version of the *Shōbōgenzō*, the *Shushōgi* (1891), which targeted a lay audience. However, even though the content of some of the text was well known for this reason, it was not until nearly forty years later that the discovery of a complete, independent manuscript of the 12-fascicle *Shōbōgenzō*, a version long rumored to exist but apparently lost for centuries, started to generate new theories about the relation between the various editions. Referred to now as *shinsō* or "new draft,"[8] it was composed almost entirely during the late Eiheiji period after the 75-*Shōbōgenzō* (or *kyusō*, old draft) was completed in 1246 and following Dōgen's return from Kamakura. The 12-*Shōbōgenzō* represents a very different discursive style which puts an emphasis on the doctrine of causality, as did other works from the late period, supported by citations from early Buddhist Abhidharma as well as Mahayana sutras (in addition to the *Lotus Sutra* Dōgen frequently cites) rather than strictly Ch'an sources. It is not clear whether this version was conceived of as a supplement to or a replacement for the 75-*Shōbōgenzō*.

The manuscript of the 12-*Shōbōgenzō* was discovered in 1927 at Yōkōji temple in Noto Peninsula in Ishikawa prefecture, a temple founded by fourth Sōtō patriarch Keizan and an important center for the sect in the medieval period. It was copied in 1445 from a 1420 recopy of the original version that was compiled by Ejō. The existence of the 12-*Shōbōgenzō* as an independent version of Dōgen's magnum opus, standing in addition to the 75-fascicle text as the most widely accepted version, was long known or at least strongly suspected because of the apparent reference in the cryptic colophon of "Hachidainingaku." Written in 1252 as the final composition before Dōgen's death and transcribed and edited in 1255 by Ejō, this fascicle was included in yet another version of the *Shōbōgenzō*, the undated 28-*Shōbōgenzō* that was apparently compiled by Gien in the thirteenth century. The colophon also appears in slightly altered form in the *Kenzeiki*.

According to the colophon provided by Ejō, Dōgen's hope was to create a 100-fascicle text, but this was never realized: "The fascicles of the *Kana* [or *Kaji*] *Shōbōgenzō* [in Japanese vernacular as opposed to the *Mana* (or *Shinji*) *Shōbōgenzō*, also known as *Shōbōgenzō sanbyakusoku* collection of 300 kōan cases in *kanbun*] that I have composed previously will be revised," Dōgen is quoted as saying, "and by adding new fascicles to the [revised] older ones I intend to create a 100-fascicle text."[9] Ejō then describes the composition of twelve new fascicles:

The "Hachidainingaku" is the twelfth of the new fascicles. After composing this fascicle, our former master's condition gradually deteriorated, and the writing of new fascicles came to a halt. Therefore, this and several other recent fascicles represent the last teachings of our former master. Unfortunately, many of the revised manuscripts for the [projected] 100-fascicle text are not available, and this is deeply regrettable. Those who wish to honor the memory of our former master should uphold the twelfth fascicle [or twelve new fascicles]. This fascicle [or these fascicles], expressing the final teachings of Sakyamuni, contains the last instructions of our former master.[10]

The colophon makes some interesting suggestions about the importance of the 12-fascicle text, but its meaning and purpose are ambiguous. On the one hand, this passage indicates a clear distinction between the old and new fascicles of the *Shōbōgenzō*, and it suggests Dōgen's need to revise the former, while indicating that the latter package of twelve fascicles is not only more recent and timely but also the most consistent with Sakyamuni's original teachings. The colophon seems to associate the 12-fascicle text with the goal of creating a 100-fascicle text, while negating the role of the early, unrevised fascicles.

Of the twelve "new" fascicles referred to in Table 7, ten were written during the 1250s, and Ejō compiled most of these during the 1255 summer retreat two years after Dōgen's death. The other two from the 1240s were originally alternative versions of fascicles contained in the 75-fascicle text but were later apparently selected by Dōgen for inclusion in the 12-fascicle edition. There are unconfirmed reports that the 12-fascicle text had been kept alive and transmitted through the centuries in some of the sect's sublineages stemming from Keizan's branch, which may have prized this version over the other editions of the *Shōbōgenzō*.

Perhaps Dōgen, who had produced *jishu* sermons throughout most but

---

TABLE 7. 12-Fascicle *Shōbōgenzō* Text (dates of composition or editing in parentheses)

1. Shukke kudoku (ed. 1255)[a]
2. Jukai (ed. 1255)
3. Kesa kudoku (1240)[a]
4. Hotsu bodaishin (1244)[a]
5. Kuyō shobutsu (ed. 1255)
6. Kie sanbō (or Kie buppōsōbō)(ed. 1255)
7. Jinshin inga (ed. 1255)[a]
8. Sanjigo (?)[b]
9. Shime (ed. 1255)
10. Shizen biku (ed. 1255)
11. Ippyakuhachihōmyōmon (n.d.)
12. Hachidainingaku (1253)

---

[a] Reworked version of a 75-SH fascicle
[b] Reworked version of a fascicle in other *Shōbōgenzō* editions

Note: Contents and dates of composition of the 12-*Shōbōgenzō*: seven fascicles were edited in 1255, two were from the 1240s, one is from 1253, and two are undated. The 95-fascicle edition consists of the 75-*Shōbōgenzō* plus the 12-*Shōbōgenzō* in addition to eight other fascicles: *Bendōwa* (1231), *Hokke-ten-hokke* (1241), *Bodaisatta shishōbō* (1243), *Shōji* (n.d.), *Yuibutsu yobutsu* (n.d.), Beppon (Supplementary) *Shinfukatoku* (n.d.), Beppon *Butsukōjōji* (n.d.), and Beppon *Butsudō* (also known as *Dōshin*, n.d.). There is also a 92-fascicle edition that lacks the three supplementary fascicles.

not all phases of his career, envisioned a composition based on the model of the major kōan collections, such as the *Pi-yen lu*, which contained 100 cases and influenced his way of appropriating Chinese Ch'an. However, the existence of multiple *Shōbōgenzō* versions indicates, again, that there is no clear sense of what Dōgen himself considered the best compilation or the one that would come closest to realizing the 100-fascicle goal. Therefore the colophon leaves some issues uncertain. For example, it does not rule out altogether the value of the older fascicles. Since it declares that some rewrites are unavailable, it is not clear where things stood at the end of the revision process at the time of Dōgen's death or how much Ejō may have interpolated, knowingly or not, into the alterations. It is also unclear whether the next-to-last sentence refers to upholding the "twelfth" fascicle alone, which reflects Sakyamuni's view, or the entire 12-fascicle text.

According to Ishii Shūdō, the unresolvability of this issue is exacerbated in light of the colophon for the *Hōkyōki* cited here in Chapter 1, in which Ejō comments on his joy tinged with sorrow at finding the lost text and suggests that there may be more manuscripts by the master undiscovered or left unfinished.[11] Another aspect of the provisional quality of the *Shōbōgenzō* is that the colophons for several of the fascicles in the 12-fascicle text subsequently found in various temple manuscripts state that they were still in the process of being revised and edited.

Because of questions about the "Hachidainingaku" colophon, most scholars have continued to focus on the 75-fascicle text even after the discovery of the 12-fascicle text. They have assumed that Dōgen was involved in an ongoing process of revising the *Shōbōgenzō* fascicles, some of which were placed either by Dōgen or by Ejō in the 12-fascicle text in order to create a work appropriate for the audience at Eiheiji, which was composed largely of laypersons and new initiates converting from rival esoteric sects. The conventional view is that Dōgen was trying to create a significantly revised edition of the *Shōbōgenzō* in the final stages of his career, after returning from the unsuccessful mission of preaching before Hōjō Tokiyori in Kamakura in 1248, when he was apparently disappointed that Zen rhetoric of nondualism beyond the distinction of good and evil could be used to sanction unethical (militaristic) behavior. These fascicles were more detailed and precise, by means of additional citations and references from Mahayana and Abhidharma scriptures, as well as more introductory in explaining the basic Buddhist doctrines of karma, causality, and impermanence, in addition to rules of monastic discipline and ritual, which may have been relatively unfamiliar to Dōgen's audience in rural medieval Japan.

Therefore, although its composition was chronologically later, from a conceptual standpoint the 12-fascicle text has been seen as a kind of preliminary work containing practical instructions paving the way for, and essentially being compatible and consistent with, the more philosophically nuanced writings in the 75-fascicle text that were studied by higher-level monks. However, a new emphasis has been placed on the 12-*Shōbōgenzō* in giving it priority as the most genuine expression of Dōgen's philosophy by the methodological movement known as Critical Buddhism (*Hihan Bukkyō*). This movement involves mainly the approach of Komazawa University scholars Hakamaya Noriaki, also a former Sōtō priest, and Matsumoto Shirō, although numerous Sōtō and other Buddhist scholars have been engaged in this debate.[12]

The Critical Buddhist method, which is associated with the Renewal Theory of Dōgen studies to be discussed here later, argues that the 12-*Shōbōgenzō* represents a new awakening or "change of heart" or "spiritual change" (*henka*) in Dōgen's attitude in stressing the inexorability of karmic causality and retribution. Critical Buddhism argues that at this stage Dōgen rejected all traces of the pantheistic doctrine of original enlightenment thought that he came to realize pervaded the 75-*Shōbōgenzō*. Traditionalists have criticized the Critical Buddhist view in maintaining that the 12-*Shōbōgenzō* and 75-*Shōbōgenzō* are consistent yet complementary in targeting different audience sectors. Ishii Shūdō has tried to carve out a compromise view by agreeing that the 12-*Shōbōgenzō* represents a degree of change in Dōgen's attitude, although perhaps not as drastic as Critical Buddhism suggests. Ishii also points out that it is important not to isolate the 12-*Shōbōgenzō* but to see its role in connection with other texts of the late period, the *Eihei kōroku* and *Hōkyōki*. In light of the criticism, Matsumoto has tried to step back from the idea that there was a blanket criticism of the 75-*Shōbōgenzō* as suggested by Hakamaya, and he points out that there were different degrees of adherence to original enlightenment thought in that text.

60-Fascicle Shōbōgenzō *and Other Editions*

The debate concerning the relation between the 75-fascicle and 12-fascicle texts highlights the fact that there are other configurations, which also need to be taken into account for an understanding of the overall significance of the *Shōbōgenzō*. Perhaps the most significant of these is the 60-*Shōbōgenzō* (or 60-fascicle text), which has long been seen as a prominent version compiled in the early days of the Sōtō sect. The main theory about the origin of this edition is that the editor, Giun, a disiciple of Jakuen at Hōkyōji temple, who became the fifth patriarch of Eiheiji, seems to have deleted some (but not all) fascicles in the 75-*Shōbōgenzō* that were hypercritical of rival Ch'an lineages. The existence of this version, which was strongly supported by the Tokugawa-era Sōtō scholastic Tenkei Denson, may indicate that there was awareness early in the tradition of Dōgen's sometimes excessive rhetoric, as well as the need to evaluate the founder's real intentions about the formation of the *Shōbōgenzō*. For example, as shown in Table 8, 11 fascicles from the 75-*Shōbōgenzō* that were not included in the 60-fascicle edition contain sharp criticism of rival schools,

TABLE 8. Fascicles Deleted in the 60-*Shōbōgenzō*?

Fascicle	Target of Criticism (or Praise)
Shinfukatoku	Te-shan
Sansuikyō	Yün-men
[a]Sesshin sesshō	Lin-chi and Ta-hui (praises Tung-shan)
[a]Shohō jissō	3 Teachings are One, Lao Tzu and Chuang Tzu (praises Ju-ching and also Yüan-wu)
[a]Butsudō	5 Schools of Zen Sect, Lin-chi, Te-shan, Chih-tsung and *Jen-tien-yen-mu* (praises Shih-t'ou, Tung-shan and Ju-ching)
[a]Mitsugo	Lin-chi and Te-shan (praises Hsüeh-tou, Ju-ching's predecessor)
[a]Bukkyō (Buddhist Sutras)	Lin-chi and Yün-men, Tung-shan (four thoughts and four relations, three phrases, three paths, and five relative positions, Confucius and Lao Tzu briefly) (praises Sakyamuni and Ju-ching)
[a]Menju	Yün-men lineage; in an appendix, two lesser known monks, Cheng-ku and Fo-kuo Wei-pai (praises Tung-shan and Ju-ching)
[a]Sanjūshichihon bodaibunpō	Zaike (Lay) and Shukke (Monk) are One, "Zen sect"
[a]Daishugyō	Lin-chi and Te-shan
[a]Jishō zanmai	Ta-hui

[a] Indicates fascicles composed in 1243–1244 in Echizen

Note: These 11 fascicles, not included in the 60-*Shōbōgenzō*, contain direct, fundamental criticism of Zen masters, schools, texts, and theories.

especially Lin-chi and Ta-hui. Of these, nine were from the first three quarters of a year after the move to Echizen. Perhaps this deletion was done deliberately, either by Dōgen himself or in collaboration with Ejō, in order to create a more perfected text during his lifetime, or by later generations of interpreters who retrospectively sought to sanitize his writings.

It was long believed that the 60-*Shōbōgenzō* was compiled by Giun, who wrote a preface and verse commentary in 1329 that was handed down in his lineage through the fifteenth century. However, a recent theory proffered by Kawamura Kōdō maintains that this version consists of Dōgen's first-draft arrangements of the fascicles included in the 75-*Shōbōgenzō*, whose order and wording were later revised. According to Kawamura, there are interlinear notes in manuscripts of the 60-fascicle version that disclose how at least some of these fascicles were altered for inclusion in the 75-fascicle version. Kawamura maintains that Ejō edited this edition years later according to Dōgen's own selection of fascicles before he died. This theory suggests that the 60-*Shōbōgenzō* is the "real" text and the 75-fascicle edition is secondary, but it is not clear whether this claim is also meant to imply that Dōgen himself excised the controversial fascicles, a key point in interpreting the 60-fascicle version.[13]

An important implication of Kawamura's theory is that the 12-*Shōbōgenzō* is also derivative in that it contains five new fascicles added to seven fascicles of the 60-*Shōbōgenzō* that were not contained in the 75-*Shōbōgenzō*. The seven fascicles are "Sanjigo," "Shime," "Shukke kudoku," "Kuyō shobutsu," "Kie sanbō," "Hotsubodaishin" (a rewritten version of "Hotsumujōshin," also included in the 60-*Shōbōgenzō*), and "Kesa kudoku" (a rewritten version of "Den'e," not included in the 60-*Shōbōgenzō*). In other words, Kawamura reverses the conventional view by arguing that the 12-*Shōbōgenzō* should be seen not as something Dōgen worked on late in life but as an edition that subsequent editors constructed or extracted from the 60-*Shōbōgenzō*.

Another important compilation is the 28-*Shōbōgenzō*, also known as the *Himitsu* (or Secret) *Shōbōgenzō*, which was probably compiled by one of Dōgen's disciples whose identity is not known. This contains some of the fascicles left out of the 60-*Shōbōgenzō* but included in the 75-*Shōbōgenzō*, as well as several of the 12-*Shōbōgenzō* fascicles. In this version, seventeen fascicles are from the 75-*Shōbōgenzō*, six are from the 12-*Shōbōgenzō*, and five, including "Yuibutsu yobutsu," are not in a known collection. Furthermore, the 84-*Shōbōgenzō* compiled in 1419 by Bonsei, an early attempt at creating a comprehensive edition, contains fascicles in the same sequence as the 75-*Shōbōgenzō*, in addition to seven fascicles from the 12-*Shōbōgenzō* and one each from the 60-*Shōbōgenzō* and 28-*Shōbōgenzō*. Extant copies of manuscripts of this edition are dated from 1644 and 1718.

Mizuno argues against seeing the four main versions—the 75-, 60-, 28-, and 12-fascicle collections—as being separate entities at odds with one another. Rather, they can be grouped together in the following way: The 75-fascicle and 12-fascicle texts complement but do not duplicate one another and have probably been studied as a single textual entity in some circles, and similarly the 60-fascicle and 28-fascicle texts can be so conjoined. These two groupings—that is, the 75 + 12 and the 60 + 28 texts—each include all but a handful of the fascicles contained in the all-inclusive 95-*Shōbōgenzō*. Figure 13 was adapted by Hakamaya from an original diagram designed by Mizuno that tracks the interaction between groups of fascicles and the way they were compiled by editors. Whereas Mizuno was neutral about the relation between collections, Hakamaya's aim is to demonstrate the priority, or superiority, of the 12-*Shōbōgenzō* as a reflection of Dōgen's true intentions.[14]

My suggestion is to expand Mizuno's effort at taking a comprehensive view by seeing intertextual connections between writings that may seem disparate or even conflictive. This approach must be applied not only to the *Shōbōgenzō*, but also to a broader focus on the *Eihei kōroku* as well as other texts that Dōgen was composing at the time that the various alternative versions of the *Shōbōgenzō* were being formed.

Shōbōgenzō Fascicles and Texts

Flowchart of editing and editions of Shōbōgenzō texts from *Dōgen to Bukkyō, Junikanbon Shōbōgenzō no Dōgen* by Hakamaya Noriaki 1992, p. 192 (influenced by categories [A-I] in Mizuno 1973).

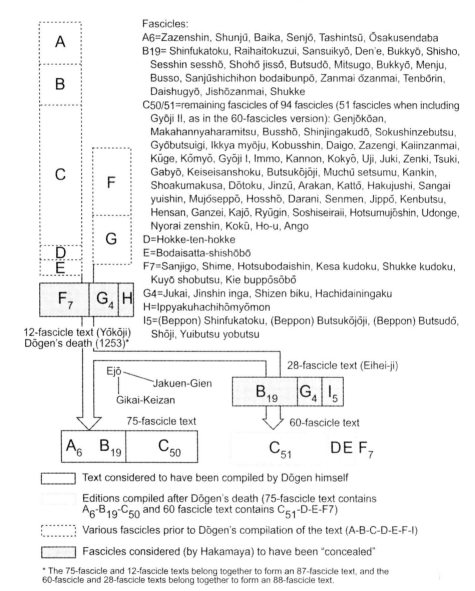

Fascicles:

A6=Zazenshin, Shunjū, Baika, Senjō, Tashintsū, Ōsakusendaba

B19= Shinfukatoku, Raihaitokuzui, Sansuikyō, Den'e, Bukkyō, Shisho, Sesshin sesshō, Shohō jissō, Butsudō, Mitsugo, Bukkyō, Menju, Busso, Sanjūshichihon bodaibunpō, Zanmai ōzanmai, Tenbōrin, Daishugyō, Jishōzanmai, Shukke

C50/51=remaining fascicles of 94 fascicles (51 fascicles when including Gyōji II, as in the 60-fascicles version): Genjōkōan, Makahannyaharamitsu, Busshō, Shinjingakudō, Sokushinzebutsu, Gyōbutsuigi, Ikkya myōju, Kobusshin, Daigo, Zazengi, Kaiinzanmai, Kūge, Kōmyō, Gyōji I, Immo, Kannon, Kokyō, Uji, Juki, Zenki, Tsuki, Gabyō, Keiseisanshoku, Butsukōjōji, Muchū setsumu, Kankin, Shoakumakusa, Dōtoku, Jinzū, Arakan, Kattō, Hakujushi, Sangai yuishin, Mujōseppō, Hosshō, Darani, Senmen, Jippō, Kenbutsu, Hensan, Ganzei, Kajō, Ryūgin, Soshiseiraii, Hotsumujōshin, Udonge, Nyorai zenshin, Kokū, Ho-u, Ango

D=Hokke-ten-hokke

E=Bodaisatta-shishōbō

F7=Sanjigo, Shime, Hotsubodaishin, Kesa kudoku, Shukke kudoku, Kuyō shobutsu, Kie buppōsōbō

G4=Jukai, Jinshin inga, Shizen biku, Hachidainingaku

H=Ippyakuhachihōmyōmon

I5=(Beppon) Shinfukatoku, (Beppon) Butsukōjōji, (Beppon) Butsudō, Shōji, Yuibutsu yobutsu

Text considered to have been compiled by Dōgen himself

Editions compiled after Dōgen's death (75-fascicle text contains A6-B19-C50 and 60 fascicle text contains C51-D-E-F7)

Various fascicles prior to Dōgen's compilation of the text (A-B-C-D-E-F-I)

Fascicles considered (by Hakamaya) to have been "concealed"

* The 75-fascicle and 12-fascicle texts belong together to form an 87-fascicle text, and the 60-fascicle and 28-fascicle texts belong together to form an 88-fascicle text.

FIGURE 13. Overview of Versions of the *Shōbōgenzō*

The Eihei Kōroku

As abbot of Eiheiji, Dōgen focused his attention primarily on delivering the *jōdō* sermons in the *Eihei kōroku*, a crucial text which until very recently has been so overshadowed by the *75-Shōbōgenzō* that it was almost entirely neglected in Western scholarship. For example, the *Eihei kōroku* was not mentioned one time in the main narrative section of Hee-Jin Kim's generally excellent seminal study published in 1975, *Dōgen Kigen—Mystical Realist* (recently reissued as *Eihei Dōgen: Mystical Realist* with a new introductory essay by the author), which translated and commented extensively on numerous passages from *Shōbōgenzō* fascicles.[15] There has been little discussion of the crucial transition from the *75-Shōbōgenzō* to the *Eihei kōroku* or the implications for understanding the move from Kyoto to Echizen, let alone its relation to the *12-Shōbōgenzō*, another late text Kim does not mention. However, Taigen Dan Leighton and Shohaku Okumura have produced an excellent recent translation, which should help give the *Eihei kōroku* its due as having status commensurate with that of the *Shōbōgenzō*.

Part of the reason for the oversight is that there are two main editions of the *Eihei kōroku*, but neither one plays a role comparable to that of the prestigious *Goshō* as an early authoritative interpretation of the *Shōbōgenzō*. The first is the 1598 edition attributed to the monk Monkaku, which is generally considered the authentic version that is the basis for the main modern edition of the collected writings, the *Dōgen zenji zenshū*.[16] There is an edition believed to be older than the Monkaku, known as the Sozan edition, but this is undated and not verified. The Sozan edition seems to be almost wholly consistent with the Monkaku edition, so that most scholars feel that it was the model used by Monkaku and generally refer to the texts interchangeably. The second edition of the *Eihei kōroku* is the 1672 version edited by Manzan Dōhaku, one of the leaders of the eighteenth-century revival of Sōtō scholarly studies. This is also known as the *rufubon*, or popular edition.

The Manzan edition is considered questionable partly because it seems to have been derived from a prominent but controversial abbreviated version of the text known as the *Eihei goroku*. The *Eihei goroku* was apparently created in China in the 1260s, about a decade after Dōgen's death, when one of his leading disciples, Giin, who was a convert from the Daruma school, went to Mount T'ien-t'ung to show Dōgen's Ch'an Dharma brothers samples of the master's works. It was later published in 1358 by Giun, also known for his commentary on the *60-Shōbōgenzō*. Thus it is the earliest edition of at least some of *Eihei kōroku* material in circulation, but it is not truly representative of the source text.[17]

The *Eihei goroku*, which consists of selections of about 20 percent of the longer text, became one of the most frequently cited works (much more so than either the *Eihei kōroku* or the *Shōbōgenzō*) in the Sōtō sect's scholastic and esoteric commentarial traditions of the Kamakura/Muromachi era. Medieval Sōtō hermeneutics produced the generic category of *shōmono* writings, with several important subgenres representing different styles and levels of commentary on the original materials. An emphasis on the *Eihei goroku* persisted until a renewed interest in studying the original texts of the sect's founder was spearheaded by Manzan and Menzan, among other Tokugawa scholastics. During this revival, both the *Shōbōgenzō* and the *Eihei kōroku* started to receive greater attention. This development helped pave the way for modern textual studies, although scholars today must struggle to overcome inaccuracies and sectarian biases embedded in the early modern accounts.

The *Eihei kōroku* is a diversified text containing different styles of composition. Despite numerous and at times significant discrepancies between the Monkaku/Sozan and Manzan/*rufubon* editions, especially in the numbering of the passages, particularly in vol. 1, and in the exact wording of numerous passages, particularly in vol. 10, the contents of *Eihei kōroku* editions that were collected by various editors over a long period follow the same basic structure. The sermons along with collected verse evoke, allude to, or comment directly on a vast storehouse of Chinese Ch'an kōans and other kinds of records. Unlike the *Shōbōgenzō*, which is a unique genre that has no model or precedent in China because it is a collection of *jishu* sermons, which were generally left unrecorded in Ch'an monastery collections, the *Eihei kōroku* was patterned after the typical Ch'an recorded sayings texts, though with a different sense of proportionality for the respective subgenres. These contain a record of a master's formal sermons, poetry collections, and other miscellaneous utterances and compositions.

The first seven volumes of the *Eihei kōroku*, as listed in Table 9, include a collection of 531 *jōdō* sermons that were originally delivered at the opening of the Dharma Hall at Kōshōji temple in 1236 and continued through the Eiheiji years until 1252. As was indicated, several periods were omitted when a Dharma Hall was not available, including Dōgen's first year in Echizen in 1243–1244 and during his eight-month mission to Kamakura in 1247–1248. Therefore, the portion of the *Eihei kōroku* dedicated to *jōdō* sermons contained in volumes edited by several disciples is representative of a span of fifteen years of Dōgen's career. However, as in the case of the 75-*Shōbōgenzō*, it is important to recognize that the great majority of *jōdō* sermons were from a more compressed time frame beginning with the abbacy at Daibutsuji/Eiheiji in the mid-1240s.

There seem to be important differences between sections of the first seven volumes of sermons, based on editorship. For example, the sermons in vol. 1 recorded by Senne, who is better known for contributing to the *Goshō*, tend to be very brief and allusive, whereas those in vols. 5 through 7, edited by Gien, have a distinctive quality in terms of length, style, and content that may reflect shifts in Dōgen's attitudes as well as the editor's outlook. It is also clear that

TABLE 9. List of *Eihei kōroku* Volumes

1. Kōshōji goroku (*jōdō* sermons, nos. 1–126 from 1236 to 1243, rec. Senne)—two-year hiatus during transition from Fukakusa to Echizen with no Dharma Hall
2. Daibutsuji goroku (nos. 127–184 from 1245 to 1246, rec. Ejō)
3. Eiheiji goroku (nos. 185–257 from 1246 to 1248, rec. Ejō)—includes 8-month hiatus during mission to Kamakura
4. Eiheiji goroku (nos. 258–345 from 1248 to 1249, rec. Ejō)
5. Eiheiji goroku (nos. 346–413 from 1249 to 1251, rec. Gien)
6. Eiheiji goroku (nos. 414–470 from 1251, rec. Gien)
7. Eiheiji goroku (nos. 471–531 from 1251 to 1252, rec. Gien)
8. Miscellaneous (20 *shōsan* from Daibutsuji/Eiheiji, 14 *hōgo* from Kōshōji, *Fukanzazengi*, rec. Ejō and others)
9. Kōshōji collection (90 kōan cases with *juko* comments from 1236, rec. Senne and others)
10. Kanbun poetry collections (5 *shinsan;* 20 *jisan;* 125 *geju* from 1223 to 1253, rec. Senne and others)

Note: A list of the contents and dates of composition for the *Eihei Kōroku*. The first seven volumes are collections of *jōdō* sermons from Kōshōji, Daibutsuji, and Eiheiji, and the last three volumes collect various kinds of lectures and poetry.

beginning with the second volume, Dōgen extensively cites Hung-chih and Ju-ching as models in delivering sermons for special ceremonial occasions.

The eighth volume of the *Eihei kōroku* contains two other kinds of sermons in *kana*: Dharma talks (*hōgo*) delivered at Kōshōji, and from the Echizen period a style referred to as *shōsan* (lit. "before a small assembly"), which is somewhat different from a style with the same designation contained in the *Shōbōgenzō zuimonki*. Verse comments (*juko*) on 90 kōan cases that were created in 1236, a year after the compilation of the *Mana Shōbōgenzō*, are included in vol. 9. Vol. 10 contains 150 *kanbun* poems including 50 verses written in China and 100 verses from later periods of Dōgen's career, especially the Echizen phase. Therefore this section of the *Eihei kōroku* is particularly interesting because it covers the full length of Dōgen's career, spanning 30 years, and the poetry composed in China is the earliest example of Dōgen's writing and the main creative effort from his travels abroad.

The Shōbōgenzō Zuimonki *and* Eihei Shingi

Two other collections that span a number of years in the making and are crucial for understanding the unfolding of Dōgen's career in relation to Chinese Ch'an include the *Shōbōgenzō zuimonki* from the middle period and the *Eihei shingi*, which is primarily from the late period. The *Shōbōgenzō zuimonki* consists of about 120 passages in six volumes, which are mostly *shōsan* sermons recorded and collected by Ejō, a former follower of the proscribed Daruma school. Ejō became Dōgen's main disciple after the death and at the behest of his previous mentor, Kakuan, a first-generation disciple of Nōnin, and Ejō collected the sermons over a period of about three and a half years from fall 1234 until spring 1238. It is important to note that during this phase of the Kōshōji abbacy, no *jishu* sermons of the *Shōbōgenzō* and only a small handful of *jōdō* sermons were delivered.

The *Shōbōgenzō zuimonki* sermons began the year Ejō joined Dōgen's community upon the deathbed recommendation of Kakuan (this was also the time the *Gakudōyōjinshū* was produced and *senshū nembutsu* practice was prohibited by the government). In 1235, the year Dōgen also created the *Mana Shōbōgenzō* and Enni traveled to Sung China, the sermons in the second and third volumes of the *Shōbōgenzō zuimonki* were delivered. The following year, when the Kōshōji Monks Hall was opened and Ejō was named head monk and probably delivered his own sermons, most of the material in the next two volumes was gathered. The text was completed during 1237, when *Tenzokyōkun* was also produced. On the eighteenth day of the fourth month of 1238, a new *Shōbōgenzō* fascicle was delivered, "Ikkya myōjū," the first in several years, and three additional fascicles appeared the following year. Therefore the termination of the *Shōbōgenzō zuimonki* marked the resumption of the *Shōbōgenzō*.

Like many Dōgen texts, the *Shōbōgenzō zuimonki* is a product (or perhaps in terms of accuracy, a "victim") of Tokugawa-era editing. The manuscript was left unpublished for over 400 years and a limited edition was first printed in 1651. Menzan worked on the text for over 50 years before publishing in 1769 his revised version, which has become known as the *rufubon* edition. There are several variations of this edition, including a modern one edited by Watsuji Tetsurō and published by Iwanami bunko, as well as another recent version edited by Mizuno Yaoko and published by Iwanami shoten in a series of classic Japanese texts. The *rufubon* edition differs considerably from a 1380 manuscript that was discovered at Chōonji temple in Aichi prefecture in 1941 and used as the basis for the text that appears in the *Dōgen zenji zenshū*.

All the versions contain six fascicles and approximately the same number of entries. In his textual criticism, Ikeda Rōsan, by comparing three other editions, provides his own analysis of what the ideal text would look like (see Table 10).[18] The main debate is not so much a matter of the number of items, since the various texts have more or less the same content despite differences in numbering, but rather it concerns the placement of the first volume, which appears as the sixth volume in the Iwanami bunko edition, which in turn serves as the basis for the two main English translations.[19] However, Ishikawa Rikizan shows that the placement of this volume in the opening slot is crucial because it more accurately reflects the sequence of composition and reveals the text as an ongoing dialogue with Ejō about differences in religious practice between the Daruma school and Dōgen's approach. Apparently, the arguments were persuasive and led several years later to the conversion of other Daruma school monks, who came to form Dōgen's main constituency.

Perhaps the most famous passage in the *Shōbōgenzō zuimonki* dealing with

TABLE 10. Editions of *Shōbōgenzō zuimonki* (by fascicle and item numbers)

Dōgen zenji zenshū edition
1–16, 2–27, 3–31, 4–14, 5–16, 6–27, T = 131

Mizuno Yaoko/Iwanami edition
1–14, 2–18, 3–21, 4–10, 5–12, 6–24, T = 99

Watsuji Tetsurō/Iwanami bunko or *rufubon* edition
6–17, 1–21, 1–26, 3–14, 4–16, 5–23, T = 117

Ikeda Rōsan's annotated edition
1–16, 2–20, 3–22, 4–13, 5–15, 6–23, T = 109

Daruma school-related issues is from about 1236. In it, Dōgen responds to a query from Ejō, who asked the master why he eliminated the practice of chanting precepts as stipulated by the *Ch'an-yüan ch'ing-kuei*. In contrast to the teaching of Nōnin, who was known for dismissing both meditative and disciplinary practices, Dōgen indicates that both the precepts and *zazen* should be practiced, but clearly the latter trumps the former: "When doing *zazen*," he asks rhetorically in *Shōbōgenzō zuimonki* 2.1, "what precepts are not upheld, and what merits are not produced?"[20] However, this statement does not imply a refutation of discipline.

The passage must be seen in light of Dōgen's composition of numerous writings dealing with monastic rules, some of which are included as fascicles in the *Shōbōgenzō* while others were independent essays grouped together by Tokugawa-era editors in the *Eihei shingi*.[21] The *Eihei shingi*, which spans a significant period of Dōgen's career and, like the *Shōbōgenzō* and *Eihei kōroku*, bridges both the Kōshōji and Eiheiji periods, includes six essays written from 1237 to 1249.[22]

Although only one of the essays in Table 11 was written in Kyoto, it is important to recognize that during his abbacy at Kōshōji, Dōgen also composed *Jūundōshiki*, which is included in the 95-*Shōbōgenzō*, and composed "Senmen," "Senjō," "Den'e," and "Kankin" on rules and rites, which were produced in the late 1230s and are included in the 75-*Shōbōgenzō*. At Eiheiji he composed the *Jikuinmon* in 1246, also included in the 95-*Shōbōgenzō*, and the *Eiheiji jūryo seiki* in 1249, as well as the "Ango," "Kajō," and "Shukke" fascicles, included in the 75-*Shōbōgenzō*, in addition to "Shukke kudoku," "Jukai," and "Kie sanbō" of the 12-*Shōbōgenzō*. All are heavily indebted to and liberally quote from, often with only minor variations, the *Ch'an-yüan ch'ing-kuei* and related Chinese Ch'an source texts on monastic rules and regulations.

Unlike the *Shōbōgenzō*, the *Shōbōgenzō zumonki*, and *Eihei kōroku*, which exhibit some degree of textual integrity based on a consistency in editing during Dōgen's lifetime, the formation of the *Eihei shingi* as a textual entity is entirely a Tokugawa-era construction. An early version containing only the

TABLE II. Essays Included in the *Eihei shingi*

1. *Tenzokyōkun* (instructions to cook), 1237 at Kōshōji
2. *Bendōhō* (detailed instructions for daily conduct), 1246 at Daibutsuji
3. *Fushukuhampō* (rules for taking food), 1246 at Eiheiji
4. *Eiheiji shuryō shingi* (rules for study hall or library), 1249 at Eiheiji
5. *Taidaiko gogejarihō* (instructions for seniority), 1244 at Kippōji
6. *Nihonkoku Echizen Eiheiji chiji shingi* (instructions for conduct of monastic administrators), 1246 at Eiheiji

Tenzokyōkun and *Chiji shingi* was compiled by Kōshū in 1502, and all six essays were published together for the first time by Kōshō Chidō in 1667 in a version titled *Nichiiki Sōtō shoso Dōgen zenji shingi*, which was later known as the Shohon edition of the *Eihei shingi*. This was produced as a Sōtō response to the popularity of the *Ōbaku shingi* text of the newly formed Ōbaku school supported by the shogun Tokugawa Ietsuna in 1660, which carried the imprimatur of authentic mainland discipline.[23] The *rufubon* edition of the *Eihei shingi*, published in 1794 by the fiftieth abbot of Eiheiji, Gentō Sokuchō, contains numerous comments as footnotes that are incorporated into the main text of the Shohon edition.[24]

The first essay in the collection, *Tenzokyōkun*, is especially important for its reflections on Dōgen's experiences while talking with two chief cooks in China, who were otherwise anonymous but useful for Dōgen's goal of contrasting the Chinese and Japanese styles of discipline, as well as exposing attitudes that were lax or corrupt. *Tenzokyōkun* shows Dōgen in the process of introducing the Sung Ch'an monastic model in order to develop a strictly disciplined life for monks at Kōshōji. Furthermore, *Bendōhō* deals with daily conduct in the Monks Hall; *Fushukuhampō* stresses that the role of taking food is not just a matter of eating in the practical sense but has a spiritual dimension in every aspect of activity; *Eiheiji shuryō shingi* explains the need for courteous conduct; and *Taidaiko gogejarihō* consists of 62 specific injunctions for etiquette in the presence of administrators.

The final essay, *Nihonkoku Echizen Eiheiji chiji shingi*, also known as *Chiji shingi*, contains two sections. The first half contains nearly two dozen kōans concerning previous temple administrators, but here Dōgen "highly praises some of his exemplars specifically for incidents in which they apparently violate precepts and regulations, or even are temporarily expelled from the community."[25] Dōgen cites cases that feature the irreverent, iconoclastic attitude of T'ang masters, such as the priest who during a winter storm poured cold water on a couple of itinerant monks who came to train at his temple, eventually relenting and allowing them entrée. The aim is to eliminate a tendency toward a blind obedience of regulations as an end in itself and to see that the true Zen master is willing to bend, break, or violate the rules in the name of adhering to them. The second half of the essay provides a detailed explanation, based on the *Ch'an-yüan ch'ing-kuei*, of the duties and attitudes of the managers and administrative functionaries of the monastic compound, including the four main officers: the director (*kan'in*), supervisor of monks (*inō*), chief cook (*tenzo*), and work leader (*shissui*).

Text Overview

Table 12 provides an overview of the production of Dōgen's major texts.

Recent Trends in Dōgen Studies

Critical Summary of Western Scholarship

An analysis of Dōgen's texts reveals relative strengths and weaknesses in recent developments in Western studies and explains why, despite significant progress in certain areas, some of the most basic questions about the sequence and content of Dōgen's writings have not been adequately addressed. For those who have been following the course of Zen studies, which has been experiencing a "Dōgen boom" for more than three decades, to argue that there has been deficiency, mishandling, or neglect may seem counterintuitive or even

TABLE 12. Editions of Dōgen's Main Texts

Edition	When Produced	Editor (Recorder)	Compiler	When Published
Shōbōgenzō		Ejō (plus)		
95-fascicles	1231–1252		Kōzen	1690 (Tokugawa)
75-fascicles	1233–1246		Senne	1263 (Kamakura)
60-fascicles	1233–1253		Giun[a]	1392 (Muromachi)
28-fascicles	1233–1253		Keizan	14th c. (Muromachi)
12-fascicles	1240–1255		Ejō[b]	1255? (Kamakura)
Eihei kōroku	1225–1252	Ejō/Senne/Gien		
Sozan/Monkaku			Monkaku	1598 (Muromachi)
Manzan			Manzan	1672 (Tokugawa)
Shōbōgenzō zuimonki	1234–1238	Ejō		
Chōonji			?	1380 (Muromachi)
rufubon			Menzan	1769 (Tokugawa)
Eihei shingi	1237–1249	Dōgen		
Shohon			Kōshū	1667 (Tokugawa)
rufubon			Gentō	1794 (Tokugawa)

[a] Kawamura Kōdō argues that Dōgen himself edited the 60-*Shōbōgenzō*
[b] Hakamaya Noriaki argues Dōgen edited the 12-fascicle edition

superfluous, given the profusion of translations and secondary sources that have recently appeared.

The boom began in the 1970s, when there first appeared renderings of numerous *Shōbōgenzō* fascicles along with the *Shōbōgenzō zuimonki, Hōkyōki,* and at least portions of other key texts, in addition to several major scholarly monographs and articles. Some of the more popular *Shōbōgenzō* fascicles have now been rendered into English at least half a dozen times, and there are a couple of complete though not necessarily reliable translations. However, there has been relatively little explanation of the multiple editions of the *Shōbōgenzō* containing varying numbers of fascicles or of the time and manner of their composition. Many readers are aware that there is a version with "95 fascicles" but may not realize that this is not definitive but a much later concoction stemming from a Tokugawa-era effort to preserve all of the available vernacular writings in a single edition. In Dōgen's day and in the period after his death when the first compilations were created and interpreted by followers, the *Shō-bōgenzō* was a sprawling array of fascicles in various versions, often with over-lapping contents. Connections with the *Eihei kōroku* and 12-*Shōbōgenzō* are also obscure for the majority of Western scholarship, which either conflates the 12-fascicle and 75-fascicle editions or sees them as separate texts.

Therefore it is necessary to supplement, update, and correct some of the mainstays of Dōgen studies in the West. First, it is useful to assess how much progress has been made since the time of two key works at the beginning of the boom. One is Kim's *Dōgen Kigen—Mystical Realist,* which remains the only study that provides a comprehensive overview of Dōgen's life and works, and the second book is *Dogen's Formative Years in China* (1980) by Takashi James Kodera, which is still the one in-depth study of his travels to China. There is no question that both of these pioneering books, now well over a generation old, are invaluable sources and must-reads for those studying Dōgen today. Unfortunately, however, from the perspective of the current state of the field as it has progressed in Japan, these works—rather expectedly—are somewhat outdated or deficient in failing to consider basic issues and viewpoints; yet they have not been adequately supplemented by other kinds of materials.

Kim's book remains essential reading in offering an insightful translation and analysis of key passages from most of the *Shōbōgenzō* fascicles. Some of the book's supplementary materials, such as a chronology, bibliography, and list of sources, were invaluable at the time of publication and can still be con-sulted. However, the limitations and lacunae are glaring by today's standards. Except for a very brief mention of alternative editions, it presents the 95-fascicle edition as if it were the only version and does not refer to the compilations that have been much debated in recent Japanese scholarship. There is also little mention of the *Eihei kōroku,* let alone the relation between these works and their relative importance for an understanding of Dōgen's approach to Zen theory and practice. *Dōgen Kigen* is also problematic, because it separates Dōgen's biography, which is discussed in the second chapter, from textual studies, which are dealt with primarily in the later sections of the book, especially the discussions of meditation, metaphysics, and monasticism in chapters 3 through 5, respectively.

In Kim's book, first published over 30 years ago, it is clear that he was simply unaware of debates that have subsequently emerged on a variety of topics that are crucial for an understanding of the connections between the life and works of Dōgen. Historical studies of Dōgen have reawakened a consideration of biographical issues and triggered efforts at a revisionism of hagiographical paradigms that seem to intrude on nearly every aspect of his life record. For example, questions have been raised about the circumstances of Dōgen's birth and aristocratic background; the time of his doubt about original enlightenment; his early relations with Tendai studies at Enryakuji and Onjōji temples; the issue of his meeting with Eisai; the role of *kanbun* poetry during his journey to China; complex reasons for moving to Echizen; the status of his visit to Kamakura; and the emphasis on karmic causality in the period following this visit.

This is but a sampling of the kinds of issues not fully dealt with by Kim that need to be taken into account in an examination of the range of texts produced by Dōgen. Other topics include developments in popular religious movements and folk religions in China and Japan, such as the role of *Hakusan shinkō* or religiosity based on the sacrality of Mount Hakusan, the *yamabushi* center that served as the main sacred mountain in the area where Eiheiji was established. Additional issues concerning the spread of Sōtō Zen subsequent to Dōgen include the controversy surrounding the "third generation succession" (*sandai soron*), or how the selection of the third Eiheiji patriarch was affected by rivalry between a faction representing former Daruma school members and those seeking to purify the sect from such elements. Related topics cover the evangelical function of Keizan and post-Keizan leaders of medieval Sōtō who assimilated Tendai/Shingon Buddhist and local gods and rituals; the role of *kirigami* (lit. "strips of paper") documents that were used in esoteric commentaries on kōan cases in the Muromachi era; the revival of Sōtō scholasticism in the Tokugawa era through such monks as Tenkei, Manzan, and Menzan; the formation of lay movements in the Meiji era under the leadership of Ōuchi Seiran and others; and the role of women and the significance of widespread prayer temples (*kitō jiin*) in the Sōtō institutional network in both monastic and lay life.

For example, in the chapter on biographical issues, "Dōgen's Life," Kim discusses very briefly, though insightfully, five reasons for Dōgen's move to Echizen. However, he does not delve into such complex issues as how the visit to Onjōji temple before joining Kenninji may be related to his eventual settling in the Mount Hakusan region or the impact of the Daruma school on the overall development of the Sōtō sect. Also, in explaining the Eiheiji period proper, he only very briefly mentions that several rules texts were composed during this time, as if the *Eihei shingi* was the only significant factor, and he fails to indicate the role of the *Eihei kōroku* or 12-*Shōbōgenzō*.[26]

In addition to recent advances in historical studies, another major feature of Dōgen studies in Japan that Kim's book preceded has been the rapid progress made in textual and hermeneutic studies. These advances are due in part to the discovery of a number of medieval manuscripts of seemingly lost texts, including *Bendōwa*, *Mana Shōbōgenzō*, *Sanshōdōei*, and the 12-fascicle *Shōbōgenzō*, among others. In addition, there are new theories on redating the *Fukanzazengi* and the *Hōkyōki*, and on clarifying the construction of the *Eihei shingi*. Furthermore, the sophistication of textual analysis has continued to improve. In 1974 Kagamishima Genryū published a revision of his doctoral dissertation that has become a kind of "bible" for Dōgen scholars, *Dōgen zenji to in'yō kyōten-goroku no kenkyū*, which provides a comprehensive list of Dōgen's citations from sutras and recorded sayings of Ch'an masters. Two decades later Kagamishima along with a team of editors published a new, enhanced version that gives the full text for each citation. This is but one of many examples of recent strides in creating useful hermeneutic tools.[27]

In discussing the pilgrimage to China, Kodera's book does an outstanding job of scouring traditional Japanese sources pertaining to Dōgen's biography from his aristocratic upbringing through the completion of the trip, in addition to the background of pertinent Chinese Ch'an history and thought, such as the evolution of Ts'ao-tung school theory and practice. However, Kodera's approach is characterized by an overreliance on sectarian materials without a critical discussion of these sources in light of contemporary historiographical methods, thus allowing some basic misconceptions about the itinerary for Dōgen's travels and his meetings with notable Ch'an masters and anonymous monks to be left largely unexamined. For instance, Kodera does not investigate problematic issues regarding the times and places when Dōgen was wandering about between several of the Five Mountains temples. He also tends to accept at face value aspects of the traditional account that seem blatantly hagiographical, as when Dōgen is said to have encountered a mysterious Arhat outside of Mount Ching who advised him that Ju-ching, who at the time was not yet assigned to Mount T'ien-t'ung, was the only authentic teacher in China. That is, he fails to distinguish between historiography and the hagiography of the *Kenzeiki*, as well as the differences between the latter work and its annotated supplement, the *Teiho Kenzeiki*. Kodera's translation of the *Hōkyōki* is quite useful, especially as a rare bilingual edition, but it does not analyze the dating of the text in light of the theory that this work was compiled long after Dōgen's return to Japan, near the end of his life.

Since the studies of Kim and Kodera first appeared over a quarter of a century ago, there have been numerous significant advances, including several *Shōbōgenzō* translations and groundbreaking renderings or examinations of lesser-known works. Several noteworthy contributions to the field are highly specialized in focusing on a particular text (*Dōgen's Manuals of Zen Meditation*, on *Fukanzazengi*, by Carl Bielefeldt; *Dōgen and the Kōan Tradition*, on *Mana Shōbōgenzō*, and *The Zen Poetry of Dōgen*, on *Sanshōdōei*, by Steven Heine; *The Wholehearted Way*, on *Bendōwa*, by Shohaku Okumura and Taigen Dan Leighton; *Flowers Fall*, on "Genjōkōan," by Yasutani Hakuun; and *Nothing is Hidden*, on *Tenzokyōkun*, by Jisho Warner et al.), on a received influence ("The Daruma-shū, Dōgen, and Sōtō Zen" by Bernard Faure), or on a doctrine (*A Study of Dōgen* by Masao Abe, and *Impermanence is Buddha-Nature* by Joan Stambaugh). Some of the best examinations of Dōgen have appeared in broader studies of other dimensions of the history or ideology of Zen. These include *Foundations of Japanese Buddhism (Vol. II)* by Daigan and Alicia Matsunaga, *Five Mountains* by Martin Collcutt, *Zen: A History (Vol. II)* by Heinrich Dumoulin, *The Rhetoric of Immediacy* by Bernard Faure, and *Sōtō Zen in Medieval Japan* by William Bodiford.

There have also been several important trends in Buddhist studies as a whole that affect an examination of Dōgen, especially a renewed interest in historical studies of Ch'an and Zen. These have led to a greater knowledge about a wide variety of movements, thinkers, texts, ideas, and institutional developments that are relevant for an understanding of works like the *Shōbō-genzō* and *Eihei kōroku*, which could not exist independently, that is, without extensive intertextual linkages and allusions to source texts from the Sung Ch'an canon. Some of the main areas that have been explored include early Ch'an movements in T'ang China, such as the Northern and Ox-Head schools, that continued to influence Zen thought, in addition to Sung Chinese institutions and masters such as Ta-hui and Hung-chih, whose forms of discourse greatly influenced Dōgen's approach.

An important recent trend in the social sciences is an approach that views texts not only in terms of how they represent an articulation of doctrine but as forms of discourse, that is, as expressions or reflections of underlying social conditions characterized by competing claims of authority and shifts in the structures of power. Since the early 1980s, studies in Japanese history have been reevaluating the role of Kamakura Buddhism in order to lead away from an exclusive focus on the novel ideas of a handful of the founding figures of sects, such as Dōgen and Eisai. Instead, the main effort is to examine the impact of the social and institutional background on the intellectual realm at both macro and micro levels, as well as the interaction of Buddhism with a much broader demographic group encompassing marginalized communities outside the mainstream of elite society. This includes women, irregular practitioners, laypersons, and various sorts of outcasts whose activities may benefit from or resemble the practices of reclusive or transient legitimate clergy.

Therefore Ch'an texts can be seen in light of how they were affected by political developments, including patterns of patronage and the rise and fall of government support or persecution. Also important are the effect of sectarian debates, and the reasons why a leading thinker may be addressing a specific audience of followers while excluding or refuting other sectors. A key issue for understanding Dōgen's role in the broader context of the formation of Kamakura religion is whether he is to be seen as an embodiment of the establishment because of his elite background and construction of an enduring temple and sect, or as the anti-establishment because of his break with the Tendai school and his resistance toward the shogun.[28]

The transition from examining "text as text," somewhat in isolation from its background, to "text in context," or as a discourse that is inseparable from the historical setting that helped produce it, has also generated diverse forms of cultural criticism. These methodological approaches reveal underlying or heretofore unseen agendas, priorities, and commitments in the self-expressions of religious institutions. There are several ways of applying such criticism to Zen texts. On one level, increasing sensitivity to how Orientalist and reverse Orientalist agendas may have skewed the presentation of traditional materials and reinforced stereotypes helps overcome falsely simplified sectarian polarities. This approach enables us to see through misleading oppositions held by different Zen schools, for example, between kōans and *zazen*, *vinaya* and rituals, or the purity of Chinese orthodoxy and dilution by Japanese heteropraxis. On another level, the integrity of Zen theory and practice has been called into question because of its apparent support for Japanese imperialism before World War II, as well as its contributions to social discrimination in carrying out funeral ceremonies for the outcast community and to the repression of women's rights in the treatment of nuns and laywomen.[29]

Some critics have been reevaluating Dōgen's writing to assess the relation between his premodern thought and a variety of problematic postmodern social issues, in order to determine whether his approach seen in contemporary contexts would represent a source for overcoming or reinforcing such problematic perspectives as ultranationalism, nativism (or *Nihonjinron* doctrine), and social discrimination toward women and outcasts. Critical Buddhist methodology has proposed that, while other forms of Mahayana and Zen thought contribute unwittingly to contemporary societal ills by endorsing the exclusion of some parties from the universality of the Buddha-nature, Dōgen's teachings, especially in the 12-*Shōbōgenzō* of the late period, provide at least the seed of the answer by emphasizing a view of morality that is rooted in the inexorability of karmic retribution and the value of repentance.

These kinds of reassessments of traditional images and icons have led to new ways of defining Dōgen's role as a Kamakura-era religious leader. For traditional Sōtō Zen, Dōgen has been viewed as the first patriarch who enjoyed royal prestige by birthright but abandoned Court nobility and eventually fled the capital as a show of a commitment to the authenticity of practice. When one looks at the various dimensions of his religiosity, Dōgen can also be seen as the keeper of the correct rite of transmission who preserved the heart of Chinese Ch'an tradition, language, lineage, and customs, including monastic discipline. Modern Japanese thinkers have praised him as an excellent mystical philosopher who can be compared to the great spiritualists or metaphysicians of any tradition. Social historians have drawn attention to the way Dōgen has functioned in popular consciousness as a miracle worker and folk hero, an image reinforced in the media in recent anniversary celebrations of Dōgen's life and death, while others see him as a precursor of contemporary reform movements.

Critique of the Decline and Renewal Theories

However, not all the progress made in recent Japanese scholarship by integrating biographical issues in their sociohistorical context with textual studies has led to altogether convincing results. In some prominent cases, breakthroughs in research have been linked to a particular sectarian or methodological agenda that tends to skew history even while illuminating it. Recent scholarship has focused on the question of whether, and to what extent, Dōgen underwent a significant change in thought and attitudes in his later years. Two main theories have emerged which agree that there was a decisive change, although they disagree about its timing and meaning. One view referred to as the Decline Theory argues that Dōgen entered into a prolonged period of deterioration after he moved from Kyoto to Echizen in 1243, at which point he became increasingly strident in his attacks on rival lineages and stubborn in rejecting laypersons and women. The second view referred to as the Renewal Theory maintains that Dōgen had a spiritual rebirth in his later period, especially after returning from Kamakura in 1248, when he began emphasizing the priority of karmic causality in the 12-Shōbōgenzō.[30]

The Decline Theory stresses that after Dōgen's return from China he cited Ju-ching and Hung-chih only infrequently and spoke highly of Lin-chi school patriarch Ta-hui until the time of his transition to Eiheiji. At that point, as we have seen, lavish praise of the Ts'ao-tung patriarchs accompanied by a sharp critique of their Lin-chi adversary became a central component of some fascicles of the Shōbōgenzō and, to a much lesser extent, of passages of the Eihei kōroku. The Decline Theory as articulated by Carl Bielefeldt and Heinrich Dumoulin, based in large part on studies in the 1970s and 1980s by Furuta Shōkin and Yanagida Seizan (both Rinzai scholars) as well as by Imaeda Aishin and Masutani Fumio, suggests that a descent into partisanship began with the Daruma school conversion in 1241. This tendency culminated two years later when Dōgen was more or less forced to flee from Kyoto at the time that Enni returned from China in 1241 and was soon awarded the abbacy at the formidable compound of Tōfukuji.

This theory, which could also be referred to as the Reversal Theory, sees

Dōgen abandoning the ideals of universal enlightenment encompassing lay-persons and women, for the sake of sectarian polemic in a rural monastery isolated from the capital and rival Buddhist schools. Dōgen also began exces-sively eulogizing his Chinese mentor while lambasting Lin-chi and others in opposing lineages. He was particularly harsh concerning the sublineage of Ta-hui's follower Te-kuang, who awarded transmission to disciples sent to China by Dainichi Nōnin; the latter never left Japan and was accused of advocating an experience of natural enlightenment without the need for following the precepts or ethical codes. The Decline Theory understands the late writings to consist of the last set of fascicles included in the 75-*Shōbōgenzō*, which were composed after 1243, when Dōgen moved to Echizen. Some passages in these texts are highly charged attacks on opponents and positions endorsed in his earlier works. However, the situation is complicated in that Dōgen's praise is not one-sided but is conditioned by the criticism and rewriting of Ts'ao-tung patriarchs' sayings, especially in the *Eihei kōroku* (which is part of what makes this text so important). In his final years, according to this theory, which tends to lack nuance, Dōgen dedicated himself to writing strict instructions on mo-nastic rules and rituals collected in the *Eihei shingi*, while neglecting the con-cerns of lay followers and women.

The Renewal Theory, expressed most emphatically in Critical Buddhist methodology, argues, conversely, that Dōgen had a spiritual rebirth after re-turning to Eiheiji in 1248 from a mission to Kamakura, where he found the dominant Rinzai Zen sect corrupted by its association with the rising warrior class. His subsequent writings are clear and consistent in endorsing the basic Buddhist doctrine of karmic causality and rejecting the antinomian implica-tions endemic to East Asian original enlightenment thought, which influenced Japanese Tendai and earlier forms of Ch'an/Zen philosophy, especially Nōnin's approach. For the proponents of this theory, Dōgen's best work was character-ized by his willingness to take a stand against the substantialist *dhatu-vada* (that is to say, *atmavada*) notion of the universality of enlightenment that is prized by the Decline Theory, and this work is based on a renewed commit-ment to the ethical imperative inherent in the quest for enlightenment. As was previously discussed, the theory maintains that the 12-*Shōbōgenzō*, which in-cludes rewritten versions of fascicles from the 75-*Shōbōgenzō* in addition to fascicles newly composed in the 1250s, is the pinnacle of Dōgen's literary achievements. Of all the various medieval editions of the *Shōbōgenzō*, including the 75-fascicle, 60-fascicle, and 28-fascicle editions, only the 12-*Shōbōgenzō*, Hakamaya argues, represents the fascicles that were selected by Dōgen himself just prior to his death rather than by posthumous editors.

On the one hand, the two theories have much in common. Both seek to identify the "pure" Zen master, a status that Dōgen had in Kyoto but lost in Echizen according to the Decline Theory, or attained just after the trip to Ka-makura according to the Renewal Theory. By arguing that there was a single basic change or an irreversible turning point in Dōgen's life, the theories challenge orthodox assumptions, particularly concerning the significance of the 75-*Shōbōgenzō*. The merits of this text generally remain unquestioned in both sectarian and modern secular studies that emphasize Dōgen's unchanging religious vision after his return from China, based on the doctrine of just sitting. The Decline Theory maintains that the later portions of the 75-*Shōbōgenzō* are rife with inconsistencies and partisan polemics, and the Renewal Theory sees it still struggling with and ever haunted by the influence of original enlightenment thought.

Both theories effectively demonstrate the need for examining Dōgen's ongoing struggle to reconcile conflicting tendencies including: composing in *kanbun* in order to transmit the Ch'an/Zen doctrine he learned in China or in *kana* for the sake of communicating with new groups of less-educated followers; writing instructions exclusively for monastics or with appeals to laypersons; making connections for patronage and power in Kyoto and Kamakura or longing to remain independent of political complications; and gazing past all polarities to the higher truth of nondual reality or stressing the merit gained from strict adherence to the precepts and other monastic regulations. The theories also contribute to the shifting of attention from text as a pristine, autonomous statement of doctrine with a fixed, unchallengeable canonicity, to the context of how the writing was indelibly molded by historical events and trends from a critical, even irreverent standpoint that demands a constant reevaluation of fixed assumptions.

Yet, as has been indicated, the theories appear to be in opposition over the meaning and content of the early and late periods. What the Decline Theory considers to constitute the late writings, or the tail end of the fascicles in the 75-*Shōbōgenzō*, is thought of as part of the early period by the Renewal Theory. The Decline Theory, according to Dumoulin, bemoans an "undeniable downturn" that Dōgen underwent in Echizen, when his writings became so marked by "a flaw of temper" toward his rivals that the "weaknesses in Dōgen's written work point to a weakness in leadership as the master advanced in age."[31] Referring to the same stage in Dōgen's career, the Renewal Theory finds Dōgen finally fulfilling his role as a premier Buddhist thinker and monastic leader by learning to cast aside the elements of thought that tend to violate the doctrine of causality. Thus the main area of contention is the last ten years following the move to Echizen. The Decline Theory maintains that Dōgen continued a downward slide precipitated by the political factors that caused him to leave Kyoto, whereas the Renewal Theory argues that the first stretch in Echizen was still part of the deficiency of the early Dōgen because it would take five more years and another crisis for his reawakening to take place.

Therefore, the Decline and Renewal theories not only differ in making nearly opposite assessments regarding the trajectory, positive or negative, of Dōgen's career but also disagree—or fail to recognize discrepancies—in their views of what time frame constitutes early and late periods. These theories based on more or less inverted views about the nature and timing of a decisive change are not so much opposite as they are talking past each other by using in heterological ways similar terminology concerning the early versus the late or purity versus impurity. The contradictions between the theories derive, ironically, from a common tendency to view the early period—defined as the pre-1243 75-*Shōbōgenzō* fascicles by the Decline Theory and as the entire 75-*Shōbōgenzō* by the Renewal Theory—from a mode of evaluation that is intent on setting up a contrast with the late writings.

Yet Dōgen's writings from the 1230s are not a monolithic unit with a single systematic message but a very diverse group in literary style and thematic content. They include a meditation manual (*Fukanzazengi*, 1233); several manuals on monastic rules (*Tenzokyōkun*, 1237, on instructions for the cook, and *Jūundōshiki*, 1239, on rules for the Monks Hall annex); two kōan collections, the *Mana Shōbōgenzō* and *Eihei kōroku* vol. 9 (1235 and 1236); the informal sermons in the *Shōbōgenzō zuimonki* (1238); and several other kinds of doctrinal expositions, including *Bendōwa* (1231), *Gakudōyōjinshu* (1234), and Dharma-talks (*hōgo*) contained in *Eihei kōroku* vol. 8 (1231–1243). During this period Dōgen wrote the first six fascicles of the 75-*Shōbōgenzō*, including "Genjōkōan," referred to as *jishu*-style lectures directed to a general, diverse audience. He also delivered the first 31 *jōdō* sermons included in the first volume of the *Eihei kōroku*. Both of these genres deal extensively with interpreting kōan cases cited in the aforementioned collections.

Dōgen's early writings became accelerated and diversified after the opening of Kōshōji in 1233 and its Monks Hall three years later, which established the temple as a thriving center for the new Zen school. These texts were experiments in developing a cogent method of adapting the Chinese models of theory and practice to a Japanese setting. While some efforts from this period were quickly abandoned, others were kept and refined throughout his career. The early works form a literary matrix out of which subsequent genres were developed, particularly the innovative *jishu* style of the 75-*Shōbōgenzō*, which is a hybrid formed apparently by combining sustained kōan commentary with the informal lecture style of *shōsan* (lit. "small gatherings")—as opposed to the *daisan* ("large gatherings"), resembling the *jōdō* style—found in Sung collections.

What each of the theories means in referring to early Dōgen is based on presupposed conclusions about the late period, and the result is a pattern of viewing the 75-*Shōbōgenzō* primarily in terms of where it led or how it changed. Although the crafters of the theories are generally sophisticated historians, at times their approaches violate actual sequence or conflate history with a methodological or theological position about what the 75-*Shōbōgenzō* eventually became or never really was. For example, the Decline Theory criticizes the so-called late 75-*Shōbōgenzō* fascicles that in some cases were written only one or two years after what it refers to as early fascicles, which it holds up as a standard beyond reproach. As is shown in Table 13, a crucial point is that over 75 percent or 57 of the 75-*Shōbōgenzō* fascicles were written in a period that lasted for a little over four years, from 1241 to the third month of 1244, which was when construction began on Daibutsuji.

Both theories tend to ignore or misrepresent the so-called early writings and their relation to the late period. In particular, it is questionable whether a notion of an early and thus a late 75-*Shōbōgenzō* is at all viable. Setting up a division between fascicles written just before and just after the Echizen migration can result in a neglect of the lines of continuity linking works composed in such close proximity, as well as the fact that some fascicles were actually recorded and then edited at very different times from their original oral deliv-

TABLE 13. Concise View of Dōgen's Main Literary Production

Years	Jishu	Jōdō	Other Writings
1223–1233	0	0	
In China			Kanbun verse (EK 10 portion)
At Kenninji			Shari sōdenki
At An'yōin			hōgo, Bendōwa
1233–1246 (7/18)	69	126	
Before 1233 (10/15)	(2)	(0)	Fukanzazengi, Gakudōyōjinshū
After	(10)	(31)	Mana Shōbōgenzō, EK 9, Tenzokyōkun, Shōbō-genzō zuimonki, Jūundōshiki
[a]After Daruma school monks convert in 1241	(29)	(95)	
[b]After 1243 (7/16) at Daibutsuji	(28)	(0)	Sanshōdōei (portions)
	(5)	(80)	Taidaiko, Bendōhō, Chiji shingi, Fushukuhampō
1246–1253	6	405	
Renamed Eiheiji	(1)		
Before 1247 (8/1)	(0)	(44)	
[c]After 1248 (3/1)	(0)	(281)	Shuryō shingi, Jūroku rakan genzuiki, Hōkyōki Hachidainingaku and other 12-SH texts
Total	75	531	

[a] The time of Dōgen's move to Echizen, key to the Decline Theory view of escape from sectarian pressures
[b] Dōgen's turn from *jishu* to *jōdō* style, key to the Three Periods Theory view of diverse literary genres
[c] Dōgen's return from Kamakura, key to the Renewal Theory view of spiritual rebirth based on causality

Note: Historical development of Dōgen's writings, with special emphasis on the historical formative relation between the *jishu* lectures that form the 75-*Shōbōgenzō*, which were phased out beginning in spring 1244, and the *jōdō* sermons that form the *Eihei kōroku* vols 1–7, which were accelerated beginning in 1245.

Adapted from several sources, especially Itō Shūken, "Manabi Jūnikanbon *Shōbōgenzō* ni tsuite," *Indogaku buk-kyōgaku kenkyū* 36/1 (1987): 194–201; Sugio Genyū, "Nana-jūgokanbon *Shōbōgenzō* no kihonteki kōsatsu," in Kurebayashi Kōdō, ed., *Dōgen zen no shisōteki kenkyū* (Tokyo: Shunjūsha, 1973), pp. 545–570; and Kawamura, "*Shōbōgenzō*," in Kagamishima Genryū and Tamaki Kōshirō, eds., *Dōgen no chosaku* (Tokyo: Shunjūsha, 1980), pp. 1–74.

ery. The Decline Theory often ends up referring to *Bendōwa* as a prototypical expression of the universalism of the early period, but this stylistically anomalous text is not part of the 75-*Shōbōgenzō* (although, as was previously mentioned, it is included in the 95-*Shōbōgenzō*, a Tokugawa-era construction). Another limitation in the Decline Theory is that it does not make recourse to an analysis of the 60-*Shōbōgenzō*, which includes fascicles deleted from the 75-fascicle text for being overly polarizing. Such an argument could bolster the theory's claims by showing that in the early stages of the Sōtō school, its leading commentators—and perhaps even Dōgen himself—were aware of the polemical tone of nearly a dozen fascicles.

Similarly, the Renewal Theory tends to distort history when it dismisses the facts that at least two of the fascicles contained in the 12-*Shōbōgenzō* were written during their so-called early period (1240 and 1244, respectively), and that Dōgen continued to edit the 75-*Shōbōgenzō* fascicles (including the second one, "Genjōkōan," from 1233) while he was writing the 12-*Shōbōgenzō* twenty years later, facts suggesting that he never abandoned interest in this text. Because so much attention is given to a distinctive approach to the debate about *Shōbōgenzō* editions, the Renewal Theory tends to overlook the role of other works from the late late period (that is, the period after Dōgen's return from Kamakura), including the *Eihei kōroku* and *Hōkyōki*, which might actually support their theory of a new emphasis on causation. For example, in *Eihei kōroku* no. 5.386 from 1250 Dōgen writes, "People have no sincere faith, and true mindfulness has dimmed, so that they do not trust genuine reality but merely love spiritual power. . . . If people who study Buddha Dharma have no genuine faith or true mindfulness, they will certainly dispense with and ignore [the law of] causality."[32]

By having fixed notions about what the late Dōgen means for interpreting the 75-*Shōbōgenzō*, the two theories tend to overlook other important works from both early and late periods which often express diverse ideas indicating that Dōgen was not one-sidedly pure or impure at any given stage. For example, the Decline Theory does not take into account that Dōgen wrote several monastic rules and ritual texts in the early period and that the *Shōbōgenzō zuimonki* repeatedly supports the priority of monastics over laypersons well before the migration to Echizen. In addition, the theories generally neglect the main feature of Dōgen's literary production during the entire Echizen period, both before and after the trip to Kamakura: the proliferation, beginning within a year of the opening of Daibutsuji/Eiheiji, of the *jōdō* sermons included in the first seven volumes of the ten-volume *Eihei kōroku*. Although, as we have seen, the *Eihei kōroku* has not received the attention it deserves, as the single major work of Dōgen's last nine years it is crucial for developing a theory about the late period.[33] As was shown in Table 1, the vast majority (nearly 80 percent) of *jōdō* sermons were delivered just as the *jishu* lectures were being phased out of Dōgen's monastic program.

The role of the *Eihei kōroku* in the Echizen period is presumably trouble-some to both theories. While focusing on other aspects of change in Dōgen, however important, the theories have had a blind spot with regard to how the origins of the *Eihei kōroku* are connected with the rise and fall of the composition of the 75-*Shōbōgenzō*. Yet the *Eihei kōroku* is probably the most reliable indicator of Dōgen's own attitudes in the late period because, like the *Shōbōgenzō zuimonki* though for the most part unlike the 75-*Shōbōgenzō*, it includes personal anecdotes and biographical self-reflections, some of which are contained in memorials for masters and disciples and in commemorations for ceremonial occasions.

In contrast to the view of the Decline Theory, the *Eihei kōroku* and other works from the late period show Dōgen as a vigorous Zen master in full command of his monastery who was neither antagonistic toward rival schools and unambiguously loyal to Ju-ching nor uncaring about the lay community and dedicated only to monastic life. An emphasis on the necessity of practicing *zazen* meditation is seen throughout all stages of Dōgen's career. Also some passages dealing with karma and causality in the *Eihei kōroku* may reflect a different orientation than the philosophy expressed in the 12-*Shōbōgenzō* by stressing a supernatural approach to retribution and redemption through the rites of repentance, thereby challenging the Renewal Theory's view of a monolithic stance once Dōgen underwent a once-and-for-all change of heart.

Therefore although the *Eihei kōroku* has often been viewed as a kind of shadow text, important only in fleshing out ideas expressed in the 75-*Shōbōgenzō*, it should be taken out of its shroud and seen as a crucial work recorded almost entirely after the 75-*Shōbōgenzō* was completed. Furthermore, when seen in terms of the overall development of the Dōgen canon, the *Eihei kōroku*, first composed and collected in 1236–1240 but suspended for almost two years between Dōgen's arrival in Echizen and the establishment of Dai-butsuji/Eiheiji, is not atypical but for the most part appears consistent and continuous with the themes and styles from the mid-1230s.

Toward a Theory of Three Periods

While many of the efforts of the Decline and Renewal theories are to be applauded for trying to periodize and therefore to problematize Dōgen's career, each falls short of an effective approach for several reasons. The divisions between early and late Dōgen they espouse set up a false dichotomy with an implied or explicit judgment, allowing their description of history to be infected with an ideological bias. Instead of offering an objective historical analysis, the theories interject an evaluation cloaked as historiography. A basic limitation in the approaches of Kim and Kodera is a tendency to isolate a specific compilation or historic phase without fully taking into account the overall context, including other texts and life events. Conversely, the Decline and Renewal theories are limited in putting too much emphasis on general trends in Dōgen's life and thought accompanied by an assessment of the rise or fall, or success or failure, of his project.

My approach to periodization integrates textual/philological studies of the formation and interpretations of major and minor texts, including various versions of the *Shōbōgenzō* and the *Eihei kōroku*, with social-historical perspectives of biographical issues. I point out that the diversity in literary production, as well as the complexity and ambiguity of historical events, makes it difficult for the Decline and Renewal theories to construct a view that Dōgen had a single, decisive break with his previous writings. To clarify the discrepancies and inconsistencies between the two theories, I reverse their tendency to discuss the early period on the basis of a somewhat presumed evaluation of the status of the late Dōgen by examining later developments in light of what is reflected in the early writings. According to my approach, the 75-*Shōbōgenzō* should be seen neither as a late text, as the Decline Theory argues, nor an early text, as suggested by the Renewal Theory. Rather, it occupies a crucial transitional ground that is bookended by segments in which Dōgen primarily created other works.

Extending from these observations concerning the chronology of compositions, I present an alternative theory of periodization, which has several components. First, this theory maintains that there are Three Periods rather than two main periods (as shown in more detail in Tables 14 and 15 [see Part II]):

1. An early, pre-75-*Shōbōgenzō* period (1223–1233), which begins with the trip to China and the composition of Chinese verse and continues through the return to Kyoto and the composition of a couple of short texts, including *Bendōwa*, before and during the opening of Kōshōji.
2. The middle period (1233–1246), which includes the formation of the *Shōbōgenzō zuimonki* and the 75-*Shōbōgenzō* (without regard for the post-Echizen subdivision of this text proposed by the Decline Theory), in addition to other works experimenting with styles of kōan commentary, including the origins of *jōdō* sermons and the bulk of the *Eihei shingi*.
3. A late, post-75-*Shōbōgenzō* period (1246–1253), which covers the opening and naming of Eiheiji, in addition to the trip to Kamakura that is stressed by the Renewal Theory, and which includes the composition of the *Eihei kōroku*, the 12-*Shōbōgenzō*, and the *Hōkyōki*.

The second element of this theory is to view the texts, including the *Shōbōgenzō*, not as autonomous entities, but as participating in "fields of discourse" in terms of when the time of their composition intersects with other works as well as biographical events and sociohistorical conditions. Fields of discourse embrace the interaction and intertextuality of compilations of texts and subtexts relative to stages and substages as part of a general theory of the periodization of Dōgen's career. This technique shows, for example, that what Dōgen was writing at the time of the move to Echizen can best be seen in relation to a variety of contexts, including his relation with the Daruma school and other movements and institutions in early Kamakura Buddhism.

An example of how this approach is effective is the case of the *Mana Shōbōgenzō*. This text, which was lost for centuries, may seem an oddity that is out of place with Dōgen's other works, particularly the vernacular *Shōbōgenzō*. But if juxtaposed in the early middle period with the ninth volume of the *Eihei kōroku*, completed a year later, as well as the lectures contained in the *Shōbōgenzō zuimonki* begun in 1236, a pattern becomes clear. Around the time of the Kōshōji Monks Hall opening, Dōgen was experimenting with different ways of presenting kōans to his audience in Japan, which was beginning to be infiltrated by former members of the Daruma school. This activity resulted in the *jishu* and *jōdō* styles of lectures.

The third aspect of the theory is that the periods and subphases are not well understood because the links to China have been misrepresented. It is crucial to clarify the rises and falls in Dōgen's pattern of citing Ju-ching and Hung-chih, which takes surprising twists and turns, revealing that he is committed to the Ch'an model and showing how he uses it—or selectively chooses parts—for partisan reasons in the Japanese context.

The fourth and final aspect of the Three Periods Theory is the further division of the main periods of Dōgen's career into subperiods in order to offer a more detailed and nuanced analysis. The general designations of early, middle, and late periods can be too broad, and they blur rather than highlight subtle points of distinction and transition. The Decline and Renewal theories reflect misleading and contradictory conceptions of what constitutes the periods of Dōgen's career and deal with the sequence in a somewhat inappropriate way by suppressing subperiods, especially what I call the "middle middle" period. This is the phase of transitioning from Kyoto to Echizen, from 1241 to 1244, marked by the composition of the vast majority (two-thirds) of 75-*Shōbōgenzō* fascicles and other important writings, including the Japanese poetry collection. This complicated time is arguably the most creative period in Dōgen's career from the standpoint of literary output, yet it was also the time when he became preoccupied with using Ju-ching as a vehicle for defining his sect.

From the standpoint of descriptive neutrality that looks for a balanced view regarding continuity and discontinuity, it is necessary to highlight the middle middle period as representing neither a simple break nor a smooth transition. Such an approach helps one see the various writings from subperiods not as a matter of either the progression or the diminishing of Dōgen's skills, but as part of an unfolding of thoughts and compositions that express timeless mystical truths yet are relative to particular contexts.

TABLE 14. Periodization of Dōgen's Career (3 Main Periods and 7 SubPeriods or Fields of Discourse)

Early Period 1223–1233—Formative (China and Kenninji years)

Teaching: Doctrine of *shikan taza*, and proclaiming new Zen meditation approach in Japan, as well as exploring ways of using and interpreting kōans
Texts: early *hōgo, Bendōwa, Fukanzazengi,* 75-*Shōbōgenzō* "Genjōkōan" and "Makahannyaharam-itsu"
a. **Early Early 1223–1227 (fall)**
Career: China travels at Mount T'ien-t'ung and other Five Mountains temples; experience of *shinjin datsuraku* under Ju-ching and viewing of *shisho* materials
Texts: part of *Eihei kōroku* vol. 10 (section of Chinese poetry collection), *ichiya Hekiganroku;* Myōzen relics and lineage documents
b. **Late Early 1227–1233 (fall)**
Career: return to Kenninji where Jakuen arrives and Ejō visits; dwelling in Fukakusa hermitage (An'yōin)

Middle Period 1233–1246—Transitional (Kōshōji/Shōbōgenzō years)

Teaching: Weaving kōan citations into informal (*jishu*) sermons in *kana*, with emphasis on liter-ary (*bungakuteki*) and natural (*shizenteki*) themes in following Ju-ching, and monastic rules
Texts: 75-*Shōbōgenzō* (6 fasc.), *Eihei kōroku* vols. 2–3, *Bendōhō, Shuryō shingi, Fushukuhampō* later included in *Eihei shingi*
c. **Early Middle 1233–1241 (spring)**
Career: Establishing of Kōshōji temple (1233), where Ejō becomes disciple (1234) and Monks Hall is opened on 10.15.1236
Texts: *Eihei kōroku* vol. (1), 8, *Gakudōyōjinshū, Mana Shōbōgenzō, Eihei kōroku* vol. 9 (*juko*), *Ten-zokyōkun, Jūundōshiki, Shōbōgenzō zuimonki,* 75-*Shōbōgenzō* (12 fasc.)
d. **Middle Middle 1241–1244 (spring)**
Career: Conversion of Daruma school monks, return of Enni to Japan, receiving *Ju-ching yü-lu*, patronage of Hatano Yoshishige initiated; move to Echizen province through winter of 1243–1244 at temporary hermitages; construction of Daibutsuji begun
Texts: 75-*Shōbōgenzō* (57 fasc.), *Eihei kōroku* vol. 1, Japanese poetry collection, *Taidaiko*
e. **Late Middle 1244–1246 (summer)**
Career: Daibutsuji temple opened on 7.18.1244 and resumption of formal sermons or *jōdō* in *kanbun*

Late Period 1246–1253—Developmental (Eiheiji/Eihei kōroku years)

Teaching: New emphasis on causality with focus on ritual purity and monastic discipline
Texts: *Eihei kōroku* vols. 5–7, 12-*Shōbōgenzō* (most fascicles), *Hōkyōki*
f. **Early Late 1246–1248 (spring)**
Career: Naming of Eiheiji temple on 7.10.1246, visit to see Hōjō Tokiyori in Kamakura and re-turn to Eiheiji on 3.13.1248
Texts: *Eihei kōroku* vols. (3), 4, *Chiji shingi* (in *Eihei shingi*), *Jūroku rakan genzuiki*
g. **Late Late 1248–1253 (fall)**
Career: Following return, moon-viewing self-portrait in eighth mo. 1249, Gien becomes editor of *Eihei kōroku*, final years at Eiheji, ill health and death in Kyoto

---

In addition, this approach identifies a "late early" field or subperiod in the early 1230s, which includes *Bendōwa*, the original "Genjōkōan," and *Fukanzazengi*, as well as an "early middle" field in the mid-1230s. This subphase covers three texts that highlight the role of kōan cases: the *Mana Shōbōgenzō*, the ninth volume of the *Eihei kōroku*, and the *Shōbōgenzō zuimonki*, in addition to the *Gakudōyōjinshū*. There is also a distinction between a general late period, covering the entire Eiheiji stage, and a more specific "late late" phase, which refers to the final years after the Kamakura trip, when Dōgen developed a new focus on causality in the final portions of the *Eihei kōroku* along with the 12-*Shōbōgenzō*, the *Hōkyōki*, and the *Eihei shingi*.

The seven subperiods outlined in Tables 14 and 15 (two each for the main early and late periods, and three subperiods for the middle period in order to highlight the move to Echizen) are intended to represent a flexible framework for organizing historical materials rather than definitive units. The guiding principle is to identify in Dōgen's literary production or career path points of transition that create a division between previous writings and activities and those that follow. Each moment of transition is distinctive and valuable for how it stands out from the preceding and succeeding dimensions and for the way it contributes to the flow of Dōgen's career.

While some of the boundaries seem quite clear, such as the return from China marking the end of the early early period and the naming of Eiheiji as the beginning of the early late period, other subdivisions can more readily be contested. For example, it could be possible to start the late late period not after the return from Kamakura in the spring of 1248, but rather with the change in the editorship of the *Eihei kōroku* from Ejō to Gien in 1249, over a year later. The Three Periods Theory goes beyond the matter of intertextuality linking works from a subperiod to focus on the religious vision reflected by the writings. It recognizes that Dōgen's primary aim was not to produce texts as an end in itself, but rather to create a monastic setting that accomplished several goals reflected in the textual materials. Dōgen's central concern underlying the points of transition was to establish a full-scale monastic community effectively guided by a highly ritualized approach to meditation practice and doctrinal teachings.

These goals included the introduction and appropriation of Chinese Ch'an approaches to monastic ritual and discipline in the context of Japanese Buddhism and the establishment of an autonomous temple institution that was independent of political influence yet supported by donors and the participation of laypersons in ceremonies and rites of repentance. Dōgen's texts cannot be successfully interpreted unless they are seen in light of the monastic function and their contribution to the formation of Zen styles of training in Japan, as well as the relation of Kōshōji and Eiheiji with contemporary Daruma school and Rinzai temples that were also part of the transmission and transition from Sung Ch'an to Kamakura Zen. The main elements of change in his writing are not based so much on shifts in ideology but reflect attempts to work with different literary genres associated with the growth of Kōshōji and Eiheiji temples by altering the style rather than the content of instruction.[34]

Although each period has its own level of significance, I will stress that the *early early* (China travels), *middle middle* (move to Echizen), and *late late* (after return from Kamakura) phases are crucial for an overall understanding of the impact of China on Dōgen's productivity. Ch'an remains an influence that he plays off by accepting and modifying yet never rejecting their main elements in an ongoing give-and-take process that, if anything, increases in importance toward the end of Dōgen's career.

PART II

Theory of Periodization

Overview of Main Periods of Dōgen's Career

TABLE 15.

Period	Place	Issue	Temple	Main Text	Doctrine	Sources
1a. Early Early (1223–1227) Departure from Japan in spring	China	Doubt	Mt. Tien-t'ung	Chinese verse	*Shinjin datsuraku*	Monk–lay interaction
1b. Late Early (1227–1233) Return in fall	Kyoto/ Fukakusa	Japanese sect	Kenninji/ Anyō'in	*Bendōwa, hōgo,* and verse	*Shikan taza*	Quadriloque (w/ Nōnin, Eisai, Tendai)
2a. Early Middle (1233–1240) Opening Kōshōji in fall	Fukakusa	Monks Hall	Kōshōji	*Shōbōgenzō zuimonki, Fukanzazengi,* "Genjōkōan"	Zazen (over Precepts)	Encounter dialogues
2b. Middle Middle (1241–1244) Daruma school conversion in spring	Fukakusa/ Echizen	Move	Kōshōji/ Kippōji	75-*Shōbōgenzō,* waka poetry	Ju-ching as model	Transmission of lamp records
2c. Late Middle (1244–1246) Daibutsuji constructed in spring	Echizen	Dharma Hall	Daibutsuji	*Eihei kōroku, Bendōhō* (in *Eihei shingi*)	Monastic rules and Hung-chih as model	*Ch'an-yüan ch'ing-kuei*
3a. Early Late (1246–1248) Eiheiji named in summer	Echizen/ Kamakura	Diverse audience	Eiheiji	*Eihei kōroku, Chiji shingi**	Hung-chih as model/foil	Sung masters' records
3b. Late Late (1248–1253) Return from Kamakura in spring (Gien ed. *Eihei kōroku* 1249)	Echizen/ Kyoto	Post-Hōjō visit	Eiheiji	12-*Shōbōgenzō Eihei kōroku, Hōkyōki,* and verse	Karmic causality and repentance	Early Buddhist literature

* Part of the *Eihei shingi* collection

3

The Early Period

Dōgen Went to China

The first main period of Dōgen's career is the formative stage, covering his initial training in China and the development of ideas upon his return to Japan on establishing authentic Sung-style practice in what would emerge as one of the major new movements of Kamakura Buddhism. This period encompasses two subperiods. The first is the "early early" subperiod (1223–1227), which covers the travels to China and the experience of *shinjin datsuraku*, which are examined here from a critical historiographical standpoint, not to try to debunk the trip but to clarify our understanding of the impact of Chinese Ch'an on Dōgen's entire career development. For this stage, the only legitimated writings are fifty *kanshi* poems and a dedication to Myōzen, since the "One Night *Blue Cliff Record*" is considered apocryphal. The main works traditionally attributed to the time of the return from China in late 1227 have been redated in recent scholarship. These include *Fukanzazengi*, a brief but important meditation manual modeled on Tsung-tse's *Tso-ch'an i* contained as an appendix to the *Ch'an-yüan ch'ing-kuei* that is now moved ahead to 1233, and *Hōkyōki*, which is most likely from the end of Dōgen's life. Therefore, the key literary issue that needs to be examined is not so much what Dōgen wrote about but concerns what texts written at later stages have to say about the earliest period.

The second or "late early" phase (1227–1233) began when Dōgen settled back in Japan, for the first couple of years at Kenninji temple and then at An'yōin hermitage in Fukakusa beginning in 1230. In the early part of the decade Dōgen commanded a small Kannon temple in the same town, which became the site where his first full-fledged monastic setting was established at Kōshōji temple on 10.15.1233, which marks the end of the early period. In addition to a few minor writings, including several of the *hōgo* presented for a nun and a layman and collected in *Eihei kōroku* vol. 8,[1] Dōgen produced his first major work, *Bendōwa*. This essay attempts to declare his independence from the Daruma school and other Buddhist sects while also creating a sense of continuity with both Heian Japanese and Sung Chinese Buddhism, especially but not exclusively to the Ch'an school. *Bendōwa* reveals Dōgen exploring and experimenting with literary and pedagogical techniques to convey his understanding of the Dharma to a broad audience. This text has been seen as prototypical by many commentators, yet it is problematic for various historical, textual, and stylistic reasons. Therefore it should not be taken as the basis of a theory about the essence of "early Dōgen," particularly regarding his views on issues ranging from endorsing or distancing from original enlightenment thought to accepting the precepts or the role of laypersons and women.

The Pre-China Stage: Dōgen's Doubt

The initial stage of Dōgen's career could be backdated from 1223 for about a decade to 1212–1213, when, according to traditional accounts, especially the *Kenzeiki* and *Teiho Kenzeiki*, Dōgen's life experience stimulated his spiritual seeking and his decision to become a monk (*shukke-sha*, lit., "one who makes home departure") in the Tendai school on Mount Hiei. Born into aristocracy, which meant that he had an early education in classical Chinese literary texts, both Buddhist and non-Buddhist, Dōgen was orphaned with the death of his father when he was two years old and his mother when he was seven. Deeply troubled by the incessant impermanence in seeing the smoke from incense drifting in the air at his mother's funeral, five years later in 1212 Dōgen declined the offer of Matsudono Sonkō (relation uncertain) to train for the ministry in the imperial court. After visiting Ryōkan Hōgen, an uncle on his mother's side, he decided to renounce the secular world and enter Senkōbōin temple at Yokawa-hannyadani. He took the tonsure on 4.9.1213 and received the 58-article bodhisattva precepts the following day from Kōen, who had just become the abbot of Enryakuji, succeeding the renowned Buddhist monk/historian Jien, author of the *Gukanshō*.

Having quickly become dissatisfied with practices at Mount Hiei, Dōgen then visited Kōin, who was abbot at Onjōji of the Tendai Jimon branch that was linked with Heisenji temple near Mount Hakusan. This step suggests that the roots of Dōgen's decision to move to Echizen three decades later can be traced back to some of the institutional connections forged during the earliest days of his career. In any case, Kōin directed him to study Zen meditation at Kenninji, where the *Teiho Kenzeiki* reports he had a meeting with Eisai shortly before the latter's death in 1215, although this assertion is not consistently supported by other traditional biographies. The sources do agree, though, that on 6.25.1217, about a year after the passing of Kōin, Dōgen began six years of training at Kenninji under Myōzen. After about four years, on 9.12.1221, Dōgen received the seal of transmission (*inka*) in the Huang-lung stream of the Lin-chi school, and the two monks apparently began preparing for the trip to China. Yet it is not clear whether Myōzen was really Eisai's primary successor, since temple records do not confirm this. As with Ju-ching, it seems that Myōzen's primary claim to fame is as a mentor of Dōgen, who referred to both teachers with the respectful term *senshi*, or revered teacher.

What Did Dōgen Read?

The events that took place before the China trip are not considered part of the early early period because there is no evidence of Dōgen producing texts and little mention of his activities or autobiographical reflections in subsequent writings.[2] The key to understanding the pre-China stage, therefore, does not involve what he was writing at the time or even what he wrote about that stage in later works. Rather, it is a matter of speculation regarding what he was likely to have been reading that would help set the stage for the development of his remarkable ability in citing Ch'an texts that is so characteristic of both the *jishu* and *jōdō* sermons produced during the middle and late periods.

Traditional sources indicate that as a child, Dōgen studied Chinese poetry as well as early Buddhist Abhidharma literature, and while training at Mount Hiei, twice read (and probably memorized) the entire *Tripitaka*. As a Tendai novice, Dōgen must have specialized in the *Lotus Sutra*, which he continued to prize and cited over fifty times in various writings, referring to it as "king of the sutras."[3] Reading the *Tripitaka* and *Lotus Sutra* may have been standard fare for Mount Hiei monks, but what is not so clear is how many new Ch'an materials were available beyond early T'ang sources based primarily on pre-Hui-neng/Southern school doctrines. Those materials were long extant but overlooked in Japan, though an interest seems to have been reawakened by the end of the twelfth century that triggered Dainichi Nōnin's writings and the emergence of the Daruma school. Part of the perceived deficiency of Nōnin was that his views were based on outdated materials.

Sung Ch'an was known for its tremendously inventive and voluminous literary output, which surpassed that of other Buddhist sects, producing dozens of texts that featured records of encounter dialogues in transmission of the lamp records, recorded sayings, and kōan collections. Would Dōgen have been exposed, while still in Japan, to any of the genres of the Ch'an texts published in the eleventh and twelfth centuries? In other words, which Sung Ch'an records, if any, had Eisai introduced, and how much of them might Dōgen have been able to study in the early years of training? Access to these works while he was at Kenninji would strengthen the argument that Dōgen may not have actually had to make the journey to China to acquire his facility in citing them.

According to a passage in the *Shōbōgenzō zuimonki* (5.8), while at Kenninji, Dōgen studied the main Chinese Buddhist monk biography texts, the *Kao-seng chuan* and *Hsü kao-seng chuan*, which were crucial for understanding the early period of Ch'an history in the T'ang dynasty, including the formative stages of Ch'an but prior to the development of the main schools. Dōgen notes how impressed he was with the selfless attitude and highly disciplined approach of Chinese masters compared with that of teachers in Japan, who were just "so much dirt and broken tile." However, he does not refer and was probably not exposed to the updated Sung version of this genre. The *Sung kao-seng chuan*, published in 988, contains additional materials crucial for our understanding of the history of Ch'an, yet it may not have made it to Japan by this point.

It is likely that the only example of a genre of Sung Ch'an writings transmitted to Japan before Dōgen's trip was Eisai's appropriation of the *Ch'an-yüan ch'ing-kuei*, which he cites extensively and on which he patterns some sections in the *Kōzen gokokuron*. According to numerous passages in the *Shōbōgenzō zuimonki* in describing what Dōgen observed during his initial residency in China, the *Ch'an-yüan ch'ing-kuei* was used as a model for the strictly disciplined behavior found at Kenninji. The Sung rules text also contains numerous chapters on the tea ceremony that were also an influence on Eisai's *Kissa yōjoki*, the text that introduced tea to Japan. Tsung-tse's text was also the primary influence on the essays included in the *Eihei shingi*, as well as other writings such as *Fukanzazengi* on meditation and "Jukai' on the precepts.

Eisai was also greatly influenced by pre-Sung texts available in Japan, such as Yung-ming Yen-shou's tenth-century *Tsung-ching lu* (J. *Sugyōroku*), which sought to combine Ch'an meditation with chanting and related ritual activities aimed at attaining the Pure Land.[4] This text also had an important impact on Nōnin (as well as Enni), and it is difficult to judge which of the early Zen leaders was the first to reference it. Because Eisai did not introduce transmission of the lamp records or kōan collections, it is misleading to assume that the training Dōgen received under Myōzen at Kenninji, which incorporated Tendai and Shingon practice, bore much resemblance to Rinzai school kōan-curriculum practice as it developed in the later Kamakura era. This practice was formed only after Ch'an literature was introduced by subsequent pilgrims like Enni and Shinchi and it became widespread at Rinzai Zen temples.

Doubts about Dōgen's Doubt

What led Dōgen to join Myōzen in making what was at that time a precarious journey to China? The two monks apparently hoped to emulate the travels of Eisai, who gained firsthand knowledge of Ch'an Buddhism during his two trips, which were 20 years apart in the late twelfth century. The interim was a lengthy stretch in which not many Japanese Buddhists were traveling to the mainland—an exception was Shunjō—because of constant internal political turmoil and conflicts between leading factions in Kyoto and Kamakura. With the end of the Jōkyū War between ex-Emperor Go-Toba and the shogun Yoshitoki, which lasted from 1221 to 1222, the opportunity for travel opened up,[5] and Myōzen decided to lead the tour despite the grave illness of one of his teachers.

For Dōgen, according to the oft-cited account in the *Kenzeiki*, the trip— after several years of itinerant roaming between Mount Hiei, Onjōji, and Kenninji—was stimulated by his frustration with the apparent gap between theory and practice evident in the various Tendai and Zen Buddhist factions in Japan, a feeling reflected in the "Great Doubt" (*taigi*):

> My doubts arose after reading numerous sutras and sastras. Both
> the exoteric and esoteric teaching maintain that "[all sentient] beings
> originally share the Dharma-nature and naturally have the body of
> self-nature." If this is the case, then for what reason would all the
> buddhas of the Triple World have to aspire to buddhahood?[6]

Even if apocryphal, this passage is crucial for understanding the development of Dōgen's religiosity and its manner of linking Chinese Ch'an and Japanese Buddhism on two levels. There is a theoretical or metaphysical level of significance, which refers to a broad question about the nature of ultimate reality and its relation to the mundane realm in light of the Buddhist doctrine of two truths (absolute truth beyond duality and provisional truth within duality). In addition, a practical or concrete level of significance concerns Dōgen's more specific struggle to incorporate various elements of religious training and monastic regulations in order to create a spiritual life that reflected the resolution of his Doubt.

On the metaphysical level, Dōgen wondered whether or not there is a contradiction between the all-encompassing presence of a fundamental Buddha-nature and the need for continuing practice to attain enlightenment. If we all are already buddhas by virtue of our possession of an innately pure spiritual nature, then why has every seeker needed to train in meditation in order to acquire enlightenment? Furthermore, why have all those who have attained enlightenment continued to renew this experience through additional practice? These doubts may have referred not only to Tendai teachings that emphasized esoteric rites but also to doctrines espoused by Nōnin and the Daruma school, which denied the need for meditation.

The sense of turmoil Dōgen experienced within Tendai practice, which seemed to harbor a gap between the ideal realm of a universal Buddha-nature and manifestations in the phenomenal realm that were not spiritually pure, led him to view Chinese Ch'an as a necessary corrective to problematic approaches in Japanese Buddhism. However, the extent to which Dōgen freed

himself from the sway of original enlightenment ideology and the impact of
the Tendai school—a topic hotly debated by the Renewal Theory, which argues
that such a liberation did not occur until after the Kamakura mission—requires
an examination of broader implications regarding monastic life.

Concrete questions raised by the Doubt center on the role of diverse practices used to overcome suffering and attain nirvana in seeking a middle way
between original enlightenment and acquired enlightenment (*shikaku*). These
practices involve clarifying the number and function of the precepts, which are
a central part of classical Buddhism, combined with the study of kōans and
styles of sermons, which are unique to the Ch'an/Zen method of transmission.
Additionally, Dōgen problematized the role of the temple as a social institution
and its degree of dependence or independence from central religious and civil
authorities.

Eisai and the Daruma School

To understand further how lingering doubts about the efficacy of original enlightenment were a driving force that led Dōgen to China, it is important for
us to consider the context of early Japanese Zen and its conflicts with the Tendai
establishment. By the time Dōgen entered Kenninji over twenty years after
Eisai's Zen doctrine was first proclaimed, much had changed in the conditions
of the sect, yet the developmental situation remained fluid and challenging.
On returning from the second trip to China, which lasted four years, Eisai
found that Zen was being harshly criticized by conservative factions of the
dominant Tendai sect, who were adamantly opposed to the formation of new
religious movements considered a threat to Mount Hiei's hegemony. In 1194
Eisai was grouped along with the Daruma school that Nōnin founded in the
1180s, and both movements, seen as representative of the teachings of Bodhidharma (J. Daruma), were considered subversive cults and were proscribed.
Tendai leadership waged a similar campaign against Hōnen's Pure Land
school, which was beginning to flourish by the end of the twelfth century.
Prohibited by the establishment in 1207, Hōnen along with a number of
nembutsu-practicing disciples including Shinran were exiled for a time.

To protest the injunction of 1194, Eisai began working on the *Kōzen gokokuron*, a polemical tract published in 1198 (the same year as Hōnen's *Senchaku hongan nembutsu shū*), which distinguished his approach from that of a
less legitimate rival, Nōnin, who harbored antinomian tendencies, while also
making the case for the efficacy of Rinzai Zen in the function of national
affairs. In this, his main extant writing, Eisai argues that *zazen* meditation had
been practiced in Japan as early as the seventh century in the teachings of
Dōshō, who learned it from the great Chinese translator and traveler to India,
Hsüan-tsang. He also points out that *zazen* was utilized by Saichō based on

the teachings of T'ien-t'ai patriarch Chih-i, so that Eisai was simply reintroducing a long-lost Japanese practice.

As Albert Welter shows, "Eisai's whole presumption [was] of Zen as both the lost source and the fulfillment of Tendai teaching" based on what he had learned in China from Fa-yen stream teachings.[7] Eisai used the *Ch'an-yüan ch'ing-kuei* as a tool to demonstrate the rigorous self-discipline inherent in his view of Zen as a means of "protecting the country." The preface of the treatise opens with an iteration of the importance of "Buddhist rules governing moral behavior (*kairitsu*) taking precedence over the practice of meditation." Furthermore, "Moral precepts and monastic discipline cause Buddhism to flourish forever . . . [and] are the essence of Zen."[8]

Eisai was successful in having the ban against him lifted and in establishing Jufukuji in the new capital as well as Kenninji in the old capital at the turn of the century. However, when Dōgen left Japan in 1223, there was still no "pure Zen" (*junsui Zen*) temple, as opposed to a "mixed Zen" (*kenju Zen*) style of training that incorporated esoteric rites or acceptance of Zen as an autonomous sect. Training at Kenninji, officially listed as a branch temple (*matsuji*) affiliated with the Tendai school, was based on eclectic practices combining Zen meditation and discipline with Kenmitsu (exoteric-esoteric) ritualism. Jufukuji was even more oriented toward the esoteric traditions and had less of a Zen identity.

In order to be transmitted to Japan, Sung Ch'an had to be adjusted to the new environment and the impact of local rites and beliefs. Nevertheless, in spite of efforts to accommodate it through the assimilation of Kenmitsu practices, Tendai criticism of Eisai continued throughout his life because of his emphasis on the utility of Zen as the exclusive path to the Dharma, as well as the fact that his disciples wore robes that followed the customs of a foreign country. Eisai also gained a mixed reputation for using spiritual powers to affect the wind and weather during the construction of Kenninji. Furthermore, though Eisai's contribution to bringing Ch'an to Japan in citing from the *Ch'an-yüan ch'ing-kuei* was greater than Nōnin's, the role of transmitter of Sung Ch'an literature was played to a much greater extent by both Dōgen and Enni.

By the beginning of the thirteenth century the Daruma school came under fire from both Tendai authorities and Eisai's fledgling Rinzai school for several practical as well as ideological reasons. Nōnin was so discredited that he was given just a brief mention in historical materials of the period, particularly in Kokan Shiren's 30-volume history of Buddhism, the *Genkō shakusho* of 1372. The only extant complete biographical sketch is from the Tokugawa era, and it provides only a bare outline of some of the key events.[9] Since Nōnin did not travel to China and therefore did not receive direct Dharma transmission from a Ch'an master, the Buddhist institutional hierarchy never accepted his credentials based on self-enlightenment. He was not exposed to, and so was not a useful vehicle for the dissemination of the kinds of texts that were representative of the dynamic new style of Sung dynasty Ch'an religious discourse.

Some of the works Nōnin cited were apocryphal, misnamed, or associated with the Bodhidharma-based Northern school, which was repudiated by the Southern school of Ch'an after the emergence of the *Platform Sutra* constructed by Shen-hui and attributed to Hui-neng. With Nōnin lacking pedigree, his familiarity with Ch'an was probably limited to works from an era well before the iconoclastic Hung-chou school teachings of Ma-tsu and Lin-chi were incorporated into Sung transmission of the lamp records and kōan collections. Northern school ideology had been kept barely alive by Saichō's Japanese Tendai lineage. Its texts, which had long existed in Japan but were ignored before Nōnin dealt with them, did not enjoy a glorious revival based on the fact that he was citing them.

Nōnin's reliance on outdated or questionable materials encouraged rivals to consider him unorthodox and irregular. Despite the lineal connection that two of his followers gained with the Ta-hui stream that advocated the practice of kōan-introspection (*kanna zen*), Nōnin was unable to contribute to the transmission of ingenious kōan cases based on encounter dialogues attributed to T'ang masters or a distinctive style of training that featured charismatic sermons and insightful commentaries. Therefore Nōnin did not bring a sense of scriptural authority or creativity to the Buddhist scene at a time of intense competition from other upstart religious movements, which were all under pressure from the Tendai mainstream to demonstrate their value to the state, in addition to doctrinal orthodoxy. However, Nōnin created his own texts, especially the recently discovered *Jōtō shōgakuron*, which is of great historical interest for what it reveals about early Zen's relation to Chinese Ch'an and Japanese Tendai, in addition to the *Hōmon taikō* and the *Kenshō jōbutsuron*.[10]

The Daruma school, as outlined in Table 16, espoused a philosophy that was provocative for radically affirming the phenomenal world as coterminous with absolute reality. Nōnin's approach was considered to have antinomian implications, which in Confucian-based, family-oriented East Asian cultures was perennially the bane of home-leaving Buddhist recluses. Buddhist monks generally took pains to emphasize to the leaders of mainstream society their commitment to conventional social ethics that were invaluable in regulating monastic life. Nōnin's view, summed up by the saying, "Fundamentally there are no passions, from the outset we are enlightened," had a resonance with such Ch'an teachings attributed to Ma-tsu and other T'ang masters as "Everyday mind is Buddha" or "This very mind is the Way." Bernard Faure also emphasizes the connection of the Daruma school to the heterodoxical Northern school of Ch'an, which was to a large extent based on relic worship and various sorts of ritualism. Ishii Shūdō, on the other hand, shows that Nōnin's approach is remarkably similar to T'ang era Southern school doctrines, which include the teachings of Ma-tsu and Lin-chi on sudden enlightenment experienced in

TABLE 16. Daruma School and Dōgen

1180s	Origins of school
1189	Dainichi Nōnin, centered at Sambōji temple in Settsu, dispatches two disciples to China to gain for him a transmission seal from the Ta-hui lineage
1191	Eisai begins attacks on the Daruma school, leading to the *Kōzen gokokuron* (1198)
1194	Daruma school along with Eisai's movement officially proscribed
1196	Possible date of Nōnin's death
1198	Ban lifted for Eisai but not Daruma school
1200	Nōnin's disciple Kakuan forms a community at Tōnomine in Yamato
1222	Ejō joins Tōnomine community
1228	Tōnomine buildings burned down by monks from Kōfukuji temple in Nara
1234	Kakuan dies; on deathbed, he enjoins Ejō to see Dōgen at Kōshōji temple (Ejō had visited Dōgen at Kenninji in later 1220s but decided not to join him at that time); Ekan leads band of followers to Hajakuji, a Tendai temple in Echizen province
1235	Ejō begins recording Dōgen's lectures, resulting in *Shōbōgenzō zuimonki* (1238)
1241	Ekan, along with other former Daruma school followers from Hajakuji, Gikai, Giin, Gien, Gijun, Gison, and Giun, join Dōgen at Kōshōji temple in Fukakusa
1243	Dōgen's community leaves the Kyoto area for Echizen, settling at Daibutsuji temple in 1244 (changed two years later to Eiheiji) near Hajakuji
1246	Dōgen delivers a memorial for Kakuan (not in his lineage) in *Eihei kōroku* 3.185
1251	Dōgen delivers a memorial for Ekan (not in his lineage) at the request of Gijun, in *Eihei kōroku* 7.507
1264	Gien travels to Mount T'ien-t'ung to show monks the *Eihei kōroku* and select *Eihei goroku*
1267–1272	Gikai serves as third abbot of Eiheiji
1270s–1314	Gien serves as the fourth abbot of Eiheiji when Gikai steps down, because of the third-generation succession controversy (*sandai sōron*)
1292	Gikai abbot of Daijōji, practicing syncretism; Keizan becomes his disciple
1320s	Keizan builds Yōkōji and Sōjiji in Noto peninsula into regional Zen centers
1467–1477	Ōnin War period marks end of any independent Daruma school activities, but there is evidence that Sambōji remained a stronghold during the Edo period

everyday life, that were inherited by Sung masters like Ta-hui and can be seen as denying the need for meditation. Furthermore, Faure stresses the continuing impact Nōnin exerted on Dōgen, but for Ishii, Dōgen rejected the Daruma school as well as Ta-hui because of their emphasis on natural enlightenment.

In many respects, the metaphysics of equalizing the absolute and phenomenal realms in Nōnin's thought was not so dissimilar from the basic Tendai doctrine of original enlightenment, which asserted that sentient beings and all other aspects of existence innately possess the absolute nature. The Daruma school could be seen as an extension of the Tendai doctrine of *endonkai* (perfect and sudden precepts), which dispensed with the need for the *Pratimoksha* precepts and was sometimes associated with lax moral tendencies, such as the "passions are awakening" (*bonnō soku bodai*) outlook that gave rise to so-called "evil monks" (*akusō*). The Daruma school, subject to ongoing persecution, including the destruction of its main temples by Tendai mercenaries in 1228, became a kind of underground cult with adherents taking refuge in a couple of sanctuaries in the Yamato and Echizen areas. Yet the school persisted for decades, in part by joining forces with Sōtō Zen when Dōgen settled at Eiheiji, which was situated near Hajakuji, a Tendai temple where the Daruma school followers who converted to Dōgen's movement in 1241 were dwelling (see Table 17). Faure takes this point a step further by arguing that the connection to the Daruma school caused a sea change in Dōgen's religiosity:

> This collective conversion changed dramatically the nature of Dō-
> gen's teachings and decided the future of the Sōtō sect. Not only
> was Dōgen's criticism of the Rinzai tradition a direct result of his
> desire to convince his new audience of the superiority of his brand
> of Zen, but his sudden transfer to remote Echizen in 1243, and the
> subsequent sectarian stiffening of his doctrine, were due in part to
> the fact that the Daruma-shū had a strong following in that prov-
> ince.[11]

According to a prominent theory, there remained affiliates of the Daruma school all the way to the period of the Ōnin War of 1466–1467, when much of Zen monasticism, including powerful elements of the elite Japanese Five Mountains system, was damaged in the political upheaval.

In any case, the continuing impact on Dōgen is reflected by the fact that in 1246 he gave *jōdō* sermon no. 3.185, the first entry in *Eihei kōroku* vol. 3, at

TABLE 17 Daruma School Lineage

15 disciples

Ta-hui————Te-kuang————5 disciples

(Transmission received via Renchū and Shōben)

Dainichi Nōnin————Kakuan————Ejō————Giun
+ 5 disciples

Ekan and 6 disciples
from Hajakuji in Echizen
converted to Dōgen, 1241

Ekan
Gikai————Keizan
Giin
Gien
Gijun
Gison
Giun

the request of head monk Ekan in memorium for his late teacher, Kakuan,[12] and in 1252 he gave sermon no. 7.507, which was requested by Gijun as a memorial for Ekan:

> The old crane nests in the clouds, not yet awakened from sleep.
> Frost piles up on snow in the icy cauldron.
> For adorning his reward in the buddha land, nothing is needed
> Besides the slight fragrance of practice during one stick of incense.
> Tell me, what is the situation today of you patch-robed monks?
> After a pause, Dōgen said: Stop saying that the other shore is not before
> your eyes. This single staff is the bridge.[13]

The Early Early Period: Dōgen in China

Dōgen apparently was very much concerned about antinomianism pervading doctrine and subverting practice both in and out of the Zen school, a tendency that stood in sharp contrast to the image of strict discipline at Kenninji based on the twin pillars of training in *zazen* and adherence to the precepts. Because of the absence of writings during or about the first Kenninji phase, the early early period proper begins in 1223 with Dōgen's departure to Japan to resolve his Doubt. How did the journey to the Ch'an Five Mountains temples allow him to come to terms with the conflicts he sensed and lead to the construction of Zen religiosity integrated into the Japanese context? Unfortunately, the primary sources speak only retrospectively about the trip, which must be seen in light of historiographical questions regarding the apparent unreliability and Marco Polo-like quality of traditional accounts.

Dōgen and companions left Kenninji in the second month of 1223. The trip from the point of embarkation in Kyushu to the port at Ning-po took about 40 days. On arriving in China, Myōzen quickly disembarked and entered training at Mount T'ien-t'ung, while Dōgen's entry was long delayed and he spent several months portside. The delay was caused by illness (diarrhea) according to one source (*Shōbōgenzō zuimonki* 6.19) or by a lack of proper credentials according to others, especially the *Kenzeiki* and the *Denkōroku*. Eventually Dōgen was able to land, and over the following months he made brief visits to a series of centers of the Ch'an Five Mountains network, where Eisai was known to have traveled, especially Mount A-yü-wang and Mount T'ien-t'ung while Wu-chi was still abbot, as well as Mount T'ien-t'ai. He is also said to have gone to Mount Ching, which would later become Enni's training ground, and there he is said to have met with abbot Che-weng. Despite auspicious moments and flashes of insight usually precipitated by conversations with anonymous monks rather than with the patriarchs, Dōgen was left with a spiritual void until his meeting and training with Ju-ching in the summer of 1225.

The Role of the Precepts

In the early days of the trip, Dōgen struggled with a variety of obstacles to his religious quest. A major difficulty in being accepted into the Chinese monastic community was that, unlike Myōzen, he had not received the combined precepts, in succession, before entering China. In fact, since the time of Saichō, the 250-article *Pratimoksha* precepts as spelled out in the *Ssu-fen lü* (J. *Shibun-ritsu*, in *Taishō* vol. 22, no. 1428) were not offered in the Mahayana-centric Tendai temples on Mount Hiei. There, only the 58-article bodhisattva vows spelled out in the *Fan-wang ching* (J. *Bonmōkyō*, in *Taishō* vol. 24, no. 1484) were considered necessary and made available. The Tendai bodhisattva-based *endonkai* ("complete and sudden precepts") represented a notion very close to the idea of "formless precepts," endorsed in the *Platform Sutra*, which was also known in Japan as the "one-mind precepts" or *isshinkai*.[14] According to this approach, the *Pratimoksha* was designed to regulate the outer behavior of monks in training, whereas in the Tendai and early Ch'an view this concern was relegated to the level of ordinary or relative truth. From the standpoint of absolute or ultimate truth, there is a full internalization of the precepts, which vitiates the need for external guidelines altogether or allows them to be seen merely as a kind of metaphorical reflection of what is essentially an interior state of mind. Therefore the bodhisattva instructions, which were more abstract and far less specific, were considered sufficient, although the Daruma school apparently eliminated these.

Even though early Chinese Ch'an sources such as the *Platform Sutra* seemed to agree with Japanese Tendai on the issue of not needing the *Pratimoksha* precepts, which in fact could be considered counterproductive in that they distracted from a focus on absolute truth, Eisai found during his journeys to the mainland that the reigning practice of preceptual transmission differed on this matter. To qualify for admission to the *samgha*, a Ch'an novice was required to adhere to the 3-article refuges, the 5-article *upasaka* precepts, and 10-article *sramanera* precepts taken in succession before one received the *Pratimoksha*'s 250-article *bhikku* precepts and the 58-article bodhisattva precepts at the age of 20. Neither the *Ch'an-yüan ch'ing-kuei* nor the practice at Five Mountains temples gave an indication of the formless-precept position. However, despite Eisai's strong advocacy for the practice that he experienced in China, Kenninji as a new Tendai-based temple would not have been allowed to administer the *Pratimoksha* precepts, which remained available only at temples in Nara that followed the model of combined precepts.

Myōzen had apparently traveled to Tōdaiji in Nara, where temples still administered the Hinayana precepts. His pilgrimage occurred some years before, during the early phase of his study with Eisai, and so was not directly related to an anticipation of the trip taken with Dōgen. Although we must be skeptical of the account of Myōzen, which presumes that the precepts were available for the asking since he was not a member of a Nara-based sect, a key question concerns why Dōgen, knowing of the rules in Chinese monasteries, would not have made the same preparations as Myōzen. Arriving in China without the combined precepts meant that as a novice Dōgen barely ranked above scores of irregular, itinerant practitioners who roamed the various temples. Once Dōgen disembarked in the fifth month of 1225 after the summer retreat had already been under way, it is not clear how or why he was accepted into Mount T'ien-t'ung. Perhaps his acceptance was due to Myōzen's intercession or to a petition filed by Dōgen.

Shortly after he joined the monastery, another procedural issue led to Dōgen's filing an official challenge to the monastic system in an appeal that, according to the *Kenzeiki*, went all the way up to the imperial level for review.[15] Apparently, once Dōgen's precepts were accepted, he still felt dissatisfied with the seniority system practiced in China. Since he had already been a monk for ten years in Japan, he had a claim to seniority according to the rules of the monastic system, despite lacking the Hinayana precepts. The Chinese system was based on age rather than length of time since the precepts were received, as is indicated in the classic monastic rules attributed to Pai-chang, the *Ch'an-men kuei-shih* (J. *Zenmon kishiki*), which was a precursor of the *Ch'an-yüan ch'ing-kuei*. Because of the Chinese custom, he was subordinated to novices and was below the rank of any of the newcomers who had the combined precepts.

Dōgen lost the appeal because other Japanese monks visiting China had endured the same treatment. There are even indications that two years later Ju-ching, who generally favored his aspiring young Japanese disciple, requested that he line up with the Taoists and other non–Buddhist practitioners behind the regular monks and nuns.[16] Despite receiving this treatment, Dōgen, like Ju-ching, became concerned about the corruption and laxity in personal habits (e.g., long hair and uncut fingernails) that he witnessed among some of the monks in China, as was reported throughout the *Shōbōgenzō zuimonki* and *Hōkyōki*, as well as in *Shōbōgenzō* "Senmen," "Gyōji," and other fascicles.[17]

At some point in his career—it is not clear when this was initiated, although it was definitely in operation during the later years of the Eiheiji period—Dōgen began advocating a new system of administering 16-article precepts (*jūrokujōkai*). Dōgen's system includes three main items: (1) the three jewels or refuges (taking refuge in Buddha, Dharma, Samgha); (2) the three pure precepts (not sustaining evil, sustaining good, liberating sentient beings); and (3) the ten major or heavy precepts (not to kill, not to steal, not to lie, not to commit sexual acts, not to partake of intoxicants, not to defame male and female monastics or lay followers, not to covet, not to resist praising others, not to be stirred to anger, not to revile the three treasures).[18] This system differs significantly from what other schools in China and Japan, both Ch'an/Zen and non-Zen (Tendai, Pure Land, Nichiren), were performing. Various Buddhist

師ハジメテ
建仁開山
千光禅師
二相見

FIGURE 14. Traditional View of Dōgen's Imperial Challenge (*Teiho Kenzeiki zue*)

schools administered either additional or a different set of precepts, or they dispensed with the behavioral codes altogether.

Sōtō tradition has long held that Dōgen's system was based on the precepts he received directly from Chinese Ch'an mentor Ju-ching as part of the transmission process that took place several months after his enlightenment experience of casting off body-mind (*shinjin datsuraku*) during the summer retreat of 1225. Did Dōgen really learn the system of 16-article precepts from Ju-ching? According to the *Hōkyōki* sections 5 and 49, Ju-ching allowed the novice from Japan to occupy the bodhisattva-*sila* seat, a consent indicating that his years of living under Japanese Tendai were accepted as legitimate qualifications even though he lacked the necessary Ch'an credentials and would not have been considered a monk by typical standards. However, the *Hōkyōki* passages are quite vague and ambiguous about the use of the term "bodhisattva precepts" and whether this refers to a general sense of Mahayana practice or a specific set of behavioral codes. In any case, this would have been an extraordinary phenomenon in the Chinese Ch'an circle of the period and was far different treatment than Dōgen received under then abbot Wu-chi when Dōgen first visited Mount T'ien-t'ung in 1223. Since Dōgen's case already differed from the accepted procedure for the transmission of the precepts within the Chinese Ch'an community, was it possible that Ju-ching transmitted a distinct set of precepts to Dōgen, different from the styles used in both countries?

In considering these issues, we find it is highly dubious that Dōgen was instructed in the 16-article precepts by his Chinese mentor. As a monk in the Ts'ao-tung school who was then abbot of Mount T'ien-t'ung, one of the main temples in the Five Mountains monastic institution, Ju-ching no doubt adhered to a tradition spelled out in the *Ch'an-yüan ch'ing-kuei*, which required the combined precepts for all monks as unambiguously enunciated in the first two sections of the first fascicle covering "Receiving the Precepts" and "Upholding the Precepts." Perhaps Ju-ching made an exception for the foreign disciple in not requiring the *Pratimoksha* precepts to enter training, but it is nearly impossible to imagine that he would have created a new system of transmission just for Dōgen's benefit. Dōgen's approach not only could not have been realistically transmitted by Ju-ching, but it went against the grain of both the Ch'an school and the approach Eisai brought back from China and established in Japan. In fact, the issue of the precepts is the single area where Dōgen's religiosity diverges rather drastically from Chinese Ch'an. The fact that Dōgen cites extensively from the *Ch'an-yüan ch'ing-kuei*, including the opening passage of the "Jukai" fascicle, the main text that articulates the 16-article precept method, calls attention to the basic inconsistency concerning Dōgen's relation to Chinese Ch'an.[19]

Not only did Dōgen differ from the Ch'an Five Mountains system, but he was also at variance with the approach endorsed by the Rinzai school's temples in Japan, which followed Eisai's combined precepts, as well as the internalization approach of the formless or one-mind precepts. The main question in an evaluation of Dōgen's approach is whether the system of 16-article precepts, devoid of the *Pratimoksha* precepts, represented a compromise position created out of the strength of conviction or confusion and convenience. At the same time, perhaps there is a simple explanation in that Dōgen may have incorporated and institutionalized a streamlined approach that was at least being discussed in non-Ch'an circles in both China and Japan, even if not considered "monk-making" in the sense of conferring legitimacy to a new member of the monastic community in the pre-Dōgen era. But why?

Kagamishima Genryū, perhaps the leading Dōgen scholar of the postwar period, concludes that Dōgen himself came up with a way of streamlining and simplifying the precept system in order to break free from the hegemony of the Japanese Tendai school. Kagamishima points out that there is no record of the transmission of the 16-article precepts in the history of Chinese Ch'an Buddhism, nor were they ever mentioned in the *Ju-ching yü-lu* or any other Ch'an text.[20] Kagamishima observes that it would have been exceptional for Ju-ching to recognize Dōgen's status, but at the same time highly unlikely that this recognition meant a change of the Ch'an precept system:

> What Ju-ching did reflects that he understood the position of the Japanese bodhisattva precepts through Dōgen and expressed his own agreement [with it]. Nevertheless, Ju-ching's recognition of the position of Japanese bodhisattva precepts is not tantamount to the negation of the combined precepts as accepted by the Chinese Ch'an tradition. It was impossible for Ju-ching to retransmit the *sramanera* precepts to Dōgen, who already had received the pure bodhisattva precepts.[21]

Key to Kagamishima's argument is that Dōgen formulated a new approach because he did not have the personal experience needed to be able to require the combined precepts for his disciples.

Recently a document with 16-article precepts was found in Shoren'in, a Tendai temple in Kyoto, so there is some possibility that Dōgen's approach to having 16 articles is based on one of the Tendai precepts styles. It is possible to speculate that in non-Zen Buddhist schools as well as Tendai in Japan there were different combinations, including the 10-article major precepts along with such expressions of devotion as the three refuges, the three pure precepts, and ritual repentances, which is very close to Dōgen's approach.[22] If the 48-article minor precepts were eliminated, they may have been so because these are very general, open-ended exhortations for compassionate attitudes rather than rules governing behavior in the strict sense, and therefore easily dispensable once the six articles of the refuges and pure precepts are accepted. However, it is doubtful that such combinations would have been considered, before Dōgen, to be monk-making.

If Dōgen's view is to be considered a constructive compromise, which left him differing with both Chinese and Japanese Buddhist schools, was this view closer to the Five Mountains approach (both the Chinese and Japanese versions) of combined precepts? Or was it similar to the Tendai and early Ch'an tendencies toward an internalization of the precepts that was also endorsed in an extreme and controversial form by Nōnin? According to the latter view, a realization of the essential meaning underlying specific perceptual instructions vitiates the need for receiving them. In any case, it is a very different sort of compromise than the respective syncretistic approaches in the Rinzai sect of Eisai and Enni.

Itinerary for the Itinerancy

An investigation of Dōgen's itinerary in China and what this shows about his relationship with Chinese Ch'an masters helps us develop a focus on how Dōgen later appropriated the texts and perhaps invented the significance of his mentor in the crucial transitional, evangelical period of the early 1240s. A key factor here, as He Yansheng's award-winning book *Dōgen to Chūgoku Zen shisō* shows, is the question of the corruption of the Ju-ching records and the extent to which they were heavily edited or fabricated by Tokugawa-era Sōtō scholastics.[23]

The following is a reconstruction of the sources for the itinerary in China based on the research of Itō Shūken, who supports an earlier date (fall 1223 to winter 1224) for the time of the itinerant journey to various temples, and Ikeda Rōsan and Kagamishima Genryū, who support the date of the following year (1224–1225, before Dōgen settled into Mount T'ien-t'ung under Ju-ching's leadership). In this listing, the primary source is indicated in parenthesis, and the asterisk indicates that the item is particularly questionable in terms of dating or basic historicality:[24]

YEAR: 1223

2.22

Dōgen travels with Myōzen as well as Kakunen and Ryōshō from Kenninji to Kyushu to depart Japan for Sung China (Myōzen oshō kaichō okugaki)

3 mo.

Departs from Hakata Port

4 mo.

Arrives at Ching-yüan prefecture in Ming-chou province ("Senmen")

Suffers from diarrhea while aboard ship but overcomes illness through power of concentration (Shōbōgenzō zuimonki 6.19)

Myōzen visits teacher, Miao-yün, at Ching-te szu temple (Myōzen oshō kaichō okugaki)

5.4

Meets cook from Mount A-yü-wang while staying on board at port of Ming-chou Ching-yüan city who speaks of "exerting the Way" (*bendō*) (Tenzokyōkun)

5.13

Myōzen joins Mount T'ien-t'ung (Shari sōdenki) [but Dōgen is apparently disallowed because he lacks full precepts]

7 mo.

Joins Mount T'ien-t'ung at end of summer retreat and trains under Wu-chi, and speaks to Mount T'ien-t'ung cook, who speaks of why "now" is the time to work (Tenzokyōkun)

After close of summer retreat, he again meets the Mount A-yü-wang cook, who visits Mount T'ien t'ung to see Dōgen on his way back home west on retirement and instructs "nothing concealed in the entire universe" (Tenzokyōkun)

From Shih-kuang, Dōgen hears about the *shisho* document of Wu-chi (Shisho, Teiho Kenzeiki)

*Files official complaint with emperor about seniority system in the Mount T'ien-t'ung monastery (Teiho Kenzeiki)

Fall

From Ryūzen, another monk from Japan, sees *shisho* document of the *chuan-tsang-chu*, a descendant of Fa-yen Ch'ing-yüan of the Yang-ch'i branch of the Lin-chi school (Shisho)

Visiting Mount A-yü-wang, sees vision of full moon while looking at portraits of 33 patriarchs but does not comprehend the meaning (Bussho)

*Visits Mount Ching and meets abbot Che-weng, with whom he has dialogue (Kenzeiki)

*Learns from an elderly monk about greatness of Ju-ching (Tōkokuki, Teiho Kenzeiki) [the monk may have been at Arhat Hall, and he may have been considered the reincarnation of an arhat]

[Ikeda and Kagamishima both date this at another time, 1224, because it needs to be after Wu-chi's death and Ju-ching's ascension to abbacy]

Ju-ching leaves Jui-yen temple (Ju-ching yü-lu)

10 mo.

Ju-ching becomes abbot for second time at Ching-tzu temple (Ju-ching yü-lu)

Meets two Korean practitioners in Ching-yüan (okugaki of Den'e and Kesa kudoku) [Ikeda dates this as 1224]

Sees robe ceremony in China (okugaki of Den'e and Kesa kudoku)

YEAR: 1224

1.21

Is shown *shisho* document of Wu-chi by Chih-sou, who smuggles it out (Shisho)

Before 3 mo.

*In Pao-ch'ing era, travels "on a cloud" to Wan-nien temple on Mount T'ien-t'ai (Shisho) [but this could be seventeenth year of Chia-ting era]

*Hears of "plum twig" dream of abbot at Mount Ta-mei and has his own similar dream (Shisho)

*Returns to Mount T'ien-t'ung from Mount T'ien-t'ai [Kagamishima dates this as 1225]

Before 4 mo.

*Wu-chi dies (Ju-ching yü-lu) [or this could be 10 mo.]

7.5

Myōzen performs memorial service for Eisai at Mount T'ien-t'ung (Shi-dōki)

From 7.15 to 8.1

Ju-ching leaves Ching-tzu and enters Mount T'ien-t'ung and gives inaugural sermon (Ju-ching yü-lu) [Dōgen thus begins training in Ju-ching-led monastery]

7–8 mo. or fall

*Visits Mount P'u-t'o island (Eihei kōroku vol. 10)

*Travels to various mountains in Ming-chou, Hang-chou, and T'ai-chou [according to Ikeda and Kagamishima]

11.25

Imperial edict declaring new era (Sung-chi)

YEAR: 1225

1–2 mo.

*Meets Che-weng at Wan-shou, P'an-shan at Hsiao-ts'ui-yen near Mount T'ien-t'ai (Shisho) and stops at Hu-sheng on Mount Ta-mei [dream of plum blossom occurs now, according to this dating]

Before 4 mo.

*Ju-ching has a dream of Tung-shan incarnation appearing before him (Kenzeiki)

*Returns to Mount T'ien-t'ung from travels to various mountains (Shisho)

5.1

Burns incense and prostrates for first time in Miao-kao-t'ai, the private residence of "old Buddha" Ju-ching of Mount T'ien-t'ung, as part of face-to-face transmission (Menju)

5.27

Myōzen dies (Shari sōdenki)

5.29

Discovery of over 360 relics of Myōzen (Shari sōdenki)

During summer retreat

"Realizes act of prostrating to, and humbly receiving upon my head, this Buddhist Patriarch; it was a realization only between a Buddha and a Buddha" (Busso)

Has enlightenment experience of *shinjin datsuraku*, or casting off body-mind (Kenzeiki)

Visits Mount A-yü-wang and again sees vision of full moon while looking at portraits of 33 patriarchs but this time understands the meaning although the Chinese monks do not (Busshō)

"From now on" he is invited to Ju-ching's *hōjō* to receive instructions and special teachings (Hōkyōki)

"When I was in China," Ju-ching offers appointment as temple attendant, but Dōgen as a foreigner declines, deferring to Chinese monks (Shōbōgenzō zuimonki 1.1)

7.2
Begins recording *Hōkyōki*

7 mo.
Che-weng dies

9.18
Receives Busso shōden bosatsu kaisahō (Kaisahō okugaki)

YEAR: 1226

3 mo.
Hears nighttime sermon of Ju-ching at Miao-kao-t'ai and hears about ascetic practices of Fa-chang of Mount Ta-mei (Shohō jissō) [see also Eihei kōroku no. 2.128, Shōbōgenzō zuimonki 3.30, Gyōji 2]

Hears Ju-ching speak of his 65 years (*Hōkyōki*)

YEAR: 1227

Spring
Receives Shisho document from Ju-ching (Shisho zu)

Receives Dharma Robe of Fu-yung Tao-k'ai, texts of *Pao-ching san-mei* and of *Wu-wei hsien-chüeh*, and Ju-ching's portrait (Kenzeiki)

Ju-ching no longer abbot of Mount T'ien-t'ung, resides in hermitage (Ju-ching yü-lu)

7.17
*Ju-ching dies (Ju-ching yü-lu)

Fall
*Dōgen leaves to return to Japan (Kenzeiki) [a debate over whether this was before or after Ju-ching's death]

*Receives *Pi-yen-chi* (J. *Hekiganroku*) of Yüan-wu with aid of Hakusan Gongen Myōri (Kenzeiki)

*Subdues tiger, and heals sick with aid of Inari, while traveling (Kenzeiki)
*On return, during typhoon receives aid from Kannon (Teiho Kenzeiki)
10.5
Resides again in Kenninji temple (Shari sōdenki)
*Fukanzazengi and Fukanzazengi shujutsu yūrai

The following is a year-by-year summary of sources: For 1223 there was *Myōzen oshō kaichō okugaki, Shari sōdenki,* "Senmen," *Shōbōgenzō zuimonki, Tenzokyōkun,* "Shisho," "Busshō," Keizan's *Tōkokuki, Teiho Kenzeiki, Ju-ching yü-lu,* and "Kesa kudoku" and "Den'e" okugaki. The year 1224 was covered by "Shisho," *Ju-ching yü-lu, Kenzeiki, Shidōki, Eihei kōroku* vol. 10, and *Sung-chi.* For 1225 there was "Shisho," "Menju," *Shari sōdenki,* "Busso," "Busshō," *Hōkyōki, Kenzeiki,* and *Busso shōden bosatsu kaishō okugaki;* from 1226, "Shohō jissō" and *Hōkyōki.* Finally, 1227 included *Shisho zu, Kenzeiki, Teiho Kenzeiki,* and *Ju-ching yü-lu.* Additional sources for information on China include *Gakudōyōjinshû,* "Baika," "Ganzei," "Nyorai zenshin," and Keizan's *Denkōroku,* among others.

In considering problematic elements of the traditional account, we note that of the seventy illustrations in the *Teiho Kenzeiki zue* nearly a third cover the trip to China, and of these almost half are hagiographical, indicated by the asterisk in Table 18.[25]

An interesting feature of Dōgen's early biography including his China itinerancy is that it is marked by the death of so many of the key players, including parents and teachers (see Table 19). A number of these deaths would have occurred at such a short time after the alleged meeting that these accounts feed doubts about the historicity of the records of Dōgen's activities.

Meetings with Remarkable and Unremarkable Men

Dōgen's experience during his first two years in China was characterized primarily by a series of encounter dialogues with a variety of monks who became, at least for the moment, his teachers, even if in some cases what they taught was taken in a negative way or as an approach to avoid. According to diverse sources, Dōgen met some of the most prominent masters of the time, including Wu-chi, abbot of Mount T'ien-t'ung; Che-weng, abbot of Mount Ching; and the abbot of Mount Ta-mei. In addition to the leaders of Five Mountains temples, who did not always impress him, Dōgen also met and learned from a number of practitioners whom he mentions in his writings and refers to as anonymous, unknown, or "no name" monks.[26] For Dōgen, of course, the most remarkable teacher was Ju-ching, who is usually considered somewhat less than that by the standards for evaluating the merit of the teachings of Sung masters, which is generally based on their recorded sayings collections.[27]

TABLE 18. List of *Teiho Kenzeiki zue* Illustrations of China

---

1. Leaves by boat from Hakata with Myōzen and others, after departing on 2.22.1223 from Kenninji
2. Still on ship at Ming-chou port in the fifth month; meets the cook from Mount A-yü-wang
3. Joins Mount T'ien-t'ung after the summer retreat, though still lacking Hinayana precepts, with Wu-chi as abbot
4. Ranking of monks—as foreigner, Dōgen is kept at end of line even though he has seniority in terms of when he took the precepts
*5. Petitions the emperor for a reversal of the ruling about seniority
6. Robe ceremony—while doing *zazen* at Mount T'ien-t'ung another monk every morning places the robe on his head and recites the *kasaya gatha*
*7. Visits Mount Ching, lead temple in the Five Mountains monastic system, during the following year's summer retreat
*8. Talks to an old monk and hears about greatness of Ju-ching
9. Visits Wan-nien ssu temple at Mount T'ien-t'ai, site where Eisai practiced
*10. Has dream at Mount Ta-mei about receiving plum blossoms, foreshadowing a great encounter
*11. Ju-ching dreams of meeting a new embodiment of Tung-shan
12. Face-to-face meeting with Ju-ching—their spiritual encounter
13. Death of Myōzen and attendance at his funeral
14. Experience of *shinjin datsuraku* based on Ju-ching's strict style of training
15. Prostrates in appreciation of Ju-ching
16. At Mount A-yü-wang, for the second time seeing the image of the patriarchs manifested as a round moon
*17. Legend of subduing the tiger through the power of the Dharma
*18. Healing of Dōshō through the beneficence of Inari
19. Receives *Shisho zu* in winter of 1227 before return to Japan; becomes 51st-generation patriarch
*20. Copying of *ichiya Hekiganroku* with assistance of Hakusan Gongen Myōri
*21. Appearance of One Leaf Kannon during monsoon at sea while returning to Japan

---

Nara Yasuaki theorizes that the delay Dōgen experienced in entering the Ch'an system ultimately worked to his advantage.[28] Myōzen died in 1225; Nara feels that the challenge of joining the rigorous Chinese monastery immediately and undergoing the strenuous discipline of the summer retreat that began less than two weeks after his arrival in China caused Myōzen great stress and led to his deterioration. In contrast, Dōgen's inability to enter Mount T'ien-t'ung until after the summer retreat, which ended in the middle of the seventh month, gave him the opportunity to adjust to the Chinese language, culture, and monastic style.

Meanwhile, Dōgen's stay on the boat docked at the harbor led to the first significant encounter dialogue he experienced, in the fifth month of 1223, according to *Tenzokyōkun* written over a decade later.[29] This was the first of two instructive conversations with the chief cook or *tenzo* of Mount A-yü-wang, who again visited Dōgen at Mount T'ien-t'ung that first summer on his way back to his home province since he was retiring from the monastery. Dōgen

TABLE 19. Deaths of Key Figures in Dōgen's Early Life and Career

Father, 1202 (age 2)
Mother, 1207 (age 7)
Eisai, founder/abbot of Kenninji, 1216 (one year after supposed meeting)
Kōin, abbot of Onjōji, 1216 (shortly after meeting)
Ryōkan, uncle, 1217 (five years after meeting)
Wu-chi, abbot of Mount T'ien-t'ung, 1224 (one year after initial meeting)
Myōzen, mentor at Kenninji, 1225 (two years into China trip)
Che-weng, abbot of Mount Ching, 1225 (one or two years after meeting)
Jien, abbot of Enryakuji, 1225 (about 12 years after meeting)
Ju-ching, abbot of Mount T'ien-t'ung, 1227 (two years after starting training)

was also very much impressed by Mount T'ien-t'ung's own cook. Both *tenzo*, who were willing to forgo the privilege of rank, demonstrated a positive work ethic and commitment to single-minded dedication and perseverance in pursuit of mundane tasks that exemplify the interconnectedness of all things with the true reality of the Dharma. In addition to the conversations with the cooks, another experience that deeply impressed Dōgen was his viewing of five different *shisho* documents representing three branches of the Lin-chi school (the Yang-ch'i and Yün-men branches, as well as three forks of the Fa-yen stream). As is recorded in the "Shisho" fascicle, Dōgen saw the items listed in Table 20.[30]

In weighing the historicality and the religious implications of the fascicle, it is interesting to note that "Shisho," which links Dōgen to the Lin-chi school without actually providing him with the necessary credentials, was composed on 3.27.1241, just around the time that a number of Daruma school followers who linked their Ch'an lineage to Te-kuang joined Dōgen at Kōshōji.[31] This fascicle (edited by Ejō on 2.15.1243) was first a written record rather than a sermon. It was subsequently delivered twice as an oral preaching, on 12.12.1241 at Kōshōji (edited on 10.23.1243 at Yoshiminedera in Echizen) and on 9.24.1243 at Yoshiminedera (no information available on the editing). These events show that discussing lineage became increasingly important as Dōgen collected disciples and then entered new territory in Echizen. This fact is especially important when we consider that two other fascicles focusing on the face-to-face transmission with Ju-ching were from this same transitional period: "Busso," delivered on 1.13.1241, and "Menju," on 10.20.1243.

The next part of the traditional account of Dōgen's trip focuses on his *tangaryō*, or itinerant travels and conversations with leading masters and anonymous monks at various locations. The aim of the itinerancy was to visit the places where Eisai had trained and to look for a true teacher since Wu-chi was ailing and apparently had treated Dōgen as merely an intrusive foreigner. The goal of the narrators of the itinerary seems to be to place Dōgen in proximity

TABLE 20. Five Transmission Documents Dōgen Viewed in China

1. Fa-yen of the Yang-ch'i branch, from the *chuan-tsang-chu* monk, with the assistance of the Japanese monk Ryūzen, in fall of 1223 at Mount T'ien-t'ung.

2. Yün-men branch from Tsung-yüeh Ch'ang-tao, later to become abbot briefly of Mount T'ien-t'ung after death of Wu-chi Liao-p'ai in 1223 (Dōgen remarks that this document "looks different").

3. Shih-kuang, the director of Mount T'ien-t'ung monastery under Wu-chi, shown secretly from Chih-sou, a junior monk who smuggled it out on 1.21.1224 (Dōgen notes that this is magnificently adorned and written by Te-kuang, Wu-chi's teacher).

4. Kuei-shan from Yüan-tzu, successor to Tsung-chien as abbot of Wan-nien monastery at P'ing-t'ien on Mount T'ien-t'ai, in 1225 (the abbot tells Dōgen about his dream of an eminent monk who resembled Fa-chang of Mount Ta-mei to whom he handed a branch of plum blossoms and said, "If you meet a true man, you should not hesitate to give him this branch"; the document was written on plum silk, and Dōgen feels it conveys the "invisible favor" of Buddhas and patriarchs).

5. Fa-yen branch from Wei-yi Hsi-t'ang of Mount T'ien-t'ung, formerly head monk of Kuang-fu, known for teaching laymen and coming from the same region as Ju-ching, in 1225 (Dōgen notes that it is a "rare privilege" to see this kind of ancient writing).

with prominent Ch'an monasteries and figures, particularly at Mount Ching, and to show how he was left unimpressed with some of the famous abbots, especially Che-weng.

The dialogue with Che-weng did not satisfy Dōgen's need for an authentic teacher but rather became emblematic of his dissatisfaction with China. "According to the *Denkōroku*," Nara writes, "the first discussion with Che-weng developed as follows":

> Che-weng, serving as head monk of Wan-shou monastery, said, "When did you arrive in the land of Sung China?" and Dōgen replied, "In the fourth month last year." Che-weng said, "Did you come here following the crowds?" and Dōgen replied, "Well, I came here with my companions; is there something wrong with that? I think this is a good thing." Che-weng said, clapping together the palms of his hands, "You are a young novice who is never at a loss for words." Dōgen replied, "Maybe it is so. But what is the matter with that?" Che-weng said, "Let's sit down for a while and drink a cup of tea." Dōgen was disappointed with Che-weng and his experience at the Buddhist temple on Mount Ching.[32]

Dōgen had another disillusioning meeting, with P'an-shan of the Ta-hui lineage, whom he met at Hsiao-tsui-yen and asked, "What is Buddha?" The master responded, "He is inside the temple," and Dōgen said, "If he is inside the temple, can he be in every grain of sand in the river?" The master replied, "He is in every grain of sand in the river." "The matter is settled," concluded Dōgen, meaning that he was disturbed by the lack of a compelling response from the master.[33]

As with the two cooks whom he met shortly after arriving in China, Dōgen learned the most from anonymous monks who showed a simple, single-minded determination to pursue the Dharma. In *Shōbōgenzō zuimonki* 1.4 he tells us that he met a monk from Szechuan in Sung China who came east to the temples of Chekiang with no provisions or possessions. Somebody recommended that he return to his homeland to get properly clothed, but he refused because of his determination to stay at the Five Mountains. Dōgen comments that this monk was typical of Buddhist trainees in China—unlike the case of Japan—who did not worry about poverty or any other obstacle to their practice.

In no. 3.15 of the same text Dōgen relates the story of another monk from Szechuan, who asked why Dōgen was studying recorded sayings and kōan collections:[34] "What's the use of reading these Zen sayings?" Dōgen responded, "To understand the old masters," and the monk said, "What is the use of that in the long run?" Dōgen comments that he stopped reading the Zen sayings and other writings because "you don't need to use a single word [to express the Dharma], and I was able to gain a great awakening to the great matter." In a postscript to *Shōbōgenzō* "Kesa kudoku" from 1240, which comments positively on a robe-folding devotion he observed in China that was not known in Japan, Dōgen notes that he was also impressed when he met two Koreans, Chi Hyun and Kyung Oon, "who had come to Ching-yüan in 1224, not as monks but scholars from a[nother] small out-of-the-way country."[35]

According to the traditional account, Dōgen was so discouraged by the lack of wisdom in the famous masters, although he was impressed by the integrity of some but by no means all of the rank-and-file, that he was contemplating returning to Japan in 1224. As Nara explains, during his itinerancy Dōgen thought to himself, "No one in China and Japan is my equal." Then a remarkable event happened when he was at Mount Ching with a monk who was standing at the Arhat Hall, or who was himself the incarnation of an Indian arhat in Keizan's presentation. Nara writes:

> According to the *Tōkokuki* (from the selected writings by Keizan), at one time Dōgen met an old man in front of the hall of the arhats on Mount Ching. He was called Rōshin [Japanese pronunciation]. The "shin" (from Rōshin) means jewel. It was a name that makes us somehow imagine a pilgrim coming from India or the lands to the west of China. They started to have a lively chat. Dōgen explained that, although he had gone all the way to Mount Ching, he felt sad that he had not found someone in which he could place all his confidence as a teacher. Rōshin said, "In the country of the great Sung

dynasty the only one who possesses true insight for teaching the Dharma is Ju-ching. If you go see him, that will be a great opportunity for your training in Buddhism." That is the way the conversation is recorded in the *Denkōroku* [another work by Keizan]. Yet, Dōgen was doubtful. He didn't feel like going off to visit Ching-tzu temple where Ju-ching was residing as abbot, which was some distance away from Mount Ching. The *Denkōroku* states, "More than a year passed before he had the time to study with the master." Then, Dōgen decided to return to Mount T'ien-t'ung, and he would begin summer retreat there for the first time. He immediately left Mount Ching.[36]

At this point in the traditional account, the controversial issues involving dating and itinerary make it difficult to pin down exactly where and when Dōgen was traveling, especially as the narrative begins to involve more out-of-the-ordinary experiences following the arhat episode. Three dreams guided Dōgen to find the ultimate teacher, Ju-ching. The first dream was told by Yüan-tzu at Mount Ta-mei and was kept secret until it was finally disclosed by Dōgen in *Shōbōgenzō* "Shisho" in 1241. According to this account, Dōgen had an overnight stay at Hu-sheng monastery on Mount Ta-mei on his way back to Mount T'ien-t'ung from Mount T'ien-t'ai.

A key question is, how did he get from Mount Ching, where he met the arhat, to Mount T'ien-t'ai? Was it by land or by sea? This last question becomes pressing, since the sea route theory would require two trips to Mount Ching. In some accounts, the old monk at the Arhat Hall recommends Ju-ching after Dōgen has learned of Wu-chi's death in the late summer or fall of 1224, although at that time Dōgen would not have realized that Ju-ching would soon be appointed abbot of Mount T'ien-t'ung, and he was apparently not eager to try out yet another new temple.

In any case, the Mount Ta-mei patriarch handed Dōgen a branch of plum blossoms because the patriarch had had a dream in which a master whom he supposed to be the disciple of Ma-tsu, who founded the monastery, told him to give a plum tree twig to an authentic seeker who would come by boat to study in China. That night, Dōgen reports, he also had a mystical dream in which the original Mount Ta-mei patriarch handed him a branch of blooming blossoms that were more than a foot in diameter as reflected in the patriarch's mirror, which is "the most reliable of instruments," and Dōgen takes this to be the flowers of the *udambara* (*udonge*).[37] The third dream occurred, Dōgen learned, when the night before his return to Mount T'ien-t'ung in the fourth month of 1225, where Ju-ching had been installed as abbot for just about a month, the Chinese master dreamed that Tung-shan appeared in the form of a reincarnation.[38]

Another episode with supernatural implications is Dōgen's account in the "Busshō" fascicle of a vision of the round full moon at Mount A-yü-wang temple while he was looking at portraits of the 33 patriarchs. This section of the fascicle follows a lengthy philosophical discussion of an anecdote in the *Ching-te ch'uan-teng lu* vol. 1, in which Nagarjuna manifests as the moon. Dōgen says that "in former days, while traveling as a cloud," he went to Mount A-yü-wang in the first year of his journey to China, but when he saw the paintings, he did not understand the meaning and nobody was available to explain it.[39] Then he returned to this site about two years later, during the summer retreat of 1225, apparently a short time after his enlightenment experience under Ju-ching.

One question that is raised concerns why Dōgen would have returned to Mount A-yü-wang at this point, especially during the retreat, when it might be expected that monks dedicated to an intensive and sacred period of meditation (*geango*) would not be likely to leave their home temple. Surely, once Dōgen had taken up training under Ju-ching he would not be looking to explore other alternatives. A possibility is that the two temples at Mount T'ien-t'ung and Mount A-yü-wang, located in close proximity, would have shared resources, or that the relic was so prominent—Dōgen refers to visiting the "beautiful sites" of the compound—that he took time to see this for what was probably a second time.[40] In any case, according to "Busshō," this time he alone among the monks understood the vision, whereas the others either took it too literally or did not see it at all. Dōgen sensed the deficiency of Chinese Ch'an Buddhists, including the temple abbot, Ta-kuang, for whom there is "no nostrils in their complexion" and "no sword in their laughter." This episode marks the moment in the traditional account when Dōgen is clear in and confident of his spiritual authority and superiority. It will also serve his partisan agenda a decade and a half later by putting down members of a rival lineage from the vantage point of what he endorsed, retrospectively, in terms of what was relevant to his struggles at the time in Japan.

Face-to-Face Transmission?

Dōgen's first summer retreat would not take place until the following year (1224), when he entered Mount Ching, according to some of the sources, leaving him invigorated and primed for his eventual meeting with Ju-ching. This meeting occurred the same month Myōzen died in 1225. With the death of the senior, fully ordained monk from abroad, Dōgen would have been faced with a crisis in losing his status as Myōzen's attendant and becoming just another unordained novice like thousands of other unofficial (or unrecognized) quasi-monks in China. Unsupervised and unordained novices normally would not even be allowed in the Guest Hall (*undō*), let alone the Monks Hall. Nevertheless, Dōgen was helped by Ju-ching's allowing him to stay at the temple, and this second retreat became the time of his enlightenment experience of *shinjin datsuraku* in 1225.

One of the main issues in one's evaluating the trip from the standpoint of religious conviction based on lineal genealogy reflects on Dōgen's relation to Ju-ching and the credibility of the claim of direct, face-to-face transmission. Dōgen, whose experience of *shinjin datsuraku* was never recorded in his writings but appears in later biographies, praises Ju-ching as the one exception to the general mediocrity and disappointment he found in China and as the kind of leader who appears only "once in a thousand years," according to *Eihei kōroku* no 2.128.[41] Furthermore, Dōgen argues that the transmission received from his mentor "resolved the one great matter," according to *Bendōwa*,[42] and "is only present in our Tung-shan house; others have not experienced it even in a dream," as in *Shōbōgenzō* "Menju"[43] and "Butsudō."[44]

Much of what is known about Ju-ching (1163–1227) is from Japanese sources, including *Shōbōgenzō* "Gyōji" (part 2) and Keizan's *Denkōroku*, in addition to the *Ju-ching yü-lu*. He was a patriarch in the Chih-hsieh line of the Ts'ao-tung school that Dōgen transmitted to Japan. The other main Ts'ao-tung lineage, the Hung-chih line, was subsequently transmitted to Japan by Tōmyō E'nichi. Ju-ching was born in 1163 in Yüeh-chou in Chekiang province. He first practiced in 1181, according to "Gyōji" (part 2), under the lineage of the twelfth-century reviver of the Ts'ao-tung school, Fu-yung Tao-k'ai, and then he trained under Sung-yüan Ch'ung-yüeh and Wu-yung Ching-ch'üan, the latter a disciple of Lin-chi school leader Ta-hui, whom Dōgen severely criticized in *Shōbōgenzō* "Shohō jissō." Ju-ching was enlightened in 1184 under Hsüeh-tou of the Ts'ao-tung school and was a monk at Mount Ching in 1193 under a Lin-chi lineage abbot. After that he became abbot at several Five Mountains temples, although, like Fu-yung Tao-k'ai, he was said to have turned down the purple robe granted by imperial decree. He served as abbot at Ch'ing-liang in Chin-ling in 1210; at Jui-yen in T'ai-chou in the fall of 1215; at Ching-tzu in Lin-an in Hang-chou in the spring of 1216, which he left in the fall of 1220; at Jui-yen again in the spring of 1222 for a short residency; at Ching-tzu again in the winter of 1223 for a nine-month stay; and finally at Mount T'ien-t'ung Ching-te ssu in the fall of 1224.

Did Dōgen experience something truly unique and special with Ju-ching that led him to negate other lineages, or did he exaggerate the importance of this relationship? Or is it even possible that the role of Ju-ching was invented, if not by Dōgen alone then by subsequent sectarian leaders who controlled the editing of the works of both Dōgen and Ju-ching? Although the full implications of the latter point are beyond our scope, the question arises: On the one hand, if his connection with Ju-ching was so special, why did Dōgen not discuss it, with a couple of prominent exceptions, until the transitional years of the early 1240s? On the other hand, if he were engaged in inventing his lineal tradition in China for sectarian purposes in Japan, why would he select Ju-ching, who from all other indications was not so highly regarded? One possibility is that Dōgen did have a significant experience with Ju-ching but then, at a critical turning point late in his career, came to focus on this encounter as being exclusive to his school for sectarian reasons.

What Dōgen Wrote

In regard to the questions about the historicity of the trip to China, the main argument in support of the journey seems to be Dōgen's own significant literary production that clearly owes so much to the records of his Chinese mentor and predecessors, along with other Sung Ch'an textual materials. Dōgen's main works—beginning with the *Mana Shōbōgenzō* collection of 300 cases and including the *Shōbōgenzō* and *Eihei kōroku*—comment extensively on hundreds of kōan collection and recorded sayings texts, including citations or allusions to passages that are quite obscure. If one examines the full extent of his writings, there is an overwhelming question: Would all these texts have been available in Japan, so that Dōgen could have comprehensively studied and absorbed them at Mount Hiei or Kenninji without having taken the trip to China?

It does seem likely, on the basis of comments in the *Hōkyōki* (no. 39), that once in China—and this is perhaps the best evidence that he went there—Dōgen studied the Ch'an transmission of the lamp texts indicated in Table 21 and developed an ability to cite dialogues from these at will.

The *Tsung-men t'ung-yao chi* is listed with an asterisk in Table 21 because it is not mentioned by Dōgen, yet Ishii Shūdō demonstrates that when Dōgen's citation of dialogues is carefully analyzed, the single main source is actually

---

TABLE 21. Transmission of Lamp Records Dōgen Studied

1. *Ching-te ch'uan-teng lu* (J. *Keitoku dentōroku*), from 1004, by Fa-yen school monk Tao-yüan and presented to Emperor Chen-tsung

2. *T'ien-sheng kuang-teng lu* (J. *Tenshō kōtōroku*), from 1036, by Lin-chi school supporter Li Tsun-hsü (this contains the *Lin-chi lu*) and presented to Emperor Jen-tsung

* *Tsung-men t'ung-yao chi* (J. *Shūmon tōyoshū*), from 1090 (also dated as late as 1133), produced by the Huang-lung lineage

3. *Chien-chung Ching-kuo hsü-teng lu* (J. *Kenchū seikoku zokutōroku*), from 1101, by Yün-men school monk Fo-kuo Wei-po and presented to Emperor Hui-tsung

4. *Tsung-men lien-teng hui-yao* (J. *Shūmon rentōeyō*), from 1183, by Lin-chi school, Ta-hui/Yang-ch'i lineage monk Hui-weng Wu-ming

5. *Chia-t'ai p'u-teng lu* (J. *Katai futōroku*), from 1204, by Yün-men school monk Lei-an Cheng-shou and presented to Emperor Ning-tsung

* Indicates that Dōgen does not refer to but probably studied this text

the *Tsung-men t'ung-yao chi* and not one of the better-known texts.[45] The *Tsung-men t'ung-yao chi* was probably not considered one of the main Ch'an texts, and much of its content was incorporated into the *Tsung-men lien-teng hui-yao* as the Huang-lung lineage gradually died out. However, according to Ishii, this and the *Ching-te ch'uan-teng lu* were published and distributed as a pair of texts at Ming-chou around the time of Dōgen's arrival, with the latter focusing on listing kōan cases rather than offering a hagiography of leading monks. Also "Kokyō" is an example of a *Shōbōgenzō* fascicle that cites numerous kōan cases beyond what is found in this or other oft-cited transmission of the lamp records.

Dōgen's intensive reading of Ch'an records at once makes the account of the "One Night *Blue Cliff Record*" attractive and undercuts its credibility. A key feature of the legend is how the Mount Hakusan deity plays such a central role. Mount Hakusan is in the region where Eiheiji was established and is the "mother" peak in the sacred network of mountains that included the site for Dōgen's temple.[46] Another major peak included in the network is Mount Sekidōzan at the southeast of the Noto peninsula, which is where Sōtō Zen was spread by Keizan to the temples, Yōkōji and Sōjiji, in the fourteenth century. However, the earliest version of this legend attributed the power to a local Chinese deity, Ta-chuan hsüeh-li (J. Daigenshuri), which was a tutelary god in the form of a snake or dragon protecting a mountain near the relic of Mount A-yü-wang, as well as seafarers using local waterways. The legend was preserved but, as the medieval versions evolved, the Chinese tutelary figure was changed to an anthropomorphic depiction of a Japanese god representing the region of Dōgen's move to Echizen from the period of his career during which the role of Chinese Ch'an was becoming prominent. This kind of myth-making, like a similar story of Daitō Kokushi copying the *Ching-te ch'uan-teng lu* (J. *Keitoku dentōroku*) in a month, is one of numerous examples of other-worldly occurrences that supposedly took place in China being used to reinforce a localization of sacrality and its power.[47] Even if seen as a symbol of how Dōgen introduced Ch'an texts to Japan, these hagiographical accounts cannot help but reinforce the questionability of traditional claims about the historicity of Dōgen's travels.

The authenticity of the "One Night *Blue Cliff Record*" has been much debated. It is clear that the reporting of this event developed in Dōgen hagiographies at a rather late date, a fact tending to negate the veracity of the account. On the other hand, a manuscript that was for a long time kept secret and held for centuries by the Sōtō sect has now been inspected by D. T. Suzuki and others in modern times. Yet this version differs from standard versions of the text in the sequence and some of the wording of the cases. We are left with the impact of the legend—whether or not he actually ever copied the *Blue Cliff Record*—highlighting the fact that Dōgen singlehandedly introduced to Japan the kōan tradition expressed through a variety of texts he produced in the first half of the thirteenth century.

The *kanbun* poetry Dōgen wrote in China, which makes no mention of the teaching of Ju-ching or practice at Mount T'ien-t'ung, does not give a sense of his acquiring knowledge of the Sung transmission of the lamp records or kōan collections. There are a few poems alluding to Ju-ching in the *kanshi* collection, but these were all written during the Echizen period. There are six verses, consisting of two groups of three (nos. 10.78–80 and 10.81–83), that respond retrospectively to prompts Ju-ching had given his assembly at Mount T'ien-t'ung as part of a poetry contest typically held at Ch'an temples influenced by the secular literati.[48] In the section of poems of "self-praise" (*jisan*) or comments on portraits of himself, there are two direct and two indirect references to Ju-ching: no. 1 in this section refers to Dōgen "pulling Ju-ching's nose" and no. 9 mentions that Dōgen is a "child of Ju-ching," whereas no. 6 and no. 10 allude to Mount T'ien-t'ung and "walking in the Chinese style," respectively. In addition, no. 5 of five verses contained in the section on "praise of the patriarchs" (*shinsan*) is dedicated to Myōzen.

The vast majority of the *kanbun* verses composed in China are for civil officials and other nonmonastics who must have been supporters of Five Mountains temples. An interesting example is a condolence call for a pious layman mourning the death of his son:

> When he opens his true eyes, the pupils are clear,
> Looking at his face, he seems steady,
> Tears having already been shed,
> Though his son has entered the land of the dead,
> Lord Yama! You won't catch him crying.[49]

The following verse transforms typical Chinese lyrical imagery for a Buddhist pedagogical purpose:

> Treading along in this dreamlike, illusory realm,
> Without looking for the traces I may have left;
> A cuckoo's song beckons me to return home;
> Hearing this, I tilt my head to see
> Who has told me to turn back;
> But do not ask me where I am going,
> As I travel in this limitless world,
> Where every step I take is my home.[50]

The cuckoo's sound is an image in Chinese verse suggesting a positive, much welcomed reminder of the need to return home, but its meaning is reversed by Dōgen, the Zen wanderer.

The Late Early Period: The Case of *Bendōwa*

Ju-ching retired from the abbacy in the spring of 1227, but there is a controversy about whether he died on 7.17.1227 or a year later and, if the former, whether Dōgen departed China just before or a couple of months after his mentor's demise. With the redating of *Fukanzazengi* and *Hōkyōki*, the first and only writing at the time of his return is a short essay on bringing back Myōzen's relics, the *Shari sōdenki*, written on 10.5.1227. In this piece, Dōgen makes several interesting points. First, he recalls that Myōzen abandoned the Kenmitsu teachings on Mount Hiei, which amounted to "merely counting letters," when he joined Kenninji. Second, he gives the dates for when they left Japan and reached China, which is the only record of these facts, but then asserts that before his death Myōzen "came to be respected in all the nine regions of China," most certainly an exaggeration. Then Dōgen states that the cremation ceremony held on 5.29.1225 was extremely well attended by monks from all over Sung China and that, as would be expected for such a luminary (despite his foreign status), the ashes yielded "over 360 white crystalline fragments [Skt. *sarira*, J. *shari*]." Dōgen goes on to make the claim that, "Even though it is over six hundred years since the Buddha Dharma was first transmitted to Japan, until now we had not heard of relics remaining among the ashes of a Japanese monk." Finally, he bestows a portion of the relics to Sister Chi of Kyoto, a nun who had been a "devoted student of Myōzen."[51]

Dōgen's collection of Chinese poetry contains 26 verses from the pre-Echizen period, but the majority of these are probably from the years shortly after his return but before he established Kōshōji, and most either were dedicated to Zen monks or were in celebration of nature. For example, no. 10.71 uses the image of plum blossoms beginning to flower under the snow as a symbol of spiritual renewal, like the pines and bamboo. This image later becomes one of Dōgen's most often-used metaphors, evoked in dozens of verses and sermons, especially the *Shōbōgenzō* "Baika" fascicle. One of the six verses composed while Dōgen was in residence at An'yōin temple in Fukakusa in 1230 uses imagery that evokes the *Shōbōgenzō* "Muchū setsumu" fascicle on "Disclosing a Dream Within a Dream":

> Drifting pitifully in the whirlwind of birth and death,
> As if wandering in a dream,
> In the midst of illusion, I awaken to the true path;
> There is one more matter I must not neglect,
> But I need not bother now,
> As I listen to the sound of the evening rain,
> Falling on the roof of my temple retreat
> In the deep grass of Fukakusa.[52]

Another verse from this period in the group of self-praise poems appears in calligraphy attributed to Dōgen on a portrait of him that is owned by Hommyō temple in Kumamoto prefecture; it is signed by "Monk Dōgen of Kenninji, the third year of Karoku [1227]":

> The cold lake reflecting the clear blue sky for thousands of miles.
> A gold-scaled fish moves along the bottom in the quiet of night,
> Swimming back and forth while fishing poles snap off—
> On the endless surface of water appears the bright white light of the
>   moon.[53]

Of the 14 *hōgo* sermons contained in the eighth volume of the *Eihei kōroku*, six were written during the late early period, and the rest are from 1234–1243. The rhetoric in no. 1 recalls *Bendōwa* from the same period in emphasizing the role of enlightenment in everyday affairs by asking rhetorically, "Why aren't taverns and houses of prostitution the classrooms of the Tathagata?"[54] The second sermon, delivered for a monk named Enchi in 1231, also recalls *Bendōwa*, and three sermons (nos. 8.4h, 8.9h, 8.12h) were delivered for a nun, Ryōnen, who apparently was studying kōan cases. Dōgen offers a mixed message about the value of kōan records, which, he says, should not be reduced to the use of catch phrases or buzz words. The manuscript of no. 8.12h is in Dōgen's own hand and dates from 1231, surviving at Kasuisai temple in Shizuoka prefecture. The sixth sermon was apparently delivered to a layman in Kyushu, and so it may have been written shortly after Dōgen disembarked on the southern island at the time of his return, although if it is the same lay follower for whom "Genjōkōan" was written, the date would be a few years later.

Tendai Breakaway

The high point of the late early period is the composition of *Bendōwa*, written in 1231 at An'yōin in Fukakusa; it is the initial statement of the resolution of the Doubt on metaphysical and practical levels. Although often referred to as an ideal introduction to Dōgen's thought, this text is actually problematic in that it was apparently neglected or lost for over 400 years until discovered in the seventeenth century. A manuscript was stored at the residence of a noble family in Kyoto and was found with the assistance of monk Kanno Sosan, who belonged to this family in the late seventeenth century, and Gesshu Soko then made his own copy. Manzan, a disciple of Gesshu, must have received this copy, and he included *Bendōwa* in the 89-fascicle edition of the *Shōbōgenzō* in 1684. A few years later *Bendōwa* was included in the Honzan edition of the *Shōbōgenzō*. The text was copied and commented on by Menzan in the *Shōbōgenzō Bendōwa Monge* in the eighteenth century, after which it was given a prominent position by being included as the first fascicle in the 1811 version of the 95-*Shōbōgenzō*. The role of *Bendōwa* was further highlighted in commentaries by Nishiari Bokusan, an important Sōtō master of the Meiji era, who ranked it in importance with "Genjōkōan" and "Busshō," although it has not been included in the 75-fascicle edition that is usually led off by the "Genjō-kōan" fascicle.

This *kana* text consists of two main parts, both of which stress the superiority of *zazen* practice as the only true gate to the Dharma. The first quarter of *Bendōwa* is an introductory essay that proclaims the ability of *zazen* to attain the state of awareness known as self-fulfilling samadhi (*jijiyū zammai*).[55] The opening section proclaims the resolution of Dōgen's Doubt on the theoretical level by arguing for the continuing process of *zazen* training based on the doctrine of *shusho ittō*, or the oneness of practice-attainment taking place at every single moment of ongoing meditation. According to one of Dōgen's most famous sayings about the necessity of practicing *zazen*, "The Dharma is amply present in every person but cannot be realized without practice." The Dharma, or the experience of enlightenment, does not occur before or after but is coterminous with the authenticity of renewed meditative practice. In later Sōtō interpretations of Dōgen's thought, this basic idea gets combined with the notion that meditation is not just a seated posture but encompasses all the activities of *gyōjū zaga* (walking, standing, sitting, lying). It is also linked with the notion of *honshō myōshū*, or the unity of original enlightenment and wondrous practice, a term frequently associated with but not explicitly stated in Dōgen's writings.

The second part or final three quarters of the text consists of 18 questions and answers in which Dōgen comments on many of the main tenets of Zen while countering possible objections from or offering critiques of a number of rival or, according to Dōgen, heretical standpoints. Nearly all of the queries concern the relation between *zazen* and the precepts, *nembutsu*, or some other main feature of Buddhist training. A not-so-hidden agenda is a refutation of the Daruma school, which denied the need for following the precepts altogether without necessarily replacing them with an imperative to practice *zazen*. However, the only brief mention of Ju-ching is in the essay portion, which indicates that while practicing under his mentor, Dōgen "resolved the great matter of religious training (*ishō sangaku no daiji*)" through the experience of *shinjin datsuraku*. No other specific reference to the master is offered.

While introducing the style of training that eventually became the Sōtō sect, in *Bendōwa* and subsequent works Dōgen was dismissive of labels that implied sectarian divisions within Zen or even the autonomy of Zen in relation to Buddhism as a whole, in addition to divisions between clerics and laypersons as well as between male and female practitioners. A concern with declaring universality and avoiding charges that he was not inclusive, which was evident during the early stages of his leadership in Japan, indicates that Dōgen may have had anxiety about Tendai supervision and government restrictions and pressures on new sects. Dōgen's attitude may have also reflected the Ch'an approach in China, which was not exclusivist in the sense of endorsing the selection of a single style of training, as was characteristic of the new Kamakura-era movements. As was seen in the transmission of the lamp records, Sung Ch'an promoted a multibranched approach to lineage that incorporated all schools and streams, including rival movements, in order to give at least the appearance of unity despite partisan infighting. Furthermore, in seeking to be accepted by mainstream Confucian society as a nonsubversive cult, Ch'an masters often admired and emulated some elements of the behavior of civil rulers and, in some cases, the reverse was also the case.[56]

Dōgen's resolution of the Doubt on the practical level must be seen in light of the complex issue of how both China and Japan, in different ways, had a centralized regulatory system for religions. Part of the key to the success of Ch'an/Zen was its ability to adapt and adjust to the sociopolitical context and to win support from civil authorities and patrons. Dōgen's innovation in creating a Sung-style monastery in Kamakura Japan based on a novel approach to the relation between monastic stewardship and external regulatory powers seems to be grounded on how well he had sized up—or understood from the explanations of Ju-ching—the way things worked in China. The situation in China is discussed rather extensively in *Hōkyōki* section no. 32, which remains a valuable source for understanding this part of the history of the Ch'an institution that is for the most part left unexamined in Chinese sources from the period.

Chinese Buddhist temples were much more loosely divided than Japanese sects on broad institutional lines based on kinds of sponsorship. "Private" or Heritage temples in China were referred to as *Vinaya* (C. Lü, J. Ritsu) temples, which was a misnomer, because they represented diverse monastic traditions of which the *Vinaya* or Precept school was an example. "Teaching" or Doctrinal temples belonged mainly to the T'ien-t'ai school (this was a far different institutional function than the Tendai sect that dominated Japan and that enjoyed imperial ties from its base on Mount Hiei). Also "Public" or Meditation temples where Ch'an was practiced were subject to government regulation as well as support. T'ien-t'ai was grouped as a Public rather than Private temple lineage but had lost power and prestige by the Southern Sung.

The Public Ch'an temples, especially those in the prestigious Five Mountains category, were supervised in the selection of abbots, who were appointed by authorities by means of an external search for the best candidate rather than anointed from within according to lineal heritage, as was the case of the Private temples. Because of this selection process, Ch'an temples were not strictly segregated into Lin-chi and Ts'ao-tung branches. For example, abbot Wu-chi of Mount T'ien-t'ung was a member of the Ta-hui lineage of the Lin-chi school, although Ts'ao-tung masters such as Hung-chih previously served there. This did not mean that there were no ideological rifts or partisan, polemical debates between lineages, however, as in the case of debates about dynamic activity in relation to meditation between Hung-chih and Ta-hui.

Japan had a religious system of government-regulated sects collectively referred to by Kuroda Toshio as the Kenmitsu system; it included eight officially sanctioned groups (the six Nara sects as well as the Tendai and Shingon sects founded by Saichō and Kūkai, respectively, in the Heian era). This system made it difficult for Zen and other new movements to gain recognition of their identity and status as autonomous entities separate from Tendai. That is one main reason why both Eisai and Enni yielded to forces encouraging syncretism with esoteric rites; another reason is that this pattern is what they had experienced in China. The motive for the assimilation of esotericism driving Sōtō evangelists influenced by Keizan was a pragmatic approach, not unlike the roles of Eisai and Enni, based on efforts to expand the sect into areas previously controlled by Tendai and Shingon Buddhism.

Quadrilogue

It seems that Dōgen learned lessons from the negative consequences the Daruma school suffered, which derived from its lack of genuine affiliation or knowledge of Ch'an thought and practice. This point is evident in his asserting the doctrine of face-to-face transmission (*menju*), an experience Nōnin never had, as the only legitimate way to earn and perpetuate the transfer of a lineage. According to the "Menju" fascicle written at a hermitage in the Echizen mountains during the eleventh month of 1243, the experience of *menju* could be attained only by virtue of sitting meditation (*zazen*), a training method Nōnin failed to espouse. Dōgen's case was unlike that of the Daruma school founder, who sent disciples to China to gain transmission in the Ta-hui lineage but never had a personal encounter with a Ch'an master. As was discussed above, it is said that while in China, Dōgen met and conversed with two important Five Mountains abbots, Wu-chi of Mount T'ien-t'ung and Che-weng of Mount Ching, yet was left unsatisfied and on the verge of returning prematurely to Japan before discovering Ju-ching as an authentic teacher. Dōgen's rejection of these two important figures entered into the traditional account of his trip probably because they were both disciples of Te-kuang, who awarded transmission to Nōnin's followers who were in search of sectarian legitimacy.

The *Jōtō shōgakuron* along with Eisai's *Kōzen gokokuron* and the *Bendōwa* are prime examples of styles of argumentation utilized in defense of Zen against Tendai criticism around the dawn of the early Kamakura period. In that sense, the three texts and their authors are allied. All three texts employ a catechistic question–answer format to explain the distinctive quality of Zen in comparison with other sects, as well as its role in protecting Japan. Like other Kamakura religious movements, including the Pure Land and Nichiren schools, Eisai and Dōgen both take a selectionist (*senjaku-shugiteki*) attitude in asserting the single practice (*shugyō*) of *zazen*, or rigorous, sustained training in meditation during shorter and prolonged sessions monitored by monastic leaders to test the determination of the monks as a path to enlightenment. This method of religious practice was to be selected by followers over and against other approaches, such as *nembutsu*.[57]

Historical perspective makes it clear that Nōnin's approach was different from that of the other Zen teachers in not affirming *zazen*, perhaps because he was preoccupied with breaking free of Tendai but lacked formal training in China. The tendency of the Daruma school to forgo the need for *zazen* was referred to in Dōgen's early writings, especially *Bendōwa* and "Sokushin ze-butsu" (1239), which was the fourth fascicle of the 75-*Shōbōgenzō* completed, as the "naturalist heresy" (or Senika heresy, *senni-gedō*). According to Dōgen, this is the deficient view, which represents a throwback to pre-Buddhist *atman* philosophy affirming a soul unaffected by change as well as the natural occurrence of enlightenment, of its own accord, in all aspects of phenomenal reality, without the need for authentication through cultivation of the spiritual prowess of the mind. Two of the eighteen dialogues in the second part of *Bendōwa* are dedicated to an indirect refutation of the Daruma school. Like Eisai, Dōgen did not designate Nōnin as the target of criticism, perhaps because the school was too controversial even to be mentioned.

The severe reaction Dōgen expressed against the Daruma school, consistent with Eisai's *Kōzen gokokuron*, derived from a concern that failing to distance from this controversial approach could jeopardize the development of more legitimate Zen movements. Since neither Eisai nor Dōgen refer to Nōnin and so little is known about him, it is also possible to imagine that he was made into a caricature or, further, manufactured as a straw man by those who were eager to have the finger pointed elsewhere.

In addition to a continuing commitment to meditation, two main areas of discipline were considered crucial to the establishment of the regimen of Ch'an/Zen monasticism. The first is adherence to the precepts, which Nōnin also disavowed, in contrast to Eisai's conservative position, based on the combined precepts, and Dōgen's innovative but still somewhat traditionalist view of the 16-article precepts. The second area is the formation of monastic rules (*shingi*) based on the *Ch'an-yüan ch'ing-kuei*, which were unique to the Zen system and went beyond the *vinaya* requirements in regulating nearly every aspect of the daily routine as well as ceremonial occasions and administrative hierarchy.

In all three areas, Nōnin fell short of providing consistent guidelines or instructions. The Daruma school's emphasis that the ultimate could be attained by living in ordinary reality without the need for authentication and transcendence through dedicated ritual practice no doubt went to an extreme. Its rejection of the need for the precepts, which could be "left behind" by the attainment of the Zen mind, was suspect from all quarters and led to the proscription of 1194. On one level, Dōgen may well have appreciated that in his own way Nōnin tried to establish a "pure" style of training that for the most part eliminated the need for esoteric rituals. However, he no doubt felt that the absence of an emphasis on any kind of training, including meditation, was unwholesome, and he realized that the vacuum in praxis ironically opened the door to a fascination with esotericism. Dōgen saw that one of the implications, or possible contradictions, of Daruma school ideology was its view that enlightenment would result in the attainment of this-worldly benefits through the worship of relics and ceremonialism associated with regalia. In contrast to Nōnin, Eisai was an adamant proponent of both precepts, which he felt would compensate for any laxity or corruption among the monks, and of *zazen*, whereas Dōgen was a strong supporter of monastic rules, which he considered essential for establishing a Sung-style religious community, and meditation. Eisai and Dōgen agreed on the role of *zazen* and were in fundamental accord about the need for self-discipline and communal regulation, yet they disagreed on how to prioritize these components of monasticism. Table 22 shows that while Eisai emphasized—or perhaps was forced to do so—esoteric rites as primary institutional rituals, Dōgen introduced *jōdō* sermons as a vehicle for kōan commentaries into the Zen monastic setting for the first time in Japan, as he asserts in *Eihei kōroku* 5.358 from 1249.

Bendōwa *Seen Through the Decline and Renewal Theories*

Bendōwa, now considered Dōgen's first work, is crucial for both theories about change in the later Dōgen, which hold this text up from inverted standpoints as the epitome of the ideology of the (falsely labeled) "early *Shōbōgenzō*." For the Decline Theory it expresses Dōgen's belief in a liberal, pan-Buddhist universalism embracing all people without exception.[58] For the Renewal Theory it is the main example of how original enlightenment thought infiltrated into Dōgen's work in such notions as "original realization" (*honshō*), "original face" (*honrai menmoku*), and "original ground" (*honji*).[59] However, despite Dumoulin's statement that "the short and typical *Bendōwa* book on practice . . . may be taken as the first foundational section of the *Shōbōgenzō*,"[60] this anomalous

TABLE 22. Comparison of Priorities of Eisai and Dōgen

Category	Eisai	Dōgen
Gate to Dharma	Precepts	Zazen
Temple regulations	Shingi	Shingi
Everyday practice	Zazen	Precepts
Style of training	Syncretic	Kōans
Rituals	Mikkyō	Sermons (jishu and jōdō)

text should not be equated with or turned into a theory of the early Dōgen, for several reasons.

Bendōwa does display some distinctive features, but these are not of sufficient import so as to construct a theory of an early Dōgen. First, in the medieval period *Bendōwa* was never treated as part of the 75-*Shōbōgenzō* and its question–answer format is quite different from that of the *jishu* sermons. As Dumoulin partially acknowledges, *Bendōwa* was also not included in any of the other major Kamakura/Muromachi editions of the *Shōbōgenzō*, including the 60-, 28-, and 12-fascicle versions, and its inclusion in Tokugawa editions is due mainly to the fact that it is a *kana* work. Still, this may be appear to be begging the question: even if *Bendōwa* is technically independent of the 75-*Shōbōgenzō*, the issue remains whether or not it is representative of an early period of thought that was subsequently compromised, according to the Decline Theory, or unfortunately cultivated, as in the Renewal Theory.

To address this issue, it is not at all clear that the message of the text is really so different from that in subsequent works. *Bendōwa* is dedicated primarily to espousing the benefits of a ritualized form of *zazen* practice, a theme that was never altered or abandoned in Dōgen's exhortative works from *Fukanzazengi* to the *Shōbōgenzō zuimonki*, the *Eihei kōroku*, and other later works such as *Bendōhō* (1245) and other essays in the *Eihei shingi*. A major issue for the Decline Theory is that *Bendōwa* seems to endorse a "refreshingly ecumenical," universal outlook embracing laypersons and women, which was later drastically changed.[61] However, there are just three of eighteen questions (nos. 12, 14, 15) dealing with this topic, and the role of women is mentioned only in one brief sentence, which asserts the equal potential of all people to practice *zazen* regardless of whether they are male or female, or of high or low social status. The early *hōgo* lectures for nun Ryōnen are also indicative of an interest in women. However, the 75-*Shōbōgenzō* "Raihaitokuzui," which was the other text to affirm the role of women, was not written until 1240, already the beginning of a period of change according to the Decline Theory, and this fascicle also suggests, perhaps ironically, that demons, pillars, and foxes are worthy representatives of the Dharma. If we take Dōgen's references throughout his career to *shukke* (renunciation, lit. "home departure," in contrast to *zaike*, lay life, lit. "remaining in the home") in a gender-free sense that the term may imply, it seems that his treatment of nuns may never have changed.

The main point is that *Bendōwa* consistently asserts the need for sustained *zazen,* and while it grants laypersons the ability to practice meditation, this is not necessarily a sanctification of everyday, secular life, which Dōgen consistently criticizes for producing only ephemeral, illusory benefits. Dōgen's aim of establishing the nondual doctrine of the oneness of practice-attainment occurs in a complex ideological context involving several important issues, including: (1) resolving a debate about the role of the *vinaya* by asserting the priority of the Mahayana precepts with their emphasis on forgiveness over Hinayana precepts in question no. II; (2) absorbing the influence of Sung Ch'an masters who attempted to train and convert Neo-Confucian scholar-officials (the main example of lay meditation cited in question no. 14 is a Neo-Confucian); (3) refuting the Mappō theory of the age of degeneracy, which suggests that few or perhaps even no one is capable of self-realization; and (4) dismissing such practices as reciting sutras, chanting, or performing mantras in questions no. 3 and 12.

Dōgen's position expressed here and elsewhere represents an egalitarian declaration of a universal potential that requires constant exertion to be actualized; although everyone is capable of *zazen*, the monastic lifestyle is clearly more conducive for sustained practice. Kim suggests, "Dōgen held, from the very beginning to the very end, that monkhood was the ideal possibility of model of the rightly transmitted Buddhism, which transcended both monkhood and laity in their ordinary senses; Dōgen's universe was envisioned in terms of monkish elitism."[62] As was previously mentioned, in a *Shōbōgenzō zuimonki* passage from the mid-1230s, *zazen* forms the basis of and takes priority over all other aspects of religious practice, including the precepts.[63] In the 12-*Shōbōgenzō*, Dōgen argues that monastics will still attain enlightenment even if they violate the precepts. *Bendōwa* is seminal to the extent that Dōgen continued to maintain the view that everyone could practice *zazen*, as demonstrated by an *Eihei kōroku* passage (7.498) from the early 1250s celebrating the isolation of Eiheiji: "Whether they are bright or dull, wise or foolish, [Zen trainees] should dwell in steep mountains and deep valleys."[64]

Dōgen seeks a delicate balance on the Mappō issue, which was a prevalent Buddhist doctrine by the late Heian era that was often used to explain the social turmoil and political upheaval as well as the drastic changes in the religious environment at the outset of the Kamakura era. On the one hand, in question no. 15 he denies the notion of an innate incapacity to achieve enlightenment; through the practice of *zazen* everyone has the potential. At the same time, without again naming the doctrine, he does seem to evoke the doctrine of Mappō as a means to acknowledge and attack the limitations and flaws in the initial Japanese attempts either to appropriate or to reject Zen, especially in nos. 8 and 11.

In addition, there are two attitudes which the Decline Theory associates with Dōgen's change in Echizen that are already in evidence in *Bendōwa* and other writings from the early period. First, Dōgen explicitly praises Ju-ching as his mentor in *Bendōwa*, *Gakudōyōjinshū*, the *Shōbōgenzō*, and the *Eihei kōroku*, and he cites a Ju-ching verse in the very first 75-*Shōbōgenzō* fascicle, "Makahannyaharamitsu" from 1233. The Decline Theory has made a good point in showing the shift in attitude regarding Ju-ching during the 1240s but may have gone to an extreme by overlooking points of continuity. Second, in *Bendōwa*, Dōgen undertakes a severe and even scathing rejection of his rivals in Japan, especially the Shingon, Kegon, and Tendai schools as well as *nembutsu* practitioners. Although the Decline Theory is correct in pointing out that the explicit criticism of other Zen patriarchs did not emerge until around the time of the Echizen migration, it is also clear that throughout his career Dōgen as the founder of a new Kamakura movement was preoccupied with issues of sectarian identity and institutional integrity.

Furthermore, in contrast to the Renewal Theory's claims about the role of original enlightenment ideology in *Bendōwa*, it must be noted that Dōgen never specifically mentions (either to endorse or to refute) original enlightenment in this or any other text. Therefore any understanding of the impact of the doctrine is based on speculation from literary clues that appear in related terms and ideas. It is true that *Bendōwa*'s use of several "*hon*-words," as well as the notion that the practice of *zazen* by one person for a single instant illuminates the entire universe at all times, sound like examples of *hongaku* ideology. Yet questions no. 10 and 16 also contain the first instance of Dōgen's criticism of the so-called Senika heresy, which resurfaces in the 75-*Shōbōgenzō* "Sokushin-zebutsu," for endorsing a substantialist way of thinking in asserting that "the body is ephemeral, yet true nature is eternal." *Bendōwa* also cites traditional Buddhist anecdotes illustrating the function of karmic retribution; these include the stories of a hunter who is punished and a prostitute who is redeemed and transformed into a nun, both of whom figure prominently in several 12-*Shōbōgenzō* fascicles. Also from 1239, "Ikkya myōju," endorses, however briefly, the doctrine of "not obscuring causality" (*fumai inga*),[65] or an affirmation of the inexorability of cause-and-effect, which the Renewal Theory argues did not appear until the 12-*Shōbōgenzō* "Jinshin inga," which comments on Pai-chang's "wild fox kōan."

On the other hand, even if it is conceded that certain aspects of *Bendōwa* are unique when compared with subsequent works, it appears that some changes along the lines suggested by the two theories began shortly thereafter with the opening of Kōshōji and became especially noticeable as soon as the Monks Hall opened in 1236. At that point Dōgen began writing instructions on monastic ritual, including two 75-*Shōbōgenzō* fascicles, "Senjō" and "Senmen" (both 1239), which deal with washing the body. In addition, the *Shōbōgenzō zuimonki* from the Kōshōji period contains several passages critical of laypersons. For example, when asked whether laypersons responsible for corruption or conflict can remove their transgressions by confessing or giving offerings to monks, Dōgen replies that any misfortune arising from the situation "is not the fault of the monastics or of Buddhism but it is the laymen themselves who are in error."[66] Moreover, there are no further references after 1231 to *hon*-words, in either a positive or negative sense, although other features of Tendai *hongaku* imagery are frequently used throughout the *Shōbōgenzō*, including the 75- and the 12-fascicle editions as well as in the *Goshō* commentaries.

Therefore, as we move on to the middle period in the next two chapters, *Bendōwa* should be neither inflated in importance nor conflated with the writings of other periods or later texts, but should be seen as a starting point for a career that at once foreshadows and is changed by subsequent developments.

4

The Middle Period, Part I

The Kyoto Cycle

The second main stage or middle period of Dōgen's career extends from the establishment of his first temple in Kyoto through the completion of his move to Echizen, and it encompasses the initial explosion of literary productivity featuring a rich variety of styles and themes composed in both *kanbun* and *kana*. This remarkably fruitful and complex general period is so crucial for an understanding of Dōgen's overall career trajectory that it needs to be divided into three subperiods or phases—rather than two, as in the cases of the early and late periods—each of which is marked by a profusion of diverse forms of expression. Since the most notable literary product is the *jishu* sermons collected in the 75-*Shōbōgenzō,* which was produced almost entirely during the middle middle phase, the theory of periodization is particularly helpful in clarifying the roots of the text and disputing the interpretive approaches of the Decline and Renewal theories. An examination of the chronology of composition reveals that the *Shōbōgenzō* should be regarded not as a work spanning a lifetime, but rather as a text that was developed during a highly compressed time frame characterized by particular concerns and agendas, especially in promoting Ju-ching as the exemplary Zen master and monastic leader.

The first subperiod is the early middle period (1233–1241), which begins with the opening of Kōshōji in the town of Fukakusa in the outskirts of Kyoto and includes Dōgen's experiments with various ways of establishing monastic rules or *shingi* while commenting on the precepts and presenting and interpreting kōans. This phase starts with a couple of prominent shorter works composed in 1233,

Fukanzazengi and "Genjōkōan," each of which highlights a kōan case that is cited as a means of articulating the nature of Zen training. It continues with more sustained and elaborate attempts to transmit the kōan tradition to Japan in lengthy though lesser known works from the mid-1230s, including the *Mana Shōbōgenzō* collection of 300 cases without commentary and the ninth volume of the *Eihei kōroku*, containing 90 cases with verse comments (*juko*).

Perhaps the primary work of the early middle period is the *Shōbōgenzō zuimonki*, which contains over 100 informal sermons that frequently cite or allude to kōan cases and also comments extensively on the status of the Ch'an/Zen monastic institution. Although the writings contained in the 75-*Shōbōgenzō* were initiated then, this phase, which lasted about eight years, yielded a total of only twelve fascicles, none of which were composed over the four years during which the *Shōbōgenzō zuimonki* sermons were delivered. Nevertheless, some of the most prominent of the 75-*Shōbōgenzō* fascicles known for citing kōans were part of this group, beginning with "Genjōkōan." In addition, several *shingi*-style pieces were composed at this time, including *Tenzokyōkun* contained in the *Eihei shingi*, the *Jūundōshiki* included in the 95-*Shōbōgenzō*, the 75-*Shōbōgenzō* fascicles "Senjō," "Senmen," and "Den'e," and the 12-*Shōbōgenzō* "Kesa kudoku." It is also noteworthy that the delivery of formal *jōdō* sermons was initiated in the Dharma Hall of Kōshōji during this phase.

The diversity of texts in the early middle period set the stage for the prolific production of *Shōbōgenzō* fascicles during the middle middle period (1241–1244). The overwhelmingly significant transitional stage of Dōgen's career covers the final years in Kyoto and the unfolding sense of uncertainty, or perhaps even turmoil, Dōgen must have felt in this conflictive environment leading up to and including the days of the move to Echizen. If the early middle period is marked by experimentation with various kinds of literary styles and ways of introducing both kōans and monastic rules, this phase features the composition of the vast majority (57) of the 75-*Shōbōgenzō* fascicles, with fully half being composed during the itinerant period of late 1243 through early 1244. These informal *jishu* sermons demonstrate Dōgen's remarkable facility in culling and citing the voluminous Sung transmission of the lamp records, which contained the encounter dialogues on which he provided inventive commentary.

This chapter covers the early middle period and the initial developments of the middle middle period, and the next chapter begins by exploring in detail possible explanations for Dōgen's flight from the capital, a crucial point for an understanding of the production of the *Shōbōgenzō*, which dominates this crucial phase of his career.

The Early Middle Period: Experimenting with Kōans and Rules

The initial works of the middle period, *Fukanzazengi* and "Genjōkōan," show Dōgen's first attempts, and perhaps the earliest such efforts in the history of Japanese Buddhism, to integrate kōans into his teaching. These two writings, which exhibit many common elements in that they are succinct discourses intended to proclaim a vision of the essence of Zen based on ongoing meditative practice, have quite distinct literary styles reflecting different targeted audiences. *Fukanzazengi*, or *Universal Recommendation for Zazen*, is an independent work (later included at the end of the eighth volume of *Eihei kōroku*) composed in *kanbun* that primarily instructs monks according to the teachings of the *Tso-ch'an i*, a brief meditation manual that serves as an appendix to the *Ch'an-yüan ch'ing-kuei* by Tsung-tse. It is a purposefully derivative work, with some important variations from the source text.[1] "Genjōkōan" or "Spontaneous Realization of the Kōan" (variation: "The Kōan Realized in Everyday Life"), the first fascicle in the 75-*Shōbōgenzō* and 60-*Shōbōgenzō* texts, is a letter composed in *kana* for an otherwise unknown layman from Kyushu in a highly original and elliptical style that has no real precedent in the Ch'an/Zen tradition.

As in the case of *Bendōwa*, the literary styles of both of these early texts were abandoned after the initial effort, although Dōgen continued to maintain and to develop his interest in the content. Much of the material of *Fukanzazengi* was replicated ten years later in a *kana* fascicle of the 75-*Shōbōgenzō*, "Zazengi," and other parts were discussed more extensively in another fascicle, "Zazenshin." Also the term *"genjō,"* as well as a number of the fascicle's images and themes concerning the realization process and the meaning of time, are frequently mentioned elsewhere, most notably in the "Busshō," "Uji," and "Zenki" fascicles, and it is interesting that Dōgen was still editing "Genjōkōan" near the end of his life.

Resolving the Great Doubt

What all of the late early and early middle period texts share is an attempt to highlight Dōgen's sense of Doubt about the need for practice, given the universality of the Dharma, and to indicate the resolution of this fundamental matter by evoking the basic Buddhist doctrine of the middle way in expressing a paradoxical kōan case. *Fukanzazengi* opens with a lengthy passage, not found in the Chinese source text, that asks in several tersely worded rhetorical questions why the process of seeking to attain enlightenment is necessary if the Way is from the start ever present. The heart of the essay is a brief evocation of a kōan, which is discussed more extensively at the beginning of "Zazenshin," about the power of nonthinking or without-thinking (*hi-shiryō*) in contrast to

the conventional opposition between ordinary thinking (*shiryō*) and its negative, the withdrawn state of not-thinking (*fu-shiryō*) or absence of thought.

In the kōan case, when master Yüeh-shan, while deep in meditation, is
asked about how it is possible to think of not-thinking, he responds, "By nonthinking." The kōan on nonthinking was one of Dōgen's favorites; it appears
in *Mana Shōbōgenzō* case 124, and in the "Soshi seiraii" and "Zanmai ōzanmai"
fascicles as well as *Eihei kōroku* 5.373. According to T. P. Kasulis, nonthinking
represents a "nonpositional state" that assumes "no intentional attitude whatsoever: it neither affirms nor denies, accepts nor rejects, believes nor disbe-
lieves." Kasulis further argues that nonthinking constitutes a realization of the
"pure presence of things as they are" in his rendering of the complex term
genjōkōan.[2]

After a lengthy commentary on nonthinking, the "Zazenshin" fascicle continues with an interpretation of a related case that is also cited in the "Kokyō"
fascicle (as well as *Mana Shōbōgenzō* case 202), in which Ma-tsu in response
to a query from Nan-yüeh likens polishing a brick to sitting in meditation. In
these fascicles, written in the early 1240s,[3] Dōgen, in a way that will become
characteristic by the time of his uniquely creative middle middle period, reverses the conventional reading of the case so that Ma-tsu is considered to be
enlightened at the outset rather than at the conclusion of the narrative. Furthermore, in the "Kokyō" interpretation, the metaphor of the brick is used, not
to show the futility of *zazen* in failing to contribute to sudden awakening, but
rather as a positive example of the need for continuing to practice meditation
beyond enlightenment. This experience should not be dichotomized into sudden and gradual dimensions in a way that stifles the need for ongoing practice.

"Genjōkōan" begins with a query similar to *Fukanzazengi*'s by asking how
it is that the Dharma, transcending oneness and manyness, stands beyond the
oppositions of sentient beings and buddhas, birth and death, and delusion and
awakening, and "nevertheless, blossoms fall amid attachment and weeds
spring up to our chagrin."[4] Dōgen then offers a series of extended metaphors
to show the overcoming of each of the three main polarities: the moon reflected
in the water is like the relation between beings, who are deluded about realization, and buddhas, who have a great realization of delusion; the sequence of
firewood turning into ash but not becoming firewood again symbolizes the
relation between living and dying, which are at once sequential and nonse-
quential stages; and fish swimming in the water or birds flying in the air
resemble the unfolding of continuous realization, which is a dynamic process
yet is experienced as a sense of homecoming.

The fascicle concludes by citing an obscure kōan in which a master fan-
ning himself shows that while the wind (symbolizing the Dharma) may be
permanent, it does not circulate (or attain enlightenment) without one's exerting the effort to make it happen (through sustained practice). Although "Genjōkōan" in a strict sense cites just a single case, this fascicle is crucial for an

understanding of Dōgen's overall approach to kōan interpretation in two ways. First, the title evokes the idea of a more dynamic sense of the term than the typical view of kōans serving as precedents extracted from the past records and used as means of stimulating awakening. The second level of significance is that the fascicle itself, in raising paradox after paradox concerning the topics of self and other or illusion and reality, such as "To study the self is to forget the self" or "When one side is illumined, the other side is dark," becomes a kind of prolonged, intricate kōan case.

Another work from the first years of the early middle period, the *kanbun* text *Gakudōyōjinshū*, composed in the third month of 1234, contains ten sections of instructions on studying the Way from the first moment of aspiring to pursue realization through the renewal of practice. The eighth section, on the conduct of Zen monks, briefly alludes to several kōans. These include Hui-neng's asking his challenger to reveal "the look on his face before he was born" and the second patriarch Hui-k'o's cutting off his arm in front of Bodhidharma to show his dedication and attainment of "the marrow" of the first patriarch's teaching in gaining transmission.[5] This section also cites the *Mu* kōan and provides a rather typical interpretation that is altered significantly by Dōgen in the middle middle period's renowned "Busshō" fascicle of 1241, which explores the topic from multiple philosophical perspectives.[6]

Where Is Ju-Ching?

In the writings from the early and mid-1230s, there is scant acknowledgement of Ju-ching. The works already cited do not mention the Ch'an mentor, even in the *Gakudōyōjinshū*'s fifth section, on "Finding a true teacher for the study of the Way," which refers to the need to travel to Sung China since there are no genuine masters in Japan. An exception among the early works is the "Makahannyaharamitsu" fascicle, first delivered in 1233 and edited in 1242, when Dōgen is said to have received a copy of the *Ju-ching yü-lu*. In commenting on the *Heart Sutra*, this fascicle briefly cites an obscure verse by Ju-ching dealing with emptiness that is symbolized by a Buddhist bell. This poem is also cited in the "Kokū" fascicle and *Hōkyōki*, where Dōgen refers to the original verse in sections 38 and 39. Dōgen says that as an inexperienced foreigner, when he studied the various Ch'an writings he "found nothing so supremely profound in other Ch'an writings" as Ju-ching's poetic expression, a rather remarkable comment about this small verse. Also *Eihei kōroku* 9.58 from 1236 includes a rewriting of Ju-ching's poem:[7]

> The bell looks like a mouth, gaping,
> Indifferent to the wind blowing in the four directions;
> If you ask about the meaning of wisdom,
> It only answers with a jingling, tinkling sound.

Dōgen's version provides more rhetorical flourish, with an emphasis on the continual ringing of the bell and the elimination of any trace of duality between instrument and sound. His verse uses tautology and onomatopoeia to make the conclusion more concrete and practical:

> The bell is a voice articulating emptiness,
> Playing host to the wind blowing in the four directions,
> Expressing in its own elegantly crafted language
> The tintinnabulation: the ringing of the ringing. . . .

While the verses show some aspects of what Dōgen was doing and think-ing in China, there are numerous *jōdō* sermons that reveal his approach to inheriting and transmitting the teachings to Japan. For example, in no. 1.48 (which appears as no. 1.1 in the Manzan edition of the *Eihei kōroku* and is also the first sermon in the *Eihei goroku*), Dōgen reflects on Ju-ching in the self-deprecating language he uses elsewhere, and he also offers a couple of brief yet frequently noted verses that highlight the teaching that he brought back from China:

> [Dōgen] said, This mountain monk [Dōgen] has not passed through many monasteries. Somehow I just met my late teacher Ju-ching. However, I was not deceived by T'ien-t'ung [Ju-ching]. But T'ien-t'ung was deceived by this mountain monk. Recently, I returned to my homeland "empty-handed" (*kūshū genkyō*). And so this mountain monk has no Buddha Dharma. Trusting fate, I just spend my time:
>
> > Every morning, the sun rises in the east.
> > Every evening, the moon sets in the west,
> > Clouds gathering over the foggy peaks,
> > Rain passes through the surrounding hills and plains.
>
> [Also:] A leap year comes every fourth year, a rooster crows at dawn.[8]

Ejō and the Shōbōgenzō Zuimonki

As the Kōshōji community continued to grow with more offices and officers/administrators in place, additional texts were needed to guide and regulate the new institutional developments. The texts also sought to indoctrinate followers being initiated—many of whom probably had not received training at Kenninji or other temples with a Zen orientation—with a knowledge and understanding of both kōan records and monastic rules, the two key features of Ch'an relig-iosity imported from China by Eisai and Dōgen.

Of the numerous disciples Dōgen attracted at Kōshōji, the most important was Ejō, who converted to Dōgen's movement from the proscribed Daruma school and who recorded in the *Shōbōgenzō zuimonki* some of Dōgen's informal lectures or *shōsan* delivered from the end of 1234 to the spring of 1238. Ejō had visited Dōgen at Kenninji in the late 1220s, apparently instructed to join Dōgen by his teacher, Kakuan, who died in 1234; at that time, however, he was turned away as a permanent follower, since Dōgen did not yet lead his own movement. He became a disciple at Kōshōji, which had a Monks Hall and other trappings of a Sung-style temple in 1236 after successful fundraising (*kanjin*) efforts mentioned in two passages from the year before—the promotional essay *Kannon dōri'in sōdō kanjin* and *Shōbōgenzō zuimonki* 3.12.[9]

Shōbōgenzō zuimonki 5.5, from 1.28.1237 (variously dated 12.27.1236), indicates that Ejō was invited then for the first time to take the head seat at Kōshōji and present a lecture to the assembly. Following Dōgen's preaching on the nature of Zen transmission, Ejō took up the fly-whisk (*hossu*) and began his discourse on a kōan case assigned by Dōgen, Tung-shan's "three pounds of flax" kōan. However, Ejō, the devoted follower and lifelong compiler of the vast majority of Dōgen's sermons, is not on record as being called upon again for such an opportunity.

The *Shōbōgenzō zuimonki*, which emerged as the major work of the mid-1230s, includes teachings about institutional structure and training as well as commentaries on kōan records. It is a rare example of writings prior to Dōgen's receiving the *Ju-ching yü-lu*, emphasizing the Chinese master's commitment to consistent discipline and persistent *zazen* meditation, although this topic appears in only a handful of passages. Of the approximately 120 sermons and lectures in this collection, just four are specifically on Ju-ching as a model figure, although they do not cite any of his teachings, which presumably were not then available in written form in Japan. It is important to see this ratio in light of the fact that over 40 passages deal with various aspects of Buddhism and society in China, including the practice of Ch'an as well as numerous comments on religion and culture more generally, and at least 14 treat Eisai and the religiosity of Kenninji.

The text's first passage, no. 1.1, as shown in Table 23, mentions that Dōgen was invited by Ju-ching to be his attendant, but as a foreign novice he declined the opportunity "since it would indicate a lack of suitable candidates in China." Several sermons proclaim the good fortune of practicing under an authentic Ch'an master who was a model teacher. In no. 2.16 Dōgen says, "While staying in Sung China in the assembly under Ju-ching, we had lengthy discussions during which I came to know of his life and teachings, and I realized the truth by practicing *zazen* day and night with a real Zen teacher. Should I live a short life and die suddenly, it would not be in vain."[10] Also no. 3.30 states that Ju-ching practiced *zazen* until about eleven o'clock at night and then got up at two-thirty or three, and started in again.[11] In this lengthy passage Dōgen praises Ju-ching for not being easygoing with regard to meditation schedule and for shaming monks by striking them or ringing a bell and summoning an attendant to stir and awaken them. Also during a candlelight lecture before the

TABLE 23. Chronology of Key Passages in *Shōbōgenzō zuimonki*

1234:	no. 1.1 in fall, Ejō begins recording—reports Dōgen invited to be Ju-ching's head monk (Also *Gakudōyōjinshū*, 3.9; prohibition of *senshū nembutsu*)
1235:	nos. 2.5–8, on "violating precepts," "taking the precepts," "repentance"; no. 2.21, "Seven or eight years since I returned from China"; no. 3.3, "Establishing a temple is one of the most important things a person can do"; no. 3.12, "Now I am trying to build a monastery and am asking people for contributions" (Also *Mana Shōbōgenzō*; Ejō receives "Busso shōden bosatsukai"; *Kannondōriin Sōdō konryū kanjin so*; Bakufu prohibits arms for warrior monks; Kōen dies, 9.20; Enni and Eizon enter Sung; insurrection by Kōfukuji warrior monks, 12.23)
1236:	no. 4.12, "I have already spent ten years without possessing anything at all"; no. 5.5, "On the eve of last day of the twelfth month, Dōgen invited Ejō to serve as head monk of Kōshōji temple" (Also Monks Hall opens, 10.15; Ejō gives sermon; first *jōdō* sermon)
1237:	no. 6.19 cites Ta-hui, as also recorded in *Kenzeiki* (Also *Tenzokyōkun, Shukke ryaku sahō*)
1238:	no. 6.27, concluding record (4.18, "Ikkya myōjū")
[1239:	*Jūundōshiki*, 4.25; "Sokushinzebutsu," 5.25; "Senjō" and "Senmen," 10.23]

whole assembly, an attendant asked if exhausted monks could sleep and Ju-ching replied, "Absolutely not!"

Furthermore, in no. 2.9 Dōgen says that Ju-ching would strike the monks with his slipper and scold them to keep them from dozing off during *zazen*.[12] They were grateful for the reprimand, and then he lectured them about removing delusions, and when he finished his lecture the monks all wept. This theme of Ju-ching as sermonizer extraordinaire is echoed elsewhere, especially in the "Shohō jissō" fascicle and in *Eihei kōroku* no. 2.128, both of which were composed shortly after the importation of Ju-ching's record to Japan. One theory is that in disappointment with the recorded sayings, Dōgen sought to inflate the intangible qualities of Ju-ching as a charismatic speaker since these could not be documented or evaluated in an objective fashion.

The real significance of the *Shōbōgenzō zuimonki* is not so much its emphasis on Ju-ching as its creating a picture of Zen training based on three pillars of training, *zazen, shingi* (or precepts in a general sense), and kōan study. However, this text makes no systematic attempt to link the elements of *shingi* and kōans or to use the latter as a means of illustrating the former, as is found in preceding and subsequent works. In fact, considerable ambiguity or contradiction is expressed throughout the text about the role of other practices in relation to *zazen*, which invariably takes priority. In addition to the comment, cited earlier, that when one is doing *zazen* all of the precepts automatically are being upheld, implying that the inverse is not the case, there are several passages disparaging a reliance on words and letters, which would imply a criticism of interpreting kōans (as well as composing or reading poetry). Nevertheless, throughout the *Shōbōgenzō zuimonki* the practices of obeying the precepts and interpreting kōans are proffered as being essential to the religious quest.

The Initial Monastic Rules Texts

The *Shōbōgenzō zuimonki* foreshadows the emphasis that Dōgen would develop on *shingi* as a key to discipline, combining self-generated internal spiritual prowess and external codes that guide the minute details of conduct from personal hygiene to interaction between junior and senior monks. The text contains numerous references to Chinese Ch'an monks and monasteries being consistently held up as superior to Buddhist practice in Japan in terms of their authenticity of commitment to vows of poverty and humility and lack of any trace of corruption. In *Shōbōgenzō zuimonki* 1.3, for example, Dōgen praises a monk from Szechuan province who was so poor that his trousers were made of a cheap grade of thin paper and could be heard tearing by his fellow monks. In no. 3.7 (echoing no. 3.3), which also praises Eisai for the "most splendid of words" in advocating a fair distribution of resources, Dōgen discusses how Mount T'ien-t'ung under the leadership of Hung-chih collected an assembly of hundreds of monks who were willing to share their meager portions. Hung-chih earns a rare mention in Dōgen's works for the 1230s, but he will become a primary focus of attention a decade later. The Sung master commented to skeptics, "Everyone has a mouth to feed."

Two *Shōbōgenzō* fascicles from this period dealing with an aspect of *shingi*, "Den'e" and "Kesa kudoku," composed in consecutive nights of 1240 (even though they are included in different editions of the *Shōbōgenzō*),[13] comment on the making and wearing of the Buddhist robe. Dōgen discusses a special robe ceremony he observed in China and also notes that there were two Korean lay disciples at the temple who seemed especially dedicated to seeking the Dharma. On the other hand, Japan comes under fire in *Tenzokyōkun*, which says that once Dōgen returned to Kenninji he was distraught at the inadequacy of the chief cook in comparison with the Chinese model. Furthermore, the *Shōbōgenzō zuimonki* mentions on several occasions, especially in no. 4.4, that in the "seven or eight years" since he returned to Japan, a disturbing degree of idleness and corruption had entered into the Japanese monastic system.

The message of the *Shōbōgenzō zuimonki* is not one-sided, because Dōgen also criticizes some aspects of Chinese monasticism and in some cases praises Japan over China, especially the leadership of Eisai as founding abbot of Kenninji temple. Apparently following Ju-ching's lead, if the writings of *Hōkyōki* and other sources are an indication, Dōgen is particularly keen on criticizing Chinese monks for growing long hair and fingernails or otherwise deviating from mainstream regulations and etiquette. For instance, no. 3.20 suggests that "only one or two out of several hundred or even a thousand disciples under a great Ch'an teacher ever actually gained true enlightenment," in part because, according to no. 3.27, they tended greedily to "sort the wheat and rice, separating the good from the bad and making their meals from the good alone."

This rhetorical pattern is followed in the "Senmen" fascicle, first delivered as a sermon in 1239 and presented again on 10.20.1243 while Dōgen was in the midst of settling in the Echizen mountains. The text at first greatly admires Indian and Chinese methods of cleaning, but the second half is dedicated to praising Japanese monks for using a toothbrush, a device he says was unknown in China, where the "stench was difficult to bear."[14] However, the only mention in these early *shingi*-oriented *Shōbōgenzō* fascicles of Ju-ching is a reference to the master of Mount T'ien-t'ung establishing as the time for washing the face the third period of the third watch, or some phase of the middle of the night.

The *Shōbōgenzō zuimonki* and related texts, therefore, set up a relativity of standards whereby Kenninji practice prior to Dōgen's trip, when it was led by the likes of Eisai and Myōzen, is preferred to its current, post-pilgrimage state of deterioration. China almost always takes priority over Japan (an exception is no. 4.12, which praises Japanese supporters for not lavishing monks with donations that may spoil them), but Chinese Buddhism is also divided into varying degrees of authenticity. Mount T'ien-t'ung rules supreme, yet, with the exception of Ju-ching and Hung-chih (who gets one mention, cited earlier) and several T'ang masters such as Hsüeh-feng, it is the generally sincere though anonymous monks with whom Dōgen has instructive conversations whom he prefers to elite abbots and priests. Furthermore, the criticisms of this period are not partisan in the sense of attacking a particular person or lineage, as will be found in some of the writings from the middle middle period.

The "Senjō" fascicle from the same year as "Senmen," which similarly deals with the topic of cleaning (washing and wiping), is interesting because it begins with a kōan that is also cited in *Mana Shōbōgenzō* case 101 as well as in the "Immo" and "Hensan" fascicles. A monk practices for eight years to understand the master's teaching about enlightenment. When asked if practice and realization are necessary conditions since enlightenment is nondual and inexpressible, the key line of dialogue is the monk's response: "It is not that practice and realization are not necessary, but the state [of enlightenment] can never be defiled by them"; it is said that after this dialogue he practiced for another eight years. The reply draws a connection between rites of purification associated with hygiene or physical cleaning that is obviated by the metaphysical condition of purity or innate spiritual cleansing beyond defilement.[15] This is the kind of view that Critical Buddhism takes to task for its shades of original enlightenment ideology.

In any case, *Tenzokyōkun* is the composition that makes most advantageous use of citations, interpretations, and allusions to kōans in support of the discipline of *shingi* by putting a special emphasis on the attitude or state of mind of the chief cook rather than on just his actions. According to Collcutt, "In his regulations, Dōgen always explains not only what should be done but how and why it should be done. He emphasizes a constant mindfulness that makes even the simplest of actions, whether washing the face, cleaning rice, or cutting vegetables, as conducive to Zen enlightenment as meditation, prayer, or sutra reading."[16] While citing the *Ch'an-yüan ch'ing-kuei*, the text evokes kōan cases, including one involving Tung-shan.[17] Perhaps more significantly, it also puts forward several interesting dialogues Dōgen had with two cooks from Mount T'ien-t'ung and Mount A-yü-wang during the early part of his stay in China, especially one that concludes with the cook's admonition, "Nothing concealed throughout the universe!" In that sense, Dōgen invented his own kōan case or at least reported new ones, a tendency that despite all his creativity is not repeated in writings from subsequent periods.

Diversity of the Early Kōan Texts

The *shingi* and kōan material is not merged again until the extensive discussion of a couple of dozen cases in the introductory section of *Chiji shingi* in 1249. By the end of the early middle period, however, it is clear that commenting on kōans is the main focus of the *Shōbōgenzō*. How did Dōgen come to demonstrate virtuosity with kōan commentary, and what were the steps that led in this direction? Stepping back to view the mid-1230s, we find that the *Shōbōgenzō zuimonki* has a mixed message on the use of kōans in relation to other aspects of Zen practice. On the one hand, there are several prominent passages that criticize kōans, such as no. 2.13, which maintains they are a distraction, and no. 6.27, which insists that *zazen* is the only true path whereas kōans make enlightenment more distant. However, positive assessments appear in nos. 3.20 and 6.23, both of which indicate that concentration on a case is conducive to the path. Furthermore, this text is notable for citing several cases, including "Pai-chang's wild fox" and "Nan-ch'üan kills the cat" in no. 2.4, "Matsu polishing the brick" in no. 3.28, "Chih-t'i's one finger Zen" in no. 4.4, "Tung-shan's three pounds of flax" in no. 4.5, "the color of grass in Ch'eng-nan" in no. 5.2, and "jumping off the 100-foot pole" in no. 6.24.[18]

The role of kōans in the *Shōbōgenzō zuimonki* must be seen in light of other kōan texts from the period. Recent discoveries of several complete manuscripts of the three-volume *Mana Shōbōgenzō*, each volume containing 100 cases, have dramatically altered our understanding of Dōgen's approach to kōans throughout his career. For centuries there had been rumors but they were generally considered spurious despite the existence of several Tokugawa-era commentaries; then the middle section of the *Mana Shōbōgenzō* collection was discovered in 1934 at the Kanazawa Bunko Institute. In the 1980s several Muromachi manuscripts were found in various Sōtō temples, finally authenticating the text's status as Dōgen's first major work on kōans.[19] Composed in 1235, the *Mana Shōbōgenzō* introduces the title *Shōbōgenzō* (C. *Cheng-fa yen-*

tsang), borrowed from a collection of 600 cases produced by Ta-hui, whom Dōgen praises in *Shōbōgenzō zuimonki* and later severely criticizes; *Mana Shō-bōgenzō* is a list of traditional cases without commentary, but the majority of the cases in this collection became the basis for extensive prose and verse interpretations in later works. This development shows how Chinese kōan interpretations helped shape the hermeneutic method in Dōgen's subsequent writings, beginning with the *Eihei kōroku*, vol. 9, verse comments composed in 1236 and continuing with the *jishu* lectures in the 75-*Shōbōgenzō* of the middle period as well as the *jōdō* sermons in the *Eihei kōroku* volumes of the late period.

Now that the authenticity of the *Mana Shōbōgenzō* text is confirmed, the two main questions that have been addressed in recent scholarship pertain to the influences it reflected and generated: (1) what was the major source, from which Dōgen selected his choices, from among the various Sung Ch'an records containing the anecdotes and dialogues that form the basis for almost all kōans, and (2) what was the purpose of the *Mana Shōbōgenzō* and its impact on Dōgen's other writings that contain kōan commentaries?

The question about sources is important for an understanding of the influences Dōgen received in China as well as how he viewed the nature of the transmission to Japan. As the first disseminator of kōans in the history of Japanese Zen, who brought back the "One Night *Blue Cliff Record*," Dōgen has a paramount role. Interestingly enough, the *Mana Shōbōgenzō* does not actually contain any kōans corresponding to those in the *Blue Cliff Record* (*Pi-yen lu*, 1128).[20] Like the compilers of the major Sung collections, the *Ts'ung-jung lu* (J. *Shōyōroku*, 1224) and the *Wu-men-kuan* (J. *Mumonkan*, 1228), Dōgen culled kōan cases directly from transmission of the lamp writings. According to Kagamishima Genryū and Kawamura Kōdō, the primary source for the *Mana Shōbōgenzō*, as for the Chinese collections, was the first of a long series of transmission texts, the *Ching-te ch'uan-teng lu* (J. *Keitoku dentōroku*, 1004), a conservative work in terms of style but a breakthrough in content in encompassing masters representing the multiple branches of Ch'an. The *Ching-te ch'uan-teng lu* was written on an imperial commission and consists of hagiographical materials covering, selectively, more or less the entire lineage of patriarchs in a refined, baroque style.[21]

However, as was indicated in chapter 3, Ishii Shūdō (and Ishii Seijun) argue that the main source was a different transmission of the lamp text, the *Tsung-men tung-yao chi* (J. *Shūmon tōyōshū*, c.1100, variously dated 1093 or 1130).[22] The *Tsung-men tung-yao chi*, which was the model for the *Tsung-men lien-teng hui-yao* (J. *Shūmon rentōeyō*, 1166), is much better known because of the role it played in the Japanese Rinzai sect's canon; it was composed not for official reasons but as a study tool in monastic training. It is a rather unconventional representative of the transmission of the lamp genre in limiting the hagiographical passages to the opening sections. The remainder of the voluminous text contains an extensive listing of kōans minus either historical background material or philosophical commentary.

The *Tsung-men tung-yao chi* was the main transmission of the lamp text consulted by the Huang-lung (J. Ōryō) school of the Rinzai sect in which Eisai became the first Japanese patriarch, and it is possible to imagine that Dōgen was influenced by this work during the time of his early, pre-China studies at Kenninji temple, founded by Eisai in Kyoto. Another theory is that there was an edition containing the *Ching-te ch'uan-teng lu* and the *Tsung-men tun-yao chi* that was widely distributed at the port city of Ning-po, and that Dōgen encountered it as soon as he arrived in China. The bottom line of the controversy, regardless of how it might be resolved, is that Dōgen inherited a rich, expansive body of traditional kōan cases (*kosoku-kōan*) that was shared by different texts and schools but that also gave rise to diverse and often highly factionalized interpretations and styles of composition.

There is an even more complex dispute, as is indicated in Table 24, in regard to the purpose of the *Mana Shōbōgenzō*, or why and for whom the text was compiled. Kagamishima and Ishii Seijun maintain that Dōgen collected the *Mana Shōbōgenzō* for instructional purposes and that it lacks commentary because it was used in a setting of private, individual teaching sessions so that no written comments were required. It was not until the following years that Dōgen realized that he needed to record his kōan interpretations for posterity, either by writing them out prior to oral delivery or by having his remarks transcribed by disciples. According to Kagamishima, the *Mana Shōbōgenzō* was intended specifically for Jakuen, the Chinese monk who had been a fellow disciple of Ju-ching. Jakuen came to Japan as a follower of Dōgen in the early 1230s and probably expected the teaching there to resemble the Sung style.

But Ishii Seijun, citing a passage from a *hōgo* in the *Eihei kōroku* (8.4h), probably from the early 1230s, maintains that the *Mana Shōbōgenzō* was not targeting any particular person but was a base for giving instructions on kōan learning to a wide variety of followers, including advanced monks, novices, and laypersons, most of whose identities are no longer known.[23] On the other hand, Kawamura and Ishii Shūdō see the *Mana Shōbōgenzō* as part of Dōgen's preparations for writing elaborate kōan commentarial texts. For Kawamura (as well as Tsunoda Tairyū), the *Mana Shōbōgenzō* can be regarded as a series of notes or memos Dōgen kept in preparing for the *Shōbōgenzō*. Ishii Shūdō points out that it is also necessary to consider the role of the *Eihei kōroku* vol. 9's verse comments (*juko*) on kōans written just one year after the *Mana* as a bridge linking the *Mana Shōbōgenzō* and the 75-*Shōbōgenzō* texts. Of the 90 cases included in the *Eihei kōroku* vol. 9, 65 appear first in the *Mana Shōbōgenzō*.[24] Following up on the notion of bridge texts, Ishii Seijun also emphasizes that many of the kōans cited in the *Mana Shōbōgenzō* and *Eihei kōroku* vol. 9 appear in the early *jōdō* sermons included in *Eihei kōroku* vol. 1 as well as the *Shōbōgenzō zuimonki*.[25]

TABLE 24. *Mana Shōbōgenzō* Sources and Purposes

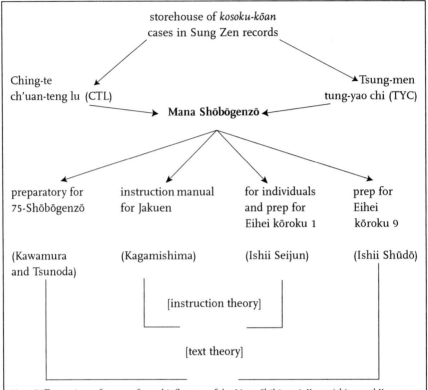

storehouse of *kosoku-kōan*
cases in Sung Zen records

Ching-te
ch'uan-teng lu (CTL)

Tsung-men
tung-yao chi (TYC)

Mana Shōbōgenzō

preparatory for
75-Shōbōgenzō

instruction manual
for Jakuen

for individuals
and prep for
Eihei kōroku 1

prep for
Eihei
kōroku 9

(Kawamura
and Tsunoda)

(Kagamishima)

(Ishii Seijun)

(Ishii Shūdō)

[instruction theory]

[text theory]

Note: Different views of sources for and influences of the *Mana Shōbōgenzō*. Kagamishima and Kawamura agree on CTL as the main source of cases, but the former believes the text was created for Jakuen and the latter along with Tsunoda sees it as preparatory for the 75-*Shōbōgenzō*; Ishii Seijun and Ishii Shūdō maintain that TYC is the main source, either aimed for individual instruction or as preparatory for *Eihei kōroku*, vol. 9.

A compromise view combining the insights of the four scholars sees the *Mana Shōbōgenzō* as the beginning of a long process in which Dōgen was crafting a variety of texts appropriate to the different levels and perspectives of his followers. During this period he was joined by two key disciples—in addition to Jakuen—who would go on to be the main editors and interpreters throughout his career and beyond his lifetime: Ejō, whose editing credits include the *Shōbōgenzō zuimonki* as well as the 75-*Shōbōgenzō* and 12-*Shōbōgenzō* and part of the *Eihei kōroku* texts; and Senne, whose background was in Tendai thought and who edited several of the mid-1230s works, including *Eihei kōroku* vol. 1 and *Eihei kōroku* vol. 9. After Dōgen's death, Senne became the main commentator on the 75-*Shōbōgenzō;* his works interpreting the text helped give it a prominent position in the history of Sōtō studies.

It is also important to keep in mind the increasing numbers of disciples who arrived once the Kōshōji Monks Hall was opened. Although before this phase Dōgen might have had time for private tutoring sessions, as Kagamishima and Ishii Seijun suggest, after 1236 he needed to find ways to address larger audiences. First he tried his hand at *kanbun* verse comments, yet he never wrote *jakugo* commentary, the "capping phrase" or layer of interlinear verses commenting on other prose and poetic comments that are featured in the *Pi-yen lu* and *Ts'ung-jung lu*, as well as in the works of leading Rinzai masters in Japan such as Daitō.[26] Again, the absences are telling, for Dōgen also never wrote Sung-style prose commentary (C. *nien-ku*, J. *nenko*) on kōans, and after the experiment of *Eihei kōroku* vol. 9 he did not return to the *juko* style. It is possible that Dōgen was not fully confident in his ability to create certain commentarial styles in literary Chinese, although throughout his career he did compose other styles of *kanbun* poetry, contained in *Eihei kōroku* vol. 10, emphasizing lyrical, natural, and meditative themes. The sermons in *Eihei kōroku* vols. 1–7 also contain some *kanbun* verse commentaries on the main lectures.

Seven of the ten *Shōbōgenzō* fascicles composed in 1239 and 1240 highlight the role of kōans, and two of these emphasizing the role of nature deserve special mention for their vision of religious training. One is "Sansuikyō" on "Mountains and Rivers Sutras," which is highly critical of Sung misunderstandings and presents a theory of interpretation that refutes the view that kōans are absurd, nonsensical utterances, instead of seeing them as expressions of realization.[27] The other is "Keisei sanshoku," which opens by citing a famous Ch'an verse on the "Sound of Streams, Colors of Mountains," but in the concluding sections veers from the topic of naturalism to emphasize an important but overlooked element of *shingi*, that is, the role of repentance, in the concluding sections of the fascicle.[28] This emphasis foreshadows and shows a cross-period consistency with the themes of karmic causality stressed in the 12-*Shōbōgenzō* and other writings of the late late period.

Transition to the Middle Middle Period

The middle middle period is characterized by intense creativity coupled with the emergence of a partisan polemical standpoint in promoting the value of Ju-ching while denigrating the approaches of rival lineages—two tendencies that cannot easily be separated; it encompassed the move to Echizen and all of the transitional modes this represented. The mysterious and seemingly oxymoronic quality of this remarkably dynamic yet controversial phase has spawned numerous theories regarding the question of change or continuity in Dōgen's approach; this issue will be explored in the next chapter.

During this period Dōgen did not create more kōan collections—unless the 75-*Shōbōgenzō* is considered one!—but he continued to cite numerous cases, dialogues, and biographical anecdotes culled from transmission of the lamp records and other Sung Ch'an sources as the basis for interpreting various issues and problems in Zen theory and practice. The Decline and Renewal theories do not adequately track the evolution or assess the variety of Dōgen's literary styles.

The *jōdō* style, in which the master addresses the congregation from the high seat in the Dharma Hall, was delivered in the daytime according to a strictly prescribed schedule on New Years, new and full moon, Vesak, and other ceremonial occasions, including memorials.[29] This kind of sermon was usually rather brief and often included a demonstrative gesture. Among the records of T'ang leaders such as Lin-chi and Te-shan there are many examples of masters striking, shouting at, or slapping disciples, or of precocious followers performing these acts on their teachers. In the *Eihei kōroku*, Dōgen sometimes draws circles in the air or throws down his stick or fly-whisk. The *jōdō* can also include formal verse comments on kōans, but in general they do not so much explain or interpret kōan cases as allude to their meaning by evoking a key phrase, such as, to cite some of Dōgen's favorites, "mind itself is Buddha" from a Ma-tsu dialogue or the "red-bearded barbarian" from a Pai-chang dialogue.

As was discussed in chapter 1, the various informal lecture styles delivered in vernacular are known variously as *shōsan*, the only one mentioned in the *Ch'an-yüan ch'ing-kuei*, and *fusetsu, bansan,* or *jishu* styles, which also followed a schedule though not as strictly. These lectures were often delivered at night in the Abbot's Quarters or some other convenient place to a select group of either advanced disciples seeking intensive instruction or more introductory students. Lay disciples might be in attendance at either the formal or informal addresses, and it was more likely that wealthy patrons would come to hear the public, ceremonial *jōdō* and that those interested in philosophy would attend the private, pedagogical *jishu*.

The majority of colophons refer to the 75-*Shōbōgenzō* fascicles as *jishu*, which literally means making pointers before a general assembly, but this term really indicates a hybrid style that is at once consistent with yet somewhat different from the way the term is used in Sung collections, for several reasons. The informal lecture styles offered a forum for lengthier and more detailed discourses on the intricacies of kōan interpretation and often featured paradoxical wordplay and other literary techniques used in a poetic atmosphere, sometimes including the composition of verse. As is demonstrated in the recorded sayings of Ta-hui and numerous other Sung masters, the informal sermons often gave the abbot a chance to present in a frank, caustic manner, comments that were fiercely critical of rival or erroneous viewpoints, though these generally targeted doctrines and did not identify particular persons. However, generally in Chinese works these sermons were not extensively recorded, and apparently they would not have been composed, delivered, edited, redelivered, reedited, and so on, as was the pattern with numerous *Shōbōgenzō* fascicles, which is what makes this such an exciting and important text in the transition from Ch'an to Zen. Another difference with Ch'an sources is that by composing in *kana*, Dōgen allowed for an additional level of wordplay in commenting on the Japanese pronunciation of Chinese script, comparable to the interlinear function of *jakugo* in *kanbun* texts.

By writing thematic essays that used kōan cases as illustrative of doctrinal topics rather than as the exclusive focus of analysis—thereby inverting the typical structure of kōan collections, featuring a case and employing philosophy and hagiography as commentary—Dōgen developed a teaching style that recaptured the original, spontaneous flavor of dialogical exchanges that form the core of most kōans. He eliminated hermeneutic, epistemological, or psychological distances between interpreter and the material being interpreted as well as the disciples receiving instruction. This style afforded a direct, dynamic interplay with the sources—but not with persons, unless the audience of monks would be considered as constituting this sector—neither merely enunciating nor pronouncing judgment on kōans but transmitting them with a genuine sense of give-and-take. In so doing, Dōgen entered into the Alice-in-Wonderland-like, upside down, duplicitous world of disingenuous blasphemy, in which insults are praise and slaps are gestures of kindness, and like his Sung predecessors, he often deliberately revised or altered the source dialogues with creative, critical comments about what the original participant could, should, or would have said in response to probing queries.

Historical Criticisms of the Decline Theory

Because of the creative literary and philosophical skills they evince, the writings of the middle middle period—although not identified as such—have long been viewed by sectarian scholars and modern philosophers such as Tanabe Hajime and Nishitani Keiji as the supreme accomplishments that established Dōgen's reputation.[30] According to the Decline Theory, however, the period as a whole was marked by a stark reversal from the universal outlook in Dōgen's early works compounded by a tendency toward strident partisan polemic following the Echizen migration. The Decline Theory, by showing how Dōgen singled out specific lineages for harsh criticism while lavishly praising Ju-ching, is a good corrective to apologetic approaches that see the 75-*Shōbōgenzō* only as a pristine, autonomous expression of philosophy unconditioned by the vicissitudes of historical circumstance. For example, Table 8 in chapter 2 shows the extent to which *Shōbōgenzō* fascicles targeted apparent rivals among the Ch'an schools. Yet the question remains whether the theory goes too far in charging that Dōgen, "late and sudden[ly]," developed a "startling new doctrine" that is "vexing" because it reveals a formerly eminent Zen master who had slumped into a deep "depression" or even "sinility" that clouded all the words and deeds for the last major segment of his life.[31]

Despite its attempt to stress the role of history over pure abstraction, the Decline Theory is plagued by a problematic approach to historical issues in several respects: (1) a misrepresentation of the chronology of the highly compressed period of the 75-Shōbōgenzō writing and an inconsistency about when the late period began in contrast to the early works, which result in (2) a one-sided, selective reading of multileveled religious texts that also reflects (3) a weddedness to a reflexive polarized understanding of the reasons behind the Echizen migration and a tendency to interpolate psychological motives for complex, ambiguous historical situations, leading finally to (4) a failure to recognize or interpret the full rage of writings in the late, post-Shōbōgenzō corpus.

First the Decline Theory stumbles in misrepresenting the chronology of the composition of the 75-Shōbōgenzō, as is indicated in the following comment:

> This collection, widely regarded as Dōgen's magnum opus and a masterpiece of religious writing, is often treated as a single work, but it must be remembered that it is not more than a random collection—or more properly, several such collections—of independent texts, and that the composition of these texts, the bulk of which were first presented in the form of lectures, spans a period of some two decades, covering almost the entirety of Dōgen's teaching career.[32]

This comment is correct in its assessment of the dispersed and fragmentary nature of the text, but the remark that it is "not more than a random collection" because it spanned "a period of some two decades" is too strong. As was shown in chapter 2, it is technically true that "Genjōkōan" was revised as late as 1252 and that the final jishu lecture contained in the 12-Shōbōgenzō "Hachidainingaku" was written in 1253. However, the implication that there was a prolonged time span is vitiated by the fact that 63 fascicles of the 75-Shōbōgenzō were written between 1240 and spring 1244; as is highlighted by Table 25, all but three fascicles (or 4%) are from 1239 to 1246 and only six were written at Eiheiji during a single year.

Therefore the following remark by Dumoulin is also misleading: "The work he did in Kōshōji shows Dōgen at the peak of his life. Toward the end of the decade we see signs of a change in the making."[33] The problem here is that the "peak," which refers to fascicles such as "Raihaitokuzui," which is favorable to women, did not actually occur until 1240–1241, when the "end of the decade . . . change" would have already taken place. Dumoulin is also problematic in saying that Dōgen "fell into a depression . . . [or] dark time he was going through. The year that Dōgen spent in Kippōji marked a low point of his life and a break in the quality of his literary pursuits as well. It is not that there

TABLE 25. 75-Fascicle *Shōbōgenzō* (fascicle number in parenthesis)

1233 [2]	Makahannyaharamitsu (2), Genjōkōan (1)[a]
1238 [1]	Ikkya myōju (7)
1239 [3]	Sokushinzebutsu (5), Senjō (54), Senmen (50)
1240 [6]	Raihaitokuzui (28), Keiseisanshoku (25), Shoakumakusa (31), Sansuikyō (29), Uji (20), Den'e (32)
1241 [9]	Busso (52), Shisho (39), Shinfukatoku (8), Kokyō (19), Kankin (30), Busshō (3), Gyōbutsuigi (6), Bukkyō [Buddhist Teachings] (34), Jinzū (35)
1242 [16]	Daigo (10), Zazenshin (12), Butsukōjōji (26), Immo (17), Gyōji (16), Kaiinzanmai (13), Juki (21), Kannon (18), Arakan (36), Hakujushi (40), Kōmyō (15), Shinjingakudō (4), Muchūsetsumu (27), Dōtoku (33), Gabyō (24), Zenki (22)[a]
1243 [22]	Tsuki (23), Kūge (14), Kobusshin (9),[b] Kattō (38) (*Move to Echizen in seventh month*), Sangaiyuishin (41), Butsudō (44), Mitsugo (45), Shohō jissō (43), Bukkyō (Buddhist Sutras) (47), Mujōseppō (46), Menju (51), Hōsshō (48), Baika (53), Jippō (55), Kenbutsu (56),[c] Hensan (57),[c] Zazengi (11), Ganzei (58),[c] Kajō (59),[c] Ryūgin (61),[c] Sesshinsesshō (42), Darani (49)
1244 [10]	Soshiseiraii (62),[d] Udonge (64), Hotsumujōshin (63), Nyoraizenshin (65), Zanmai ōzanmai (66), Sanjūshichihon bodaibunpō (60), Tenbōrin (67), Jishō zanmai (69), Daishugyō (68), Shunjū (37)[d] (*last fascicle by 3/9*)
1245 [5]	Kokū (70), Ho-u (71), Ango (72), Tashintsū (73), Ōsakusendaba (74)
1246 [1]	Shukke (75)

1233–1243 (7/1) at Kōshōji; 1243–1244 at Kippōji; 1245–1246 at Daibutsuji/Eiheiji
[a] Delivered to laypersons
[b] At an outside temple
[c] At Yamashibudera
[d] At a mountain retreat

Note: A breakdown of when the 75-*Shōbōgenzō* fascicles were written to show how this activity was compressed into a few years, with the writing ending completely by 1246. The number in parenthesis after the title indicates the fascicle number, and the number in brackets after the date indicates the total compositions for the given year. Note that the fascicle number at times does and at times does not correspond to the sequence of composition. There may be some minor differences with comparable lists due to undated or rewritten manuscripts and to variant editions. For contents of the 12-fascicle *Shōbōgenzō*, see Table 7 in chapter 2.

are no valuable passages in the late books of the *Shōbōgenzō*, but the downturn is undeniable."[34]

The Decline Theory often cannot make up its mind about when the late period began, and it refers to fascicles written prior to Echizen as either "early" or "late" depending on whether or not they reflect a partisan outlook that substantiates the theory of a reversal in Dōgen's outlook. For example, Bielefeldt cites "Shisho" as a late fascicle even though it was composed in 1241. He also says that "Gyōji," a fascicle that is relatively free of polemic, was written "as late as 1242," but on the next page he refers to "Daigo," which is critical of Linchi, as being written "as early as . . . 1242."[35] The fact is that the late Echizen period, at least as the term is used by the Decline Theory, lasts a total of eight months, from the eighth month in 1243 when the migration was completed to the third month/ninth day in 1244 when construction of Daibutsuji began.

During this time 28 fascicles, or over one third of the entire 75-*Shōbōgenzō* corpus, were recorded primarily at the Kippōji and Yamashibudera temples, temporary rural hermitages where Dōgen and his followers holed up for a long winter hiatus. No more fascicles were written in 1244, and the six fascicles written in the following year or so (five in 1245 and one in 1246) do not exhibit the features that come under criticism. Thus it is certainly possible to view this brief period as a creative peak, perhaps the greatest in Dōgen's career, rather than as a time of decline. It was also the phase during which Dōgen created the bulk of his Japanese and Chinese poetry collections celebrating the natural splendor of Echizen, particularly the Mount Hakusan area.[36] In any case, just as the Decline Theory is vague about the extent of the early period, it leaves obscure the issue of the duration and termination of the "late" period. The question of why Dōgen abandoned the 75-*Shōbōgenzō* in the mid-1240s and concentrated on the *jōdō* sermons goes unnoticed and unaddressed. Furthermore, the Decline Theory does not deal with the fact that Dōgen cites Lin-chi in a very positive way in the 12-*Shōbōgenzō* "Shukke kukoku" (ed. 1255), which was written later than its version of what constitutes the late period. Also in a passage in *Eihei kōroku* 7.437 from the final years, Dōgen argues that "the unsurpassable right transmission of the buddhas and patriarchs is not delimited by a notion of a Zen sect."[37]

This is not to deny, however, that there are some 75-*Shōbōgenzō* passages that seem reprehensible for the way they treat Lin-chi, and especially Ta-hui; the most egregious example is "Jishō zanmai," which is disingenuously skeptical about the authenticity of the latter's transmission. We may appear to be begging the question. If the Decline Theory is basically correct in that the *Shōbōgenzō* is increasingly infected by strident polemic as Dōgen's thought continued to deteriorate, even if it is unclear about the date that the change of heart transpired, then perhaps its only mistake lies in failing to condemn the entire 75-*Shōbōgenzō* or the writings of the middle period both before and after the Echizen migration. However, the theory is undermined by several other aspects of its interpretation. First, it does not take into account that the nature of the *jishu* style, as evidenced by the recorded sayings texts of Ta-hui and other Sung Ch'an masters, fosters the kind of frank repudiation of opponents expressed by Dōgen. At the same time, the Decline Theory sometimes misses the playful, tongue-in-cheek tone of Dōgen's writing, as in a "Daishugyō" passage that casts doubt on the fox metamorphosis recorded in the "wild fox kōan" (*Wu-men kuan* case 2) by arguing that if all masters who made mistakes were so transformed, then Lin-chi, Te-Shan, and their followers would surely have been turned into vulpine shapes.[38]

But the main problem is that the theory tends to be overly selective with the material it considers deficient, often offering a one-sided reading that takes certain passages out of context and exaggerates their importance while suppressing other evidence. For example, the "Butsudō" fascicle is criticized for supporting the Tung-shan lineage leading to the founding of the Sōtō sect while refuting lineages stemming from Lin-chi that influenced the rivals Dōgen was trying to dissuade or convert.[39] But a close reading reveals that the real aim of the text, consistent with *Bendōwa*, is to show that the existence of true Zen is ontologically prior to fragmented genealogies, and it cites both Tung-shan and Lin-chi in parallel ways to emphasize that neither of the masters stressed the role of sectarian lineages, so that designations such as Rinzai school or Sōtō school are erroneous,[40] a notion confirmed by some historical studies of Sung Ch'an.[41] Similarly, the theory criticizes "Shisho" (written before the Echizen migration) for the way it scoffs at Lin-chi, but the fascicle really targets his "remote followers" (*onson*), who "nowadays" (*ima*) misrepresent their teacher; in other words, it warns against rogue factions rather than Lin-chi himself or his legitimate lineage.[42]

Although the sectarian approach was heightened at this juncture, in the "Butsudō" fascicle from 9.16.1243, during the period when Dōgen and his followers were staying in temporary hermitages in Echizen shortly after they left Kyoto, he emphasizes that Ju-ching's intention is to espouse not polarization, but rather an inclusive pansectarian view:

> My late master, the old buddha, is the first to have shown concern over this decline [in Ch'an]. In a *jōdō* semon he said to the assembly, "There are monks today who talk solely of there being differences in the customs of the lineages of Yün-men, Fa-yen, We-yang, Lin-chi, and Ts'ao-tung, and that these schools are different from each other. But this is far from the Buddha Dharma or the Way of the patriarchs."[43]

In general, the Decline Theory does not discuss how the passages in question are contained in fascicles that deal with a variety of themes, including the role of language and the meaning of time, and that offer diverse messages concerning the issue of what constitutes authentic, legitimate Dharma transmission. In "Shisho," "Menju," and other fascicles Dōgen is concerned to warn his followers against relying on either false prophets, such as priests not ordained in China, or on the external paraphernalia of religiosity, whether sutras or relics. This was not necessarily an inappropriate claim given the religious climate in early Kamakura Japan, especially in the countryside, and these sentiments echo the teachings of Lin-chi (not to mention the Buddha).

The best correction to the Decline Theory is to explore various reasons for Dōgen's move to Echizen. Doing this in the next chapter will open up multiple possible interpretations of the rich diversity of writings and views of Ju-ching and Chinese Ch'an that emerged in the middle middle and subsequent periods, as expressed in *Shōbōgenzō*'s *jishu* and *Eihei kōroku*'s *jōdō* sermons.

5

The Middle Period, Part II

The Echizen Cycle

This chapter continues the discussion of the middle middle period, including Dōgen's move to Echizen and the production of the *Shō-bōgenzō*. Questioning the Decline Theory's view of the sequence and content of texts brings us back to the issue that forms the linchpin of the theory: the question of why Dōgen left Kyoto for Echizen in the summer of 1243, perhaps the most significant and also the most mysterious event during the midpoint of his career. There is not a single reference or attempt to explain the move in Dōgen's own writings, so an explanation must be reconstructed from a variety of sources, some more reliable than others. Rather than our seeking a simple or single understanding of the matter, it is important to survey and assess in a thick-descriptive way a conflux of interlocking events that took place in the early 1240s. These apparently caused a major sense of upheaval that must have led to the shift in Dōgen's thinking about Ju-ching and a new emphasis on the Ts'ao-tung school lineage of China in establishing his movement in Japan.

One of the important features of the middle middle subperiod is that, just as the *Shōbōgenzō* reached a peak of philosophical creativity, some of the writings were also characterized by what appears to be excessively shrill partisan rhetoric in putting forward the model of Ju-ching's patriarchy while denigrating rival lineages. This stance may be the reason that certain fascicles were not included in the *60-Shōbōgenzō*. Therefore it is important to examine closely which fascicles were composed at Kippōji and Yamashibudera in Echizen, and how and why these came to be part of various versions of the *Shōbōgenzō*.

The third phase of the general middle period is the late middle subperiod (1244–1246), beginning with the construction of Daibutsuji in the spring of 1244. With the opening of the Dharma Hall that summer, the delivery of the 75-*Shōbōgenzō*'s *jishu*-style sermons began to subside as just six new fascicles were composed, several of them focusing on monastic rules. Thereafter, *jōdō* sermons, which had been on hiatus during the move when a main hall was not available, became the primary form of expression in the new temple. In addition, *Bendōhō*, one of the chapters included in what eventually became the *Eihei shingi*, was composed. Recognizing that this period was a productive phase, albeit somewhat limited in scope, marked by a transition to new forms of writing and religiosity rather than by a lack of creativity, helps defeat one-sided evaluations in the Decline and Renewal theories. Both views tend to obscure a balanced approach to understanding diverse yet consistent developments in Dōgen's career by overestimating the importance of particular texts isolated from their respective field-of-discourse context.[1]

Exploring Reasons for the Move to Echizen

The main corrective to the Decline Theory is the need to understand the complex reasons for the move to Echizen as well as the significance of developments in the post-move periods. The move is portrayed in the Decline Theory as a disappointing, even devastating defeat for the aspiring and ambitious Zen master, who had been on the verge of great success in the capital and was probably accompanied by only a handful of disciples and forced to evangelize a reluctant, uneducated rural audience. The Decline Theory has made an extremely valuable contribution in showing that Dōgen's writing at the time of the migration was motivated by, or at least cannot be dissociated from, the political factors in an era in which exile to Echizen and other remote provinces was by no means atypical.[2] But does this lead to a conclusion that a partisan drive lay at the heart of much of the 75-*Shōbōgenzō* rhetoric?

Recent studies in Japan have shown that the reasons behind the transition need to be explored in depth, and no doubt they involve factors reflecting the impact of Chinese Ch'an in addition to Dōgen's relations with Japanese Buddhism and culture. The problem is that the historical events are complex and poorly recorded; furthermore, some of the Decline Theory's assumptions are undermined by recent research. For example, a political text supposedly penned by Dōgen in 1241 to plead the Sōtō cause before a local official, the *Gokoku shōbōgi*, which is the main work traditionally cited to account for the move based on persecution by the dominant Tendai factions, now appears to be either apocryphal or a fiction. There are no extant editions, and it is never referred to in other writings by Dōgen or in his biographies, only briefly in external histories such as a citation in a fourteenth-century collection of Tendai texts that erroneously indicates that the year of the move was 1246.[3] No other corroborating references to such an attack have been found.

It seems that Dōgen and a band of followers, who may have been a small, dedicated group or a larger caravan of about 100 including lay assistants or servants, departed Kyoto by foot for a complex journey on the seventh day of the seventh month. They traveled from Fukakusa, located southeast of the capital, around the tip of Lake Biwa, and then north through the provincial barrier at Arachi. Passing through difficult mountain terrain, including the imposing 1,900-foot Kinobe Pass, they arrived in Echizen by 7.16.1243 after about eight or nine days of travel. Over the next months, the group of monks took up residence at temporary hermitages, including Kippōji, the main site, and Yamashibudera, which was used for about six weeks beginning in late fall. In the third month of 1244 construction began, and by the eighteenth day of the seventh month a permanent temple at first named Daibutsuji was completed, which included a Dharma Hall for the delivery of *jōdō* sermons resumed after a hiatus of over a year.

The move to Echizen is a black hole in that Dōgen's own writings provide no reference whatsoever by way of explanation, rationale, or even description for what seems in retrospect to be a dramatic departure from Kyoto. As Bodiford points out, "Three months later [than a sermon he gave outside Kōshōji for his patrons, the "Kobusshin" fascicle] Dōgen abandoned Kōshōji to lead his disciples to the mountains of rural Echizen. Nowhere in his writings does Dōgen suggest what reasons might have led to this drastic change in venue."[4] In examining the last fascicle and its colophon written before the move ("Kattō") as well as the first fascicle after it ("Sangai yuishin"), Bodiford notes that "neither text mentions any relocation." Nevertheless, he suggests that "this move was not an endeavor undertaken lightly." The summer retreat (*ango*) was held in full that year at Kōshōji, and the smoothness in completing the transition despite an arduous journey indicates that advance preparations had been made. This evidence tends to undermine assertions that the move was done not deliberately but rather quickly in response to an attack stemming from religious and political hostility.

We simply do not know, and we will most likely never discover, what Dōgen or others were thinking. Dōgen may have felt frustration and disillusionment when he first moved—if so, Dumoulin's characterization of his state of depression has merit, although in the end it is nothing more than a psychological interpretation based on inference and speculation. In contrast to this standpoint, however, the only autobiographical reference, an *Eihei kōroku* passage (2.128), suggests the opposite view: that with the founding of Daibutsuji/Eiheiji, Dōgen experienced exhilaration and joy at the opportunity to preach the Dharma as he had learned it in China.[5]

In the spirit of thick description, we can identify several factors that contributed to the move as shown in Table 26. One event was the 1241 mass

TABLE 26. Factors and Conditions Involved in the Echizen Move

1. 1241: Conversion of Ekan, Gikai, Gien, Gijun, and other Daruma school monks
2. 1241–1243: Return of Enni Ben'en from China beginning in 1235 and abbacy at Tōfukuji
3. 1241–1243: Increasing connections and preaching at samurai patron Hatano Yoshishige residence ("Zenki") and temple, Rokuharamitsuji ("Kobusshin")
4. 1242: Receiving *Ju-ching yü-lu* from China and perhaps sense of disappointment
5. No reference or explanation of move in Dōgen's works before or after, including the "Kattō" and "Sangai yuishin" fascicles produced in the intercalary seventh month
6. Main source about Dōgen's decision, *Gokoku shōbōgi*, now discredited
7. Takes pathway through Kinobe Pass with a handful of followers or perhaps up to 100 in entourage from 7.7.1243 to 7.16.1243
8. Eleven fascicles not included in 60-*Shōbōgenzō* that contain direct, fundamental criticism of other Zen masters and teachings based on practice or *gyō* (See Table 8 in chapter 2)
9. Much later, an association is made in the Sōtō tradition between the sacred peak of Mount Hakusan and Dōgen's copying the "One Night *Blue Cliff Record*" when leaving China

conversion to Dōgen's movement on the part of former members of the Daruma school. The Daruma school had been proscribed in 1194, yet although the ban was never officially lifted, its membership persisted despite ongoing persecution and the burning of its temples. Most of the remaining disciples joined the Kōshōji community from their residence at the last stronghold of Hajakuji temple, located very close to where Eiheiji was established. The effort to attract former followers of Nōnin and appeal to monks from diverse backgrounds may have caused Dōgen to forge a new approach to sectarian identity based in part on the proclamation of a separation and difference from the Tekuang lineage that gave transmission to Nōnin.

As Imaeda Aishin points out, before Dōgen ever practiced Zen but had experienced his Doubt about original enlightenment at the Tendai center at Enryakuji on Mount Hiei, according to traditional biographies, he studied under abbot Kōin at Onjōji,[6] stemming from the lineage of Enchin, a follower of Ennin, the famous pilgrim who traveled to China and kept a journal of his adventures in the ninth century. According to Imaeda—and it must be pointed out that this part of his argument seems not to be either supported or refuted by mainstream scholarship in Kamakura Buddhist studies—the branch of the Tendai church in Hakusan, centered at Heisenji temple (or Hakusan Tendai), was affiliated with Onjōji.[7] Several of the Daruma school followers who joined Dōgen at Kōshōji studied at Hajakuji near Heisenji and may well have passed through Onjōji on their way to Fukakusa. As shown in Table 27, there was an Enryakuji-Rinzai axis and an Onjōji/Heisenji-Sōtō axis, which may have influenced Dōgen's change in attitude and in any case created a connection with Hakusan religiosity.

Another factor was the return of Enni from China in 1241 and his being awarded in 1243 the stewardship of the Rinzai school's Tōfukuji temple, which

TABLE 27 Relation Between Tendai Factions

Sanmon Tendai at Enryakuji on Mount Hiei	Jimon Tendai at Onjōji in Otsu	Hakusan Tendai at Heisenji on Mount Hakusan
	Rivalry Alliance	
Dōgen left at 14 and may have remained in conflict due to its later support for Tōfukuji	Dōgen visited at 15 and perhaps maintained a lasting affiliation	Location of Daruma school followers at Hajakuji near Hatano estates, and site of Daibutsuji/Eiheiji

had the sanction of the Tendai school, an element of support Dōgen lacked in his leadership of the Sōtō school, a situation perhaps causing him to be demoralized. A third factor is the rise in importance of Hatano Yoshishige and his clan as the primary patrons of Dōgen. At the time of the move, Hatano was more powerful than his previous supporters yet still limited in his capacity to influence political affairs in the capital. Dōgen's early patronage at Kōshōji was limited to a minor nobleman, Kujō Noriie, and a nun, Shōgaku, who were both probably distant relatives. Hatano was a *bakufu* retainer who served on the council at the Rokuhara district, the major political unit in Kyoto, very near Fukakusa, where Dōgen occasionally preached to his group; he gave at least two recorded lectures for Hatano, one at his residence ("Zenki") and one at the Rokuharamitsuji temple located near Kenninji in central Kyoto ("Kobusshin").

Hatano's family served as the military land-stewards (*jitō*) for the Echizen estates of the Konoe family of the Shihi domain, affiliated with the the Miidera line temple of Saishōkō'in, whom Dōgen presumably met in Kyoto. Hatano also had close ties with Kenninji and Miidera temples as well as Hakusan Tendai, based at Heisenji. Perhaps he and his family, including cousin Kakunen, another Dōgen patron who held land in the town of Shihi and supported the construction of Eiheiji on a family-owned estate, played some role in forging a greater alliance between the Miidera/Jimon and Heisenji factions of Tendai. Eiheiji was established with a structure independent of government supervision, with financial support from the patrons and labor assistance from a community of lay participants in repentance and other rituals. Hatano also sponsored Dōgen's visit to Kamakura in 1247–1248, another key feature of Dōgen's traditional biography that is questioned by some modern scholars.

A fourth factor contributing to the move was a new estimation of Ju-ching following Dōgen's receiving a copy of the mentor's recorded sayings that had recently been edited and brought from China. According to *Eihei kōroku* 1.105 from 8.6.1242 (Senne, the compiler of this volume of the *Eihei kōroku*, notes,

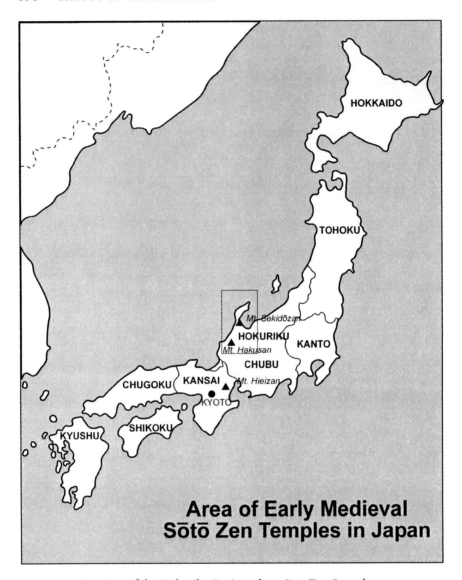

FIGURE 15. Location of the Hokuriku Region where Sōtō Zen Spread

Note: Spread occurred after the founding of Eiheiji in the vicinity of Hakusan, the sacred mountain near Echizen province. Also locates two other important sacred mountains: Hieizan (Mount Hiei), the center of Tendai Buddhism, and Sekidōzan in the Noto peninsula.

"Many words were not recorded," which suggests that Dōgen spoke more but only wrote down what is included here):

> The teacher Dōgen stood up, lifted the recorded sayings [of Ju-ching] above the incense, and said: Great Assembly, this is T'ien-t'ung [Ju-ching], who has leaped over the eastern ocean, causing great waves

to astonish fish and dragons. But even though fish and dragons are astonished, they do not hide themselves. How shall we express this? Have these words and sayings previously arrived here? If you say they have not yet been spoken, it is essential that the pure great ocean assembly verify [Ju-ching's sayings].[8]

As was indicated earlier, a common theory is that Dōgen apparently felt that this version gave an inadequate picture of Ju-ching's teaching and he wanted to enhance and revise the image of his mentor. It is interesting to note, however, that a few months before the arrival of the record, Ju-ching was evoked by Dōgen to reinforce sectarian perspectives. For example, in "Gyōji" (part 2) from 4.5.1242 Dōgen quotes his mentor, in a passage that is not found in his recorded sayings, as severely criticizing Te-kuang:

> In former days, I hung my traveling staff at Mount Ching when the head monk was Fo-chao Te-kuang. In the lecture hall, he said to his disciples, "About Zen Buddhism you should not seek another's views, but try to realize it for yourselves." So saying, he paid no attention whatsoever to what happened in the Monks Hall. The junior and senior monks were also unconcerned, and busied themselves with the reception of government officials. He was quite ignorant of the Buddha Dharma and was instead attached to fame and fortune. If we could, as he says, grasp the Buddha Dharma by ourselves, then why have the sharpest monks gone searching for a true teacher? Really, Te-kuang has never even experienced Zen. Now, in every area we find those who have not awakened their bodhi-seeking mind who are followers of Te-kuang. It is regrettable that the Buddha Dharma is not found among them.[9]

Dōgen comments, "When my late master spoke like this, Te-kuang's descendants were in the assembly but did not resent him for saying this." In the same fascicle he adds the following scathing critique of Ch'an monks outside his own lineage:

> Now in all parts of Sung China, the skinbags who profess to be Buddhist practitioners . . . are as numerous as rice, flax, bamboos, or reeds. I have never heard any of them except my late teacher persuade monks to the practice of the true *zazen*. . . . Some head monks of great temples are quite ignorant of Ju-ching. Although born in China in the cradle of civilization, they are akin to birds and beasts because they idle away their time and do not practice *zazen*. What a pity to mistake their wild talk for the teachings of Buddhas and Patriarchs.[10]

The various factors all contributed to creating a historical context, but they do not in themselves explain fully why Dōgen made the move, which was so monumental for his entire career and pattern of religious practice, at that particular time in his career. Did external forces compel him or did he go of his own free will? Was the move a sign of weakness in that he fled from a struggle to remain near the capital, or of strength because he was seeking a true Buddhist path of solitary contemplation? What alterations in his approach were either reflected by or a consequence of the move? There are no clear answers from the records of Dōgen or his biographers for what was apparently instigated for a variety of reasons. These range from Ju-ching's injunction to avoid secular corruption and Dōgen's desire to dwell in the lofty mountains to sectarian turf battles with the Rinzai and Daruma schools as well as patronage patterns that linked him to the Echizen area. However, speculation gives rise to different interpretations, often depending on the perspectives of the observers and the ideological or methodological agendas they represent. Is the move simply inexplicable, or are there actually almost too many factors that seem to apply?

The various reasons given to explain the move can be grouped into three main categories; they are the Withdrawal Hypothesis, which suggests Dōgen chose to leave the capital; the Desperation Hypothesis, which is a variation of the Decline Theory, emphasizing the effect of political turmoil; and the Hakusan Tendai and Hakusan Shinkō Hypotheses, focusing on institutional and indigenous religiosity associated with the premier sacred peak of the Echizen region. Each of the reasons can be criticized for overlooking or distorting a key historical element in Dōgen's career (see Table 28).

Withdrawal Hypothesis: Is Eiheiji "Mount T'ien-t'ung East"?

The traditional, sectarian explanation is that the move was motivated by Dōgen's pure longing to uphold Ju-ching's injunction to escape the confusion and turmoil of the capital (which is so eloquently described in Chōmei's Hōjōki of 1212) and to remain free from secular corruption by establishing an ideal monastic community in the natural splendor of Echizen. There he discovered what can be referred to as a mystical *axis mundi* in the remote mountain forests.[11] In support of the emphasis on renunciation from worldly connections, there are several prominent examples of teacher Ju-ching and disciple Dōgen expressing disdain for false monks, even within the upper echelons of the Buddhist hierarchy, who are prone to give in to temptation, greed, or longing for power rather than have a supreme dedication to pursue the Dharma. For instance, both Ju-ching and Dōgen declined the offer to wear the purple robe proffered by imperial authorities at key turning points in their careers. In texts written in Kyoto, Dōgen exhorts Zen practitioners to dwell among the crags and white rocks found only in secluded mountain landscapes (*Bendōwa*) and

TABLE 28. Possible Reasons for Dōgen's Move from Kyoto to Echizen

Withdrawal Hypothesis

Sectarian View: heeding Ju-ching's admonition to dwell in solitude away from secular corruption in remote mountains, even with few followers
Japanese Aesthetic View: yearning for a mountain hermitage in deep mountain forests, which provide a sanctuary from turmoil and setting for spiritual renewal
Criticism: Eiheiji is quite a different monastic setting than Mount T'ien-t'ung

Desperation Hypothesis

Skeptical Partisan View (Withdrawal Thesis—"Exile Mania"): escape from persecution by Tendai church and intimidation by emerging rival Rinzai Zen at Tōfukuji established by Enni near Kō-shō
Patterns of Patronage: land donated by samurai patron Hatano Yoshishige and clan linked to Hōjō regency
Criticism: disregards institutional developments at Eiheiji as high point of career

Hakusan Tendai and Hakusan Shinkō Hypotheses

Tendai Linkages: connections between Onjōji (Miidera) Tendai movement in Otsu near Kyoto and Heisenji Tendai in Mt. Hakusan (as opposed to Enryakuji Tendai on Mount Hiei)
Folk Religious View: attraction of Mt. Hakusan religiosity (Hakusan *shinkō*) and connections with proscribed Daruma school at Hajakuji whose followers joined Dōgen
Criticism: may be more relevant for post-Dōgen developments of Sōtō Zen

suggests that mountain abodes are the natural setting for Zen masters ("San-suikyō").[12]

According to *Hōkyōki* no. 10, Ju-ching admonishes, "You must first make your dwelling in steep mountains and dark valleys."[13] In a similar passage recorded in *Kenzeiki* he instructs, "Do not live near the capital or by rich and powerful persons. Avoid emperors, ministers and generals. Stay in the deep mountains far removed from worldly affairs and devote yourself to the education of young monks, even if you have only one disciple. Do not terminate the transmission I have given you."[14] Yet sectarian scholars have also long been well aware of the argument that Dōgen, as the leader of a new movement, was embroiled in a political conflict with the Tendai establishment on Mount Hiei and may, in fact, have been driven away from Kyoto. These scholars portray Dōgen sympathetically as a heroic victim who eventually rose above his opponents, in part through Hatano's patronage.

In his effort to gain a place for contemplation that was free of secular distractions, Dōgen may also have been inspired by the poetic tradition he had studied as a child, having been brought up with a late-Heian style aristocratic education. Japanese poetry, which was in part derived from Chinese aesthetics grounded in eremitic and reclusive traditions, celebrated the intense sense of privacy and solitude (*sabi*) that can be experienced only in secluded, natural areas. This was a theme well expressed in Dōgen's own verse composed in both Japanese and Chinese, as well as in *Shōbōgenzō* fascicles that evoke the serenity of the natural environment as the ideal backdrop for undisturbed ascetic meditation, including "Keisei sanshoku" and "Baika" (the latter written at Kippōji).

It is possible to imagine that Dōgen felt that only mountain seclusion would provide the unadorned simplicity needed to foster the path to enlightenment. According to one of Dōgen's Japanese *waka* poems, he never gave up a sense of longing for the refinement of the capital, whose beauty had an appeal that rivaled Echizen's:

Miyako ni wa	All last night and
Momiji shinuran	This morning still,
Okuyama no	Snow falling the deepest mountains;
Koyoi mo kesa mo	Ah, to the see autumn leaves
Arare furi keri.	Scattering in my home.[15]

Ienaga Saburō explains the Japanese view of nature as a mirror and a model for humans, an experience attained "in a secluded grass-thatched hut in the mountains (*yamazato*) where secular dust of worldly life does not reach," and nature has a supremely soteric (*kyūsai*) value.[16] Similar sentiments are expressed in a *kanbun* verse from this phase:

> For so long here without worldly attachments,
> I have renounced literature and writing;
> I may be a monk in a mountain temple,
> Yet still, I am moved in seeing gorgeous blossoms
> Scattered by the spring breeze,
> And hearing the warbler's lovely song—
> Let others judge my meager efforts.[17]

However, the Withdrawal Hypothesis argument is somewhat undermined by a careful consideration of the relation between Eiheiji as the pioneer Sōtō Zen temple and the Chinese Ch'an model on which it was supposedly in large part based. One of the main elements of traditional records of Dōgen's career is the notion that he established Eiheiji in the mid-1240s in the snowy mountains of Echizen province on the basis of the model he experienced while training at Mount T'ien-t'ung in China two decades before. As has been indicated, according to the *Hōkyōki* and *Kenzeiki*, he was admonished by his Chinese mentor Ju-ching to remain withdrawn from the corruption of mainstream society in a secluded natural setting. In "Shohō jissō," following an account of one of Ju-ching's spontaneous midnight sermons accompanied by a detailed description of the halls and platforms of Mount T'ien-t'ung, Dōgen refers to his "having crossed innumerable mountains and rivers" to reach the locale where Eiheiji was established.

From the traditional account, it would seem fair and appropriate to imagine that Mount T'ien-t'ung was the model for a remote, reclusive site for Eiheiji, which could be considered an eastward version of the Chinese Ch'an temple. However, considerations of georitual perspectives—that is, how the geographical settings of the respective sites seen in light of social environment and cultural context affect the implementation of ritual activities—indicate that although the temples have some common features, the differences and discrepancies in style, over and beyond basic cultural distinctions, are significant and even glaring. The following is a brief discussion of location, institutional history and styles of practice at the thirteenth-century temples.

A. LOCATION, LOCATION, LOCATION. Mount T'ien-t'ung is not situated in the secluded mountain forests, as were many Buddhist temples in China. Rather it is, first of all, close to the large cosmopolitan port area of Ning-po, which in turn is in close proximity to then capital Hang-chou. Second, it is not in the deep, reclusive mountains but is set at the base of a small hill in the expanse of the T'ai-pai mountain forests. Mount A-yü-wang is on completely flat ground, so the term "mountain" in this case is used more as a literary conceit to evoke an atmosphere than as a description. Both monasteries at that time were surrounded by dozens of other temples throughout the Hang-chou and Ming-chou provinces populated by full-time and part-time residents who were among the literati and civil servantry. Furthermore, the climate in the area south of Shanghai is considerably warmer and milder than the Echizen mountains.

B. SECT AND INTER-SECT. Whereas Eiheiji has been a head temple of the Japanese Sōtō sect since its inception and continuing without any slight variance ever since, the situation is quite different in the case of Mount T'ien-t'ung. The Chinese temple, which had a 700-year history before becoming affiliated with the Ch'an school in the first decade of the eleventh century, veered back and forth from Lin-chi and Ts'ao-tung connections depending on who was appointed abbot by the authorities responsible for religious administration. For most of its 1,000-year Ch'an history, it has been associated with the Lin-chi stream, though today it is known primarily for Dōgen's role there, which lends an impression that it is primarily of Ts'ao-tung affiliation. Ju-ching himself is "trans-sectual" in that he had trained at and was abbot of Lin-chi temples and was by no means a strict adherent to one school of thought and refuter of another. It appears that "bad blood" in the Hung-chih versus Ta-hui rivalry just a couple of generations before did not affect the time of Ju-ching's abbacy. Dōgen's affection and connection to him was based on his particular style of preaching rather than on a sectarian standpoint. Lin-chi abbots served before and after Ju-ching's leadership.

C. INSTITUTIONAL STRUCTURE. Despite differences of instructional structure in regard to lineage affiliation and of instructional style in regard to training methods and transmission rites, both temples adhered to the seven-hall monastic compound construction emphasizing the function of the Monks Hall and Dharma Hall (and Abbot's Quarters), as well as the delivery of formal and informal sermons in relation to seasonal and other ceremonies. Nevertheless, there were significant differences in form: Mount T'ien-t'ung stressed *zazen* and precepts more than the kōan cases or regimented discipline and chores that were found at Eiheiji. The Chinese temple also incorporated relics and esoteric ritual elements, in addition to a different approach to lay rituals, repentance, and ordination ceremonies. However, it was in subsequent generations that the assimilation of indigenous and folklore elements of religiosity made many Sōtō prayer temples (*kitō jiin*) in Japan even further removed—and for different reasons than in Dōgen's case—from the ritual style at Mount T'ien-t'ung.

Desperation Hypothesis and Mount Hakusan Hypothesis

Whereas the Withdrawal Hypothesis emphasizes the role of personal choice, the Decline Theory view—referred to in terms of this issue as the Desperation Hypothesis—characterizes the move as a matter of Dōgen fleeing from Kyoto in humiliation because Tendai monks were persecuting him; it notes also that he had fallen into a hopeless competition with the rapidly expanding Rinzai sect. Decline Theory scholars cite sources mentioning that Kōshōji, the first temple in Japan to have a Chinese Ch'an-style structure accommodating the delivery of *jōdō* sermons, was about to be burned down by Tendai opponents from Mount Hiei in 1243, much the same as the Daruma school center at Tōnomine was destroyed in 1228 by jealous monks from the Nara area.

Referring to this point, Kosen Nishiyama and John Stevens, translators of one of the first versions of the *Shōbōgenzō* in English, argue that "the neighboring monks on Mount Hiei were neither compassionate nor friendly and began to harass Dōgen and his followers, accusing them of 'innovations.' They descended on the monastery and attempted to burn it down in the summer of 1243. Needless to say, Dōgen was quite apprehensive about the future of his community and the safety of their present location."[18] An intriguing question is whether this ill will projected by Mount Hiei in 1243 would have been directed toward Dōgen or the Daruma school monks; he was reduced to an ambivalent, never really comfortable association with them because some of them may have had mixed loyalties.[19]

In support of skeptics who see Dōgen leaving Kyoto in humiliation, it seems likely that he felt intimidated or threatened by Enni, whose supporter, regent Kujō Michiie, envisioned Tōfukuji as a combination of the stately Tōdaiji and Kōfukuji temples in Nara. Michiie was bent on attacking other new sects as heretical outcasts out to do evil or as "worms inside eating the lion." The practice at Tōfukuji was supposed to be based on Enni's conviction that *zazen* represented the true path to enlightenment, yet it was destined to embrace syncretic tendencies stemming from Tendai and Shingon influences, much like Eisai's temples. Nevertheless, in sheer size and grandeur derived from the magnificent style of Sung temples, it clearly dwarfed Kōshōji. With the ascendancy of Enni, Dōgen realized that he would never be accepted by the Buddhist establishment.[20]

However, the textual basis for the claim that Kōshōji was going to be destroyed has been seriously challenged by modern studies. Even though the evidence for this claim is spurious, the argument has gained staying power because it seems to fit into two quite different agendas. The first is that of Sōtō traditionalists who see Dōgen as a victim of persecution in his lonely struggle to preserve the fragile purity of Zen, akin to other Kamakura-era religious heroes. The second agenda is that of modern historians who may be smuggling into their discussions criticisms cast by a rival sect.

A problem with the latter theory is that not only does it imply that Dōgen suffered an early defeat in fleeing Kyoto, but it often gets coupled with the view that Dōgen's career continued to spiral on a downhill course after the traumatic impact of this transition. The suggestion that his time at Eiheiji was altogether unproductive and represented a degeneration of his skills is a conclusion that could be drawn only on the basis of a complete neglect of the achievements represented by the late late texts, including the *Eihei kōroku*, the 12-*Shōbōgenzō*, and shorter Eiheiji compositions. These works show that Dōgen may have changed or revised but never abandoned or lost, and indeed may have expanded or enhanced his ability to express a religious vision of Zen practice.

A third hypothesis about the move to Echizen draws on elements of folk religiosity in that it is also possible that Dōgen's move was not a matter of fleeing Kyoto in response to negative factors alone but was motivated by a more positive desire to relocate near Mount Hakusan (see Figure 16). However, this probably was not only a strictly eremitic function, as sectarian accounts indicate, but was done for the sake of promoting a vision of monastic life. The large snow-covered, Fuji-like peak of Mount Hakusan in northwest Japan was a center of the *shūgendō* or *yamabushi* cult based on ascetic techniques carried out on distant mountains. Throughout the Hakusan region there were literally hundreds of Buddhist temples and hermitages, many of which had assimilated Shinto or folk gods, as well as small mountain peaks considered "offspring" of the main summit, to which they were considered to be connected by geomantic energy lines.

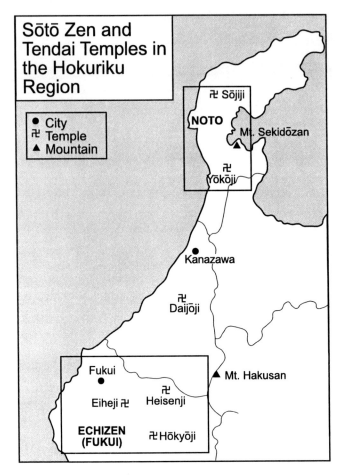

FIGURE 16. Close-up of Hokuriku Region

Note: Region subdivided into two main areas: the Echizen mountains and the Noto peninsula.

Adapted from Imaeda Aishin, *Zenshū no rekishi*, Nihon rekishi shinsho (Tokyo: Shibundō 1966), p. 181.

By the thirteenth century, Heisenji temple, located in the foothills of Mount Hakusan and linked to the Hakusan Jinja shrine, was also home to ritual activities associated with Onjōji temple and Jimon Tendai. In the generations after Dōgen, Sōtō Zen spread due north of Kaga province into the Noto peninsula around the area near Mount Sekidōzan, another sacred mountain in the Mount Hakusan network. Keizan's two main temples were located in the southern (Yōkōji) and northern (Sōjiji) tips of the peninsula, and smaller temples were situated approximate to the mountain's sacred energy source. Generations of monks after Keizan were successful in disseminating Sōtō Zen into the Tohoku, Kanto, and Chugoku areas, with local regional centers eventually based in the main cities of Sendai, Tokyo, and Nagoya, respectively. Even today, Eiheiji novices (*unsui*) perform some of their training on Mount Hakusan, and a sacred spring from the mountain brings water to Dōgen's stored remains as a daily offering.

This view proposed by Imaeda, which can be referred to as the Hakusan Tendai Hypothesis, shifts the focus away from the circumstances surrounding the flight from Kyoto to the question of what attracted Dōgen to the new area; it presumes that Dōgen already had significant links to Echizen through both Hatano and the Daruma school converts. Imaeda maintains that Dōgen moved mainly in order to establish a connection with Hakusan Tendai, which was an alternative institution that provided some relief from problems suffered at the hands of the main church on Mount Hiei.[21] As is shown in Figure 17, the Hakusan Tendai network, which extended from the northwest region (Hokuriku) down to Lake Biwa's northeast shores, was based at Heisenji, the point of embarkation for mountain pilgrimages, which was less than 25 km. from

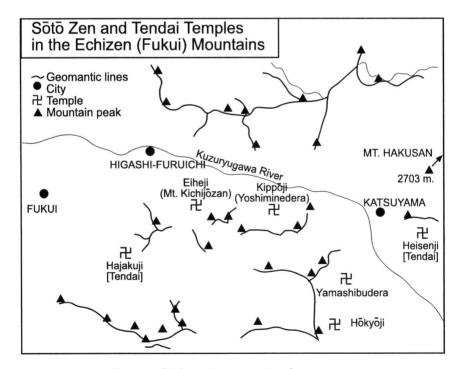

FIGURE 17. Close-up of Echizen Mountain Temples

Note: According to some theories, the geomantic lines link the peaks in the area, as well as five important temples.

Adapted from Imaeda, *Dōgen: Zazen hitosuji no shamon*, p. 147; and Imaeda, *Zenshū no rekishi*, p. 47.

Eiheiji and even closer to Kippōji and Yamashibudera. Mount Kichijōzan, renamed by Dōgen from the original name, Mount Sanshōzan, after his return from Kamakura, was no doubt part of the Hakusan network of sacrality.

The Hakusan Tendai Hypothesis is in some ways a variation of the Desperation Hypothesis associated with the Decline Theory in arguing that Dōgen went to Echizen in part out of weakness and vulnerability during political turmoil. A related standpoint, suggested by Satō Shunkō, builds on Imaeda's emphasis on the role of Hakusan but steers the discussion back to the notion of choice. This view, which can be referred to as the Hakusan Shinkō Hypothesis, stresses that, in addition to possible affiliations with the Tendai church (it is not clear where Hakusan Tendai stood in relation to the religious battle in the capital), Dōgen was probably influenced by the environment of popular religiosity and folk amalgamations of the Hakusan region (or Hakusan shinkō). These included a wide variety of yamabushi practices and folk beliefs, such as geomancy, which were gradually absorbed into the Sōtō school.[22] For example, as is illustrated in Figure 18, Satō examines how the sect spread to Yōkōji and Sōjiji temples, both founded by Keizan in the Noto peninsula along geomantic lines at the base of Mount Sekidōzan (also known as Isurugiyama), one of numerous sacred mountains associated with Hakusan shinkō, which had its own longstanding shūgendō tradition. It is also interesting that Mount Hakusan and Mount Sekidōzan stand in a direct line on a 45-degree angle northeast of Mount Hiei.

It may be, partially in contrast to and partially in support of Imaeda's argument, that there were alliances between the Hakusan Tendai and both factions in the capital. Extending from this notion, one might consider that Dōgen actually moved to Echizen with the consent (or even at the request) of the Kyoto religious establishment; perhaps an arrangement was worked out such that Dōgen was assigned or awarded the Hakusan area as a site for evangelizing. Satō further analyzes in detail the evolution of the legend in Muromachi-era hagiographies that the Hakusan gongen (avatar of Buddha) guided Dōgen's copying of the "One Night Blue Cliff Record" just prior to his return to China. The Hakusan Shinkō Hypothesis stresses the role of the "localization" of religious influences involving shamanistic rites, regional deities, and other aspects reflecting highly localized divergences in shrine worship as well as the link between Buddhist meditation and mountain ascetic practices. This notion will continue to be a major topic in future Sōtō studies.[23]

For the most part, however, the impact of the assimilation of local religiosity as well as esoteric elements derived from former mikkyō (Tendai and Shingon) temples that were converted to Sōtō can be attributed to post-Dōgen leaders, particularly Keizan and his followers, who began the rapid expansion of the sect. The point here is that even if Dōgen was, in effect, removed from Kyoto because of political factors, as the Decline Theory argues, his decision

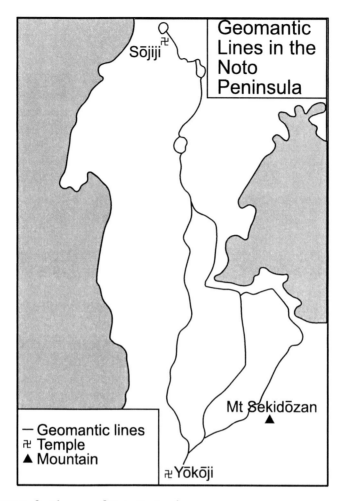

FIGURE 18. Close-up of Noto Peninsula

Note: Area where Keizan spread Sōtō Zen in the early fourteenth century.

Adapted from Satō Shunkō, "Hakusan shinkō to Sōtō-shū kyōdan shi," 20 parts. *Sanshō* 556–585 (VII: 30).

to head for Echizen has proved to be a shrewd maneuver from an institutional standpoint. Furthermore, it appears that at least some of Dōgen's writings in the late period may have been geared to accommodate an audience accustomed to features of Hakusan religiosity, including the cult of arhats (*rakan*) and mountain numinosity.

The transition to Echizen, partly in response to Daruma school monks who came from Hajakuji to Kyoto, may have convinced Dōgen that significant advancement of his sect could be gained in the Hakusan vicinity, an opportunity that could not be passed up. Another twist that links the Decline Theory with the Hakusan Hypothesis is that, perhaps out of desperation, Dōgen turned to the Daruma school followers as the only hope for keeping alive his sect after it was run out of the capital. Bernard Faure takes this point a step further by arguing that the connection to the Daruma school caused a sea change in Dōgen's religiosity:

> This collective conversion changed dramatically the nature of Dō-gen's teachings and decided the future of the Sōtō sect. Not only was Dōgen's criticism of the Rinzai tradition a direct result of his desire to convince his new audience of the superiority of his brand of Zen, but his sudden transfer to remote Echizen in 1243, and the subsequent sectarian stiffening of his doctrine, were due in part to the fact that the Daruma-shū had a strong following in that province.[24]

Aside from giving too much credence to the impact of the Daruma school, the problem with this assertion is that it fails to mention the context of Chinese influences that formed the necessary background from which the Dōgen-Sōtō-Daruma connections were forged. For example, if Dōgen's intention was mainly to please the Daruma school monks, it would appear quite odd for him to begin a shift to preaching in kanbun, which was a dialect that these monks, less educated than the Kyoto elite, could hardly understand. Perhaps this change was part of his strategy to impress them with his China credentials, but in any case it highlights the increasing importance of Chinese Ch'an influences through the phases following the move.

Features of the Middle Middle Period

Emergence of Ju-Ching as Ch'an Model

Regardless of what could be pinpointed as the primary motivating factor for the move to Echizen, an analysis of the sequence of Dōgen's writings clearly shows that it was at this crucial and extremely challenging juncture that he began eulogizing Ju-ching in a heightened manner and cultivating an interest in Ch'an models. Dōgen seemed to be shifting his approach in other ways during the transition to Echizen by putting less emphasis on the universality of enlightenment and the ability to attain spiritual freedom by laypersons (zaike) and women and stressing instead the need to become a monk and practice the lifestyle of a home-leaver (shukke).

As was mentioned, Dōgen notes receiving Ju-ching's recorded sayings in the summer of 1242, although the first indication of renewed interest was in Shōbōgenzō "Gyōji" (part 2), which was written several months before this and contains four citations.[25] The list in Table 29, when seen in light of Table 5 in

TABLE 29. Dōgen's Citations or Allusions to Ju-ching

Shōbōgenzō	References/Allusions Only	Citations
Makahannyaharamitsu, 1233–1	Bendōwa, 1231	EK 2.147, 1246
Senjō, 1239–1	Shōbōgenzō zuimonki, 1236	EK 2.179, 1246
Shisho, 1241–1	Senmen, 1239	EK 3.194, 1246
Kankin, 1241–1	Busso, 1241	EK 4.318, 1249
Gyōji 2, 1242–4	Busshō, 1241	ᵃEK 4.319,
Gabyō, 1242–1	Zazenshin, 1242	1249
Kobusshin, 1243–1	Darani, 1243	EK 5.379, 1250
Kattō, 1243–1	Menju, 1243	ᵃEK 5.390, 1250
	Jippō, 1243	ᵃEK 5.406,
	Zanmai ōzanmai, 1244	1250
After Move to Echizen		EK 6.424, 1251
		EK 6.432, 1251
ᵃButsudō, 1243–2	Others	EK 6.437, 1251
ᵃShohō jissō, 1243–2		EK 6.438, 1251
ᵃBukkyō (S), 1243–2	Tenzokyōkun, 1234–2	EK 6.469, 1251
ᵃMujō seppō, 1243–1	Chiji shingi, 1246–1	EK 9.86, 1235
ᵃKenbutsu, 1243–1	Shuryō shingi, 1249–1	EK 7.502, 1252
Baika, 1243–8		ᵃEK 7.503, 1252
Hensan, 1243–1		ᵃEK 7.522, 1252
Ganzei, 1243–7	Eihei Kōroku	EK 7.530, 1252
Kajō, 1243–5		EK 10.80 (3)
Udonge, 1244–2	Memorials	EK 10.84
Tenbōrin, 1244–1		
Ho-u, 1245–1	EK 2.184, 1246	
Ango, 1245–1	EK 3.249, 1247	References
Ōsaku sendaba, 1245–2	EK 4.274, 1248	
Kokū, 1245–1	EK 4.342, 1249	EK 1.48, 1236
	EK 5.384, 1250	EK 1.105, 1241
	EK 4.276, 1251	EK 1.118, 1241
	EK 7.515, 1252	EK 2.128, 1245
		EK 2.148, 1245

ᵃ Indicates the source is not in *Ju-ching yü-lu*

Chapter 1, shows that the other *Shōbōgenzō* fascicles containing multiple citations stem from the period following the reception of the record. Although there were some references to Ju-ching in writings dating back to the early 1230s, the full acknowledgment and celebration—or possibly idealization and exaggeration—of the mentor came at this time. A reliance on allusions to Ju-ching expressed in *Shōbōgenzō* fascicles from the 1240s continued to proliferate throughout the later stages of Dōgen's career in *Eihei kōroku* sermons from the 1250s. Note that memorials for Ju-ching were not begun until 1246 but were then continued for seven years until the end of Dōgen's career, when illness forced him to stop preaching. Generally, these are brief and cryptic.[26] However, an evocation of Ju-ching's authority, more frequently than one might suppose, is not far removed from critique and revisionism of the master.

Of the compositions from the early 1240s, the "Baika" and "Ganzei" fascicles consist almost entirely of commentary on the mentor's teaching. "Baika," which evokes lyrical imagery as a symbol for enlightenment, is dedicated to remembrances and citations of the sayings of Ju-ching, who apparently spoke frequently about the symbolism of the plum tree, whose fragrant blossoms appearing at the end of the winter season are a harbinger of spring, and thus renewal. This fascicle was originally a sermon delivered on 11.6.1243 during the year of Dōgen's move to Echizen, when he was staying in a temporary hermitage before settling into a permanent temple. According to the colophon, three feet of snow fell that day, and we can only imagine that Dōgen was perhaps a bit despondent and seeking out sources of inspiration.[27]

In addition to reflecting on the natural image, Dōgen recalls his feelings during the time of his studies in China when he realized that not many native Chinese had the ability or opportunity to take advantage of their contact with such an eminent teacher and how fortunate he was as a foreign novice:

> In sending the [monks] away [Ju-ching] said, "If they are lacking in the essentials, what can they do? Dogs like that only disturb others and cannot be permitted to stay in the monastery." *Having seen this with my own eyes and heard it with my own ears* [emphasis added], I thought to myself: Being natives of this country, what sin or crime must they have committed in a past life that prevents them from staying among us? What lucky star was I born under that, although a native of a remote foreign country, I was not only accepted in the monastery, but allowed to come and go freely in the abbot's room, to bow down before the living master and hear his discourse on the Dharma. Although I was foolish and ignorant, I did not take this superb opportunity in vain. When my late teacher was holding forth in Sung China, there were those who had the chance to study with him and those who did not. Now that my late teacher, the old master, is gone, it is gloomier than a moonless night in Sung China. Why? Because never before or since has there been an old master like my late teacher was an old master.[28]

Dōgen appreciated the qualities of openness and flexibility that afforded him a unique avenue for accessibility to the abbot. In *Hōkyōki* he reports that Ju-ching invited him to come to the Abbot's Quarters on demand and without reservation, something that would have been a rare privilege. According to a passage in the *Shōbōgenzō zuimonki*, Ju-ching offered Dōgen the slot of head monk but he declined in deference to native seekers. In *jōdō* no. 2.184 from 1246, a memorial sermon, Dōgen expresses self-deprecation in celebrating Ju-ching's wisdom:

When I entered China, I studied walking like someone from Handan. I worked very hard carrying water and hauling firewood. Do
not say that my late teacher deceived his disciple. Rather, T'ien-t'ung
was deceived by Dōgen.[29]

There are several main aspects of Ju-ching's influence on Dōgen. Perhaps
the best-known example of master–disciple interaction is the transformational
experience of *shinjin datsuraku*, or casting off body-mind, as depicted in the
Kenzeiki and the *Denkōroku*. Dōgen's enlightenment was triggered by the strict
manner of training, whereby Ju-ching insisted on the total commitment and
dedication of disciples to the practice of meditation. The moment of *shinjin
datsuraku* occurred when the monk sitting next to Dōgen was scolded by Ju-
ching for dozing off while doing *zazen* during a *sesshin* held as part of the
summer retreat, although there is one theory that it transpired earlier as a kind
of "satori at first sight" when the master and disciple first met.

The importance of the doctrine of *shinjin datsuraku* is referred to in a
passage that appears in *Hōkyōki* as well as in other texts, including *Bendōwa*,
"Gyōji," and several passages in the *Eihei kōroku*. According to Ju-ching, who
confirmed Dōgen's personal insight during a private meeting in his quarters,
"To study Zen under a master is to cast off body-mind through single-minded
sitting meditation, without the need for burning incense, worshipping, reciting
the *nembutsu*, practicing repentance, or reading sutras. . . . To cast off body-
mind is to practice sitting meditation (*zazen*). When practicing single-minded
sitting meditation, the five desires will be set aside and the five defilements
will be removed."[30]

There has long been a debate about whether Dōgen heard Ju-ching correctly or modified his phrasing deliberately. Ju-ching and other Ch'an masters
of the time were not known to utter the words "casting off body-mind" but did
occasionally use a similar locution, "casting off the dust from the mind," which
might imply a subject–object dualism in that the pure mind is defiled and
must be freed from contaminated objects. The two expressions sound alike
(they are identical in Japanese pronunciation, *shinjin*, and have a slight variance
in Chinese, in which "body-mind" is *shen-hsin* and "dust from the mind" is
hsin-ch'en). To Dōgen's ear as a nonnative speaker of Chinese, it may have been
easy for him to confuse the phrases. It is also plausible that he had what can
be called a creative misunderstanding or sought deliberately to modify Ju-
ching's utterance in order to free it from dualistic overtones. Dōgen's interpretation could then well be a part of his tendency to evoke and rely on the
authority of Ju-ching yet also to distance himself and proclaim his autonomy.

East Asian training traditions generally emphasize that a disciple needs to
be able to surpass his teacher, who must be magnanimous enough to encour-
age and acknowledge the value of the comeuppance. In some cases there is an

exchange of ironic insults or blows. A classic example in Ch'an occurs when Pai-chang refers to his disciple Huang-po, who was in turn the teacher of Lin-chi, as nothing but a "red-bearded barbarian" or a "wild fox" to indicate praise and admiration after Huang-po slapped him. In other cases the act of going beyond one's mentor is demonstrated in a deliberately subtle fashion. For example, in the poetic technique of *honkadori* (allusive variation), the junior poet makes only a seemingly minor but very significant alteration in the verse of his mentor.[31]

Perhaps an even more important influence than the specific occasion of his personal breakthrough in shaping Dōgen's overall religiosity was his sense of awe at Ju-ching's teaching style. The main image of Ju-ching that emerges in the writings of this period is that of a master who breaks out of the mold of a formal monastic setting to deliver dynamic, spontaneous sermons. Dōgen considered Ju-ching's approach uniquely compelling for the charismatic appeal and sincere authenticity he projected. Unlike many Ch'an masters, who stuck to regulations and schedules even for informal sermons, Ju-ching was inspired to preach in different places of the temple compound at odd times of the day, including late hours. He gave lectures not only in the Dharma Hall on a fixed schedule but any time of day or night when the inspiration struck.

Shōbōgenzō "Shohō jissō" was presented by Dōgen in 1243 after "eighteen years had swiftly passed" since a remarkable occasion of mystical exaltation during the fourth watch of the night in the third month of 1226.[32] At that time, Ju-ching gave a midnight sermon in the Abbot's Quarters, when Dōgen heard the drum beating, with signs hung around the temple announcing the event. Monks were burning incense and waiting anxiously to hear, "You may enter [the abbot's room]." The sermon concluded with the saying, "A cuckoo sings, and a mountain-bamboo splits in two."[33] Dōgen says that this was a unique method of intense, personal training not practiced in other temple districts. In several other passages in the *Shōbōgenzō* and *Eihei kōroku*, Dōgen describes the excitement and thrill of studying with someone of Ju-ching's stature who attracted followers from all over China. In addition to Dōgen, Ju-ching invited disciples to approach his quarters at various times when he or they felt the need for instruction. Therefore Ju-ching demonstrated supreme discipline along with ingenious innovation. It is interesting to note that the 75-*Shōbōgenzō* fascicle "Kōmyō" from the six month of 1242 was delivered at two o'clock in the morning, as Dōgen proudly declares in the colophon, while the monks listened attentively as a heavy storm poured down during the rainy season.[34]

60-*Fascicle* Shōbōgenzō

Dōgen's portrayal of Ju-ching is suspect in terms of accuracy and is problematic because of its connections to partisan rhetoric, and these factors perhaps form the roots of the 60-*Shōbōgenzō* edition, which seems to represent an attempt to weed out of the text whole fascicles that may be considered unreliable or untenable. First, it is questionable whether Dōgen's enthusiasm for Ju-ching's sermon style is warranted. Perhaps in emphasizing the extraordinary informal method of Ju-ching, Dōgen is acknowledging that his mentor's recorded discourse was rather pedestrian and not as stellar as that of better-known Chinese masters, and so he wanted to stress that the unrecorded pedagogy was what made Ju-ching sensational.

Another dubious aspect of the Dōgen–Ju-ching relationship is the fact that there are numerous examples of Ju-ching's sayings, including the "Baika" passage cited earlier, not found in the recorded sayings of the mentor. According to the analysis by He Yansheng, this text no doubt was drastically reconstructed, or even fabricated, by Tokugawa-era Sōtō editors precisely to create a match-up, yet these sections are still missing in some glaring cases. The fascicles in which Dōgen cites passages not in the *Ju-ching yü-lu* deal to a large extent with a sectarian agenda of criticizing the Ta-hui lineage in "Shohō jissō" and the other branches of Ch'an in "Butsudō" and "Bukkyō" [Buddhist Sutras]. In these passages, which Dōgen may have misquoted or even invented, Ju-ching sounds considerably more partisan and combative in tone than in passages that can be traced to the *Ju-ching yü-lu*.[35] As was seen in Table 8 in chapter 2, all of these fascicles are excluded from the 60-*Shōbōgenzō*. In another excluded fascicle, "Menju," delivered just two weeks prior to "Baika," Dōgen stresses that he gained face-to-face transmission, which was "transmitted only to my monastery; others have not dreamed of it." There is a rather belligerent tone attributed to Ju-ching, who is said to refer to incompetent monks as "dogs," evoked as part of Dōgen's claim for the authentic status of his own temple. Furthermore, inconsistencies are evident in some of the doctrines Dōgen attributes to Ju-ching and in what is expressed in the recorded sayings, as Nakaseko Shōdō demonstrates, raising doubts as to whether Ju-ching, especially in comparison with other Ch'an luminaries, was really a master who had as great an impact as Dōgen asserts.[36]

Therefore, much of Dōgen's eulogizing of Ju-ching can be accounted for as a way of using Ch'an as a rhetorical device for creating a sectarian identity in Japan grounded exclusively in Ts'ao-tung/Sōtō teachings. Dōgen was excessively critical of teachers from other lineages, some of whom he had previously praised. Dōgen scathingly attacked the eminent master Ta-hui, although half a decade earlier, in the *Shōbōgenzō zuimonki*, he had admired Ta-hui's commitment to continuous, diligent practice. In "Jishō zanmai," another fascicle excluded from the 60-*Shōbōgenzō*, written in the winter of 1244, Dōgen goes so far as to challenge the authenticity of the enlightenment of Ta-hui, who he says could not recognize the Dharma even in a dream. He further asserts that only those in the Tung-shan (that is, the founder of Ts'ao-tung/Sōtō) lineage can have a genuine experience. Other fascicles of this period also give harsh treatment to various Lin-chi masters while praising Ts'ao-tung teachers.

Table 30 lists the masters associated with the Lin-chi/Rinzai sect who are severely criticized in the controversial fascicles, including T'ang dynasty monks Lin-chi, Yün-men, Te-shan, and Kuei-shan, in addition to Ta-hui and his teacher Yüan-wu of the Sung dynasty. At the same time, T'ang dynasty Ts'ao-tung/Sōtō patriarch Tung-shan receives great praise, along with Sung dynasty masters Ju-ching and Hung-chih. There are half a dozen other fascicles in both editions that express some criticisms, but the tone in these cases is generally indirect and focused on theoretical differences rather than on ad hominen attacks. See Appendix VI for a complete listing of the 75-fascicle and 60-fascicle texts, and note that seven fascicles from the 12-*Shōbōgenzō* are included in the 60-*Shōbōgenzō* along with two fascicles from the 95-*Shōbōgenzō*. While the origins of the 60-fascicle edition are obscure and may stem from as early as Dōgen himself or as late as Giun, a fourteenth-century Sōtō patriarch and fifth-generation abbot of Eiheiji, we sense an interest in the formative days of the sect in a diminishing of the harsher polemical elements of the *Shōbōgenzō*.

At the same time, this approach was not altogether one-sided; there are many examples of Dōgen's writings during this period in which he evoked the life and teachings of a wide variety of Ch'an masters without regard to their lineal status and contrasted them with the deficiency of practitioners in Japan. For example, "Keiseisanshoku," which is included in the 60-*Shōbōgenzō*, cites numerous Chinese masters from various lineages who were notable for dwelling in mountain forests. Yet even here, there is a sectarian edge to the writing. Dōgen describes how those who seek fame and fortune were labeled "pitiful" by Ju-ching, who probably borrowed this phrase from the *Suramgama Sutra*. Dōgen goes on to comment, "In this country of Japan, a remote corner of the

TABLE 30. Fascicles with Criticism of Lin-chi School

Lin-chi	Te-shan	Yün-men
Sokushin zebutsu	Sokushin zebutsu	Sansuikyō
Daigo	Shinfukatoku	Kattō
Bukkōjōji	Bukkōjōji	ªKenbutsu
Gyōji	Kattō	ªBukkyō S
ªSesshin sesshō	ªButsudō	ªMenju
ªButsudō	ªMitsugo	
ªBukkyō S	ªMujō seppō	Yüan-wu
ªMitsugo	ªDaishugyō (12-SH)	
ªMujō seppō		Bukkōjōji
ªKenbutsu	Kuei-shan	Kattō
ªDaishugyō (12-SH)		ªShunjū
	Kattō	

ª Indicates not included in 60-*Shōbōgenzō*

ocean, people's minds are extremely dense. Since ancient times, no saint has ever been born here, nor anyone wise by nature."[37] This fascicle also emphasizes the need for repentance as a means for overcoming spiritual deficiency, words that may have been intended to send a message about the powerful impact of karmic retribution to monks converting from the Daruma school, which apparently disdained the precepts and monastic rules in the belief that all beings are originally endowed with the Buddha-nature.[38]

The Late Middle Period

It is easy to see why this subperiod, which began with the construction of Daibutsuji, tends to be overshadowed by the richness and variety of the towering yet somewhat controversial and conflicted accomplishments of the middle middle period. The Decline Theory is fueled by the fact that Dōgen's career did undergo a dry period lasting about a year—from spring 3.9.1244, the date of the composition of the "Daishugyō" fascicle, to 3.6.1245 and the composition of "Kokū"—when there were no *jishu* or *jōdō* sermons delivered and no other kinds of writings produced. Perhaps this was so because the opening of the new temple was time-consuming and did not allow for the formation of a new pattern of discourse or interaction with disciples.

During the next year and a quarter, several trends became evident in what would prove to be a productive phase of compositions, especially in the field of discourse generated by kōans and rules explored in the *Shōbōgenzō*, *Eihei kōroku*, and *Eihei shingi* texts. From a literary or philosophical standpoint, the creative fires burned less brightly at this time. However, when the work is understood as a change from creative wordplay to development of a unique administrative approach in establishing Sung-style monasticism in a Japanese context, there emerges a compelling rebuttal to the Decline Theory (an utter lack of productivity) and the Renewal Theory (continued troubled pattern prior to the mission to Kamakura).

A key feature of this phase is a continued focus on kōan interpretation in several of the final group of 75-*Shōbōgenzō* fascicles. These include "Tashintsū," which provides an extended discussion of the supranormal power of reading others' minds, which is also cited in *Eihei kōroku* 9.27, and "Kokū" on spatiality, which discusses Ju-ching's bell verse cited in "Makahannyaharamitsu," *Eihei kōroku* vol. 9, and the *Hōkyōki*. In addition, "Ōsakusendaba" is a kōan-oriented fascicle that is interesting for evoking Hung-chih, who is also cited in "Shunjū" from 1244, and for mentioning the fact that Ju-ching refers to him as his "old master" (*kobutsu*), a foreshadowing of Dōgen's focus on Hung-chih that would develop in short order. These writings tend to continue the criticism of Sung Ch'an practice, though in a more general and less vociferous and partisan way than is found in fascicles from the Kippōji cycle.

During the late middle period Dōgen also began to rely heavily on different sources, including the *Ch'an-yüan ch'ing-kuei*, which was also cited in a couple of *Shōbōgenzō* fascicles in the late 1230s, and the recorded sayings of Sung predecessors, especially Hung-chih.[39] An emphasis on monastic rules greatly influenced by the *Ch'an-yüan ch'ing-kuei* is evident in early 1244, when Dōgen wrote what eventually became the fifth chapter of *Eihei shingi*, the *Taidaiko gogejarihō*, a brief essay containing instructions on how junior disciples should behave deferentially toward senior monks at summer retreats. During 1245–1246, when Dōgen was settled at Daibutsuji, he added several writings in this vein. One of the main examples is *Bendōhō*, which became the second chapter in the *Eihei shingi* and contains detailed instructions on daily conduct, particularly on practicing *zazen* both morning and night as well as the etiquette of washing and folding the robe. A lengthy passage near the end of the essay provides a thorough explanation of meditation that is also found in *Fukanzazengi* as well as in the "Zazengi" and "Zazenshin" fascicles (the latter citing and revising a prominent Hung-chih verse).

In addition, several of the *Shōbōgenzō* fascicles from this phase are very much *shingi*-oriented material, especially "Ango," delivered in 1245, which instructs monks on the summer retreat and includes a brief mention of how Ju-ching made a modification in some of the procedures. Another example is "Shukke" from 1246, the last of the 75-*Shōbōgenzō* fascicles, in which Dōgen seems to assert for the first time the priority of the monastic (*shukke*, lit., one who has made home departure) lifestyle: "Remember, if we have made a home departure, then even breaking the precepts is preferable to not breaking the precepts as a layperson."[40] Another short rules text, *Jikuinmon*, on guiding behavior while cooking in the kitchen, is a kind of sequel to *Tenzokyōkun*, included in the 95-*Shōbōgenzō* edition.

Renewal of the Jōdō Sermons

Dōgen's reliance on the records of Sung masters is apparent from the start of the late middle period. They are heralded in Ejō's preface to the second volume of the *Eihei kōroku*; Ejō took over editing chores from Senne, who, according to a theory, may have stayed behind in Kyoto. The preface announces that "during the following year [after the founding of Daibutsuji], Zen monks came in droves to study with Dōgen from all over the country," apparently in large part to hear him lecture.[41] We can only surmise how many followers there were. The delivery of *jōdō* sermons in 1245 followed a hiatus of a year and three-quarters, which meant that the new temple was opened for about nine months before the assembly was convened in the Dharma Hall for the master's formal discourse.

The sermons (see Table 31) frequently deal with kōans, generally cited on special occasions such as holidays or memorials, but by means of allusion rather than exegesis, evoking key phrases without extensive commentary. The records generally note that after a "long pause," during which there was probably much heated discussion and debate that is left unrecorded, Dōgen makes final remarks, which are often poetic and are accompanied by demonstrations, gestures, or body language that is mentioned in the records but eludes interpretation in textual critical studies. In other words, the effectiveness as well as the spontaneity of the jōdō style probably depended on an atmosphere of audience appreciation and participation that is difficult to reconstruct.

A central aim of the sermons was to establish a pattern of advancing the administrative needs and symbols of authority of the monastery. A prominent example is *Eihei kōroku* 2.147, which is one of numerous jōdō that highlights the role of the Zen master's staff. A full appreciation of the significance of the sermon must take into account other writings in the discursive field of the late middle period. Unlike the case of *Tenzokyōkun*, which innovatively combines styles, the kōan-based and *shingi*-based writings of this phase tend to be separated, with the prominent exception of the "Ho-u." This fascicle, in discussing the meaning of the begging bowl, cites and revises Ju-ching's commentary on a kōan, *Pi-yen lu* case 26, known as Pai-chang's "sitting alone atop Ta-hsiung peak." Both Dōgen and his mentor show a flair for a creative rewriting of this record in order to highlight their respective visions of the essence of Zen practice.

In the source record Pai-chang is asked by a monk, "What is the most remarkable thing [in the world]?" and he responds, "It is sitting [or practicing *zazen*] alone atop Ta-hsiung peak [or Mount Pai-chang]."[42] This reply seems a bit surprising, since Pai-chang is known primarily for his emphasis on rules expressed in the first (and probably apocryphal) Zen monastic code, the *Ch'an-men kuei-shih*. This text stresses the role of the charismatic abbot's sermons, which are supposed to be held twice a day, before and after the midday meal, far more than *zazen*, which is left up to the discretion of the disciple.[43] Ju-ching rewrites the response as, "It is just eating rice in a bowl at Ching-tzu ssu temple on Mount T'ien-t'ung,"[44] thus shifting the focus from *zazen* to everyday praxis and from Mount Pai-chang to his own mountain temple.

Dōgen reflects on this case at least five times in his works, three times in the late middle period (and two more during the late late period, to be discussed in chapter 6). He cites Ju-ching's revision approvingly in "Kajō" (1243), but in *Eihei kōroku* 2.147 from the same year as "Ho-u" (1245) he rewrites the concluding statement. In the context of discussing the value of wielding the Zen staff (*shujō*),[45] which metaphorically encompasses all aspects of reality, Dōgen cites Ju-ching's response, but this time he says, "I would answer by raising high my staff at Daibutsuji temple in Japan," and he then puts the staff down

TABLE 31. *Chronology of Eihei kōroku Construction*

YEAR	1/1 New Year	1/10 10th Day	1/15 Full Moon	2/15 Buddha Death	3/1 Open Hearth	3/14 Return Kamakura	3/20 20th Day	4/8 Buddha Birth	4/15 Summer Retreat	4/25 25th Day	5/1 New Moon	5/5 Boys' Fest	5/27 Memor Butsuju[a]	6/1 New Moon	6/10 10th Day	6/10 Emperor Birthday	6/15 Temple Name[b]
1236—	X	X	X	X	X	X	X	X	X	X	X	X	X	X	X	X	X
1240																	
1241	32							42	44								
1242	90h							98	118								
1243	116			121	122			75									
1244	X	X	X	X	X	X	X	X	X	X	X	X	X	X	X	X	X
1245	X	X	X	X	X	X	X	X	127								
1246	142H			146			152h	155h	158h			169	171				177
1247	216H		219	225				236H	238			242H			247		
1248	X	X	X	X	X	251		256H	257H	259		261H					
1249	303H	305	X	311	X			320H	322H	324	325	326H					
1250				367												379	
1251			412	418				427					435				
1252			481	486	489			495						504			
Total	6	1	3	7	2	1	1	9	7	2	1	4	2	1	1	1	1

YEAR	7/5 Memor. Eisai[c]	7/15 Close Retreat	7/17 Memor. Ju-ching	8/1 Tenchū Fest.	8/1 New Moon	8/6 Ju-ching Record	8/15 Harvest Moon	9/1 New Moon	9/2 Memor. Minamoto	10/1 Open[d] Temple	10/15 Open Hearth	11 mo. Winter Solstice	12/8 Rohatsu	12/10 Tenth Day	12 mo. Memor. Mother	12/25 Year End	TOTAL
1236—	X	X	X	X	X	X	X	X	X	(1)	X	X	X	X	X	X	0
1240							13H				14H	25					1–31=31
1241							77H						88				32–65; 76–89=48
1242		102		104		105	106				109	115					90–115=26
1243			X	X	X	X	X	X	X	X	X	X	X	X	X	X	66–75; 116–126=21
1244	X	X	X	X	X	X	X	X	X	X	X	X	X	X	X	X	0
1245		130										135H	136				127–141=15
1246		183h	184				189	193			199	206H	213				142–215=74
1247		248	249		250	X	X	X	X	X	X	X		X	X	X	216–250=35
1248			274				277	279			288	296H	297			302	251–275; 277–302=51
1249		341	342				344H	347			353		360				303–345; 346–360=58
1250			384				413	389	363		396		406	392	409		361–411; 413=52
1251		442	276				448	451			462		475		478		276,412; 414–480=69
1252		514h	515				521	523	524		528		506				481–531=51
TOTAL	2	7	7	1	1	1	9	6	2		8	5	8	1	2	1	531

H = direct influence of Hung-chih, h = indirect influence

LINE = beginning of Gien's editing of the EK and Dōgen's focus on the composition of the 12-fascicle *Shōbōgenzō*

a 1184–1225, disciple of Eisai and teacher of Dōgen

b Change name from Daibutsuji to Eiheiji

c 1141–1215, also known as Myōan Senkō

d The opening of Kōshōji Temple in 1236 was marked by record in the Manzan edition only.

and steps off the dais.[46] Dōgen shows here both a willingness to challenge his mentor and a ritual use of the staff as a means of proclaiming the legitimacy of his approach. Similarly, in *Eihei kōroku* 2.145, Dōgen refers to his lineage as "a diverse amalgamation . . . horns grow on the head, dragons and snakes mix together, and there are many horses and cows . . . they all discern the monk's staff and complete the matter of a lifetime." To mention a few of the many other examples, in no. 2.150 he holds up the staff and pounds it on the floor saying, "Just this is it," and in no. 2.168 he asks rhetorically, "Is there a dragon or elephant here who can come forth and meet with Daibutsu's staff?"

An important development of this period is the use of *jōdō* sermons for advancing a Sung Ch'an administrative style, especially by praising and appointing monks to key staff positions. For example, *Eihei kōroku* 2.137 expresses appreciation for the outgoing director, while no. 2.139 refers to appointing a director and chief cook (*tenzo*) and no. 2.157 appoints a new receptionist. Sermon 2.138, which shows appreciation for the cook, is interesting because Dōgen claims, "Among all the temples in Japan, I imported the rules for the cook for the first time." Dōgen had mentioned in *Tenzokyōkun* that during his stay at Kenninji just after returning from China he found that the temple had already created this position, but it was "in name only, without him really doing it at all."[47]

The *Eihei kōroku* sermons, which cite 298 kōan cases according to Kagamishima, are an outgrowth of the focus on kōans in the earlier works, including several cases frequently discussed in the 75-*Shōbōgenzō*, such as "Ma-tsu's mind itself is buddha," "Pai-chang's wild fox," and "Chao-chou's does a dog have Buddha-nature."[48] Many of the *Eihei kōroku* doctrines are also consistent with those in previous writings, including the view that sitting in *zazen* is more fundamental than the precepts. There do appear to be changes in the *Eihei kōroku* around the time of the Kamakura mission, which are both stylistic and doctrinal in a new focus on causality.

The late middle period is significant in completing a dramatic shift from *jishu* to *jōdō* sermons; it becomes clear that the key point of the later stages of Dōgen's career is not so much an emphasis on rituals to the exclusion of new ideas, as the Decline Theory suggests, or a negation of the old ideas, as the Renewal Theory argues, but *a different ritualization of the way the ideas were presented*. The *Eihei kōroku* marks the triumph of public, regulated, ritualized instruction over spontaneous, private, individual teaching. Seen from this perspective, the eight months from 1243–1244 in which Dōgen wrote over one third of the 75-*Shōbōgenzō* fascicles—or the two years, 1242–1244 (3/9), during which he wrote nearly two thirds—is a transitional stage. Dōgen busied himself and held his community together by giving informal lectures while preparing for his real work, a resumption of the formal sermons begun at Kōshōji once he was settled into his new temple.

There are several important passages that clearly express Dōgen's own view of the powerful and popular role of *jōdō* sermons based on Ju-ching's model. The first example is the second passage in the second volume, *Eihei kōroku* 2.128 from 1245, which reveals Dōgen working through the complex stages of transition from informal to formal lectures and thus provides a good indication of why the *jishu* style was phased out.[49] The passage is especially interesting not because it repudiates *jishu* in favor of *jōdō*, but because it highlights the significance of lecturing in general as the key function of a monastic community. It explains Dōgen's admiration for Ju-ching, who was skillful at delivering several styles of informal lectures, including evening sermons (*ban-san*), general discourses (*fusetsu*), and provisional lectures (*shōsan*), although it does not mention the *jishu* style specifically. Technically, this passage is not a *jōdō* style, because it was delivered in the evening, the typical time for informal lectures; it is one of a handful of evening sermons which appear at the beginning of the second volume of the *Eihei kōroku*, that is, in the earliest phase of the Daibutsuji period.

Dōgen begins no. 2.128 by recalling how master Tzu-ming Chü-yuan, in discussing the meaning of the size of monasteries, cautioned his disciples not to equate the quantity of followers or the number of monks in attendance with the magnitude of the temple. According to Tzu-ming, a temple with many monks who lack determination is actually considered small, while a temple with a few monks of great dedication is quite large. This part of the passage could be seen as reflecting a defensive posture; perhaps Dōgen was explaining why he was not attracting many followers. However, that suspicion is undercut by the preface to the second volume as well as the following excerpt from the sermon, which makes it clear that this is a statement about the need for selectively identifying quality disciples from among the multitudes.

Dōgen next contrasts several T'ang masters, all of Lin-chi lineages, it turns out, who preached worthy evening sermons to fewer than 20 monks, with unnamed contemporary leaders who preach meaningless words before hundreds of followers. He then expresses regret that "for many years [in China] there were no evening sermons." Since the golden age of Zen in the T'ang, no one was capable of delivering a lecture with the same vigor until "Ju-ching came to fore," offering "an opportunity that occurs once in a thousand years." Recalling passages in *Shōbōgenzō zuimonki* 3.30 and "Shohō jissō" about Ju-ching's charismatic style of delivery, Dōgen praises his mentor as he had since *Bendōwa*. Here, however, Dōgen does not set himself up in opposition to other lineages, but displays a multibranched approach to Zen genealogy so that any trace of meanspiritedness or bitterness, if it was ever there, is now faded.[50]

Once again, the main feature of Ju-ching's leadership that Dōgen admires was his ability to offer numerous spontaneous, off-the-cuff lectures at any time of day that the inspiration struck for an eager band of followers who must have shared in the excitement and charisma of the occasion:

> Regardless of what the regulations in monastic rules manuals actually prescribed, at midnight, during the early evenings or at any time after the noonday meal, and generally without regard to the time, Ju-ching convened a talk. He either had someone beat the drum for entering the abbot's quarters [nyūshitsu] to give an open talk [fusetsu] or he had someone beat the drum for small meetings [shōsan] and then for entering the abbot's quarters. Or sometimes he himself hit the wooden clapper in the Monks Hall [sōdō] three times and gave an open talk in the Illuminated Hall [shōdō]. After the open talk, the monks entered the abbot's quarters [hōjō]. At other times, he hit the wooden block hanging in front of the head monk's quarters [shuso] and gave an open talk in that room. Again, following the open talk the monks entered the abbot's quarters. These were extraordinary, truly exceptional experiences!

Dōgen then declares, "As a disciple of Ju-ching, I [Daibutsu], am also conducting evening meetings that are taking place for the very first time in our country."[51] Dōgen describes the excitement that was so unique in his Ch'an teacher's approach and also sets the standard for introducing various styles of sermons to Zen temples in Japan.

Dōgen then cites a story in which Tan-hsia from the Ts'ao-tung lineage notes that Lin-chi master Te-shan, from whom the Yün-men and Fa-yen lineages were descended, said to his assembly, "There are no words or phrases in my school, and also not a single Dharma to give to people." He further commented, "He was endowed with only one single eye. . . . In my school there are words and phrases [goku]. . . . The mysterious, profound, wondrous meaning is that the jade woman becomes pregnant in the night." According to Dōgen, however, "Although Tan-hsia could say it like this. . . . In my school *there are only words and phrases [yui goku]* [emphasis added]," echoing the view of the unity of Zen and language that is expressed with a more sustained though partisan argumentation in the "Sansuikyō" fascicle.

While Dōgen's statement certainly goes beyond Tan-hsia's, it does not necessarily represent criticism and, indeed, Tan-hsia's student Hung-chih is frequently quoted by Dōgen in the ensuing volumes of the *Eihei kōroku*. In fact, this phase marks the beginning of Dōgen's extensive reliance, which lasts for about three or four years, on Hung-chih's recorded sayings as well as the kōan collection, the *Tsung-jung lu*, which he helped create. In *Eihei kōroku* 2.135 Dōgen cites Hung-chih in creating his sermon for the winter solstice, and in 2.142 he cites the Sung master for the new year's sermon, while 2.148 alludes to *Tsung-jung lu* case 5 (also *Blue Cliff Record* case 30), and 2.170 alludes to *Tsung-jung lu* case 69, among other examples. The pattern is to emulate Hung-chih's sermon almost to the point of plagiarism yet conclude with a devastating albeit respectful critique—in a kind of pious irreverence—of him as well as Ju-ching and other predecessors.

Therefore *Eihei kōroku* 1.128 captures a key moment in the shifting of priorities. Dōgen explains the importance of lectures and of a master capable of delivering them with appropriate spontaneity and dynamism, shortly before settling on the *jōdō* sermon as his main lecture style. The end of an emphasis on informal lectures must make us wonder whether Dōgen abandoned the style or continued this manner of instruction during the late period; perhaps discourses in the Abbot's Quarters were either left unrecorded or lost. The 12-*Shōbōgenzō* consists of *jishu* sermons, but for the most part these were written and not presented orally, so the text appears planned and culminating, according to the Renewal Theory.

6

The Late Period

Outpost Administrator or Brilliant Innovator?

The final main stage or late period of Dōgen's career begins with the renaming of Daibutsuji temple as Eiheiji on 6.15.1246 in order to proclaim institutional autonomy and integrity, as was noted by the delivery of *Eihei kōroku* 2.177.[1] The name was apparently a reference to the Yung-p'ing (J. Eihei) era, which lasted from 58 to 75 C.E., when the first Buddhist sutra was supposedly introduced to China and Buddhist spiritual power was considered superior to that of the Taoists. This period extended through the final writings of 1253, including "Hachidainingaku," the last fascicle in the 12-*Shōbōgenzō* (an anomalous text influenced primarily not by kōan literature but by the *Yuikyōgyō* [*Taishō* no. 389], which purported to express the last injunctions of the Buddha) and several poems composed shortly before Dōgen's death. Like the early stages but rather unlike the middle middle stage of his career, which was rather monolithic in the production of the 75-*Shōbōgenzō*, the late period is marked by experimentation with diverse literary genres that draw heavily from established Buddhist literature. Nevertheless, historical analysis shows the emergence of distinct fields of discourse revealing Dōgen's ingenuity and creativity in constructing a vision of monastic life.

The late stage is divided into two subperiods. The first is the early late period (1246–1248), extending through the mission to Kamakura, which lasted for about seven and a half months, from the beginning of the eighth month of 1247 until Dōgen's return to Eiheiji on 3.14.1248. This return is the basis for one of the most prominent of the *jōdō* sermons, *Eihei kōroku* 3.251. This phase features Dōgen's continued reliance on Sung sources for inspiration and guidance, especially the records of Hung-chih, which are cited in numerous *jōdō* sermons,[2] and the *Ch'an-yüan ch'ing-kuei,* which influenced the *Fushu-kuhampō* and the *Nihonkoku Echizen Eiheiji chiji shingi* (or *Chiji shingi*). These became the third and sixth chapters of the *Eihei shingi,* respectively.

The late late phase, beginning with the return from Kamakura, has long been by far the most neglected and misunderstood period in Dōgen's career. It can now be seen as a dynamic—and perhaps even the most crucial—phase of all, marked by the composition of at least three major writings. These include: 281 or 53 percent of the 531 *jōdō* sermons collected in *Eihei kōroku* vols. 3–7 and *shōsan* sermons contained in vol. 8; the majority of the 12-*Shōbōgenzō* fascicles; and the *Hōkyōki.* In addition, poetry (both *waka* and *kanshi*) along with other short works were composed at this time. Collectively, these writings express what seems to be a new attitude toward the doctrine of karmic causality in its various ramifications, ranging from a rational or logical examination of conditioning factors to supernatural/mythological elements evoking the inviolability of retribution and possibilities for redemption through rites of repentance and miraculous feats of Buddhist symbols and saints.

Although Dōgen has long been celebrated by the Sōtō tradition as a Zen master par excellence for his leadership at Eiheiji, recent revisionist scholarship associated with the Decline Theory has suggested that there was a downward spiral from the time of the arrival in Echizen all the way to the end of his life. During this ongoing process of decline, Dōgen treated a limited set of monastic issues for a narrow audience of unsophisticated novices from remote provinces. The Decline Theory sees the earlier, freethinking Dōgen who supported the role of women and laypersons in pursuit of the Dharma, now retreating to a conservative, nay puritanical and intolerant, ideological stance. It further suggests that there were no major developments or alterations and that the only serious focus of the late period was on ritual. This approach has been buttressed by scholarship that attributes the eventual success of the Sōtō sect in spreading throughout northern and central Japan to the dissemination strategies of Keizan and his evangelical disciples, rather than to the organizational efforts of Dōgen.[3]

However, the Decline Theory fails to raise the question of why the 75-*Shōbōgenzō,* one of the great experiments in the history of Japanese letters even according to its own rather skeptical assessment, came to such an abrupt end— *and with it the partisan attacks.* For example, *Eihei kōroku* 4.304 from 1247 praises both Lin-chi and Te-shan, who were criticized so bitterly just a few years earlier. By avoiding this issue, the Decline Theory does not report that the period of Dōgen's intense criticism of rivals was short-lived and did not occur again. Nor does it indicate that Eiheiji worship did not neglect laypersons or women (as both monastics [*shukke-sha*] and lay followers [*zaike-sha*]), but frequently included villagers along with local officials at precept recitation ceremonies for monks and nuns, during which miraculous apparitions were said to appear.[4] Or, instead, it dismisses these kinds of writings altogether as indications of the deterioration of Dōgen's faculties without exploring the significance of their possible connections with folklore religiosity.

Furthermore, the Decline Theory does not attempt to show that there are several possible explanations for the termination of the 75-*Shōbōgenzō*. It may be, for example, that Dōgen at this stage of his career did not realize how significant his writings would prove for posterity. Or it could be that he lost the inspiration for the sustained argumentation characteristic of the *jishu* style, or was turned off to this kind of presentation because despite certain advantages, it brought to the surface a tendency toward hypercritical rhetoric. We must also consider that Dōgen may have continued to deliver but chose not to record *jishu* lectures because they were intended for a resumption of one-on-one, private instruction begun at Kōshōji. Or perhaps there were manuscripts from this period that were lost or destroyed. As Ejō writes in the colophon to the posthumously discovered *Hōkyōki*, "As I began drafting this, I wondered whether there might be still other [manuscripts] that have not been discovered. I am concerned that [the record of] Dōgen's unlimited achievements may be incomplete, and in my sadness fall 100,000 tears."[5] Perhaps Dōgen himself never considered the 75-*Shōbōgenzō* his main achievement, or maybe he saw it as a part of a larger goal, such as the collection of 100 fascicles, which was his fondest wish according to Ejō's colophon found in one of the manuscripts of "Hachidaingaku."[6]

While the Decline Theory conflates the end of the middle with the late period, the Renewal Theory understands that the 75-*Shōbōgenzō* was rooted in a stage of Dōgen's career from which he went on to a final and perhaps in his mind more decisive period. For the Renewal Theory, the key transition is from the composition of the 75-*Shōbōgenzō* to the 12-*Shōbōgenzō*. This theory argues that while Dōgen began the late period still in ideological doldrums, the return from Kamakura resulted in his coming to his senses by realizing the deficiency of the Mahayana doctrine of original enlightenment or universal Buddha-nature and embracing the basic Buddhist teaching of karmic causality. According to this theory, the emphasis in the latter text on a strict interpretation of causality as a refutation of original enlightenment must have always been in the back of Dōgen's mind during his earlier writing,[7] but it did not emerge emphatically as the key element in his philosophical vision until he was disturbed by the fusion of Zen and warrior culture, and consequent rationalization of violence and killing, during his visit to Kamakura. Yet the Renewal Theory tends to overlook many distinct points of continuity whereby Dōgen in the later stages expresses ideas about the monastic institution and its structure that are consistent with or an extension of positions reflected in earlier writings.[8] It neglects the significance of late texts, other than the 12-*Shōbōgenzō,* that in some ways enhance and in other ways detract from its view, and it maintains that the only real change in Dōgen's entire life occurred after the Kamakura mission, a trip that the Decline Theory argues "seems to have come to naught."[9]

Both theories do an admirable job in relativizing and contextualizing the importance of the 75-*Shōbōgenzō*. However, the Decline Theory tends toward an extreme view in negating, through a neglect of key works, the significance of the later stages, and the Renewal Theory tends toward another extreme by focusing on a few key pieces of the puzzle that comprise the late Dōgen while ignoring materials that might compromise or, ironically, strengthen its perspective. The theories focus exclusively on a single category of texts without paying attention to the entire career production, thereby offering a one-sided, skewed evaluation of the complex characteristics of the late period. Therefore borrowing insights while also reflecting on contradictions and conflicts between the Decline and Renewal Theories is useful in highlighting the important role of the late late period and constructing what I refer to as the Monastic View of Dōgen's career trajectory.

The Early Late Period: Solidifying the Monastic Model

The writings of the early late period are intent on establishing ritual precedents and are so emulative of Sung sources that many at first seem quite mundane and unoriginal, reflecting a decline due to isolation or lack of inspiration. As with the late middle period, Dōgen's overwhelming concern with formulating the policies and customs of monastic life is reflected in the *Eihei shingi* materials, particularly the *Chiji shingi*, composed in 1246 shortly after the naming of Eiheiji; it provides instructions on the functions for four main leaders of the temple: director (*kan'in*), rector (*ino*), chief cook (*tenzo*), and supervisor (*shissui*). In each of the four sections on these positions, Dōgen quotes the *Ch'an-yüan ch'ing-kuei* verbatim, or close to it, as is also the case in a number of his *shingi* writings from the *Shōbōgenzō* and elsewhere.[10] It is significant that Dōgen introduces the sets of instructions with various examples of kōan cases about the role of leadership in Ch'an temples. The kōans show T'ang masters standing in disregard and defiance of rules and regulations. Assimilating the regulations of institutional structure with an emphasis on radical individuality or anti-structure is a rather remarkable innovation in itself. Yet the sense of ingenuity is somewhat diminished by the lack of the dazzling interpretive wordplay that characterizes much of the 75-*Shōbōgenzō* fascicles. Furthermore, the main sections of the text outlining the various administrative functions appear unoriginal and underdeveloped, especially compared with the earliest of the *Eihei shingi* chapters, *Tenzokyōkun*, on the role of the chief cook written ten years earlier. As translators Dan Leighton and Shohaku Okumura note of the *Chiji shingi*, "Had [Dōgen] lived longer, perhaps the sections for the other three administrators might have been developed into separate texts parallel to [*Ten-zokyōkun*]."[11]

Nevertheless, there is another level of significance of the *Chiji shingi*, as suggested by Ishii Seijun and supported in part by the research of Ishii Shūdō and others, which is a focus on the Monastic View. Although Dōgen is sometimes known for a "clergy for clergy's sake" (*shukke shijo shugi*) approach, his rules texts indicate not only his thoughts on practice, but also his plans for integrating the lay community into the structures of monastic life. On several occasions where Dōgen subtly alters Ch'an sources in the instructional sections of the text, he does so in order to make a point about the importance of the secular community of donors and lay followers. As the list of titles of the *Chiji shingi* sections shows, even though these are not instructions preached directly to laypersons, they instruct the monks on how members of the lay community should be treated. According to the section on the role of the director, for example:

> Therefore, [we can see that] to venerate and extend a compassionate
> heart to donors and patrons was the teaching and decree of the
> World-Honored Tathagata [Sakyamuni]. Although experiencing the
> great result [of buddhahood] is possible from small causes, this is
> only within the blessing field of the three jewels.[12]

Therefore if donors make a donation (or offering) with a clear mind, they will gain the result of being respected or of attaining the same level of buddhahood as monks. Similar sentiments are expressed in the other sections.

The Monastic View explains that Dōgen experimented and made changes in the Ch'an style in dealing with the life of monks. For example, the *Eihei kōroku* adjusts the prescribed schedule for the delivery of *jōdō* sermons from the *Ch'an-yüan ch'ing-kuei* guidelines to fit the needs of the development of Zen monasticism at Eiheiji. From the numbers of sermons shown in Table 31 in the previous chapter, it is clear that the Buddha's birth (4.8), death (2.15), and enlightenment (12.8) anniversaries, in addition to memorials for Ju-ching and Eisai, were favorite events in the yearly cycle. Dōgen also consistently presented sermons for seasonal celebrations, especially in the fall (new and full moons in the eighth, ninth, and tenth months of the year).

Influence Yet Critique of Hung-Chih and Other Ch'an Masters

In analyzing the contents of the *Eihei kōroku*, there seem to be key differences in the materials collected by the three recorders of the *jōdō* sermons. In vol. 1, recorded by Senne, there are numerous short and concise sermons (about 15 percent of the total) that consist of only one or two sentences.[13] For example, no. 1.23 states, "Deeply see the blue mountains constantly walking. By yourself know the white stone woman gives birth to a child at night," and no. 1.34 queries simply, "If this greatest cold does not penetrate into our bones, how will the fragrance of the plum blossoms pervade the entire universe?"[14] Both sermons conclude with a reference to the fact that following the brief verbal utterance, "Dōgen descended from his seat."

In the second main section (vols. 2–4, recorded by Ejō), a new pattern emerges: Dōgen cites eminent Chinese Ch'an predecessors but also is willing to challenge, critique, revise, and rewrite their sayings to express his own unique understanding and appropriation of Buddhist teaching. Dōgen expresses great respect and admiration for Ch'an as practiced in China, especially a reverence for Sōtō predecessors whose sayings he regularly cites. Yet he also relishes his role as a critical commentator and revisionist of many of the leading Chinese masters, including those from his own Ts'ao-tung/Sōtō lineage. A common refrain in many of the sermons is, "Other patriarchs have said it that way, but I [Eihei] say it this way. . . ."

Ishii Shūdō finds that the main changes in the last three volumes, vols. 5–7, edited by Gien and covering the final years at Eiheiji, is that Dōgen is no longer as heavily influenced by Hung-chih's recorded sayings, which are less frequently cited, and there is a greater emphasis on causality and the citation of early Buddhist scriptures, but not any significant alteration in ideology about zazen or kōan interpretation.[15]

A close-up look at the second phase of the Eihei kōroku (vols. 2–4), which corresponds to the early late period, shows that Dōgen asserts the primacy of the discursive style of Hung-chih and wages a campaign to identify himself with the Hung-chih-Ju-ching axis that occupied the abbacy during the glory days of Mount T'ien-t'ung. This identification helped enable Dōgen to distinguish his lineage from rival Zen movements in Japan, and to support the rejection of Ta-hui because his lineage in China gave sanction to the controversial Daruma school. Unlike Ju-ching, who remained obscure except for his connection to Dōgen, Hung-chih was widely recognized as one of the premier sermonizers and poets during the peak of the Ts'ao-tung school, which had undergone a period of revival inspired by Fu-yung Tao-k'ai (J. Fuyū Dōkai) two generations before.

Whereas Ju-ching appears with much greater frequency in the Shōbōgenzō, Hung-chih's role is quite prominent in the Eihei kōroku (see Table 32). Dōgen frequently turns to Hung-chih as a model for sermons on ritual occasions, citing him in the jōdō far more frequently than in the jishu, with the prominent exception of the "Zazenshin" and "Jinshin inga" fascicles, in which Dōgen critiques and rewrites his view of meditation or causality. A major consequence of overlooking the Eihei kōroku is to neglect the importance of Hung-chih's influence, whereas Hung-chih is cited over 40 times, although allusions continued into the late late period. Dōgen cited Hung-chih three or four times on the occasion of the Buddha's birthday between 1246 and 1249, and also on

TABLE 32. Sources Cited in the *Eihei kōroku*

Text	*Eihei kōroku* No. of Citations
1. Ching-te ch'uan-teng lu (J. Keitoku dentōroku)	68
2. Hung-chih lu (J. Wanshi roku)	43
3. Tsung-men t'ung-yao chi (J. Shūmon tōyōshū)	25
4. Tsung-men lien-t'ung hui-yao (J. Shūmon rentōeyō)	24
5. Ju-ching lu (J. Nyojō roku)	10
6. Chia-t'ai p'u-teng lu (J. Katai futōroku)	7
7. Yüan-wu lu/sung-ku (J. Engo roku/juko)	9
8. T'ien-sheng kuang-teng lu (J. Tenshō kōtōroku)	9
9. Ta-hui lu (J. Daie roku)	2
10. Huang-po lu (J. Ōbaku roku)	2
11. Hsü ch'uan-teng lu (J. Zoku dentōroku)	2
TOTAL	201

other occasions such as New Year, the beginning of the summer retreat, the Boys' Festival, and the winter solstice.

The reliance on Hung-chih for the most part did not continue in the later sections recorded by Gien, a former Daruma school monk who ten years after Dōgen's death took the *Eihei kōroku* to China to have it certified at Mount T'ien-t'ung and returned with a controversial abbreviated version, the *Eihei goroku*. Table 33, juxtaposed with Table 29 in the previous chapter dealing with Ju-ching citations, makes it clear that references to Hung-chih, which are primarily concerned with ritual occasions when the master's words are a model Dōgen emulates yet sometimes revises, reach a peak in the late 1240s and seem to fade just as those to Ju-ching began picking up again in the early 1250s.

As was mentioned, it sometimes goes unnoticed that Dōgen's reverence did not prohibit Zen-style criticism of the masters he favored, though generally he fell short of blasphemy, and that Ju-ching is not immune to this treatment. In citing Hung-chih, Dōgen rarely loses the opportunity to critique or outdo him. The first main example is *jōdō* no. 2.135, a sermon for the winter solstice at Daibutsuji:

> When the old buddha Hung-chih was residing at Mount T'ien-t'ung, during a winter solstice sermon he said, "Yin reaches its fullness and yang arises, as their power is exhausted, conditions change. A green dragon runs away when his bones are exposed. A black panther looks different when it is covered in mist. Take the skulls of all the buddhas of the triple world and thread them onto a single rosary. Do not speak of bright heads and dark heads, as truly they are sun face, moon face. Even if your measuring cup is full and the bal-

TABLE 33. Dōgen's Citations or Allusions to Hung-chih

Eihei kōroku Citations	Mid-Autumn	EK 7.481, 1252
		EK 7.494, 1252
Winter Solstice	EK 4.344, 1249	EK 7.514, 1252
		EK 8.s.13, 1240s
EK 2.135, 1245	*Other Examples*	EK 8.s.20, 1240s
EK 3.206, 1246		EK 9.25, 1236
EK 4.296, 1248	EK 3.203, 1246 (full)	EK 9.88, 1236
	EK 3.246, 1247 (full)	
	EK 4.269, 1248 (full)	
New Year	EK 7.498, 1252 (full)	*Shōbōgenzō*
EK 2.142, 1246		
EK 3.216, 1247		Gyōbutsuigi, 1241
EK 4.303, 1249	*Allusions Only*	Zazenshin, 1242
		Gyōji, p. 1, 1242
	EK 2.180, 1246	Kobusshin, 1243
5.5 Day	EK 3.186, 1246	Shunjū, 1244
	EK 3.187, 1246	Ōsakusendaba, 1245
EK 3.242, 1247	EK 3.222, 1247	Jinshin inga, 1253?
EK 4.261, 1248	EK 3.223, 1237	
EK 4.326, 1249	EK 3.227, 1247	
	EK 4.264, 1248	*SBGZ Zuimonki*
Bathing Buddha	EK 4.285, 1248	
	EK 4.329, 1249	3.10, 1237
EK 3.236, 1247	EK 4.337, 1249	
EK 3.256, 1248	EK 4.340, 1249	
EK 4.320, 1249	EK 4.341, 1249	*Bendōwa*
	EK 4.344, 1249	
Summer Retreat	EK 4.397, 1250	(1231)
	EK 5.400, 1250	
EK 3.257, 1248	EK 5.403, 1250	
EK 4.322, 1249	EK 5.418, 1250	
EK 4.341, 1249		

ance scale is level, in transactions I sell at a high price and buy when the price is low. Zen worthies, do you understand this? In a bowl, the bright pearl rolls on its own without being pushed.

"Here is a story," [Hung-chih continued]. "Hsüeh-feng asked a monk, 'Where are you going?' The monk said, 'I'm going to do my communal labor.' Hsüeh-feng said, 'Go ahead.' Yün-men said [of this dialogue], 'Hsüeh-feng judges people based on their words.' " Hung-chih said, "Do not make a move. If you move I'll give you thirty blows. Why is this so? Take a luminous jewel without any flaw, and if you carve a pattern on it its virtue is lost."

The teacher [Dōgen] then said: Although these three venerable ones [Hsüeh-feng, Yün-men, Hung-chih] spoke this way, I, old man Daibutsu, do not agree. Great assembly, listen carefully and consider this well. For a luminous jewel without flaw, if polished its glow in-

creases. . . . With his fly-whisk [Dōgen] drew a circle and said: Look!
After a pause [Dōgen] said, "Although the plum blossoms are color-
ful in the freshly fallen snow, you must look into it further to understand the first arrival of yang [with the solstice]."[16]

Here Dōgen is indebted to Hung-chih's original passage, which cites Ma-tsu's
famous saying, "Sun face [or eternal] buddha, moon face [or temporal] buddha"
from *Ts'ung-jung lu* case 36, and also includes a saying about the bright pearl
that appears in the fourth line of Hung-chih's verse comment on this case.
But Dōgen challenges all the masters. After making a dramatic, well-timed
demonstration with the ceremonial fly-whisk as a symbol of authority, he
evokes the image of plum blossoms in the snow to highlight the need for
continually practicing *zazen* meditation. This statement reinforces his rewriting of the jewel metaphor to put an emphasis on the process of polishing.

To give another example, in *jōdō* no. 3.236 for "Bathing [the Baby] Buddha,"
a celebration of the Buddha's birthday in 1247, Dōgen tells that when Hung-
chih was abbot at Mount T'ien-t'ung, in a sermon delivered on the same occasion, he had cited an anecdote in which Yün-men performed the bathing
ritual and had apologized to the Buddha for using "impure water." However,
Dōgen criticizes Hung-chih's interpretation by suggesting:

> Although the ancient buddha Hung-chih said it like this, how
> should I [Eihei] speak of the true meaning of the Buddha's birthday?
> Casting off the body within the ten thousand forms, the conditions
> for his birth naturally arose. In a single form after manifesting as a
> human body, he discovered anew the path to enlightenment. What
> is the true meaning of our bathing the Buddha? After a pause [Dō-
> gen] said, "Holding in our own hands the broken wooden ladle, we
> pour water on his head to bathe the body of the Tathagata."[17]

Dōgen is also especially critical of Chao-chou, as in nos. 1.140, 4.331, and
4.339, in addition to no. 2.154, in which he first appears to be defending the
Chinese master in citing a passage from his recorded sayings against a critique
by a disciple, but then concludes by overturning Chao-chou's standpoint:

> Consider this: A monk asked Chao-chou, "What is the path without
> mistakes?" Chao-chou said, "Clarifying mind and seeing one's own
> nature is the path without mistakes." Later it was said, "Chao-chou
> only expressed eighty or ninety percent. I am not like this. If some-
> one asks, 'What is the path without mistakes?' I would tell him,
> 'The inner gate of every house extends to Chang'an [the capital, lit.,
> "long peace"].' "
>   The teacher [Dōgen] said: Although it was said thus, this is not
> worth considering. The old buddha Chao-chou's expression is cor-

rect. Do you want to know the clear mind of which Chao-chou spoke? [Dōgen] cleared his throat and then said, Just this is it. Do you want to know about the seeing into one's own nature that Chao-chou mentioned? [Dōgen] laughed, then said, Just this is it. Although this is so, the old buddha Chao-chou's eyes could behold east and west, and his mind abided south and north. If someone asked Daibutsu [Dōgen], "What is the path without mistakes?" I would say to him, You must not go anywhere else. Suppose someone asks, "Master, isn't this tuning the string by gluing the fret?" I would say to him, Do you fully understand tuning the string by gluing the fret?[18]

The phrases about not going anywhere else and "gluing the fret" allude to concrete manifestations of phenomenal reality rather than conceptual abstractions that may impede an appropriation of enlightenment experience.

In no. 3.207, Dōgen criticizes Yün-men, as well as the whole notion of the autonomy of a "Zen school" (Zen-shū), which may take priority over the universal Buddha Dharma:

[Dōgen] said: Practitioners of Zen should know wrong from right. It is said that after [the Ancestor] Upagupta, there were five sects of Buddha Dharma during its decline in India. After Ch'ing-yüan and Nan-yüeh, people took it upon themselves to establish the various styles of the five houses, which was an error made in China. Moreover, in the time of the ancient buddhas and founding ancestors, it was not possible to see or hear the Buddha Dharma designated as the "Zen school," which has never actually existed. What is presently called the Zen school is not truly the Buddha Dharma.

I remember that a monk once asked Yün-men, "I heard an ancient said that although the [patriarch of the Ox Head School] expounded horizontally and vertically, he did not know the key to the workings of going beyond. What is that key to the workings of going beyond?" Yün-men said, "The eastern mountain and the western peak are green." If someone were to ask Eihei [Dōgen], "What is that key to the workings of going beyond?" I would simply reply to him, "Indra's nose is three feet long."[19]

Note that in Dōgen's rewriting of Yün-men's response, neither expression addresses the question although each has its merits as a reflection of Zen insight. Yet Dōgen seems to suggest that Yün-men's phrasing is deficient and that his own saying is on the mark, perhaps because it is at once more indirect and absurd yet concrete and down-to-earth.

Furthermore, the reverent tone of a dutiful follower that is so apparent in the *Hōkyōki*, which deals—whenever it was composed—with Dōgen's time as a disciple, is not necessarily duplicated in the *Eihei kōroku*, where he subjects Ju-ching's interpretations of Ch'an kōans and other sayings to a process of revision and rewriting. In no. 2.179 Dōgen critiques five prominent figures, Sakyamuni and four Chinese masters, who respond to a statement of the Buddha in the *Suramgama Sutra*, chapter 9, as also cited and discussed with the same conclusion in *Shōbōgenzō* "Tenbōrin":

> [Dōgen] said, The World-Honored One said, "When one person opens up reality and returns to the source, all space in the ten directions disappears." Teacher Wu-tsu of Mount Fa-yen said, "When one person opens up reality and returns to the source, all space in the ten directions crashes together resounding everywhere." Zen Master Yüan-wu of Mount Jia-shan said, "When one person opens up reality and returns to the source, all space throughout the ten directions flowers are added on to brocade." Teacher Fo-hsing Fa-t'ai said, "When one person opens up reality and returns to the source, all space in the ten directions is nothing other than all space in the ten directions."
>
> My late teacher T'ien-t'ung [Ju-ching] said, "Although the World-Honored One made the statement, 'When one person opens up reality and returns to the source, all space in the ten directions disappears,' this utterance cannot avoid becoming an extraordinary assessment. T'ien-t'ung is not like this. When one person opens up reality and returns to the source, a mendicant breaks his rice bowl."
>
> The teacher [Dōgen] said, The previous five venerable teachers said it like this, but I, Eihei, have a saying that is not like theirs. When one person opens up reality and returns to the source, all space in the ten directions opens up reality and returns to the source.[20]

Heading East?

Whether or not Dōgen actually made the trip to Kamakura at the end of the early late phase is far more problematic in terms of historiographical documentation than the pilgrimage to China, and numerous scholars have raised serious questions about its credibility. The only references to the mission in Dōgen's writings are a set of *waka* and one *kanshi* verse, in addition to a short essay,[21] as well as the sermon, *jōdō* no. 251, to be discussed later, that is so crucial for understanding the impact of the trip on the late late period, especially for the Renewal Theory. Another bit of evidence in support of the trip is that, according to *Shōbōgenzō zuimonki* 3.13, Dōgen says that in the mid-1230s he first refused to be called to the shogun's stronghold in the temporary capital, implying that a Hōjō invitation may have come to him. At that time, he felt that going east (to the remote Kanto region) to preach to "people who don't want to study would wear me out," and that sincere, dedicated followers should be willing "to cross mountains, rivers, and seas" to come find him, an ordeal required after his move to Echizen. However, a trip in the 1230s would have probably been for evangelical purposes only, but without the support of the Hōjō, since the current regent, Tsunetoki, was not involved in promoting Buddhism, especially a decade after the death of Buddhist patron or "nun shogun" Hōjō Masako.

As shown in Table 33, with the ascendancy a decade later in 1246 of Hōjō Tokiyori, who was the first of the Hōjō rulers to have a genuine interest in Zen, in addition to holding political control over the Hatano clan—a mixed blessing given the trade-off of support and manipulation—Dōgen relented. Or perhaps he went to Kamakura not directly because of the Hōjō but at the behest or instruction of Hatano, who was apparently a *daimyō* being summoned by his warlord. Dōgen's misgivings about surrendering his integrity and autonomy seem to be expressed in the following verse, which was in the group of twelve *waka* poems apparently presented to the Hōjō's wife and first published in the *Kenzeiki* in 1472:

Shōbōgenzō	*Treasury of the True Dharma-eye*
Nami mo hiki	In the heart of the night,
Kaze mo tsunaganu	The moonlight framing
Sute obune	A small boat drifting,
Suki koso yawa no	Tossed not by the waves
Sakai nari keri	Nor swayed by the breeze.[22]

Dōgen may have first been intrigued, but by the end of the journey was terribly upset with what he considered the corruption lurking in the shogunate's misuse of Zen as a tool for the advancement of samurai culture. His ambivalence and longing to be back at Eiheiji are expressed in a *kanshi* verse written near the end of his trip to Kamakura in the early spring of 1248, after he had been away from Eiheiji for nearly eight months. He writes "on the occasion of hearing an early spring thunderstorm":

> For six months, I've been taking my rice at the home of a layman,
> Feeling like the blossoms of an old plum tree covered by the snow
>   and frost,
> Exhilarated in hearing the first sound of thunder crackling across
>   the sky—
> The five red petals of spring peach blossoms will soon be brighten-
>   ing the capital.[23]

The "layman" referred to in the first line is no doubt his patron, Hatano. Dōgen clearly misses the life of ritual purity at Eiheiji yet at the same time longs for

TABLE 34. Hōjō Periods of Rule*

Hōjō Takamasa, 1203–1205 (becomes monk)
Hōjō Yoshitoki, 1205–1224
Sanetomo assassinated, 1219
Tale of Heike, 1220
Jōkyū Incident, 1221
Hōjō Yasutoki, 1224–1242
Hōjō Masako ("nun shogun"), d. 1225
Hōjō Tsunetoki, 1242–1246
Fujiwara Yoritsune removed from office, 1244
Hōjō Tokiyori, 1246–1256
Drives from power Kujō Michiie
Offers abbacy to Dōgen
Sets up Lan-hsi in Kenchōji
Hōjō Tokimune, 1268–1284
At first favors Ritsu school, then practices *zazen*
Sets up Wu-hsüeh as founding abbot of Engakuji

*Additional regents include Hōjō Nagatoki, 1256–1264, Hōjō Masamura, 1264–1268, and Hōjō Sadatoki, 1284–1301.

a return to the capital (however, it is ambiguous whether "capital" refers to Kyoto or to the temporary capital in Kamakura).

By departing Kamakura and returning to the Echizen mountains in a matter of months, Dōgen apparently turned down the opportunity offered by the Hōjō to head Kenchōji temple and thereby to take part in the development of what became the Japanese Five Mountains system (see Figure 19). This conflict between the monk and the shogun is further explored in the recent Kabuki play *Dōgen no tsuki*, which suggests that Tokiyori, incensed by the refusal of a piece of land by the Zen master, who may have considered it a form of bribery, was about to execute Dōgen for insubordination; he was stifled in this attempt, however, by Dōgen's spiritual power, which resisted the thrust of the sword.[24]

According to the *Teiho Kenzeiki* and other traditional records, against Dōgen's instructions, one of the erstwhile Daruma school monks, named Gemmyō, who was left behind to settle accounts in Kamakura, went ahead and accepted the Hōjō's donation. As a result, Dōgen, who later declined the imperial offer of a purple robe, banished Gemmyō from Eiheiji, the appropriate punishment as indicated in the original Ch'an *shingi* code, attributed to Pai-chang, the *Ch'an-men kuei-shih* (see Figure 20). But the subsequent digging up and permanent removal of his meditation platform from the grounds of the temple was an exceptional action showing an even tougher standard than was generally followed in Sung China. Renewal Theory scholars have speculated that this episode inspired a new way of thinking in the late late period by signifying Dōgen's embracing of the doctrine of karmic causality.

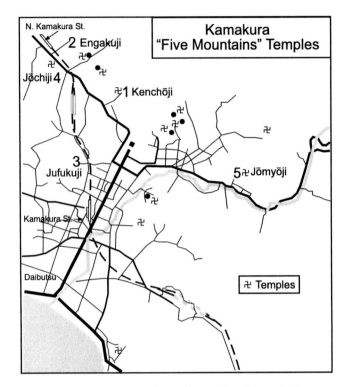

FIGURE 19. Map of Kamakura "Five Mountains"

The Late Late Period: Turn Toward Causality

This final subperiod has a dynamic quality similar to that of the move to Echizen in being characterized by (1) the challenges of a shift in location (return
from Kamakura) and sectarian rivalry (disagreements with the Rinzai school
about accepting the Hōjō's approach); (2) a change in the recording and editing
of the *Eihei kōroku* (from Ejō to Gien, beginning with vol. 5 in summer 1249);
(3) the reception of an inspiring new text (Hatano presented Dōgen with a
complete set of the *Tripitaka* canon in late 1249); and (4) the incorporation of
different kinds of students (especially laypersons receptive to miracles) in Dōgen's movement. See Table 35.

   The combination of these factors demanded an innovative approach to
instruction and helped inspire new approaches to constructing his writings
that continued to reflect older themes such as the impact of Chinese influences,
especially Sung masters and texts, while incorporating newer ones, such as a
reliance on pre-Ch'an and even pre-Mahayana sources emphasizing the theme

玄明首座ヲ
擯出シ坐禪
ノ床ヲ截リ
取セ玉フ

FIGURE 20. The Removal of Gemmyō's Space (*Teiho Kenzeiki zue*)

of karmic causality. However, it is also possible to see this phase infused with fundamental contradictions that seem to occur during the late period. Dōgen examines causal conditioning from a logical standpoint while also accepting mythological tales of retribution and repentance, and he stresses that true enlightenment is available only to monks who strictly adhere to an undistracted approach to *zazen* while also highlighting the occurrence of supernatural

TABLE 35. Main Features of Late Late Phase

Return from Kamakura, 3 mo. 1248
Gemmyō Incident, summer 1248
Gien Editorship, summer 1249
Hatano's Gift of *Tripitaka*, late 1249
Miraculous Events at Eiheiji, 1245–1251
Lay Repentance Rites Performed, 1249–1251
"Hachidainingaku," 1253

events at Eiheiji to attract lay followers. How do these elements fit together, and what is the best methodology for comprehending their connectedness? Let us first consider the role of the Chinese mentor in the late late period.

Re-Reappearance of Ju-Ching

An aspect of continuity and enhancement of earlier stages that has long gone unnoticed is that Dōgen refers to Ju-ching during the late late period more extensively than ever before, and with a greater frequency than in the middle middle period, when an intense focus on the mentor was initiated. In his unflawed loyalty to the teacher, Dōgen seems to come full circle by epitomizing not so much the trends of Chinese Ch'an in the Sung era but the selectionist approach of the Japanese Buddhist schools of the Kamakura era. Dōgen's commitment to just-sitting (*shikan taza*) initiated in *Bendōwa* remains consistent throughout his career and does not relent in the latter days despite any other apparent changes in outlook regarding his mentor and other Chinese figures and texts. For example, Dōgen continually emphasizes *zazen* and the experience of casting off body-mind, as in nos. 4.318, cited below, and 4.337:

> My late teacher [Ju-ching] instructed the assembly, "Practicing Zen with a teacher [*sanzen*] is dropping off body and mind. Great assembly, do you want to understand thoroughly the meaning of this?" After a pause [Dōgen] said, "Sitting upright and casting off body and mind, the ancestral teachers' nostrils are flowers of emptiness."[25]

However, as we have seen, Dōgen is by no means slavishly devoted to the Ch'an mentor. In no. 5.390, one of the longest and most important of the *jōdō* sermons, which is echoed in the briefer no. 6.464, he undertakes a sustained argument that revises Ju-ching's view of meditation and also criticizes and revises Pai-chang's view of monastic regulations.[26]

Although Dōgen's portrayal of Ju-ching is consistent throughout his writings, there are numerous inconsistencies between Dōgen's presentation of his mentor and what is known about Ju-ching's approach from his recorded sayings. Nakaseko Shōdō suggests that by analyzing differences in the teachings of master and disciple, we see contradictions in Dōgen's appropriation of Ju-ching. According to Nakaseko, there are two sets of doctrines: one is how Ju-ching is portrayed in Dōgen's writings, and the other is how he is expressed in the *Ju-ching yü-lu* (assuming its authenticity). As seen in the works of Dōgen, Ju-ching was a strict advocate of intensive *zazen* training, which was the only form of religious practice he consistently followed since he began training at the age of 19, according to "Gyōji" (part 2). Ju-ching is also portrayed as a severe critic of reliance on kōans as well as of the corrupt lifestyle of many of his contemporary monks. In addition, according to Dōgen, Ju-ching criticized a variety of doctrines that found currency in Chinese Ch'an. The objects of his criticism include the following:[27]

1. The unity of the three teachings (according to *Shōbōgenzō* "Shohō jissō")
2. The *kikan* or developmental, intellectual approach in the notions of the three phrases of Yün-men (*Shōbōgenzō* "Bukkyō" [Buddhist Sutras])
3. The four relations of Lin-chi, the five ranks of Tung-shan, and numerous other doctrinal formulas (*Shōbōgenzō* "Butsudō")
4. The sectarian divisiveness of the five houses of Ch'an, which defeats the unity of all forms of Buddhism (*Hōkyōki*)
5. The autonomy of the Zen sect (*Hōkyōki*)
6. A view that advocates the separation of Ch'an from the sutras (*Hōkyōki*)
7. The "naturalist fallacy" that affirms reality without transforming it (*Hōkyōki*)
8. The tendency in some forms of Ch'an thought toward the negation of causality and karmic retribution (*Hōkyōki*).

As Nakaseko points out, much of this thought stands in contrast with what is evident in the *Ju-ching yü-lu*, which is for the most part a conventional recorded sayings text reflecting the doctrines and literary styles of the Sung period.[28] In this text, there is not so much emphasis on *zazen* or the rejection of kōans, or on criticism of the laxity in the lifestyle of monks. Furthermore, Ju-ching did not dismiss Confucius or indicate that the other teachings were inferior to the Buddha Dharma, and he did not express concern with the five houses or the autonomy of Ch'an, or the view that separates Ch'an from the sutras. He did not criticize the *kikan* formulas or the naturalist heresy. Nor did he stress causality or emphasize lyrical imagery in a way that varies from what was typical for Sung Ch'an masters appealing to an audience of literati.

It is in this context that the *Hōkyōki* is seen to be of questionable authenticity and is subject to being redated as a late late text. According to Takeuchi Michio's analysis of the contents of *Hōkyōki*, as indicated in Table 36, a third

TABLE 36. List of Hōkyōki Topics
(Total=52)

Topic	No. Entries
Doctrine	17
Rituals or precepts	13
Zazen	17
Doctrine and people	3
Doctrine and practice	2

of the dialogues in the text focuses on doctrine, a third on *zazen*, and the rest on rituals, precepts, ceremonies, people, and texts.[29] Of the more than twenty items dealing with doctrine, there is a sharp criticism of *kyōge betsuden* (special transmission outside the scriptures) theory in no. 2 and no. 21, of *kanna-zen* (Ta-hui's kōan-introspection) in no. 3, and of original enlightenment in no. 4, which are views that do not seem consistent with what is known of Ju-ching. Several passages (nos. 10 and 22) emphasize the doctrine of *kannō dōkō* (reciprocal spiritual communion defining the transmission between master and disciple), which is also featured in the 12-*Shōbōgenzō* "Hotsubodaishin" fascicle. In addition, the attack on lax behavior and the wearing of long hair by monks in no. 9, as well as the affirmation of the bodhisattva precepts in no. 5, seem to reflect Dōgen-oriented rather than Ju-ching (who would have emphasized the full precepts) priorities that are echoed in the 12-*Shōbōgenzō* "Jukai" fascicle.

The Doctrine of Karmic Causality

Perhaps the most interesting feature of the *Hōkyōki* is the presence of numerous passages on the effects of karma extending through past, present, and future (*sanjigo*). For example, nos. 7 and 8 highlight the inexorability of causality (*inga*) and the problems with ignoring the immutable law, and in no. 20 Ju-ching refutes the teaching of master Ch'ang-sha, which negates the existence of karmic hindrances. This idea echoes that of the other main writings of the late late period that stress the significance of causality as crucial for appropriating the Buddha Dharma, and severely criticize those who dismiss or ignore this outlook, including numerous passages in the *Eihei kōroku* as well as the "Jinshin inga," "Sanjigo," and "Shizen biku" fascicles of the 12-*Shōbōgenzō*, which were also composed in the early 1250s. Therefore the *Hōkyōki* may appear to be—rather than a record of conversations during Dōgen's journey to China—a part of his late late period discourse.

In addition to his reaction to the quality of Zen in Kamakura, another major turning point in Dōgen's final phase was the reception of a complete copy of the *Tripitaka* (J. *Agonkyō*) at Eiheiji near the end of 1249 from his patron, Hatano Yoshishige. This event is commemorated in *Eihei kōroku* 5.361, which acknowledges the receipt, in no. 5.362 on giving thanks, and in no. 5.366, which describes the embroidered cover that was made for the texts. Once he had the *Tripitaka* in his possession, Dōgen began to focus on drawing his citations from early Buddhist texts, especially pre-Ch'an Mahayana and Abhidharma sources rather than strictly from the Ch'an canon, although the practice of studying these texts was no doubt common at Chinese Ch'an temples, especially the Five Mountains locations where Dōgen trained. The transition from Ejō's editorship to Gien's, which occurred around 9.1.1249, is another significant turning point according to some scholars, particularly Ishii Shūdō.[30] The final sections of the *Eihei kōroku* recorded by Gien generally emphasize the doctrine of karmic causality or refute syncretic or assimilative tendencies in Zen Buddhism, and this outlook has a striking resonance and consistency with that of the 12-*Shōbōgenzō* as well as *Hōkyōki*.

The late late discourse on causality opens with *Eihei kōroku* 3.251. Delivered on 3.14.1248 at the time of Dōgen's return to Eiheiji, this is a sermon that expresses an appreciation for his monk disciples after what must have seemed like a lengthy and confusing absence. Yet it is not clear that Dōgen was successful in reassuring his followers, who were apparently worried that he had preached a different or inconsistent doctrine in the court of the Hōjō:

> [Dōgen] said, On the third day of the eighth month of last year, this mountain monk departed from this mountain and went to the Kamakura District of Sagami Prefecture to expound the Dharma for patrons and lay disciples. In the third month of this year, just last night, I came home to Eiheiji, and this morning I have ascended this seat. Some people may be wondering about the reasons for my travels. After crossing over many mountains and rivers, I did expound the Dharma for the sake of lay students, which may sound like I value worldly people and take lightly monks.
>
> Moreover, some may ask whether I presented some form of Dharma that I never before expounded and that they have not heard. However, I did not preach a Dharma there that was different from what I previously expounded to you here. I merely explained to them that people who do good deeds for others and renounce all evil action will surely reap the rewards of causality. Cast away tiles and pick up jewels. This is the one matter I [Eihei] clarify, explain, believe, and practice. Followers, you must learn this truth!
>
> After a pause, [Dōgen] said, You may laugh to hear my tongue speaking of causality in so casual a fashion. How many follies have I committed in my effort to cultivate the way. Today, it is pitiful that I have become a water buffalo. This is the phrase for expounding

Dharma. How shall I utter a phrase for returning home to the mountains? This mountain monk has been gone for more than half a year. I was like a solitary wheel placed in vast space. Today, I have returned to the mountains, and the clouds [i.e., monks] are feeling joyful. My great love for this mountain is greater than it has ever been.[31]

Although this sermon, at the time it occurred, may well have seemed anomalous and confusing, it turns out to have been a harbinger of the new emphasis expressed in *jōdō* nos. 4.315, 5.381, 6.437, 7.485, 7.510, and 7.517, among others. For example, no. 6.437 from 1251 makes it clear that those who advocate the inescapable efficacy of karmic retribution alone are the true Buddhists, whereas those who reject this doctrine in favor of a metaphysical principle beyond morality and considered free from karma must be considered heretics. This passage criticizes Devadatta, a disciple of Sakyamuni who was unclear about moral standards:

At that time, the World-Honored One declared to those monks, "If there is evil conduct, there is retribution. All good and bad actions have their recompense. If the foolish Devadatta knew that there were consequences to good and evil, he would be withered with thirst, and grieve and lament his unhappiness."[32]

However, Dōgen concludes the sermon with a passage that bypasses a mechanical view of causality by evoking his mentor's doctrine of *shinjin datsuraku* as the key to resolving all ethical issues:

My late teacher T'ien-t'ung [Ju-ching] said, "*Sanzen* [practicing Zen, or *zazen*] is casting off body-mind." If you have already cast off body-mind, you will definitely not be subject to mistaken views, attachments, or arrogance. I sincerely pray on behalf of all of you.

This tends to undermine the Renewal Theory, which sees causality overriding the need for meditation in every instance.

Also, in nos. 4.383 and 5.412, echoing the 12-*Shōbōgenzō* "Shizen biku" fascicle, Dōgen criticizes the notion of the "unity of three teachings" (Buddhism, Confucianism, Taoism, *sankyō itchi*), which was a staple belief in many Ch'an lineages who were trying to assimilate and accommodate mainstream Chinese religiosity. In no. 5.390 he dismisses syncretism; in nos. 5.402 and 7.472 he refutes the "naturalism heresy" (*jinen gedō*) that equates absolute reality with all, or particular parts, of nature, or advocates an anthropomorphic view. Also, in nos. 6.447 and 7.509 he rejects spiritism (*reichi*) as opposed to rational inquiry and an examination of the human condition characteristic of the Buddha's teaching. At the same time, in no. 7.491 Dōgen rejects once again the view of a distinctive, autonomous Zen sect (Zen-*shū*), and in no. 4.335 he criticizes the distinction between different approaches to the actualization of Zen enlightenment, including Tathagata Zen (*nyorai Zen*) based on the sutras and Patriarchal Zen (*soshi Zen*) based on the special transmission outside words and letters:

> Tathagata Zen and Patriarchal Zen were not transmitted by the ancients, but only transmitted falsely in the Eastern Land (China). For several hundred years some have been clinging with delusion to this vain name. How pitiful is the inferior condition of this Age of Decline.[33]

The Renewal Theory's Assessment of 12-Shōbōgenzō

The linchpin of the Renewal Theory is an argument for the priority of the 12-*Shōbōgenzō* as the only authentic representative of the collected writings emphasizing Dōgen's apparent rewriting of several fascicles in the 75-*Shōbōgenzō* or 60-*Shōbōgenzō* texts to express a a new standpoint based on the moral commitment embodied in the post-Kamakura period.[34] There are five rewritten fascicles, listed in Table 37 according to their order in the 12-fascicle text.

The interpretation of case 4 of the rewritten fascicles expresses as much as any other single argument in their repertoire the heart of the Renewal Theory's view of Dōgen's concept of karma and its relevance for overcoming deficient standpoints in East Asian Buddhism as a whole, especially original enlightenment. The two versions both begin by citing the famous "wild fox" kōan included in Pai-chang's recorded sayings and also cited in a variety of kōan collections, including the *Wu-men kuan* (no. 2) and the *Tsung-jung lu* (no. 8), transmission of the lamp histories such as the *T'ien-sheng kuang-teng lu* (J. *Tenshō kōtōroku*) of 1036, where it first appeared, and the *Tsung-meng lien-teng*

TABLE 37. The Rewritten Fascicles of 12-*Shōbōgenzō*

---

1. "Shukke" (Home departure) first written in 1246, no. 75 in the 75-fascicle text, rewritten as "Shukke kudoku" (Merits of home departure) and compiled by Ejō in 1255, no. 1 in the 12-fascicle text (also no. 58 in the 60-fascicle text)
2. "Den'e" (Transmission of the robe), 1240, no. 32, rewritten as "Kesa kudoku" (Merits of the robe) in 1240, no. 3 (no. 41)
3. "Hotsumujōshin" (Awakening the supreme mind), 1244, no. 63, rewritten as "Hotsubodaishin" (Awakening the bodhi-mind) in 1244, no. 4 (no. 34)—in some editions both versions are called "Hotsubodaishin"
4. "Daishugyō" (Great cultivation), 1244, no. 68, rewritten as "Jinshin inga" (Deep faith in causality), compiled by Ejō in 1255, no. 7 (not in 60-fascicle text but no. 26 in the 28-fascicle text, with "Daishugyō" no. 17)
5. "Sanjigo" (Karmic retribution through the past, present, and future), 1253, in the 60-fascicle but not in the 75-fascicle text, rewritten as "Sanjigo" in 1253, no. 8 (no. 8).

yao (J. *Shūmon rentōeyō*), as well as other kōan commentaries and dozens of Sung-era recorded sayings texts. The importance of this case for Dōgen is also demonstrated by his citation in the *Mana Shōbōgenzō* and commentary in the *Shōbōgenzō zuimonki*, as well as several passages in the *Eihei kōroku*, including a verse commentary in the ninth volume.[35]

According to the narrative of the source kōan, a monk has been transfigured into a fox for 500 lifetimes as a punishment for expressing a misunderstanding of causality. In response to a disciple's inquiry, he maintained that even a person of great cultivation (*daishugyō*) does "not fall into causality" (*furaku inga*). The monk is released from this fate, and the fox corpse is buried with Buddhist rites, through the "turning word" (*ittengo*) of Pai-chang, who maintains the virtue of "not obscuring causality" (*fumai inga*). The fundamental paradox of this kōan is that by verbally denying causality the monk is victimized by karma, yet by Pai-chang's affirming its impact he gains release. As the commentary by Dōgen and other Zen masters indicates, there are several problematical points in interpreting the kōan, including the final fate of the monk (does he continue to transmigrate or attain full nirvana?) and of the fox spirit after its reversion to the vulpine shape. Dōgen also ponders the idea that the fox might have deceived Pai-chang into believing it was really a monk, in which case its corpse should not have received a Buddhist burial.

On the other hand, the basic message of the kōan about the inviolability of karmic causality, as indicated by the phrase *fumai inga*, seems quite clear. Yet most commentaries on the kōan case, including those in the *Wu-men kuan* (no. 2) and the *Tsung-jung lu* kōan collections, highlight the provisionality and ultimately the indistinguishability of the *furaku inga* and *fumai inga* responses.[36] Dōgen, in the earlier "Daishugyō" fascicle (excluded from the 60-*Shōbōgenzō* for its criticisms of Yüan-wu, Ta-hui, and Hung-chih), seems to echo that view:

> Because causality necessarily means full cause and complete effect, there is no reason for a discussion concerning "falling into" or "not falling into," "obscuring" or "not obscuring" [causality]. If "not falling into causality" is incorrect, then "not obscuring causality" is also incorrect. Nevertheless, because of a fundamental misunderstanding, [the old man] was first transfigured into a wild fox body and then released from being a wild fox. And although "not falling into causality" was incorrect in the age of Buddha Kasyapa, it may not be incorrect in the age of Buddha Sakyamuni. Although "not obscuring causality" released the wild fox body in the current age of Buddha Sakyamuni, it may not have been effective in the age of Buddha Kasyapa.[37]

Both fascicles dealing with this kōan are critical of the Senika heresy, which advocates a "return" to an original nature or source, they see the release from the fox body as a symbol of the monk resuming his true nature. Yet whereas "Daishugyō" refuses to criticize the old man's view of *furaku inga*, "Jinshin inga" of the 12-*Shōbōgenzō* repudiates Dōgen's position of a decade before in which he equated causality and the transcendence of causality. In the later work, he asserts quite emphatically that only *fumai inga* is accurate and the *furaku inga*, which amounts to the denial of causality (*hotsumu inga*), is mistaken:

> The single greatest limitation of the monks of Sung China today is that they do not realize that "not falling into causality" is a false teaching. It is a pity that even though they encounter the true Dharma of the Tathāgata correctly transmitted from patriarch to patriarch, they accept the views of those who would deny causality. They must awaken right away to the principle of causality. The expression "not obscuring causality" of the current head monk of Mount Pai-chang demonstrates that he never denied causality. It is clear that practice, or cause, leads to realization, or result.[38]

The Renewal Theory maintains that the philosophy of religion in the 12-*Shōbōgenzō* is characterized by intellectual life and scholarly learning through textual study, rather than by the intuitionism and suppression of discourse expressed in early texts such as *Bendōwa*. In other words, the later text marks a transition from *zazen* only (*shikan taza*) and "original realization and marvelous practice" (*honshō myōshū*) to "honor *prajna*" (*hannya sonchō*) and have "deep faith in causality" (*jinshin inga*).[39] The overall aim of the Renewal Theory involves more than a simple reinterpretation of the *Shōbōgenzō*. It uses Dōgen's apparent post-Kamakura change of heart as a starting point from which to challenge original enlightenment orthodoxy that has perpetuated social discrimination and tacitly supported the status quo on the basis of claims of epistemological nondiscrimination and ontological dynamism. This challenge in turn involves rethinking the meaning of the nonduality of samsara (which is causal) and nirvana (which transcends causality).

According to the Renewal Theory, the original enlightenment view reflected in Zen thought and expressed to some extent in the 75-*Shōbōgenzō*, until Dōgen realized he had not yet fully overcome the limitations in the thought of the Daruma school, actually compounds the conceptual and moral dilemmas implicit in the naturalist position. By identifying ultimate reality with concrete phenomena, the original enlightenment view asserts nonduality from the standpoint of causality swallowing up noncausality and at the same time being swallowed up by it (since it does not necessarily require spiritual purification). Thus there is no genuine freedom or nondiscrimination as claimed under the banner of universal freedom and equality. What occurs instead is an acceptance of things as they are without moral authentication or evaluative judgment. The real problem is a matter not simply of identifying polarities or of shifting the conclusion from one side to the other, but of equalizing them in such a way that the moral component of karmic causality is highlighted rather than concealed. If the morality of cause-and-effect is obscured because it is overly influenced by an emphasis on noncausality, then genuine noncausality cannot be attained.

For the Renewal Theory, Dōgen resolves this dilemma by asserting in "Jinshin inga" that "the law of causality is clear and impersonal [or selfless; *watakushi nashi*]"[40] in the sense that it is universal and inviolable and yet has an eminently subjective quality ("deep faith") in that the freedom of noncausality can be attained only through the continuing process of moral purification perfected within the realm of causality.[41] This assertion recalls the Madhyamika (*Mulamadhyamakarika* 25:9–10) view that nirvana is found in terms of causality—nirvana occurs in the midst of samsara and not as an escape from it, yet it is attained only through a fundamental change of perspective rather than the mere acceptance of causal relations. However, Dōgen's approach is based not on a nonrelational freedom from karma, but on an eminently flexible and polymorphous process in which the stages of practice and realization, while often simultaneous and overlapping, occur in irreversible sequence.[42]

Responses of Traditionalist Scholars

While many traditional Sōtō scholars have acknowledged the basic merit and impact of the issues raised by the Renewal Theory, they express mixed reactions concerning the long-term significance of this new methodology. Kagamishima Genryū, perhaps the most prominent of figures in Dōgen studies until his death in the late 1990s, who co-edited and wrote the introduction to *Jūnikanbon Shōbōgenzō no shomondai*, has appraised the Renewal Theory as an overemphatic and rather biased (*henchō*) approach to be contrasted with what he considers a more reasonable, mainstream position. This compromise view sees the 12-*Shōbōgenzō* expressing a multivalent but less significant degree of change that marks a shift in emphasis rather than a revolution in Dōgen's direction, and it stresses that the 12-fascicle text must be seen only in connection with other writings and activities from Dōgen's later period.

It is necessary to distinguish between two traditionalist positions—which will be referred to here as (a) and (b)—for a total of three positions regarding the role of the 12-*Shōbōgenzō*. At one end of the spectrum, the Renewal Theory argues that Dōgen underwent a radical and decisive change, and at the opposite end the more conservative traditionalist (a) view maintains that there was no real change and that Dōgen stayed essentially the same throughout his life after his return from China, which is also the opposite of the Decline Theory. Both of these oppositions stress a single, simple standpoint, whereas the compromise traditionalist (b) view allows for change but not in the clean-cut, once-and-for-all way that the Renewal Theory scholars claim. The first position holds that the 12-fascicle text, which was written during one relatively confined time span, supersedes earlier versions and is sufficient for an understanding of Dōgen; the second position maintains the fundamental equality of the 75-fascicle and 12-fascicle texts, while asserting the ultimate priority of the former in terms of the more sophisticated audience it targets; and the third position explores complex areas of development in Dōgen's later writings and biography that affect an understanding of the relation between the 75-fascicle and 12-fascicle texts.

What links the two traditionalist positions is a basic skepticism regarding any attempt to prove Dōgen's intentionality concerning the priority of the 12-fascicle text. From that standpoint they both make a series of guerilla raids on Renewal Theory strongholds, including interpretations of the rewritten fascicles and Dōgen's philosophy of causality. The traditional scholars have argued against the Renewal Theory and in support of the 75-fascicle text on several grounds, such as the difficulty of establishing that the "rewriting" was Dōgen's and not the editing of his disciples, and the existence of other apparently rewritten fascicles that do not appear in or express the standpoint of the 12-fascicle text. Furthermore, Dōgen's approach to the topic of causality is complex, and it is easy to mistake a shift in perspective for a fundamental change.

The leading representatives of the traditionalist (a) position include Kagamishima and Kawamura Kōdō, the latter a specialist in the textual formation of the *Shōbōgenzō* and its early medieval commentaries, who supports the 60-fascicle edition. Kagamishima and Kawamura both have argued that there is no firm evidence that Dōgen limited his message to the 12-fascicle text. Kawamura emphasizes Ejō's role as an editor and interpreter of Dōgen. Ejō's editing of the twelve fascicles two years after Dōgen's death is the only tangible evidence for the priority of the new text. Yet, as Kawamura points out, all the other evidence indicates that Ejō asserted the priority of the 75-fascicle text the year before the master's final days. If Dōgen had emphasized the importance of the 12-fascicle text as he approached death, why did Ejō not show this view in a more vigorous way than by composing a single, cryptic (and long-lost) colophon to the "Hachidainingaku" fascicle? If the Renewal Theory is correct, why did Ejō not stop altogether his editing of the earlier fascicles, which Dōgen continued to revise until nearly the end of his life? Also why did the other main disciples who were privy to Dōgen's way of thinking, Senne and Kyōgō, comment only on the 75-fascicle text? Kagamishima wonders if there may be in the near future a discovery of another version of Ejō's colophon that will further clarify—or perhaps complicate—our understanding of Dōgen's final instructions or intentions.[43]

Furthermore, Kagamishima and Kawamura emphasize that it is simplistic to argue that the five rewritten fascicles were revised for a single reason alone. The specific methods and purposes of rewriting vary significantly from case to case, but the general impression of the rewritten fascicles indicates that the respective versions express distinct but complementary rather that conflicting viewpoints on a particular topic. During the course of his move from Kyoto to Echizen, they argue, Dōgen recognized the necessity of addressing the concerns of several different types of disciple: those still needing to refine and develop their training, and those approaching the final stages of realization. For example, in the two versions of the fascicle on leaving home, the first version ("Shukke") deals with home departure from the standpoint of *jukai,* or the stage of receiving the precepts, while the second ("Shukke kudoku") examines it from the standpoint of *kudoku,* or the following stage of attaining merit.

Similarly, the "Daishugyō" and "Jinshin inga" fascicles that reach drastically different conclusions concerning the phrase *furaku inga* (not falling into causality) may be approaching its meaning from different standpoints.[44] "Daishugyō" approves of the saying from the standpoint of ultimate reality, which transcends the distinction between causality and noncausality, while "Jinshin inga" criticizes it from a more restricted realm of discourse, conventional truth, in which the tendency to avoid or escape causality must be refuted. In the final analysis, however, the two levels of discourse, ultimate and conventional, enhance and enrich one another to demonstrate a conclusion that would likely, though ironically, be supported by the Renewal Theory: the transcendence of causality is within, yet not merely within causality, like the process of disentangling vines (*kattō*) by means of entangled vines, as expressed in the 75-fascicle text's "Kattō." Therefore the traditionalist (a) position is that the *Shōbōgenzō* as a whole expresses multiple perspectives, so that the 12-fascicle text is not complete and autonomous but complementary with the 75-fascicle text in that the two texts intertwine general and specific, or introductory and advanced frames of reference without any sense of polarization between them.

Ishii Shūdō, one of the leading representatives of what Kagamishima has identified as the compromise or traditionalist (b) view, is sympathetic to but criticizes some aspects of the Renewal Theory.[45] Ishii agrees that Dōgen's approach to Buddhism is based primarily on wisdom (*chie,* Skt. *prajna*) and learning rather than on meditative contemplation, despite the fact that Sōtō is often characterized as a religion based on *zazen*-only or just-sitting, a sectarian misunderstanding traceable to fourth patriarch Keizan and projected back to Dōgen. Without being too harsh on Keizan, who since the Tokugawa era has been revered by the sect as an eminent patriarch of equal status to Dōgen, Ishii feels that the purity of Dōgen's thought was subverted by the un-Buddhistic syncretism and misleading simplification inspired by Keizan and his disciples.

Like the Renewal Theory scholars, Ishii argues that Dōgen should be understood as standing in accord with the critical approach to philosophy practiced in the Madhyamika school in India and Tibet, which seeks to overcome all one-sided fixations and delusions. In that context, Ishii cites the studies of Yamaguchi Zuihō that pointed out significant affinities between Dōgen and

South Central Asian Buddhism. He also maintains that Dōgen Zen is different from Chinese Ch'an, which has been overly influenced by Lao-Tzu and Confucius (though Ishii's view of Dōgen's Japan-ification as a purification of the syncretistic elements he found in China may be considered naïve). On the question of interpreting the *Shōbōgenzō*, Ishii endorses the Renewal Theory focus on the 12-fascicle text as a means of generating a fundamental revision of the Sōtō sect in a way that links classical theories of dependent origination to the contemporary need to take responsibility for societal problems such as discrimination and nationalism. Yet, like other traditionalists, he does not comment directly on social issues.[46]

On the other hand, Ishii shares with the traditionalist (a) position a skepticism concerning several of the main conclusions of the Renewal Theory. First, he feels that Dōgen's attitude toward original enlightenment thought stayed relatively constant after his return from China, with no clearly discernible revision of thinking following his Kamakura visit. He sees Dōgen's consistency as a position of constructive ambivalence, standing not strictly for or against original enlightenment thought, but he also seems to put more emphasis than traditionalism (a) on Dōgen's career-long struggle for an appropriate communicative style and substance. Ishii agrees with Yamanouchi Shun'yū, a specialist in Dōgen's relation to Japanese Tendai, that it is necessary to take attention away from Dōgen's Doubt, which after all stemmed from his youthful concerns and inexperience (his rather unsophisticated question is not entirely relevant to the complex historical and textual issues involved in interpreting Dōgen's understanding of original enlightenment thought).

Like traditionalism (a), Ishii is cautious not to overvalue the 12-fascicle text at the expense of Dōgen's other works. He points out that Dōgen edited and added to the 75-fascicle text until his death, so the dates of writing and rewriting (as well as the question of how much disciples contributed to the revised versions) cannot be pinned down, especially considering the variety of *Shōbōgenzō* texts. In particular, Ishii is skeptical of the role of the 12-fascicle text in relation to the so-called 100-fascicle project mentioned in Ejō's colophon, because it is not entirely clear why this project would be important. Perhaps Dōgen was trying to emulate the *juko hyakusoku* style (poetic commentaries on 100 kōan cases) and other Sung-era collections of recorded sayings, but if this is the case it does not support the Renewal Theory arguments.

Ishii's main approach centers on the interrelatedness of the 12-fascicle text and two other late Dōgen texts, the *Eihei kōroku* and the *Hōkyoki*, as well as the intertextuality involved in Dōgen's frequent references in his later works to the texts of Hung-chih, Ju-ching, and a variety of early Buddhist texts. The intratextual and intertextual dimensions reveal shifts in the style of Dōgen's approach, but not necessarily supporting the Renewal Theory, since Dōgen's citations and allusion to Sung masters in the *Eihei kōroku* increase significantly in the post-Kamakura period, and the rewritten fascicles of the 12-fascicle text use more citations from Mahayana sutras and *jataka* tales. Several scholars, including Ikeda Rōsan, show that Dōgen extensively cites traditional Buddhist (or pre-Zen) texts, especially Abhidharma, as in Table 38.[47]

The Monastic View of Dōgen's Career Trajectory

The Monastic View is an alternative standpoint, moving the discussion beyond the 12-*Shōbōgenzō* debate, which argues that Dōgen in the later years was hardly a withdrawn figure preoccupied with one topic (causality), but had developed into a genuinely innovative administrator and orchestrator of monastic ritualism functioning on multiple levels for diverse participants and audiences. In his writings, Dōgen was not so much addressing specific ideological issues such as naturalism or causality as he was intent on constructing a monastery setting that embraced a range of elements of religious practice, as well as lines of patronage and support from donors and the lay community independent of government intervention. According to Ishii Seijun, the key is to understand how Dōgen's approach was distinct from the two established monastic institutional systems at the time. One is the Five Mountains system of Chinese Ch'an, in which the appointment and supervision of administrative officers in the monastery was handled by a centralized government agency, the Religious Administrative Office. The other was the Tendai temple system—or rather the Kenmitsu (Tendai/Shingon, combining exoteric, or *kenjū*, and esoteric, or *mikkyō* elements)—of late Heian/early Kamakura as discussed by Kuroda Toshio and other scholars, in which the Imperial Court supervised and regulated the appointment of the abbot as well as the superior monks.[48] In addition to focusing on the issue of supervision, Ishii emphasizes the relation between the monks who lead the monastery and the lay community that helps support and benefits from their activities. For Ishii, Eiheiji was a "community-based" sys-

TABLE 38. 12-*Shōbōgenzō* Citations of Early Buddhist Texts

12-SH Fascicle	No. Citations
Shukke (75-SH)	5
Shukke kudoku	21
Den'e (75-SH)	4
Kesa kudoku	11
Hotsumujōshin (75-SH)	6
Hotsubodaishin	10
Daishugyō (75-SH)	3
Jinshin inga	9
Sanjigo (60-SH)	12
Sanjigo (12-SH)	15

tem following democratic principles, with the self-appointed abbot creating a rotation of administrative functionaries who were very much interactive and attuned to the needs of laypersons. I will comment critically on this method.

The Monastic View shows that the late writings fulfill the hope kindled upon Dōgen's return from China that, once a legitimate Sung-style Monks Hall and Dharma Hall were created in the mountains, he would be able to carry out the genuine Ch'an approach to monastic leadership, as reflected in the transition from *jishu* to *jōdō* sermons. The significance of the new emphasis on formal sermons is revealed in *Eihei kōroku* 5.358, which declares, "Japanese people are curious about the meaning of the word *jōdō*. I [Eihei] am the first to transmit *jōdō* sermons to this country."[49] In no. 5.378,[50] five years after the original citation in "Kokū," Dōgen returned to the Pai-chang kōan also cited by Ju-ching, as was discussed in chapter 5, about the query, "What is the most remarkable thing [in the world]?" by responding, "I [Eihei] will go to the lecture hall today." The following year, 1251, in no. 6.443 Dōgen revised the conclusion once more, this time by saying, "If someone asks me this question, I [Eihei] will respond, 'It is attending *jōdō* sermons on Mount Kichijōzan.' "[51] This statement demands a rethinking of conventional assumptions about Eiheiji religiosity in that Dōgen, unlike Pai-chang, is generally known for his emphasis on *zazen* rather than sermons. In no. 3.244 Dōgen remarks ironically, though without necessarily complaining, that despite his giving the first authentic Zen-style sermons in Japan at Eiheiji in the Echizen mountains, many onlookers denounce him by saying, "Just take a look at that preposterous rube on the mountain whose preaching is merely the talk of a 'wild fox Zen.' "[52]

Numerous passages in *Eihei kōroku* further proclaim how Dōgen brought ritual elements and patterns from China for the first time in the history of Japanese Buddhism. These include the following (in addition to nos. 2.128 and 5.358 on the role of sermons, previously cited):

> no. 2.138, on introducing the post of chief cook
>
> no. 4.319, "On Mount Kichijō there is a Monks Hall available for the first time for all Japanese to hear of its name, see its shape, enter and sit in it"[53]
>
> no. 5.406 (on 12.8.1251), "Japanese ancestors have been holding ceremonies to celebrate the birth of Sakyamuni Buddha and commemorate his death since an earlier era. However, they have not yet received transmission of the annual ceremony to celebrate his enlightenment. I [Eihei] imported Rohatsu (12.8 ritual) twenty years ago and maintained it. It must be transmitted in the future."[54]
>
> no. 8.*shōsan*.10, "I first transmitted *shōsan* sermons twenty years ago."[55]

Furthermore, in addition to other earlier examples cited in chapter 5, nearly a dozen sermons over the last few years of delivery are examples of administrative appointments or declarations, as listed in Table 39.

TABLE 39. *Jōdō* Sermons on Administrative
Positions

	1245
2.137	Appreciate director
2.138	Appreciate chief cook
2.139	Appoint director and chief cook
	1246
2.157	Appoint receptionist
2.190	Appreciate and appoint rector
3.214	Appreciate/appoint director and chief cook
	1247
(none–Kamakura mission)	

Post-Kamakura (late late phase)

	1248
4.298	Appreciation for the rector
4.299	Appreciation for the director
4.300	Appointment of a new director
	1249
4.336	Appointment of a new secretary
5.357	Appointment of a new chief cook
	1250
5.385	Appreciation for the rector
5.398	Appointment of a new head monk
5.401	Appointment of another new chief cook
	1251
6.416	Appointment of a chief cook
6.460	Appointment of a new secretary
6.467	Appointment of a new librarian

A main feature of the Monastic View is that Dōgen did not simply try to duplicate the Chinese model, something that would have been impossible in any case, but adjusted it to the Japanese context. Whereas Ch'an Five Mountains was a highly politicized system with economic implications in terms of government control of ordinations and administration, the Kenmitsu system had political implications based on an increasingly outdated economic structure involving fundraising monks (*kanjin hijiri*) who appealed to lords of manors for financial support. Seeking to avoid the pitfalls of these approaches, Dōgen developed a monastic unit based on the principles of democracy and lay inclusion; Figure 21 shows Ishii's conception of the intertwining of elements of support and labor at Eiheiji.

There are several major implications of the Monastic View. One is that Dōgen apparently did not want to control his administrative appointees, and

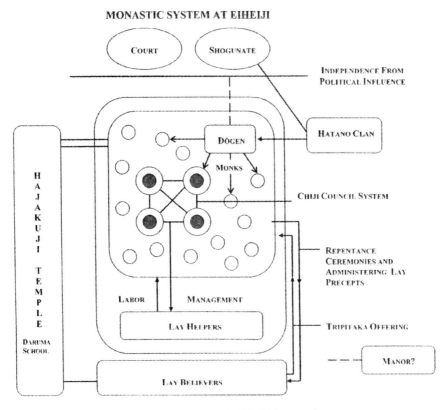

FIGURE 21. Dōgen's Eiheiji Approach

in the *Chiji shingi* he says that they should have their own autonomous council system to deal with any issue that would affect the monastery. Why does Dōgen use kōans, known for emphasizing antistructure, in the context of instructing on the quality of monastic structure? This seems to be his way of asserting that the monks appointed to a role as administrator do not occupy a kind of political position or are not appointed for such reasons, but are selected because they represent the very best of Zen spiritual insight into human nature. When Dōgen visited Sung China, all the monastic administrators were appointed by the religious administrative office, which was a political institution, and he apparently rejected this practice in kōan cases of antistructural monks who lived in the T'ang dynasty. The attitude of the T'ang masters marks a different approach from what had become longstanding custom at Mount T'ien-t'ung. In contrast to the way Mount T'ien-t'ung appointees were regulated by the Religious Administrative Office, which also had the power to certify ordinations, Dōgen himself held this authority but apparently did not regard his own role as abbot as overwhelmingly important and intended to create a horizontal rather than hierarchical relationship among monks, abbot, administrators, and trainees in the monastery.

A second characteristic of Eiheiji as an independent monastery is that Dōgen tried to differ from the *Ch'an-yüan ch'ing-kuei*, in which the supervisor is considered to lead not only all the monastic work but also matters of the monastic farm and manor (*shoen*) located outside of the temple. In an effort to be faithful to Pai-chang's original injunctions about self-sustaining monastic compounds, Dōgen does not refer to work outside temple grounds, such as manor maintenance, but instructs the supervisor only to manage lay helpers for the upkeep of the temple yard and buildings. That is, all reference to external work is eliminated in Dōgen's commentary, although we have to consider that in actual practice there may have been a manor owned and maintained as a source of income by Eiheiji in Okayama prefecture, as was the case with the large Ch'an temples in China.

The third implication of the Monastic View is that, while Dōgen's late period is seen as a time of cloistered monasticism by both the Decline Theory, because it shows a diminishing of talents, and by traditionalists, who emphasize his pursuit of purity, it actually marks a shift away from a clergy for clergy's sake approach that is characteristic of the *Shōbōgenzō*. In featuring the role of repentance meetings in which laypersons could make offerings to the *Tripitaka*, Dōgen tended to equalize their role in relation to clergy, perhaps out of democratic as well as fundraising inclinations.[56] Dōgen reached out beyond the landed gentry and manor lords who were involved with Chinese Ch'an to encompass a much broader base of support. Nevertheless, the participation of laypersons, while gaining merit, could not actually lead to their enlightenment or transmission, which was available only to full-fledged monks (who, in Dōgen's system, received the 16-article precepts). Table 40 highlights the *jōdō* sermons that are important for showing Dōgen's gradual turn to an increasing emphasis on monastic and lay ceremonialism.

In acknowledging that the Monastic View highlights complex features of Dōgen's texts and contexts often overlooked by other approaches, my criticism emerges when Dōgen's approach is contrasted not only with the then-current systems of Ch'an Five Mountains and the Kenmitsu temples in Japan, but with two crucial subsequent developments of Japanese Zen during the Ashikaga shogunate of the Muromachi era. These are the Five Mountains system, which had eleven main temples and over 300 branch or minor temples supervised by the shogunate, or *bakufu*—as in China, the role of civil authorities was paramount—and the Rinka system, including Rinzai and Sōtō temples often based on a charismatic abbot, who stressed either evangelical, cultural, pedagogical, or political functions.[57] The main point is that, while Dōgen's writings indicate that he seemed to be aspiring to achieve a community-based approach based on precepts ceremonies, we have no indication one way or the other whether this goal was actually accomplished in his life, since his time of lead-

TABLE 40. Turning-Point *Jōdō*

Early Period

1.48, 1236	Opening Kōshōji Monks Hall
1.105, 1242	Receiving *Ju-ching yü-lu*
1.126, 1243	Last sermon before flight to Echizen

Middle Period

2.128, 1245	Introducing new sermon styles
2.135, 1245	Citation of Hung-chih for first time
2.185, 1245	Memorial for Kakuan (Daruma school)

Late Period

2.177, 1246	Renaming temple as Eiheiji
2.184, 1246	First memorial for Ju-ching
3.251, 1248	Return from Kamakura (causality)
5.358, 1249	Transmission of *jōdō*
5.361, 1250	Receiving the *Tripitaka*
5.379, 1250	Ceremony to stop rain
5.390, 1250	Distances from Mahayana v. Hinayana
6.435, 1251	First memorial for Myōzen
6.441, 1251	First memorial for Eisai
6.485, 1252	On karmic retribution (*sanjigo*)
7.507, 1252	Memorial for Ekan (Daruma school)
7.517, 1253	On causality (*inga*)

ership at Eiheiji was cut short by an early demise. Furthermore, the fact that his independence was based largely on the support of the Hatano clan is acknowledged yet not fully taken into account in Ishii's evaluation.

From a long-range historical vantage point, it appears that Dōgen, like other representatives of the new Kamakura Buddhist schools, had severed himself from the Court, but this meant that the accomplishments of his temple were based on two main factors. One was an affiliation with a *daimyō* (Hatano) beholden to the Hōjō shogunate, which resembled the later Japanese Five Mountains approach, and the other was the power of his teaching as a charismatic abbot resembling predecessors in the Tendai as well as successors in the Rinka temple ranks. It must also be pointed out that the Rinka abbots of Sōtō monasteries generally integrated Dōgen-style sermons on seminal Chinese Ch'an texts with teaching methods that incorporated *mikkyō* elements. These included an instructional use of kōans based on the transmission of initiation documents known literally as "slips of paper" (*kirigami*) replete with esoteric diagrams and instructions that were a major part of the *shōmono* style of commentary.[58]

Summary of Major Theories

Table 41 sums up the major differences between five standpoints on six interpretive issues: (1) Dōgen's intention in revising the *Shōbōgenzō*; (2) the status of the rewritten fascicles; (3) the question of change in Dōgen's attitude; (4) Dōgen's view of original enlightenment thought; (5) his view of Chinese Ch'an; and (6) the main overall emphasis of his career. The five standpoints are: (1) Decline Theory, which emphasizes the 75-*Shōbōgenzō* as main text, with mixed evaluation; (2) Renewal Theory, which emphasizes the 12-*Shōbōgenzō* as the primary text; (3) Traditionalist (a), which sees complementarity of 75- and 12-fascicle texts; (4) Traditionalist (b), which sees 12-*Shōbōgenzō* in relation to *Eihei kōroku* and *Hōkyōki*; and (5) Monastic View, which emphasizes (b)'s texts in relation to *Eihei shingi*.

Neither Early nor Late

The Monastic View helps distinguish between what is important for our understanding the historical context of Dōgen's career path and what is important in itself and has an enduring legacy. The Decline and Renewal theories, based on change, tend to blur or collapse this distinction. The Renewal Theory shifts from the conventional focus on what constitutes the legacy, while the Decline Theory questions or denies that there is such a legacy. In correcting these through evoking the Monastic View, which at times is overly concerned with legacy, the Three Periods Theory argues that one should not reduce ideology to history by looking at Dōgen's life on the basis of biographical issues (*denki*), but should clarify ideology in light of history by looking at his life in light of his canon (*seiten*) and its effects. Therefore an emphasis on the historical role of the *Eihei kōroku* and other late texts may ironically lead us back to an appreciation of the intellectual role of the 75-*Shōbōgenzō*. But the 75-*Shōbōgenzō* must be seen in a new way, through lenses cut by our encountering the question of why Dōgen at the peak of composing this work abandoned it.

Dōgen's total literary output is multidimensional and, because he adopted different standpoints of doctrine and methods of instruction, there are numerous apparent contradictions, not only between periods but within a period or even in a relatively short text.[59] Nevertheless, there is a fundamental consistency in that the turning points in Dōgen's writing are associated with key developments at his temple. These include the Kōshōji Monks Hall and Dharma Hall openings and the construction of Daibutsuji, which coincide with the abrupt transition from *jishu* to *jōdō* lectures, or from the writing of the 75-*Shōbōgenzō* to the *Eihei kōroku*. Consistency overshadows the changes—the move to Echizen in 1243 and the trip to Kamakura in 1247—that are stressed in the Decline and Renewal theories. The transitions indicate that Dōgen never

TABLE 41. Comparison of Five Views of Dōgen's Ideas and Attitudes

	Decline Theory	Renewal Theory	Traditional (a)	Traditional (b)	Monastic View
Dōgen's Intention re *Shōbōgenzō*	75-fascicle text only is valid	12-fascicle text only is valid	75- and 12-fascicle texts complementary	No clear, single discernible plan	*Eihei kōroku* takes priority
Rewriting Issue	Any rewriting ignored or irrelevant	Only rewritten fascicles are relevant	Dōgen continues editing 75-fascicle texts to the end	Inter- and intratextual elements must be clarified	Rewriting in accord with *Eihei kōroku* as culmination
Question of Change	Deterioration with Echizen move	Post-Kamakura "spiritual change"	Never any real change	Minor change	Deepening of approach at Eiheiji
On Original Enlightenment	Accepts yet still struggles	Dōgen sharpens critique in 12-fascicle text	Maintains same consistent view throughout career	Continues ambivalent view	Distances from Tendai ties
View of Ch'an	Innovation dissipates with Ch'an reliance	Shows flaws of Chinese Buddhism	Surpasses Ch'an approach	Heavily reliant on Ch'an sources	Depends on yet refashions Ch'an
Main Career Emphasis	Egalitarian re women and lay followers in early days	Emphasis on karmic causality as corrective to *hongaku*	Encompassing of introductory and advanced perspectives with consistency	Explores shifting perspectives to balance influences of China and Japan	Administrative functions foremost with unity of clerical and secular interests

abandoned but continued to transform and adapt the roots of his religiosity, especially commentaries on kōans influenced by the recorded sayings of Sung masters, including both Lin-chi/Rinzai and Ts'ao-tung/Sōtō lineages. Therefore the main changes his writings underwent were not so much a matter of either a drastic reversal or a rebirth of ideology as they were attempts to work out various literary styles appropriate to the needs of diverse audience sectors in a complex monastic setting, including followers literate in *kanbun* and/or *kana*, monks and laypersons, general or public assemblies, and individual instructees.

The Renewal Theory tries to shield itself from criticism based on historical studies because it claims to be making a theological argument about "true Buddhism" (*tadashii Bukkyō*). From its standpoint, in the final analysis the 12-*Shōbōgenzō* epitomizes a reclaiming of the basic, timeless Buddhist teaching about causality, regardless of any questions raised about the chronology or political context of Dōgen's composition. The Monastic View helps one to understand the later writings from a balanced perspective as a matter of continuity with previous concerns, rather than drawing a biased estimation of mere deficiency or a heightened sense of progress. Yet, to complement and provide a more complete picture than is offered in the Monastic View, it is also important to understand the complexity of the late period in that Dōgen never abandoned his interest in poetic creativity and lyricism, as is reflected in a profuse use of the symbolism of plum blossom imagery in various kinds of prose and poetic writings, to be discussed later in the chapter. Furthermore, Dōgen's focus on karmic causality encompassed magical or miraculous elements that may seem contradictory but are in accord with what is found in other Buddhist schools from various historical periods. Throughout he maintains a critical devotion toward Ju-ching.

Supernatural Implications of Karma

The 12-*Shōbōgenzō*, when seen in connection with the *Eihei kōroku* and *Hōkyōki* as well as a series of short writings from this phase, is considerably more multifaceted than the one-sided interpretations presented by the Renewal Theory. Indeed, the view of karma expressed therein reflects an interface with popular religious conceptions of retribution and repentance in the Age of Decline. Although there are strong refutations of folk religious views expressed in "Kesa kudoku" and "Kie sanbō," which are frequently cited, it is clear from a careful reading of these and other fascicles that Dōgen was influenced by supernatural elements in early Buddhist *jataka* tales that were often translated or integrated into East Asian morality tale literature known as *setsuwa bungaku*.

In fact, many of the fascicles are concerned primarily with the ritual efficacy and ability to create miraculous transformations by reversing karma of key Buddhist symbols, especially the robe, bowl, and stupas. To a large extent, the 12-*Shōbōgenzō* is a text about rituals, a factor that tends to support the Decline Theory's picture of the late period. Yet it cannot be reduced to this single dimension either, because it contains numerous original enlightenment-like passages that have a resonance with the 75-*Shōbōgenzō* in expressing the notion, for example, that a single instant of wearing or viewing the robe will result in enlightenment. The powers of the Buddhist robe to provide spiritual protection and bring about an experience of enlightenment for those who wear or otherwise come in contact with it are also discussed in *Hōkyōki* nos. 29–31 and 34–35.[60]

The emphasis on ritualism in late late period discourse is also seen in *Eihei kōroku* 5.388, which tells a story of repentance involving demons and celestial spirits; and no. 5.379, delivered on 6.10.1250, which deals with the use of a master's supranormal spiritual power in fertility rites.[61] Here Dōgen states that his intention is to invoke a clear sky, and he says that "last year rain fell ceaselessly but now I wish for fine weather like my master at Mount Ching-liang temple [a temple where Ju-ching was abbot before serving at Mount T'ien-t'ung], who went to the Dharma Hall to wish for fine weather. When he did not go to the Dharma Hall, the Buddhas and patriarchs did not either. Today I am in the Dharma Hall, just like my former teacher." Despite citing Ju-ching in this supernatural context, Dōgen concludes with an ironic, iconoclastic commentary by pausing, sneezing, and saying, "Once I sneeze, clouds break and the sun appears." Then he raises the fly-whisk and remarks, "Monks! Look at this. The cloudless sky swallows the eight directions." The fly-whisk is a ceremonial object that symbolizes the authority of the Zen master, derived from pre-Buddhist shamanistic purification devices as well as imperial scepters; many sermons express its power to beat up a pack of wild foxes, turn into a dragon or snake, or perform other miraculous functions.

Furthermore, as indicated in Table 42, during the period after Kamakura, in 1249, Dōgen wrote a couple of short texts, the *Jūroku rakan genzuiki* and *Rakan kuyō shikibun*, celebrating the miraculous appearance on new year's day of supernatural arhats which protect Buddhism while celestial blossoms rain down on the beholders of the visions.[62] Dōgen states that such visions had been known previously only at Mount T'ien-t'ai in China, but the popular religious element expressed here also has affinities with Hakusan *shinkō*. In the brief essay the *Eiheiji sankareizuiki* he recounts three miracles that occurred at Eiheiji over the course of several years: (1) the sounding of a heavenly bell for 200 strokes, something that occurred multiple times, but on one particular occasion in 1251 the sound was so clear and vibrant that even a visiting minister (representing a nonbeliever) was able to hear it; (2) the appearance of five-colored clouds over Eiheiji, again something that had happened at Mount T'ien-t'ai; and (3) a mysterious fragrance that seemed to be a blessing that encompassed the temple.

At this point in our analysis, it becomes clear that the role of the *Teiho*

TABLE 42. Teiho Kenzeiki zue *on the Late Late Phase*

Supernatural Events

1245	(summer retreat) Flowers fall from sky during ceremony at Daibutsuji
1247	(1.15) Five-colored clouds appear over the temple[a]
1248	(4.12) Mysterious fragrance wafts over Monks Hall[a]
1249	(1.1) During Rakan veneration flowers fall, as at Mount T'ien-t'ai[b]
1251	(1.5) Bell sounds 200 strokes (happened often over eight years)[a]

Other Events from Late Late Period

1248	Bestows precepts to Hōjō, becomes basis for tale of Sōtō monk saving ghost of Hatano's concubine with lineage chart (*kechimyaku*)
1248	Banishment of Gemmyō for accepting offer of land from Hōjō
1249	Moon-viewing (*tsukimi*) self-portrait and verse composition
1249	Hatano donates complete set of *Tripitaka* to Eiheiji
1249	Dōgen declines imperial offer of purple robe and verse

[a] Included in *Eiheiji sankarareizuiki*
[b] Includes *Jūroku rakan genzuiki* and *Rakan kuyō shikibun*

Kenzeiki as well as the *Teiho Kenzeiki zue* must always be taken into account in order for us to understand the overall discourse regarding Dōgen's life and works, despite the lapse of time between his career and the production of these texts. It is necessary to see the connections between the overlapping as well as the divergent interests and methods of historical scholars (*kenkyūsha*) and sectarian or theological thinkers (*shūgakusha*).

Rhapsody in Plum

Another key feature of Dōgen's writings often overlooked in the various theories that stress that he remained constant and consistent and never varied is a lyrical quality that captures some of the finest elements of East Asian literary traditions, as in *Eihei kōroku* 4.327 on how buddhas transmit their teaching without attachment:

> In the dead of the night, the moon low in the sky,
> As Sakyamuni enters *parinirvana*, the jade forest, turning white,
> Cannot play host to a thousand-year-old crane,
> Whose glistening feathers fly right by the empty nest.[63]

Several examples in the *kanshi* collection are notable for their philosophical significance. For example, no. 10.10b, which accompanies a portrait of Dōgen painted at Kōshōji temple, makes an interesting statement on the issue of illusion and reality:

If you take this portrait of me to be real, then what am I, really?

But why hang it there, if not to anticipate people getting to know me?

Looking at this portrait, can you say that what is hanging there is really me?

Your mind will never be united with the wall [Bodhidharma's wall-gazing meditation].[64]

A *waka* verse features a wordplay on *ochikochi*, which literally means "hither and thither" but is a pivot-word that evokes "regret" (*oshimu*), perhaps for leaving Kyoto:

Azusa yumi	Dispersed, as today's
Haru kure-hatsuru	Spring light fades
Kyō no hi o	Yet stays held taut,
Hikitodometsutsu	Like a catalpa bow:
Ochikochi yaran.	My travels are never ending.[65]

A common ingredient in many of the *kana* and *kanbun* writings—both prose and poetic—that starts in the middle middle period and continues throughout later stages is the evocation of the image of plum blossoms, which are the first bloom of early spring often appearing amid late winter snow even before the seasonal weather has changed. The blossom is considered a harbinger of uplifting cyclical shift, symbolizing hope and optimism in the midst of turmoil and challenge or renewal and change while one is experiencing anxiety and despair—the emergence of enlightenment within the world of samsara. Also, plum is a key feature of the China journey narrative, where it is part of a dream sequence associated with Dōgen's visit to Mount Ta-mei, named for a famous T'ang master and disciple of Ma-tsu whose name literally means "Great Plum," as was noted by his teacher in an encounter dialogue.

An extensive use of plum blossom imagery appears in "Baika," a sermon delivered on the occasion of a three-foot snowfall which may have been demoralizing to Dōgen's followers during the first autumn of their move to the Echizen mountains, and also in "Udonge" and several other *Shōbōgenzō* fascicles as well as throughout the sermons and verses in the *Eihei kōroku*. This imagery, important in Japanese literature, probably reflected the influence of Chinese aesthetics expressed in the works of Hung-chih and Ju-ching. For example, according to *Eihei kōroku* 2.135 for the winter solstice of 1245 in a paragraph that seems to have been added later by compiler Ejō:

This mountain [temple] is located in Etsu [Province] in the Hoku-riku [northern] region, where from winter through spring the fallen snow does not disappear, at various times seven or eight feet, or even more than ten feet deep. Furthermore, T'ien-t'ung [Ju-ching] had the expression "Plum blossoms amid the fallen snow," which the teacher Dōgen always liked to use. Therefore, after staying on this mountain, Dōgen often spoke of snow.[66]

In no. 2.143 Dōgen remarks, "At dawn we are informed by the calls of mountain birds; at the beginning of spring we get the news from the fragrance of plum blossoms."[67]

In *jōdō* no. 4.279, delivered on 9.1.1248, six months after returning from Kamakura, Dōgen writes:

> The opening of the petals of plum blossoms heralds the beginning
> of spring. In the sky at dawn there is only the round, pale moon.[68]

Similarly, *jōdō* no. 4.297, a sermon delivered in 1248 for the Buddha's Enlightenment Day (traditionally celebrated in Japan on 12.8), evokes the image of plum blossoms which are beginning to come to the fruition of their growth cycle even when they are still far from visible in the midst of the winter snow. The sermon starts with an exclamation cited from the verse comment to a story about Layman Pang playing in the snow in the *Blue Cliff Record* case 42:

> The snowball hits! The snowball hits! It hits as the cold plum blossoms in the snow. On this eighth day of the twelfth month, the
> bright star in heaven and a wooden ladle on the earth appear before
> the spring.[69]

Table 43 is a partial list of the more than forty references to plum blossom imagery in the *Eihei kōroku*.

Approaching Death

Dōgen's poetic approach is also evident in his last couple of writings. On 8.5.1253, after spending most of the year ill, Dōgen, with his entourage, departed from Eiheiji at the suggestion of Hatano to seek medical assistance in the capital, as is noted by a verse recalling his comments before leaving Kamakura:

TABLE 43. Plum Blossom References in *Eihei kōroku*

1.34	4.258	5.359	7.473	9.48
2.135	4.279	5.360	7.478	9.72
2.136	4.288	5.363	7.481	10.1s
2.138	4.297	5.406	7.506	10.1
2.143	4.299	5.409	7.530	10.71
3.213	4.303	6.417	8.s.2	10.78
3.219	4.308	6.436	8.s.4	10.89
3.223	4.319	6.438	8.s.10	10.92
3.253	4.325	6.456	9.11	

For ten years I've taken my rice at Eiheiji,
For ten long months, I've been laid up sick in bed,
Now I must return from the deep mountains to the ordinary world
   to seek a cure—
The Buddha of suchness [Tathagata] guides me toward the healing
   [Buddha].[70]

The message of this and other poems near the final stages of his life is to rise above deception and desolation, as in a *waka* composed on way to Kyoto when Kinobe Pass, which was also navigated during the move to Echizen in 1243, was crossed once again a decade later:

Go-jōraku no sono hi go-shōka *kore ari shō ni iwaku*	The [final] journey to Kyoto
Kusa no ha ni	Like a blade of grass,
Kadodeseru mi no	My frail body
Kinobe yama	Treading the path to Kyoto,
Kumo obi oka aru	Seeming to wander
Kokochi koso sure.	Amid the cloudy mist on Kinobe Pass.[71]

Dōgen's death verse, a variation of Ju-ching's, who expresses calm acceptance, is indicative of Dōgen's attitude of taking on all challenges:

> For fifty-four years
> Following the way of heaven;
> Now leaping beyond,
> Shattering every barrier,
> Amazing! To cast off all attachments;
> While still alive, plunging into the Yellow Springs.[72]

To conclude our discussion of Dōgen's absorbing the influences of China, let us consider his citation of the Ch'an mentor in no. 7.522, one of the final *jōdō* sermons he delivered:

Dōgen says, I remember when my late teacher T'ien-t'ung [Ju-ching] was dwelling at Mount T'ien-t'ung and instructed the assembly with the following sermon: "Right at the very time of sitting, patch-robed monks can make offerings to all the buddhas and ancestors in the whole world in ten directions. All without exception pay homage and make offerings ceaselessly with various materials such as fragrant flowers, lamps, precious jewels, or excellent robes. Do you know and see this? If you know this, do not say you are wasting time. If you do not yet know it, do not avoid what you are facing."

    Dōgen then said: I [Eihei] graciously became the Dharma child of T'ien-t'ung, but I do not walk the same as T'ien-t'ung. And yet, I have been sitting the same as T'ien-t'ung. How can I not penetrate the expressions of the innermost hall of T'ien-t'ung? Please tell me, what is the meaning of such a statement?[73]

Therefore, like a son to a father, Dōgen neither follows nor disrupts the teaching of Ju-ching.

Appendix I: Timeline of Kamakura Religious Figures

end of Heian era | Kamakura era begins

1110 1120 1130 1140 1150 1160 1170 1180 1190 1200 1210 1220 1230 1240 1250 1260 1270 1280 1290 1300 1310 1320 1330

Saigyō 1118-1190 (*Sankashū, 1180s*)

Hōnen 1133-1212 (*Senjaku hongan nembutsushū, 1198*)

Dainichi Nōnin ?-1196? *(Jōtō shōgakuron, n.d.)*

Eisai 1141-1215 (*Kōzen gokokuron, 1198*)

Jien 1115-1225 (*Gukanshō, 1220*)

Chōmei 1155-1216 (*Hōjōki, 1212*)

Myōe 1173-1232 (*Saijarin, 1212*)

Shinran 1173-1262 (*Kyōgyōshinshū*, begun *1224*)

DŌGEN 1200-1253 *(Bendōwa*, 1231)

Enni Ben'en 1202-1280 (*Jūshū yōdō ki*, n.d.)

Nichiren *1222-1282 (Risshō ankokuron, 1260)*

Mujaku 1226-1312 (*Shasekishū, 1283*)

Ippen 1239-1289 (*Ippen shōnin goroku, n.d.*)

Gyōnen 1240-1321 (Hasshū kōyō, *1268)*

Appendix II: Chronology of Buddhism in China and Japan

1191: Eisai returns from four-year-long second trip to China

1194: Prohibition of new Zen sect

1196: Nōnin, founder of Daruma school, dies?

1198: Eisai, *Kōzen gokokuron*; Hōnen, *Senchaku hongan nembutsu shū*

1200: Eisai opens Jufukuji in Kamakura at bequest of Hōjō Masako, widow of shogun; Yoritomo bakufu prohibition of Pure Land Nembutsu sect

1201: Shinran joins Hōnen's cult

1202: Eisai opens Kenninji in the north end of Rokuhara in Kyoto with the support of shogun Yoriie

1204: *Chia-t'ai p'u-teng lu* (J. *Katai futōroku*)

1205: *Shinkokin wakashū*; Hōnen presents *Senchaku hongan nembutsu shū* to Shinran; Enryakuji burns

1206: Myōe establishes Kōzanji

1207: Bakufu exiles Shinran and Hōnen, prohibits Senshū nembutsu

1210: Ju-chng at Ch'ing-liang temple

1211: Eisai, *Kissa yōjōki*

1212: Hōnen dies; Chōmei, *Hōjōki*; Myōe, *Saijarin*

1214: Enryakuji burns Onjōji

1215: Eisai dies, Chōmei dies

1216: Kōin dies

1220: Jien, *Gukanshō*

1221: Jōkyū War, as ex-Emperor Go-Toba declares war against Hōjō Yoshitoki, who installed Kujō Michiie as shogun on the grounds that he descended from Minamoto Yoritomo; but with settlement in the following year there is rapprochement with China

1222: Nichiren born

1223: *Ts'ung-jung lu* (J. *Shōyōroku*)

1224: Shinran, *Kyōgyōshinshō*

1225: Jien dies

1227: Enryakuji denies Senshū nembutsu petition; death of Genghis Khan

1228: *Wu-men kuan* (J. *Mumonkan*); *Ju-ching yü-lu* (J. *Nyojō goroku*); Kōfukuji monks burn Tōnomine (remaining Daruma school stronghold)

1229: Ejō visits Dōgen at Kenninji

1231: Gikai joins Hajakuji

1232: Gikai receives precepts at Mount Hiei

1232: Myōe dies

1233: Mount Ching Wan-shou ssu burns

1234: Prohibition of Senshū nembutsu

1235: Kōen dies; Enni Ben'en travels to China; Eizon travels to China

1237: Nichiren makes *shukke*

1239: Ippen born; Tōfukuji Buddha Hall built

1239: Muhon Kakushin transfers from Kōyasan to Jufukuji in Kamakura

1240: *Heike monogatari*

1241: Enni returns to Japan; Mongols favor the Ch'an school

1243: Enni founding abbot of Tōfukuji

1246: Hōjō Tokiyori ascends to power; Lan-hsi Tao-lung (Rankei Dōryō) comes to Japan at request of Hōjō

1248: Shinran, *Jōdo wasan*

1249: Kenchōji opens; Muhon Kakushin travels to China

1253: Nichiren establishes new sect; *Wu-teng hui-yüan* (J. *Gotō egen*)

1254: *Wu-men kuan* brought to Japan

Appendix III: Dōgen Chronology

1200: Born on 1.2 to Minamoto Michichika and Motofusa in Kyoto

1202: Father dies

1203: Reads *Pao-yung* by Li-ch'iao

1206: Reads *Mao-shih* and *Tso-chuan*

1207: Mother dies in winter, feels sorrow of impermanence at funeral, and vows to pursue the Dharma

1208: Reads *Kusharon* (Skt. *Abhidharmakosa*)

1212: Declines Matsudono Sonkō's (relation uncertain) offer to train for the ministry; visits Ryōkan Hōgen, uncle on mother's side, decides to make shukke, goes to Enryakuji on Mount Hiei, first enters the Senkōbō at Yokawa-hannyadani

1213: 4.9, takes tonsure; 4.10 receives Tendai precepts from Kōen

1214: Experiences a profound Doubt about the relation between original enlightenment (*hongaku*) and the need for continuing practice; visits Onjōji Kōin, directed to Kenninji; possible meeting with Eisai, founder of Rinzai Zen, Huang-lung branch

1216: Kōin dies

1217: 6.25, joins Kenninji under Myōzen

1221: 9.12, receives inka and Huang-lung branch precepts from Myōzen; begins preparation for trip to China

1223: Arrives in China, begins itinerant period

1225: After death of Myōzen, joins Mount T'ient-t'ung summer retreat; experiences *shinjin datsuraku*; begins composing Chinese verse; begins recording conversations with Ju-ching collected in Hōkyōki

1227: Receives *shisho* from Ju-ching and returns to Japan to stay in Kenninji; Ichiya Hekiganroku; Shari sōdenki; Hōkyōki (redated to end of his life); Fukanzazengi (redated to 1233)

1228: Stays at Fukakusa hermitage; receives Jakuen

1229: Receives visit by Ejō

1230: Composes hōgo

1231: Resides at Anyō-in; "Ji Ryōnen ni hōgo"; Bendōwa

1233: Kannondōriin established, from Gokurakuji maintained by Fujiwara family; writes Echizen Myōkakuji chinjū, 4 mo.??; Makahannyaharamitsu; Fukanzazengi, 7.15; Genjōkōan

1234: Gakudōyōjinshū, 3.9; Ejō joins Dōgen in winter; Ejō begins recording Shōbō-genzō zuimonki

1235: Gives to Rikan the *kechimyaku* of Myōzen shoden?; gives to Ejō the Busso shōden bosatsu sahō; begin construction of Monks Hall, 12 mo.; Kannondōriin sōdō konryū kanjin-so; Mana Shōbōgenzō

1236: Establishment of Monks Hall, 10.15 lecture to assembly; appoints Ejō first head monk

1237: Tenzokyōkun, spring; Shukke ryaku sahō

1238: Completes Shōbōgenzō zuimonki; Ikkya myōjū

1239: Jūundōshiki, Sokushinzebutsu, Senjō, Senmen

1240: Raihaitokuzui, Sansuikyō, Uji, Kesa kudoku, Den'e, Keiseisanshoku, Shoaku makusa; 31 Jōdō (collected, but these began in 1236)

1241: Busso, Shisho; Ekan followers join Dōgen, including Gikai, Giin, Gien, Gijun, spring; receives Ju-ching yü-lu, spring; Hokke-ten-hokke, Shinfukatoku, Shinfukatoku-b (supplementary), Kokyō, Busshō, Gyōbutsuigi; Bukkyō, Jinzū; 48 Jōdō; Enni Ben'en returns to Japan

1242: Daigo, Zazenshin, Inmo, Bukkōjōji, Gyōji, Kaiin zammai, Juki, Kannon, Arakan, Hakujushi, Kōmyō; receives Ju-ching yü-lu, 8.5; Nyorai zenshin, Muchū setsumu, Dōtoku, Gabyō, Bukkyō (Teachings), Zenki; gives bosatsukai to Kakushin; 26 Jōdō

1243: Tsuki, Kūge, Kobusshin, Bodaisatta shishobō, Kattō; move to Echizen, 7 mo. after ango; Samgai yuishin, Butsudō, Mitsugo, Shohō jissō, Bukkyō (Sutras), Mujō seppō, Menju; Hōsshō, Baika, Jippō, Kenbutsu, Hensan, Zazengi, Zazenshin-2, Ganzei, Kajō, Ryūgin, Sesshin sesshō, Darani; 21 Jōdō

1244: Daigo-2, Soshi seiraii, Udonge, Hotsu mujōshin, Hotsu bodaishin, Nyorai zenshin, Zanmai ōzanmai, Sanjūshichihon bodaibunpō, Tenbōrin, Jishō zammai; begin construction on Daibutsuji, 2.29; Daishugyō; Taidaiko, 3.21; ceremony for opening Daibutsuji, 8.18; opening of Daibutsuji Dharma Hall, 9.1, Monks Hall, 11.3; Shunjū; o Jōdō

1245: Kokū, Ho-u; Ango at Daibutsuji; preaching to Hatano Yoshishige, 5 mo.; Bendōhō; Ango, Tajinzū, Ōsaku sendaba; 15 Jōdō

1246: Chiji shingi, 6.15; Jikuiamon, 8.6; Shukke; Fushukuhampō; 74 Jōdō

1247: Fusatsu sekkai at Eiheiji with five-colored clouds over Hōjō, 1.15; Risshun Daikichimon, spring; visits Kamakura, 8.3; Gikai head monk at Eiheiji; 10 (12) waka for Hōjō Tokiyori; Kōbō Daichi-mon; 35 Jōdō

1248: Returns from Kamakura, 3.13; renames Sanshō Peak as Kichijō Peak, 11.1; Eiheiji Ko-in kisei, 5 rules, 12.21; 51 Jōdō

1249: Jūraku rakan genzuiki (Rakan kūyō), 1.1; Shuryō shingi, 1 mo.; self-portrait gazing at the moon, 8 mo.; Jūji kisei, 9 rules, 10.18; receives Tripitaka from Hatano, EK 5.361, 362, 366; 58 Jōdō

1250: Senmen-3, 1.11; 18 hōgo for Eiheiji hermits; 52 Jōdō

1251: Flowers fall from sky hōgo; 69 Jōdō

1252: Edits Genjōkōan; falls ill in fall; 51 Jōdō

1253: Hachidainingaku, 1.6; asks Gikai to dedicate merit to Ekan from seeing shisho; becomes more ill, 7.8; presents robe he stitched to Ejō, 7.14; Hatano recommends return to Kyoto, 8.5; departs with Ejō and other disciples, leaving Gikai in charge of Eiheiji; Waka on return, 8.15; dies, 8.28; Ejō brings relics back to Echizen, 9.6; relics at Eiheiji, 9.10; Nehan ceremony, 9.12; o Jōdō

Appendix IV: Five Factions of Sōtō Zen

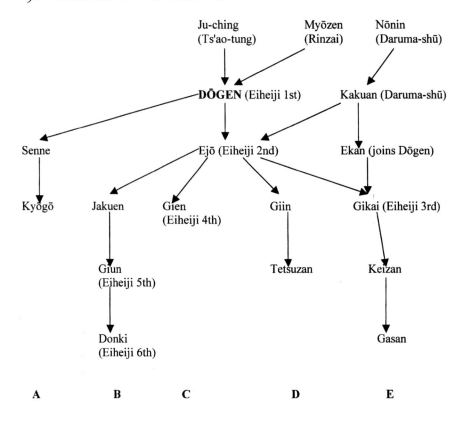

Faction A: Although it was not long lasting, the Senne-Kyōgō lineage is known for an important commentary on the 75-fascicle *Shōbōgenzō*, the *Gokikigakishō* (or *Goshō*), the first such work and the only one until the revival of *Shōbōgenzō* studies in the Tokugawa era; they left Eiheiji before 1263 for Yōkōan near Kenninji in Kyoto.

Faction B: The Jakuen-Giun lineage was based in Hōkyōji temple, founded by Jakuen, who had been Dōgen's Dharma-brother in China and came to join him in Japan; but he left Eiheiji in 1261, although Giun later returned to become the fifth abbot; Giun is known for his recorded sayings (*Giun goroku*) and his edition of the 60-fascicle *Shōbō-genzō* in addition to an interest in Dōgen's record (*Eihei goroku*) published by Donki.

Faction C: The Ejō-Gien lineage was aligned with Jakuen in opposition to the attempt by Gikai, the third patriarch of Eiheiji, to introduce esoteric rituals and chants into Zen practice; in the 1270s Gikai abdicated and Gien became the fourth patriarch.

Faction D: The Ejō-Giin lineage led to the founding of Sōtō Zen in Kyushu, based on the efforts of Giin, who built on inroads made there by Eisai; Giin made a second trip to China in 1264, which resulted in the editing of Dōgen's *Eihei goroku* by Wu-wai I-yüan, who had been one of Ju-ching's major disciples and who also compiled his teacher's recorded sayings that reached Dōgen in 1242; I-yüan wrote a eulogy for Dōgen, and Giin also got eulogies from Hsü-t'ang and Yüan-ning, prominent monks in the Five Mountains system; the text, an abbreviated, one-volume version of the voluminous ten-volume *Eihei kōroku*, was the first Sōtō sect publication released in 1358 by Donki, and it was quickly followed by Dōgen's one-volume *Gakudōyōjinshū* and Giun's one-volume *goroku* (some sources date these as 1357) (see B).

Faction E: The Gikai lineage's syncretic religiosity became the most successful by far in converting Shingon and Tendai temples and gaining multitudes of followers for the Sōtō sect, especially through the missionary efforts of the Keizan-Gasan sublineage based in Sōjiji in the Noto peninsula, which was aligned with mountain worship of Mount Sekidōzan, which was part of the sacred network of Mount Hakusan.

Note: (1) dual lineages affecting Dōgen (from Ju-ching and Myōzen), Ejō (from Dōgen and Kakuan), and Gikai (from Ejō and Ekan); (2) the affinities between both Gien and Giin and the Jakuen-Giun line, in contrast to Gikai's independence that perhaps stemmed from continued Daruma-shū influence; all the third-generation disciples studied with Dōgen, including Kyōgo, and Keizan also studied with Jakuen, Ejō, and Gien.

Appendix V: *Shōbōgenzō* Editions

95 Fascicles	A		B			Delivery	Location	Record/Edit	Editor	Pub. Date
	75 Senne	12 Yōkōji	60 Giun	28 Eiheiji	84 Bonsei					
1. Bendōwa						1231.8.15	Anyō'in	1332.2.7	Shigoku	1796
2. Makahannyaharamitsu	2		2		2	1233 ango	Kannon-in	1244.3.21	Ejō	1796
3. Genjōkōan	1		1		1	1233 8 w[b]	Kannon-in	1252	(Dōgen)	1805
4. Ikkya myōjū	7		7		7	1238.4.18	Kōshōji	1243.7.23	Ejō	1805
5. Jūundōshiki						1239.4.25	Kōshōji	—	—	1808
6. Sokushin zebutsu	5		5		5	1239.5.25	Kōshōji	1245.7.12	Ejō	1797
7. Senjō	54		54		54	1239.10.23	Kōshōji	—	—	1802
8. Raihaitokuzui	28		28	8	28	1240.3.15 r	Kōshōji	—	—	1797
9. Keisei sanshoku	25		25		25	1240.4.20	Kōshōji	1243.4.8	Ejō	1798
10. Shoaku makusa	31		31		31	1240.8.15	Kōshōji	1243.3.27	Ejō	1798
11. Uji	20		20		20	1240.10.1 w	Kōshōji	1243 ango	Ejō	1799
12. Kesa kudoku		3	41		81b	1240.10	Kōshōji	1255 ango	Ejō	1798
13. Den'e	32			12	32	1240.10 r	Kōshōji	—	—	1906
14. Sansuikyō	29			14	29	1240.10.18	Kōshōji	1244.6.3	Ejō	1798
15. Busso	52			22	52	1241.1.3	Kōshōji	1244.5.14	Ejō	1906
16. Shisho	39			19	39	1241.3.7 r	Kōshōji	1243.2.15	Ejō	1906
						1241.12.12	Kōshōji	1243.10.23	Ejō	
						1243.9.24	Kippōji			
17. Hokke-ten-hokke			12		77b	1241 ango & r	Kōshōji	1332.2.7	Shigoku	1800
18. Shinfukatoku	8			3	8	1241 ango	Kōshōji	—	—	1802
19. Shinfukatoku b				4		1241 ango	Kōshōji	—	—	1802
20. Kokyō	19		19		19	1241.9.9	Kōshōji	1243.1.13	—	1802
21. Kankin	30		30		30	1241.9.15	Kōshōji	1245.7.8	Ejō	1803
22. Busshō	3		3		3	1241.10.14 r	Kōshōji	1243.1.19	Ejō	1799
23. Gyōbutsu igi	6		6		6	1241.10.15 r	Kōshōji	—	—	1801
24. Bukkyō (Teachings)	34			13	34	1241.11.14	Kōshōji	—	—	1801
						1242.11.17	Kōshōji	—	—	

(continued)

No. & Title				Date	Place	Date copied	Copyist	Year
25. Jinzū	35		35	1241.11.16	Kōshōji	1244.2.1	Ejō	1801
26. Daigo	10		10	1242.1.28	Kōshōji	1244.2.20	Ejō	1801
27. Zazenshin	12		12	1242.3.18 r	Kippōji	1277 ango	Kangai	1797
				1244.2	Kōshōji	1277 ango	Kangai	
28. Butsukōjōji	26	1b	26	1242.3.23	Kippōji	1259 ango	Ejō	1803
29. Immo	29		17	1242.3.26	Kōshōji	1243.4.14	Ejō	1800
30. Gyōji 1 and 2	16–17		16	1242.4.5 w	Kōshōji	1243.1.18	Ejō	1797
31. Kaiin zanmai	13		13	1242.4.20 r	Kōshōji	1243	Ejō	1804
32. Juki	21		21	1242.4.25	Kōshōji	1244.1.10	Ejō	1801
33. Kannon	18		18	1242.4.26	Kōshōji	1243.2.10	Ejō	1801
34. Arakan	36		36	1242.5.15	Kōshōji	1245.6.16	Ejō	1798
35. Hakujushi	40		40	1242.5.21	Kōshōji	1243.7.3	Ejō	1799
36. Kōmyō	15		15	1242.6.2	Kōshōji	1244.12.13	Ejō	1799
37. Shinjin gakudō	4		4	1242.9.9	Kōshōji	1243.2.2	Ejō	1800
38. Muchū setsumu	27		27	1242.9.21	Kōshōji	1243.3.23	Ejō	1800
39. Dōtoku	33		33	1242.10.5 w	Kōshōji	1243.11.2	Ejō	1800
40. Gabyō	24	19	24	1242.11.5	Hatano Y.	1242.12.7	Ejō	1797
41. Zenki	22		22	1242.12.17	Kōshōji	1243.1.19	Ejō	1797
42. Tsuki	23		23	1243.1.6 w	Kōshōji	1243.7	Ejō	1801
43. Kūge	14		14	1243.3.10	Kōshōji	1244.1.27	Ejō	1800
44. Kobusshin	9		9	1243.4.29	Rokuharamits	1244.5.12	Ejō	1802
45. Bodaisatta shishōbō	28		78b	1243.5.5	—	—	—	1799
46. Kattō	38		38	1243.7.7	Kōshōji	1244.3.3	Ejō	1797
47. Sangai yuishin	41		41	1243.7.1 c	Kippōji	1243.7.25	Ejō	1800
48. Sesshin sesshō	32	27	42	1243	Kippōji	1244.1.11	Ejō	1800
49. Butsudō		9	44	1243.9.16	Kippōji	1243.10.23	Ejō	1797
50. Shohō jissō		6	43	1243.9	Kippōji	—	—	1801
51. Mitsugo		15	45	1243.9.20	Kippōji	1243.10.23	Ejō	1797
52. Bukkyō (Sutras)		25	47	1243.9	Kippōji	—	—	1798
53. Mujō seppō	46		46	1243.10.2	Kippōji	1243.10.15	Ejō	1800

| 95 Fascicles | A | | B | | | Delivery | Location | Record/Edit | Editor | Pub. Date |
| | 75 | 12 | 60 | 28 | 84 | | | | | |
	Senne	Yōkōji	Giun	Eiheiji	Bonsei					
54. Hōsshō	48		48		48	1243.10	Kippōji	—	—	1800
55. Darani	49		49		49	1243	Kippōji	1244.1.13	Ejō	1803
56. Senmen	50		50(60)		50	1239.10.23	Kōshōji	—	—	1798
						1243.10.20	Kippōji	—	—	
						1250.1.11	Eiheiji	—	—	
57. Menju	51			26	51	1243.10.20	Kippōji	1244.6.7	Ejō	1797
58. Zazengi	11		11		11	1243.11	Kippōji	—	—	1798
59. Baika	53				53	1243.11.6	Kippōji	—	—	1798
60. Jippō	55		45		55	1243.11.13	Kippōji	1245.12.24	Ejō	1800
61. Kenbutsu	56		47		56	1243.11.19	Yamashibu	1244.10.16	Ejō	1800
62. Hensan	57		37(60)		57	1243.11.27	Yamashibu	1244.12.27	Ejō	1803
63. Ganzei	58		44		58	1243.12.17	Yamashibu	1243.12.18	Ejō	1801
64. Kajō	59		43		59	1243.12.17	Yamashibu	1244.1.1	Ejō	1798
65. Ryūgin	61		51		61	1243.12.25	Yamashibu	1279.3.5	Ejō	1801
66. Shunjū	37				37	1244	mtn retreat	—	—	1801
67. Soshiseiraii	62		52		62	1244.2.4	mtn. retreat	1279.6.22	—	1798
68. Udonge	64		54		64	1244.2.12	Kippōji	—	—	1803
69. Hotsu mujōshin	63		53		63	1244.2.14	Kippōji	1279.3.10	Ejō	1800
70. Hotsu bodaishin		4	34		80b	1244.2.14	Kippōji	1255.4.9	Ejō	1800
71. Nyorai zenshin	65		55		65	1244.2.15	Kippōji	1279.6.23	Ejō	1801
72. Zanmai ōzanmai	66		10		66	1244.2.15	Kippōji	1244.2.15	Ejō	1800
73. Sanjūshichihon bodaibun	60			11	60	1244.2.24	Kippōji	1244.3.9	Ejō	1799
74. Tenbōrin	67			16	67	1244.2.27	Kippōji	1244.3.1	Ejō	1803
75. Jishō zanmai	69			17	69	1244.2.29	Kippōji	1244.4.12	Ejō	1906
76. Daishugyō	68			18	68	1244.3.9	Kippōji	1244.4.12	Ejō	1799
77. Kokū	70		56		70	1245.3.6	Daibutsuji	1279.5.17	Ejō	1803
78. Ho-u	71		42		71	1245.3.12	Daibutsuji	1245.17	Ejō	1797

79. Ango	72	57		72	1245.6.13	Daibutsuji	1279.5.20	Ejō	1797
80. Tashintsū	73			73	1245.7.4	Daibutsuji	—	—	1797
81. Ōsaku sendaba	74		10	74	1245.10.22	Daibutsuji	—	—	1805
82. Jikuinmon					1246.8.6	Eiheiji	—	—	1800
83. Shukke	75		24	75	1246.9.15	Eiheiji	—	—	1801
84. Sanjigo	8	8(60)		76(60)	1253	—	1253 ango	Ejō	1800
85. Shime	9	39		79[b]	1253[a]	—	1253 ango	Ejō	1800
86. Shukke kudoku	1	58		82[b]	1253[a]	—	1255 ango	—	1803
87. Kuyō shobutsu	5	59		83[b]	1253[a]	—	1255 ango	—	1799
88. Kie sanbō	6	60		84[b]	1253[a]	—	1255 ango	—	1799
89. Jinshin inga	7		5		1253[a]	—	1255 ango	—	1800
90. Shizen biku	10		23		1253[a]	—	1255 ango	—	1800
91. Yuibutsu yobutsu			28		—	—	1278.3.30	—	1800
92. Shōji			2		—	—	—	—	1798
93. Dōshin (Butsudō)			7[b]		—	—	—	—	1801
94. Jukai	2		21		—	—	—	—	1906
95. Hachidainingaku	12		20		1253.1.6	Eiheiji	1255.12.7	Gien, Ejō	1800
(Ippyakuhachi hōmyōmon)	11								
	75	60	28	84					

A, B = groupings of texts based on theory of Mizuno Yaoko

w = written, r = recorded, b = supplementary or alternative version

[a] Unclear dating

[b] Epistle

[c] Intercalary month

— = unknown

(60) = 60-fascicle version

Shisho—3 times, Senmen—3 times, Daigo—2 times, Zazenshin—2 times, 9 fascicle from 12-SH in 60-SH or 28-SH

(continued)

95-SHŌBŌGENZO CONTENTS

	95	75		
Anyō'in, 1231	1[a]	0	Pre-Kōshōji	Kyoto/Fukakusa Period, 1231–1243.7
Kannondōriin, 1233	2	2		
Kōshōji, 1238–	39[b]	36		
Hatano Y., 1242.12	1	1		
Rokuharamitsu, 1243.4	1	1	Kōshōji	
Kippōji, 1243.7–	23[c]	21	Temporary	Echizen Period 1243.7–1253
Yamashibudera–	5	5	Hermitages	
Mtn. retreat, 1244.3	2	2		
Daibutsuji, 1245.3–	5	5	New Temple	
Eiheiji, 1253.1	3[d]	1		
Unknown	13			

[a]Bendōwa
[b]Jūundōshiki, Kesa kudoku, Shinfukatoku-b
[c]Hotsu bodaishin, Sanjūshichihon bodaibunpō
[d]Jikuinmon, Hachidainingaku

75-SHŌBŌGENZO CONTENTS

Anyō'in	1
Kanondōriin	1
Kōshōji	37
Rokuharamitsuji	1
Hatano Y.	1
Mtn retreat	2
Kippōji	21
Yamashibudera	5
Daibutsuji	5
Eiheiji	1

Appendix VI: Comparison of 75- and 60-Fascicle Texts

75 Fascicle		60 Fascicle
1. Genjōkōan	1233.8 epistle	Genjōkōan
2. Makahannyaharamitsu	1233.ango	Makahannyaharamitsu
3. Busshō	1241.10.14 r	Busshō
4. Shinjingakudō	. 1242.9.9	Shinjingakudō
5. Sokushinzebutsu	1239.5.25	Sokushinzebutsu
6. Gyōbutsu igi	1241.10.14 r	Gyōbutsu igi
7. Ikkya myōjū	1238.4.18	Ikkya myōjū
8. Shinfukatoku	1241.ango	Sanjigo (different in 12-SH)
9. Kobusshin	1243.4.29	Kobusshin
10. Daigo	1242.1.28	Daigo
11. Zazengi	1243.11	Zazengi
12. Zazenshin	1242.3.18 r	Hokke ten hokke (in 95-SH)
13. Kaiin zanmai	1242.4.20 r	Kaiin zanmai
14. Kūge	1243.3.10	Kūge
15. Kōmyō	1242.6.2	Kōmyō
16. Gyōji	1242.4.5 w	Gyōji 1
17. Immo	1242.3.20	Gyōji 2 (sequenced)
18. Kannon	1243.4.26	Kannon
19. Kokyō	1241.9.9	Kokyō
20. Uji	1240.10.1 w	Uji
21. Juki	1241.4.25 r	Juki
22. Zenki	1242.12.17	Zenki
23. Tsuki	1241.1.6 w	Tsuki
24. Gabyō	1242.11.5	Gabyō
25. Keisei sanshoku	1240.4.20	Keisei sanshoku
26. Bukkōjōji	1243.3.23	Bukkōjōji
27. Muchū setsumu	1242.9.21	Muchū setsumu
28. Raihaitokuzui	1240.3.15 r	Bodaisatta shishōbō (95-SH)
29. Sansuikyō	1241.10.18	Immo
30. Kankin	1241.9.15	Kankin

31. Shoaku makusa	1240.8.15	Shoaku makusa
32. Den'e	1240.10.1r	Sangai yuishin
33. Dōtoku	1242.10.5 w	Dōtoku
34. Bukkyō (Teachings)	1241.11.14	Hotsu bodaishin
35. Jinzū	1241.11.16	Jinzū
36. Arakan	1242.5.15	Arakan
37. Shunjū	1244 n.d.	Hensan
38. Kattō	1243.7.7	Kattō
39. Shisho	1241.3.27r	Shime (in 12-SH)
40. Hakujushi	1242.5.21	Hakujushi
41. Sangai yuishin	1243.7.1	Kesa kudoku (in 12-SH)
42. Sesshin sesshō	1243	Ho-u
43. Shohō jissō	1243.9	Kajō
44. Butsudō	1243.9.16	Ganzei
45. Mitsugo	1243.9.20	Jippō
46. Mujō seppō	1243.10.2	Mujō seppō
47. Bukkyō (Sutras)	1243.9	Kenbutsu
48. Hōsshō	1243.10	Hōsshō
49. Darani	1243	Darani
50. Senmen	1239.10.23+	Senmen
51. Menju	1243.10.20	Ryūgin
52. Busso	1241.1.3	Soshiseiraii
53. Baika	1243.11.6	Hotsu mujōshin (in 12-SH)
54. Senjō	1239.10.23	Udonge
55. Jippō	1243.11.13	Nyorai zenshin
56. Kenbutsu	1243.11.19	Kokū
57. Hensan	1243.11.27	Ango
58. Ganzei	1243.12.17	Shukke kudoku (in 12-SH)
59. Kajō	1243.12.17	Kuyō shobutsu (in 12-SH)
60. Sanjūshichihon bodaibunpō	1244.2.24	Kie sanbō (in 12-SH)
61. Ryūgin	1243.12.25	x
62. Soshi seiraii	1244.2.4	x
63. Hotsubodaishin	1244.2.14	x
64. Udonge	1244.2.12	x
65. Nyorai zenshin	1244.2.15	x
66. Zanmai ōzanmai	1244.2.15	x
67. Tenbōrin	1244.2.17	x
68. Daishugyō	1244.3.9	x
69. Jishō zanmai	1244.2.29	x
70. Kokū	1245.3.6	x
71. Ho-u	1245.3.12	x
72. Ango	1245.6.13	x
73. Tashintsū	1245.7.4	x
74. Osaku sendaba	1245.10.22	x
75. Shukke	1246.9.15	

Appendix VII: Dōgen's Citations of Ju-ching

Topic	Cited in	Source (Ju-ching yü-lu, Taishō 48)
1. Ju-ching's Buddhist bell verse	Makahannyaharamitsu (1233), EK 9.58 (1235), Kūge (1243), Hōkyōki	132b
2. A useful or unfulfilled dream	Muchū setsumu (1242)	123b
3. Bamboos and banana plants	Gabyō (1242)	126c
4. Old master Hung-chih	Kobusshin (1243), Ōsaku sendaba (1245)	127a
5. Entangled vines	Kattō (1243), Mujō seppō (1243)	128b
6. A verse on midwinter	Baika (1243)	128a
7. Gotama poked out his eye	Baika, Ganzei (1243), Udonge (1243)	122c
8. New Year's morning starts afresh	Baika	123c
9. One word expresses the truth	Baika	123c
10. Willows are wearing belts	Baika	126c
11. Original face	Baika	131c
12. All things are clear	Baika	132b
13. By lifting an eyebrow	Baika, Kenbutsu (1243), EK 7.530 (1252)	130c
14. The great Way has no gate	Hensan (1243)	122a
15. 4000 or 5000 willow branches	Hensan, EK 7.488 (1252)	123c
16. Pure autumn wind	Ganzei	126a
17. Gouging out Bodhidharma's eye	Ganzei	121c

Topic	Cited in	Source (Ju-ching yü-lu, Taishō 48)
18. For six years he stumbled in the weeds	Ganzei	122b
19. The rainy season goes on for weeks	Ganzei	124a
20. The sun in the south grows distant	Ganzei	123b
21. This morning is the first day of the second month	Ganzei	124a
22. This Ching-te monk took his begging bowl	Kajō (1243), Ho-u (1245), EK 2.147 (1245)	127b
23. When hungry I eat	Kajō	123b
24. For half a year I took meals	Kajō	123c
25. The golden, marvelous form	Kajō	125c
26. Painted tower or tavern	Kajō	129c
27. Ling-yun saw the peach blossoms	Udonge	127b
28. A person expresses the truth and returns to the origin	Tenbōrin (1244), EK 2.179 (1246)	128b
29. On the flat earth we stack up our bones	Ango (1245)	129a
30. Steep cliff in the deep mountains	EK 3.194 (1246), EK 7.502 (1252)	125c
31. Jōdō sermon praying for clear skies	EK 5.379 (1250)	123a
32. Clouds disperse in the autumn sky	EK 10.geju 80 (Eiheiji)	122c
33. Before the gates of each house	EK 10 geju 83 (Eiheiji)	122c

(The rest of these citations cannot be tracked in the Ju-ching yü-lu)

34. Not understanding the importance of shaving	Senjō (1239)	—
35. All buddhas experience transmission of the Dharma	Shisho (1241)	—
36. I recited the collection of sutras (criticize Te-kuang)	Kankin (1241)	—
37. Pursuing the Dharma since the age of 19	Gyōji 2 (1242)	—
38. Casting off body-mind	Gyōji 2, Zanmai ōzanmai (1244), Bukkyō (S) (1243) EK 4.318 (1249), 6.424 (1251), 9.86 (1235), Hōkyōki	—
39. This is how I preach	Gyōji 2 (1242)	—
40. Not accepting the gift of silver	Gyōji 2 (1242)	—
41. There are no sectarian differences	Butsudō (1243)	—
42. None of them understands the Dharma	Butsudō	—
43. Old veterans in the ten directions	Shohō jissō (1243)	—

44. Tonight is filled with oxen	Shohō jissō	—
45. Learning the state of buddha	Bukkyō (S)	—
46. Ta-mei studying with Ma-tsu	EK 4.319 (1249)	—
47. Breath enters and reaches the tanden	EK 5.390 (1252)	—
48. Yün-men took a shit	EK 7.503 (1252)	—
49. Right at the very time of sitting	EK 7.522 (1252)	—
50. Have you ever studied the Yuikyōgyō?	Shuryō shingi (1249)	—

Notes

1. DZZ II: 481. At the beginning of this text, Dōgen says that he "visited leading priests of the Liang-chi region" (DZZ II: 461), which refers to "a circuit division that included what is now Chekiang province and adjacent areas. In T'ang and Sung times, the 'Five Mountains' or principal monasteries of Chinese Zen were located in this area on both sides of the Chi'en-tang River and Hangchou Bay. T'ien-t'ung was on the eastern side," in Norman Waddell and Masao Abe, trans., *The Heart of Dōgen's Shōbōgenzō* (Albany, N.Y.: SUNY Press, 2002), p. 9 n. 6.

2. DZZ I: 435; another example is *Hokke-ten-hokke*, included in the 95-fascicle edition of *Shōbōgenzō*, DZZ II: 497. In *Chiji shingi*, Dōgen refers to his home country of Japan as "a distant, remote island over a couple hundred thousand miles from the land of the Buddha's birth," in DZZ VI: 146.

3. One of the best discussions remains Hee-Jin Kim, " 'The Reason of Words and Letters': Dōgen and Kōan Language," in William R. LaFleur, ed., *Dōgen Studies* (Honolulu: University of Hawaii Press, 1985), pp. 54–82.

4. There is a recent, excellent English translation of the Monkaku edition of the *Eihei kōroku* by Taigen Dan Leighton and Shohaku Okumura, *Dōgen's Extensive Record: A Translation of the Eihei Kōroku* (Boston: Wisdom, 2004), which comes nearly two decades after the only previous translation by Yokoi Yūhō (Tokyo: Sankibō Buddhist Bookstore, 1987), a complete rendering of the nonstandard Manzan edition (see discussion in Chapter 2) that is very problematic in terms of reliability. A partial and somewhat misleading translation of some passages is in Thomas Cleary, *Rational Zen: The Mind of Dōgen Zenji* (Boston: Shambhala, 1993). By contrast, there are numerous complete and partial translations of the *Shōbōgenzō* and *Shōbōgenzō zuimonki*, although these are of varying quality and reliability.

5. Carl Bielefeldt, *Dōgen's Manuals of Zen Meditation* (Berkeley: University of California Press, 1988), p. 28.

6. Ishii Shūdō, "Saigo no Dōgen zenji kenkyū ni omou," *Chūgoku Sōtōshū seinenkai isshiken dai-kai kōgi roku* 60 (1994): 1–130.

7. Clifford Geertz, "Thick Description: Toward an Interpretive Theory of Culture," *The Interpretation of Cultures* (New York: Basic Books, 1973), p. 7.

8. DZZ I: 473.

9. William M. Bodiford, *Sōtō Zen in Medieval Japan* (Honolulu: University of Hawaii Press, 1993), p. 210.

10. Martin Collcutt, *Five Mountains: The Rinzai Zen Monastic Institution in Medieval Japan* (Cambridge, Mass.: Harvard University Press, 1981), p. 32. The use of the term "Five Mountains" (Wu-shan) in the case of Ch'an may be an anachronism, since the term does not officially appear in China until the Yuan dynasty.

11. The ranking of the Five Mountains temples was: (1) Mount Ching-shan Wan-shou Ch'an ssu, of Hang-chou; (2) Mount A-yü-wang-shan Kuang li Ch'an ssu, of Ming-chou; (3) Mount T'ai–pai-shan T'ien-t'ung Ching-te Ch'an ssu, of Ming-chou; (4) Mount Pei-shan Ch'ing-te ling-yin Ch'an ssu, of Hang-chou; (5) Mount Nan-shan Ch'ing tz'u pao en kuang hsiao Ch'an ssu, of Hang-chou. The system actually consisted of some 50 temples in a three-tiered ranking. Japanese temples were influenced by a small handful of Sung Chinese temples, especially Mount T'ien-t'ung, as shown by diagrams in the *Gozan jissatsu zu* held at Gikai's Daijōji temple in Kanazawa and in the *Kenchōji sashizū*. Both Sōtō and Rinzai sects were affected by the design of Mount T'ien-t'ung. See Collcutt, *Five Mountains*, pp. 175–177.

12. Patricia Buckley Ebrey, *The Cambridge Illustrated History of China* (Cambridge: Cambridge University Press, 1996), p. 144.

13. It was also a city advanced in printing and developing libraries, and in early modern times was the place where the game of Mah Jhong was developed based on traditional card and board games of chance.

14. The A-yü-wang specimen was supposedly one of 84,000 relics that King Asoka disseminated and is housed in a seven-step stupa about 20 inches high in the reliquary. The other two relics, according to temple sources which indicate that Jiang Zemin visited the A-yü-wang relic in 2002, are a tooth held in a Beijing temple and a finger joint held in Xian (formerly the T'ang capital, Chang-an). Dating the origins of the monasteries as being in the Ch'an order is more complicated than it might seem, because these are the dates in which they seem to have been awarded "Public" monastery status, and the assumption is that at that time this designation meant "Ch'an," although there is some ambiguity that remains in textual and epigraphical evidence. See Morten Schlutter, "Vinaya Monasteries, Public Abbacies, and State Control of Buddhism under the Song (960–1279)," in William M. Bodiford, ed., *Going Forth: Visions of Buddhist Vinaya* (Honolulu: University of Hawaii Press, 2005), pp. 104–105. Mount Ta-mei in the Ming-chou area also became Public at this point.

15. This fascicle includes a lengthy passage in which Dōgen describes two visits to the temple, first in the summer retreat of 1223 and again two years later during the summer when he was first training under Ju-ching. The passage indicates that Dōgen was very much dissatisfied with the lack of Ch'an insight on the part of the monks, but it is also the case that he was critical of all of the temples he visited, including

Mount T'ien-t'ung until Ju-ching arrived there in 1225. Furthermore, Mount A-yü-wang did not have the seven-hall–style monastic layout characteristic of Mount T'ien-t'ung and some other Ch'an temples.

16. These figures may have been preceded by a monk named Kakua, who is said to have played a flute when asked in an imperial meeting to expound the tenets of Zen, indicating that he must have received authentic Ch'an training in China in 1171; see Collcutt, *Five Mountains*, pp. 38–39, citing the *Genkō shakusho*.

17. According to Collcutt, the seven-hall style, which was "no more than the essential minimum skeleton of the Zen monastery," may have developed in the Sung and been transferred to Kamakura Japan, but it "does not seem have been applied to Chinese monasteries"; in *Five Mountains*, p. 186.

18. T. Griffith Foulk notes the role of Shunjō as a Tendai monk who traveled to China and returned to set up a temple in Kyoto that incorporated many of the features and instructions on running a monastery contained in the *Ch'an-yüan ch'ing-kuei*; see Foulk, "The 'Rules of Purity' in Japanese Zen," in Steven Heine and Dale S. Wright, eds., *Zen Classics* (New York: Oxford University Press, 2006), pp. 137–169.

19. Illustrated materials on the early history of the Rinzai school are contained in a partially bilingual catalogue prepared for an exhibit at the Tokyo National Museum of Art on *Kamakura Zen no genryū* (*The Art of Zen Buddhism*) (Tokyo, 2003).

20. Heinrich Dumoulin, *Zen Buddhism: A History II: Japan*, trans. James W. Heisig and Paul Knitter (New York: Macmillan, 1990), p. 32.

21. While Tendai adhered to the 58-articles bodhisattva (or Mahayana) precepts, Eisai, on the basis of Ch'an models, advocated the 250-articles *Pratimoksha* (or Hinayana) precepts as prefatory to these, whereas Dōgen developed a unique system of 16-articles and Nōnin apparently dismissed them all as irrelevant.

22. Bernard Faure, "The Daruma-shū, Dōgen, and Sōtō Zen," *Monumenta Nipponica* 42/1 (1987): 25–55.

23. *Bendōwa* refers to Dōgen studying under Myōzen at Kenninji for "nine years," which could mean that Dōgen actually started there a couple of years earlier than a reconstruction of the chronology from other traditional sources such as the *Kenzeiki* would indicate.

24. There remains a debate about whether Ju-ching died in 1227, the more current theory, or 1228, and, assuming the former, whether Dōgen's return to Japan, which is not clearly dated in the sources, was shortly before or after his mentor's death, perhaps by a matter of weeks or a couple months.

25. Shunjō, a *vinaya* master (*risshi*) who returned from China in 1211, set up Sennyūji, a monastery in Kyoto, that closely resembled the plans for such temples as Tōfukuji and Kenchōji (see note 18).

26. SZ 6.15. Note that the numbering system used for all *Shōbōgenzō zuimonki* citations is based on Ikeda Rōsan, *Gendaigoyaku Shōbōgenzō zuimonki* (Tokyo: Daizō shuppan, 1993), rather than on the version of the text used in DZZ VII: 2–151, which does not number the passages and has some other discrepancies to be discussed in Chapter 2. Also note that the main English translations are based on the so-called *rufubon* (popular) edition of the text, in which the first fascicle from the Ikeda text is the sixth and last fascicle, so that the fascicle numbers will always vary by one; in addition there are discrepancies regarding the numbering of the entries so that the

Myōzen passage, for example, appears as no. 5.12 in Reihō Masunaga, trans., *A Primer of Sōtō Zen: A Translation of Dōgen's Shōbōgenzō Zuimonki* (Honolulu: University of Hawaii Press, 1971).

27. In *Eihei kōroku*, Dōgen memorializes Myōzen on 5.27.1251 (no. 6.435) and 1252 (no. 7.504), and Eisai on 7.5.1251 (no. 6.441) and 1252 (no. 7.512). Also *Bendōwa* refers briefly to Myōzen, and in *Shōbōgenzō zuimonki* he eulogizes Eisai in nos. 1.14, 2.1, 2.8, 2.21, 3.2, 3.3, 3.7, 3.9, 4.4, 5.8, 5.10, and 6.9.

28. Collcutt, *Five Mountains*, p. 43.

29. According to Tokugawa era sources, the temple design bears anthropomorphic symbolism in that each of the seven main buildings is associated with a part of Sakyamuni's body, so that entering the temple grounds is considered the equivalent of communing directly with the Buddha. The halls include on the main axis: the mountain gate or entrance (associated with the groin), the Buddha Hall for displaying icons and hosting banquets (heart), and the Dharma Hall for sermons before the assembly (head). The right leg is associated with the bathhouse and the right arm with the kitchen, whereas the left leg is associated with the latrine and the left arm with the Monks Hall. Four additional mainstays included at Eiheiji and other Zen temples are the Abbot's Quarters, known as the "ten-foot square hut" (*hōjō*), following a passage in the *Vimalakirti Sūtra* in which an informed layman holds forth in a humble abode with the ability to outsmart bodhisattvas; the hall to commemorate the local earth deity (*dojishin*) associated with protection of the temple grounds; a bell tower (*bonshō*) that houses a large bronze bell rung at New Years and other festivals as well as purification ceremonies; and a reading room for the study of sutras and related Buddhist and literary works. The Abbot's Quarters is usually located north of the Dharma Hall, with the earth deity hall and bell tower to the right, and the reading room to the left. In addition, as Foulk points out in "The 'Rules of Purity' in Japanese Zen," the temple compounds frequently housed numerous other halls, depending on size, function, and financial strength.

30. See Nancy Shatzman Steinhardt, *Chinese Imperial City Planning* (Honolulu: University of Hawaii Press, 1990); Steinhardt, ed., *Chinese Architecture* (New Haven, Conn.: Yale University Press, 2002); and Stephen Little with Shawn Eichman, ed., *Taoism and the Arts of China* (Chicago: The Art Institute of Chicago, 2000).

31. See *Chan-men kuei-shih* (J. *Zenmon kishiki*, also known as *Pai-chang ch'ing-kuei*, J. *Hyakujō shingi*), in *Taishō* 51: 250c–251b.

32. EK 1.48 in DZZ III: 34, according to the Monkaku edition (in the Manzan edition this passage appears in EK 1.1). The main exceptions are of course Dōgen's transmission seal (see *Busso shōden bosatsukai kyōju kaibun* in DZZ VI: 212–231) as well as Myōzen's relics, and other possibilities include the robe and portrait of Ju-ching.

33. Hee-Jin Kim, *Dōgen Kigen—Mystical Realist* (Tucson: University of Arizona Press, 1975), p. 46. Myōzen's relics, which Dōgen gave away to a nun, are the most tangible item mentioned in his collected writings.

34. See Satō Shunkō, "Hakusan shinkō to Sōtō-shū kyōdan shi," 20 parts. *Sanshō* 556–575 (1990–1991); and Takeuchi Michio, *Dōgen* (Tokyo: Yoshikawa kōbunkan, 1992), pp. 153–156 (includes a photo of a page of the supposed original manuscript stored at Daijōji temple and seen in modern times by D. T. Suzuki and others on p. 155).

35. Despite ways in which the religiosity of Sōtō Zen in subsequent generations may have differed from its founder's approach by incorporating esoteric and popular religious elements, the sect was known throughout the medieval period for its commentaries on various forms of Chinese Ch'an writings, which were in many ways continuous and consistent with Dōgen's interests. Muromachi-era Sōtō records of kōan commentaries were part of the complex genre of *shōmono* works, which included hermeneutic styles geared for public or exoteric and private or esoteric audiences; see Andō Yoshinori, *Chūsei Zenshū bunseki no kenkyū* (Tokyo: Kokusho kankōkai, 2000).

36. Ishii Shūdō, "*Hyakujō shingi* no kenkyū: '*Zenmon kishiki*' to '*Hyakujō koshingi*,'" *Komazawa Daigaku Zen kenkyūjō nenpō* 6 (1995): 15–53.

37. See Kagamishima Genryū, Satō Tetsugen, and Kosaka Kiyū, eds., *Yakuchū Zen'en shingi* (Tokyo: Sōtōshū shūmuchō, 1972); and Yifa, trans., *The Origins of Buddhist Monastic Codes in China: An Annotated Translation and Study of the Chanyuan Qinggui* (Honolulu: University of Hawaii Press, 2002).

38. See Steven Heine, *Dōgen and the Kōan Tradition: A Tale of Two* Shōbōgenzō *Texts* (Albany, N.Y.: SUNY Press, 1994).

39. Kagamishima Genryū, ed., *Dōgen in'yō goroku no kenkyū* (Tokyo: Sōtō shūgaku kenkyūjō, 1995), in some ways an update of Kagamishima, *Dōgen zenji to in'yō kyōten-goroku no kenkyū* (Tokyo: Mokujisha, 1985).

40. For example, in using Japanese vernacular, Dōgen can turn a Chinese expression such as "genjō" (to become manifest) into a more dynamic verbal activity by supplementing it with "suru" (to do or make); see the discussion in Tajima Ikudō, "Sahen dōshi no hanasu—ibunka inyū no ippōbō toshite no *Shōbōgenzō* no hyōgen no ittokuchō," in Daihonzan Eiheiji, ed., *Dōgen zenji kenkyū ronshū* (Tokyo: Taishūkan shoten, 2002), pp. 807–830.

41. DZZ III: 194.

42. DZZ III: 132.

43. See Leighton and Okumura, *Dōgen's Extensive Record*, p. 211.

44. Collcutt, *Five Mountains*, p. 148, in referring to "90 or more chapters," he means that there were different editions of the *Shōbōgenzō* containing 92, 95, or 96 fascicles, in addition to other prominent editions, which will be explained in Chapter 2.

45. E-mail exchange, February 10, 2002.

46. Ishii Seijun, "Eiheiji senjutsu bunseki ni miru Dōgen zenji no sōdan un-ei," in Daihonzan Eiheiji, ed., *Dōgen zenji kenkyū ronshū* (Tokyo: Taishūkan shoten, 2002), pp. 409–440; and http://hompage1.nifty.com/seijun.

47. Bodiford, *Sōtō Zen in Medieval Japan*, p. 211.

48. Dōgen also referred to Ju-ching as "former teacher" (*senshi*).

49. DZZ II: 60 [emphasis added]. In a characteristic wordplay in a passage just prior to this one, Dōgen says, "The great way of the buddhas and patriarchs is this alone, only face-to-face [transmission] given and received, or the giving and receiving of face-to-face [transmission], beyond which there is nothing left over and nothing lacking." The fascicle also refers to the date of 5.1.1225 (DZZ II: 54).

50. Kawamura, Kōdō, ed., *Eihei kaizan Dōgen zenji gyōjō: Kenzeiki* (Tokyo: Taishūkan shoten, 1975), p. 24. This work contains five editions of the tradition biography *Kenzeiki* from 1472, juxtaposed with the *Teiho Kenzeiki* by Menzan from 1753.

51. DZZ II: 461 [emphasis added].

52. Ikeda, *Gendaigoyaku Shōbōgenzō zuimonki*, p. 203.

53. DZZ III: 69. Senne, the compiler of this volume of the *Eihei kōroku*, notes in this passage that, "Many words were not recorded." Presumably Dōgen spoke more, but Senne wrote down only what is included here. This sermon is also notable for Dōgen's emphasis on the role of language in relation to silence in communicating the Dharma; see discussion in Chapter 5.

54. DZZ I: 196–202.

55. See He Yansheng, *Dōgen to Chūgoku Zen shisō* (Kyoto: Hōzōkan, 2000); Kagamishima, *Tendō Nyojō zenji no kenkyū* (Tokyo: Shunjūsha, 1983); and Nakaseko Shōdō, *Dōgen zenji den kenkyū-sei* (Tokyo: Kokusho kankōkai, 1997).

56. In 1998 a shrine to Dōgen was constructed on the grounds of Mount T'ien-t'ung including a stele and portrait as part of a campaign to attract Japanese tourists.

57. See the "Butsudō" fascicle, for example.

58. A reliable bilingual translation is in Takashi James Kodera, *Dogen's Formative Years in China* (Boulder, Col.: Prajna Press, 1980), pp. 113–140 and 224–258 (original).

59. According to *Shōbōgenzō zuimonki* 1.1, as a foreigner Dōgen declined Ju-ching's offer to be his personal attendant in deference to senior Chinese monks.

60. DZZ VII: 48–51.

61. Mizuno Yaoko, "*Hōkyōki*," in Kagamishima Genryū and Tamaki Kōshirō, eds., *Dōgen no chosaku* (Tokyo: Shunjūsha, 1980), III: 217–240. Both colophons talk about having a mixed sense of joy at the discovery and of loss because there may be other undiscovered or missing works.

62. *Shari sōdenki*, DZZ VII: 216–218; and *Myōzen oshō kaichō okugaki*, DZZ VII: 234–235.

63. Kawamura, *Eihei kaizan Dōgen zenji gyōjō: Kenzeiki*.

64. David A. Riggs, "Life of Menzan," *Japan Review* 16 (2004): 67–100.

65. See Sakai Ōtake, ed., *Dōgen zenji eden* (Tokyo: Yūgen gaisha Bukkyō kikaku, 1984); and Nara Yasuaki, *Anata dake no Shushōgi* (Tokyo: Shōgakkan, 2001), which intersperses this text with the contents of the *Shushōgi*, in honor of memorials for Dōgen's 800th birth and 750th death anniversaries. See also Sekiryō Mokudo, *Gendaigoyaku Kenzeiki zue* (Tokyo: Kokusho inkokai, 2001).

66. Tatematsu Wahei, *Dōgen no tsuki* (Tokyo: Shodensha, 2002).

67. For a comprehensive study of the main events in Dōgen's travels and studies in China, see Satō Shūkō, "Dōgen zaisōchū no sangaku kōtei ni kansuru shomondai (jō)," *Komazawa Daigaku Zen kenkyūjō nenpō* 6 (1996): 93–121; and "Dōgen zaisōchū no sangaku kōtei ni kansuru shomondai (ge)," *Komazawa Daigaku Zen kenkyūjō nenpō* 8 (1998): 73–97.

68. Frances Wood, *Did Marco Polo Go to China?* (Boulder, Col.: Westview, 1986).

69. Other topics mentioned in the traditional biographies that are problematic range from birth to death, including his aristocratic family background and parents, meeting with Eisai in 1215, trip to Kamakura in 1247–1248, declining of the imperial offer of purple robe in the late 1240s, and final return to Kyoto with illness in 1253.

70. Wood, *Did Marco Polo Go to China?* p. 81.

71. T. Griffith Foulk, "The Ch'an School and Its Place in the Buddhist Monastic Tradition," Ph.D. Dissertation, University of Michigan, 1987.

72. Wood, *Did Marco Polo Go to China?* p. 140.

73. According to Jonathan Spence, "the book is a combination of verifiable fact, random information posing as statistics, exaggeration, make-believe, gullible acceptance of unsubstantiated stories, and a certain amount of outright fabrication," in Spence, *Chan's Great Continent: China in the Western Mind* (New York: Norton, 1998), p. 1.

74. Note that although Dōgen frequently refers to *shinjin datsuraku* as a notion that Ju-ching stressed, there is no direct testimony in Dōgen's writings mentioning his having had this experience while training in China; see Steven Heine, "Dōgen Casts Off 'What'?: An Analysis of *Shinjin datsuraku*," *Journal of the International Association of Buddhist Studies* 9 (1986): 53–70.

75. A period of itinerancy is called so because the monks arrived in the evening and left in the morning (*tanshin*).

76. Imaeda Aishin, *Dōgen: Zazen hitosuji no shamon*, NHK Books, 255 (Tokyo: Nihon hōsō shuppan kyōkai, 1976), p. 52.

77. Kagamishima Genryū, *Dōgen zenji to sono shūhen* (Tokyo: Daitō shuppansha, 1985), p. 310.

78. On the significance of this site, the Kamakura-era Hossō priest Jōkei preferred the aspiration of rebirth on Mount Fudaraku to Amida's Pure Land (Gokuraku).

79. DZZ IV: 268–270; for this and other Dōgen poems translated here, see Steven Heine, trans., *The Zen Poetry of Dōgen: Verses from the Mountain of Eternal Peace* (Mt. Tremper, N.Y.: Dharma Communications, 2005). Mount P'u-t'a is the sacred mountain where the Bodhisattva of Compassion Avalokitesvara (C. Küan-yin, J. Kannon) is said to sit, enshrined in a cavelike grotto. There is another verse in Dōgen's *kanshi* collection, called "Continuing the View of Mount P'u-t'a" (DZZ VI: 262–264), which appears as 17 verses before the other one in the standard Monkaku edition of the *Eihei kōroku* but is the following verse in the Manzan edition sequence: "The ocean waves crash like thunder below the cliff./ The visage of Kannon appears./ Who can fathom the ocean of merit?/ Just turn your gaze to behold the blue mountain."

80. A stele at a small Sōtō temple outside Kumamoto in Kyushu is supposedly at the site where Dōgen landed on the return boat from China. It is currently not on the ocean shore, because of landfill or at least a changed shoreline, presumably. The drawing of Kannon shows "One-leaf Kannon," one of 33 forms in China, who is supposed to save seafarers from drowning in the ocean. The story is that during the ocean passage from China, a storm threatened the boat, and Dōgen, sitting on the deck, chanted the "Kannon-kyō" (chapter 25 from the *Lotus Sutra*). Dōgen envisioned Kannon floating on the ocean, and the storm subsided. Then Dōgen supposedly etched the image he saw of Kannon on the ship deck using one of the 18 implements that are always carried by monks in the *vinaya*. The priest at what was then a Shingon temple did a rubbing of the etching and in 1242 took it to Kōshōji, where Dōgen was starting to make a name for himself. Dōgen agreed to inscribe his picture and wrote the verse (DZZ VII: 252): "From one flower, five petals open,/ Each petal is one Tathagata,/ His great vow is deep as the ocean,/ Turning in dedication to transport [Dōgen]." This is followed by: Year Nin'in of Ninji reign (1243), 9th month, 1st day, inscribed by Shamon Dōgen.

81. Eric Hobsbawm and Terence Ranger, eds., *The Invention of Tradition* (Cambridge: Cambridge University Press, 1983).

82. Bielefeldt, *Dōgen's Manuals of Zen Meditation*, pp. 24–25.

83. For other important studies of Dōgen and Chinese Ch'an, see also Ishii Shūdō, *Sōdai Zenshūshi no kenkyū* (Tokyo: Daitō shuppansha, 1987); Ishii, *Chūgoku Zenshūshi wa: Mana Shōbōgenzō ni manabu* (Kyoto: Zen bunka kenkyūjō, 1988); Ishii, "Recent trends in Dōgen studies," trans. Albert Welter, *Komazawa Daigaku Zen kenkyūjō nenpō* 7 (1990): 219–264; and Yanagida Seizan, "Dōgen to Chūgoku Bukkyō," *Zen bunka kenkyūjō kiyō* 13 (1984): 7–128.

84. See especially "Senmen," "Senjō," and "Den'e" in the 75-fascicle *Shōbōgenzō* and "Kusa kudoku" in the 12-fascicle *Shōbōgenzō*.

85. Despite the claim in *Eihei kōroku* 1.48 (DZZ III: 34) that Dōgen returned from China "empty-handed," the *Shari sōdenki* indicates that he returned with the relics of Myōzen, which were given away to a lay female disciple before Dōgen's arrival in Kyoto. However, as William Bodiford has pointed out to me, the *shisho* document supposedly given to Dōgen by Ju-ching and now designated a national treasure by the Japanese government most certainly is a medieval forgery. It is noteworthy that the document Dōgen describes is a long, thin scroll just like modern Chinese Ch'an "Dharma Scrolls" depicted by Holmes Welch, which is completely different from the "shisho" attributed to Ju-ching.

86. Bodiford, *Sōtō Zen in Medieval Japan*, p. 20; however, this argument may go too far in suggesting that "Seen apart from his writings, however, little separates Dōgen from the rural milieu and world of religious expectations that shaped the monastic communities of his successors and gave birth to the subsequent Sōtō traditions."

CHAPTER 2

1. DZZ VI: 152–179.

2. *Eihei Shōbōgenzō shūsho taisei*, 25 vols. plus supplements (Tokyo: Taishūkan, 1974–1981).

3. Kawamura Kōdō, *Shōbōgenzō no seiritsu-shiteki no kenkyū* (Tokyo: Shunjūsha, 1986).

4. David A. Riggs, "Life of Menzan," *Japan Review* 16 (2004): 67–100.

5. Discussion at Komazawa University, July 2001.

6. Etō Sokuō, ed. *Shōbōgenzō*, 3 vols. (Tokyo: Iwanami bunko, 1939–1943); and Etō, *Shūso toshite no Dōgen zenji* (Tokyo: Iwanami shoten, 1944).

7. Ōkubo Dōshū, ed., *Dōgen zenji zenzhū* (Tokyo: Chikuma shobō, 1970); and Terada Tōru and Mizuno Yaoko, eds. *Shōbōgenzō*, 2 vols. (Tokyo: Iwanami shoten, 1970, 1972). Among English translations, the following two cover 95 fascicles, but the latter does not adhere to the traditional sequence: Nishijima Gudo Wafu and Chodo Cross, *Master Dōgen's Shōbōgenzō*, 4 vols. (Woods Hole, Mass.: Windbell Publications, 1994–1999); and Nishiyama Kōsen and John Stevens, trans., *Dōgen Zenji's Shōbōgenzō (The Eye and Treasury of the True Law)*, 4 vols. (Sendai, Japan: Daihokkaikakun, 1975). Also the following edition contains 75 fascicles: Yokoi Yūhō, trans., *Shōbōgenzō* (Tokyo: Sankibō Buddhist Store, 1986). In addition, Yokoi translates the 12-fascicle text in *Zen Master Dōgen* (New York: Weatherhill, 1975).

8. Steven Heine, "Critical Buddhism (*Hihan Bukkyō*) and the Debate Concerning the 75-Fascicle and 12-Fascicle *Shōbōgenzō* Texts," *Japanese Journal of Religious Studies*

21/1 (1994): 37–72; and David Putney, "Some Problems in Interpretation: The Early and Late Writings of Dōgen," *Philosophy East and West* 46 (1996): 497–531.

9. DZZ II: 458.

10. Ibid.

11. Ishii Shūdō, "Saigo no Dōgen—Jūnikanbon *Shōbōgenzō* to *Hōkyōki*," in Kagamishima and Suzuki Kakuzen, eds., *Jūnikanbon Shōbōgenzō no shomondai* (Tokyo: Daizō shuppan, 1991), pp. 319–374.

12. Jamie Hubbard and Paul L. Swanson, eds., *Pruning the Bodhi Tree: The Storm over Critical Buddhism* (Honolulu: University of Hawaii Press, 1997).

13. Kawamura, *Shōbōgenzō no seiritsu-shiteki no kenkyū*.

14. Hakamaya Noriaki, *Dōgen to Bukkyō: Jūnikanbon Shōbōgenzō no Dōgen* (Tokyo: Daizō shuppan, 1992).

15. Hee-Jin Kim, *Dōgen Kigen—Mystical Realist* (Tucson: University of Arizona Press, 1975); a reference does appear in an appendix on p. 314.

16. DZZ III and IV; also, Ōtani Teppū has edited editions of both the Monkaku and Manzan versions.

17. The *Eihei goroku* contains about one-seventh of the material in the *Eihei kōroku*. See Ishii Shūdō, "*Eihei ryaku roku* kangae: Jūnikanbon *Shōbōgenzō* to kanren shite," *Matsugaoka bunko kenkyū nempō* 11 (1997): 73–128; and Steven Heine, "An Analysis of Dōgen's *Eihei goroku*: Distillation or Distortion?" in Steven Heine and Dale S. Wright, eds., *Zen Classics: Formative Texts in the History of Zen Buddhism* (New York: Oxford University Press, 2006), pp. 113–136.

18. See Ikeda Rōsan, *Gendaigoyaku Shōbōgenzō zuimonki* (Tokyo: Daizō shuppan, 1993), pp. 372–380, for a detailed, passage–by–passage analysis.

19. Reihō Masunaga, trans., *A Primer of Sōtō Zen: A Translation of Dōgen's Shōbōgenzō Zuimonki* (Honolulu: University of Hawaii Press, 1971) (one of the first English translations of Dōgen, although the earliest examples date back to the first decade of the twentieth century, when Japanese intellectuals were trying to impress the West for the first time); and Thomas Cleary, trans., *Record of Things Heard: The "Shōbōgenzō Zuimonki," Talks of Zen Master Dōgen as Recorded by Zen Master Ejō* (Boulder, Col.: Prajña Press, 1980).

20. This is stated at the conclusion of a lengthy and complex discussion of the role of the precepts as articulated in the Mahayana *Fan-weng ching* (J. *Bonmōkyō*) and the Zen *Pai-chang ch'ing-kuei* (J. *Hyakujō shingi*) to *zazen*, which is a topic he returns to over a decade later in one of the lengthiest *jōdō* sermons, *Eihei kōroku* 5.390.

21. Kosaka Kiyū, "*Eihei shingi*," in *Dōgen no chosaku* (Tokyo: Shunjūsha, 1980), III: 119–166.

22. DZZ VI: 1–168.

23. Helen Baroni, *Ōbaku Zen* (Honolulu: University of Hawaii Press, 2000).

24. Taigen Dan Leighton and Shohaku Okumura, trans., *Dōgen's Pure Standards for the Zen Community* (Albany, N.Y.; SUNY Press, 1996), pp. 21–22, 77 n. 11. Also Yifa remarks how indebted Dōgen was to the model of the *Ch'an-yüan ch'ing-kuei* in the case of *Fushukuhampō*: "With the addition of an introductory paragraph of theoretical explanations, Dōgen's text copies entire sections word for word. . . . It occasionally expands on the original with material gained from Dōgen's own observations in Chinese monasteries, such as his detailed account of the Chinese custom of taking

down the bowls from their place on the wall before eating. . . . Generally speaking roughly 85 percent of *Fu shukuhan pō* is taken verbatim from *Chanyuan qinggui*," in *The Origins of Buddhist Monastic Codes in China: An Annotated Translation and Study of the Chanyuan Qinggui* (Honolulu: University of Hawaii Press, 2002), pp. 41–42. See Yifa's table on "Influence of *Chanyuan qingqui* on Dōgen's writings" on pp. 44–45.

25. Ibid., p. 12.

26. In discussing the reasons for the flight to Echizen, Kim in *Dōgen Kigen—Mystical Realist*, pp. 57–58, briefly mentions difficulties in Kyoto, the role of Tōfukuji, Ju-ching's injunction, Dōgen's unquenchable yearning for nature, and the value of ascetic rather than lay Buddhism, which are all important ideas that require considerable amplification.

27. Kagamishima, *Dōgen in'yō goroku no kenkyū* (Tokyo: Sōtō shūgaku kenkyūjō, 1995).

28. Sueki Fumihiko, "Two Seemingly Contradictory Aspects of the Teaching of Innate Enlightenment (*hongaku*) in Medieval Japan," *Japanese Journal of Religious Studies* 22/1–2 (1995): 3–16.

29. See Brian A. Victoria, *Zen at War* (Tokyo: Weatherhill, 1998); and Victoria, *Zen War Stories* (London: Routledge/Curzon, 2002).

30. Hakamaya Noriaki endorses the Renewal Theory view that after Kamakura, Dōgen changed his approach by rejecting original enlightenment thought and embracing karmic causality, and he rewrote the 75-*Shōbōgenzō* as the 12-*Shōbōgenzō* to eliminate deficient tendencies in his previous work; see Hubbard and Swanson, eds., *Pruning the Bodhi Tree*.

31. Heinrich Dumoulin, *Zen Buddhism: A History II: Japan*, trans. James W. Heisig and Paul Knitter (New York: Macmillan, 1989), pp. 62, 104.

32. DZZ III: 258. This is a saying by the seventeenth Indian ancestor, Sanghanandi, in the *Ching-te ch'uan-teng lu* (J. *Keitoku dentōroku*), vol. 2.

33. Ishii Shūdō, "Saigo no Dōgen-Jūnikanbon *Shōbōgenzō* to *Hōkyōki*," in *Jūnikanbon Shōbōgenzō no shomondai*, pp. 319–74; and Matsuoka Yukako, *Kobutsu Dōgen no shii* (Kyoto: Kokusai zengaku kenkyūjō, 1995), pp. 435–440.

34. Putney, "Some Problems in Interpretation," pp. 513–514.

CHAPTER 3

1. There is a debate about whether the *hōgo* genre was an oral (lecture) or written (letter) style of communication.

2. Exceptions are the brief autobiographical passages at the opening of *Bendōwa*.

3. Kagamishima Genryū, *Dōgen zenji to in'yō kyōten-goroku no kenkyū* (Tokyo: Mokujisha, 1965), pp. 121–135.

4. Albert Welter, *The Meaning of Myriad Good Deeds: A Study of Yung-ming Yen-shou and the Wan-shan t'ung-kuei chi* (New York: Peter Lang, 1993).

5. Takashi James Kodera, *Dogen's Formative Years in China* (Boulder, Col.: Prajna Press, 1980), pp. 31–32.

6. Kawamura Kōdō, *Eihei kaizan Dōgen zenji gyōjō: Kenzeiki* (Tokyo: Taishūkan shoten, 1975), p. 10.

7. Albert Welter, "Zen Buddhism as the Ideology of the Japanese State: Eisai

and the *Kōzen gokokuron*," in Steven Heine and Dale S. Wright, eds., *Zen Classics* (New York: Oxford University Press, 2006), p. 83.

8. Cited in Wm. Theodore de Bary, comp., *Sources of Japanese Tradition, Volume One: From Earliest Times to 1600* (New York: Columbia University Press, 2001), p. 313.

9. Philip Yampolsky, "The Development of Japanese Zen," in Kenneth L. Kraft, ed., *Zen: Tradition and Transition: A Sourcebook by Contemporary Zen Masters and Scholars* (New York: Grove Press, 1988), pp. 140–156. This is based on the *Sesshū Sambōji shamon Nōnin den* of the *Honchō kōsōden*, vol. 19, completed by Mangen Shiban in 1702, 500 years after Nōnin's death. Also Nichiren's *Kaimokushō* of 1272 mentions and harshly criticizes Nōnin, along with Hōnen, as the two founders of Pure Land and Zen, respectively, who are said to be like mice afraid of cats (Tendai and the *Lotus Sutra*) and this attitude is repeated in the *Kyōki jikoushō* and the *Ankokuron go-kan yurai*.

10. See Ishii Shūdō, *Zen no seiritsu-shiteki kenkyū* (Tokyo: Daizō shuppan, 1991), pp. 625–714.

11. Bernard Faure, "The Daruma-shū, Dōgen, and Sōtō Zen," *Monumenta Nipponica* 42/1 (1987): 30.

12. DZZ III: 126. Kakuzen Ekan was a Dharma heir of Bucchi Kakuan, a Dharma heir of Dainichi Nōnin, founder of the Daruma school. Ejō had also been a disciple of Kakuan. Ekan became a disciple of Dōgen in 1241, bringing with him his disciples Gikai, Giin, Gien, Gison, and Gijun, among others, who all became prominent disciples of Dōgen, with Gikai also becoming the Dharma heir of Ejō. Dōgen says in the first part of the sermon (See Table 17):

> Who can equal Ekan in their conduct of filial responsibility? Today's memorial dedication will be clearly examined by the [departed] sacred spirit. The deep determination of the disciple yearning for his late teacher is known only by the late teacher. The late teacher's compassion while sympathizing with his disciple is known only by the disciple. How can someone else know it? People without [such a relationship] cannot match it. So it is said, it cannot be known with mind, it cannot be attained without mind, it cannot be reached by practice-enlightenment, and it cannot be measured with spiritual power. Having reached this ground, how can it be calculated?

13. DZZ IV: 88.

14. See Bernard Faure, *The Will to Orthodoxy: A Critical Genealogy of Northern Chan Buddhism* (Stanford, Calif.: Stanford University Press, 1997), pp. 113–118; and Jacqueline Stone, *Original Enlightenment and the Transformation of Medieval Japanese Buddhism* (Honolulu: University of Hawaii Press, 1999), p. 19.

15. Nara Yasuaki, *Anata dake no Shūshōgi* (Tokyo: Shōgakkan, 2001), pp. 47–49.

16. See David Riggs, "The Rekindling of a Tradition: Menzan Zuihō and the Reform of Japanese Sōtō Zen in the Tokugawa Era," Ph.D. diss., University of California at Los Angeles (2002), p. 110; based on his reading of a brief passage in *Shōbōgenzō* "Gyōji," part 2.

17. For example, Ikeda observes that the theme dealt with most frequently in *Shōbōgenzō zuimonki* passages is that of morality (*dōtoku*), referring to lifestyle ten-

dencies compared with two other themes, *zazen* and models of the patriarchs (*kihon*) in Ikeda Rōsan, *Gendaigoyaku Shōbōgenzō zuimonki* (Tokyo: Daizō shuppan, 1993), pp. 435–439.

18. Hee-Jin Kim, *Dōgen Kigen—Mystical Realist* (Tucson: University of Arizona Press, 1975), pp. 276–277; see also the discussion in William M. Bodiford, *Sōtō Zen in Medieval Japan* (Honolulu: University of Hawaii Press, 1993), pp. 163–173; Riggs, "The Rekindling of a Tradition," p. 179; and Shohaku Okumura, "The Bodhisattva Precepts in Sōtō Zen Buddhism," *Dharma Eye* 13 (2004): 1–3.

19. DZZ II: 294–299.

20. Kagamishima Genryū, "Zenkai no seiritsu to endonkai," in *Bukkyō ni okeru kai no mondai* (Kyoto: Heiraku, 1984), p. 273, as cited in Charles Wei-hsun Fu, "Mixed Precepts, the Bodhisattva Precepts, and the Preceptless Precept: A Critical Comparison of the Chinese and Japanese Buddhist Views of Sila/Vinaya," in Charles Wei-hsun Fu and Sandra A. Wawrytko, eds., *Buddhist Behavioral Codes and the Modern World* (Westport, Conn.: Greenwood Press, 1994), pp. 245–276.

21. Furthermore, Dōgen received "the bodhisattva precepts correctly transmitted from the Buddha" from Ju-ching, which refers to the *Fen-wang ching* uncombined bodhisattva precepts, clearly indicating that the position of Japanese Tendai precepts already had been reflected in the case of Ju-ching through Dōgen. See Kagamishima, "Zenkai no seiritsu to endonkai," pp. 278–279; Kagamishima Genryū, *Tendō Nyojō zenji no kenkyū* (Tokyo: Shunjūsha, 1983); and Fu, "Mixed Precepts, the Bodhisattva Precepts, and the Preceptless Precept."

22. See the discussion in Riggs, "The Rekindling of a Tradition," p. 178.

23. He Yangsheng, *Dōgen to Chūgoku Zen shisō* (Kyoto: Hōzōkan, 2000), pp. 111–140.

24. Itō Shūken, *Dōgen Zen kenkyū* (Tokyo: Daizō shuppan, 1998), pp. 118–120; Ikeda Rōsan, *Gendaigoyaku Shōbōgenzō zuimonki* (Tokyo: Daizō shuppan, 1993), pp. 431–434; and Kagamishima Genryū, *Dōgen zenji to sono shūhen* (Tokyo: Daitō shuppansha, 1985), p. 325.

25. Nara, *Anata dake no Shushōgi*.

26. He, *Dōgen to Chūgoku Zen shisō*, p. 17.

27. Kagamishima, *Tendō Nyojō zenji no kenkyū*.

28. Nara, *Anata dake no Shushōgi*, p. 45.

29. DZZ VI: 2–25.

30. DZZ I: 423–435.

31. Following Ejō's arrival at Kōshōji in 1234, the next wave of Daruma school followers (Gikai, Gien, Giin, and Gijun, all associated with Ekan and the temple at Hajakuji in Echizen) to come to Dōgen's temple appeared in 1241.

32. Nara, *Anata dake no Shūshōgi*, p. 57.

33. Nara, *Anata dake no Shūshōgi*, p. 63.

34. DZZ VII: 90.

35. DZZ II: 330–331.

36. Nara, *Anata dake no Shūshōgi*, p. 59.

37. DZZ I: 433.

38. Nara, *Anata dake no Shūshōgi*, p. 65.

39. DZZ I: 31–33.

40. See Nakaseko Shōdō, "*Shōbōgenzō* 'Busshō' kan no rokushushōchi to Mina-

moto no Sanetomo no shari nōkotsu mondai ni tsuite," in *Dōgen zenji kenkyū ronshū*, Daihonzan Eiheiji, ed. (Tokyo: Taishūkan shoten, 2002), pp. 518–537. The passage in "Busshō" refers to visiting "six" sites at the temple, but it is unclear whether this is meant in a literal or metaphorical sense. A key point is that travel from the home temple during the summer retreat was strictly forbidden, as itinerancy (*tangaryō*) was limited to the nine-month period of "liberation" outside the retreat period. Nakaseko refutes a theory proffered by Sugio Gen'yū that Dōgen went to Mount A-yü-wang during the summer retreat of 1225 (the year that Hōjō Masako died) to fulfill a memorial mission for the deceased shogun Sanetomo, who was installed at age eleven in 1203 and assassinated on new year's day in 1219 on the steps of the Hachiman Jingu shrine in Kamakura. Already stripped of much of his power well before his death, Sanetomo fervently dedicated himself to poetry and cultural activities, and apparently always had a dream of going to Mount A-yü-wang in China to visit the relic and even tried to set sail but the boat was defective. According to tradition, the monk Kakushin took his remains to the Chinese temple, but Sugio suggests that it was actually done by Dōgen, who later became a teacher for a brief period and administered the bodhisattva precepts to Kakushin in 1242. See Sugio, "Minamoto Sanetomo no nyōsō kikaku to Dōgen zenji," *Shūgaku kenkyū* 8 (1976): 41–46.

41. DZZ III: 72.

42. DZZ II: 461.

43. DZZ II: 55.

44. DZZ I: 471–488.

45. Ishii Shūdō, *Chūgoku Zenshūshi wa: Mana Shōbōgenzō ni manabu*; also *Shōbōgenzō* "Kokyō" is an example of a fascicle that cites numerous kōan cases beyond what is found in the main transmission of the lamp records.

46. See Satō Shunkō, "Hakusan shinkō to Sōtōshū kyōden shi"; and Bernard Faure, *Visions of Power: Imagining Medieval Japanese Buddhism* (Princeton, N.J.: Princeton University Press, 1996).

47. Daitō, who was said to have copied the text in forty days, "must have been aware that he was not only transcribing the history of Zen but participating in it as well"; in Kenneth L. Kraft, *Eloquent Zen: Daitō* (Honolulu: University of Hawaii Press, 1993), p. 48.

48. DZZ IV: 282–284.

49. DZZ IV: 264.

50. DZZ IV: 262.

51. Apparently Myōzen may never have visited the Mount A-yü-wang relic.

52. DZZ IV: 276.

53. DZZ IV: 254.

54. DZZ IV: 138.

55. DZZ II: 460–464.

56. T. Griffith Foulk, "Myth, Ritual and Monastic Practice in Sung Ch'an Buddhism," in Patricia Buckley Ebrey and Peter N. Gregory, eds., *Religion and Society in T'ang and Sung China* (Honolulu: University of Hawaii Press, 1993), pp. 147–208.

57. According to T. P. Kasulis, the experiment with the writing style of *Bendōwa* "failed" and Dōgen did not try it again, in "The Zen Philosopher: A Review article on Dōgen scholarship in English," *Philosophy East and West* 28/3 (1978): 353–373. Note also that Dōgen does not argue for or against the role of kōans in this text.

58. Imaeda Aishin, *Dōgen: Zazen hitosuji no shamon*, NHK Books, 255 (Tokyo: Nihon hōsō shuppan kyōkai, 1976), pp. 76–90.

59. See Hakamaya Noriaki, *Hongaku shisō hihan* (Tokyo: Daizō shuppan, 1989), pp. 327–337.

60. Heinrich Dumoulin, *Zen Buddhism: A History II: Japan*, trans. James W. Heisig and Paul Knitter (New York: Macmillan, 1990), p. 60.

61. Carl Bielefeldt, *Dōgen's Manuals of Zen Meditation* (Berkeley: University of California Press, 1988), p. 38. Matsuo Kenji notes that Dōgen, as well as Gien and Keizan in later generations, each produced several female disciples, in *Shin Kamakura Bukkyō no tanjō* (Tokyo: Kōdansha gendai shinsho, 1995), p. 135. See also Paula Arai, *Women Living Zen: Japanese Sōtō Buddhist Nuns* (New York: Oxford University Press, 1999).

62. Kim, *Dōgen Kigen—Mystical Realist*, p. 53.

63. DZZ VII: 66.

64. DZZ IV: 82.

65. DZZ I: 81.

66. DZZ VII: 79.

CHAPTER 4

1. See Carl Bielefeldt, *Dōgen's Manuals of Zen Meditation* (Berkeley: University of California Press, 1988).

2. T. P. Kasulis, *Zen Action, Zen Person* (Honolulu: University of Hawaii Press, 1981), pp. 73, 75.

3. 1242 and 1241, respectively.

4. DZZ I: 2.

5. DZZ V: 14–49; the sixth section of the text mentions several cases including "cutting off a finger."

6. DZZ I: 43–44.

7. DZZ IV: 22; Steven Heine, trans., *The Zen Poetry of Dōgen: Verses from the Mountain of Eternal Peace* (Mt. Tremper, N.Y.: Dharma Communications, 2005), p. 151. The Ju-ching verse was later mentioned in *Shōbōgenzō* "Kokū" in 1245 and also alluded to in the "Immo" fascicle of 1242.

8. DZZ III: 34.

9. Additional sermons, especially in the third fascicle of the *Shōbōgenzō zui-monki* delivered in 1237, comment on how monks in China receive provisions and temple maintenance from diverse sectors of society including civil authorities and lay followers but say that such support in Japan is more wholehearted and generous, ena-bling Dōgen "to survive for more than ten years"; see DZZ VII: 238–241.

10. See DZZ VII: 74.

11. See DZZ VII: 99.

12. See DZZ VII: 69–70.

13. Additional rules texts from the same year are *Jūundōshiki* and *Kannon dōri-in sōdō konryūkanshinsho*.

14. DZZ II: 37–53.

15. DZZ II: 80–81.

16. Martin Collcutt, *Five Mountains: The Rinzai Zen Monastic Institution in Medieval Japan* (Cambridge, Mass.: Harvard University Press, 1981), p. 148.

17. According to this case from the *Tung-shan lu*, Hsüeh-feng once practiced as *tenzo* under master Tung-shan. Once when he was washing rice, Tung-shan asked him, do you wash the sand away from the rice, or the rice away from the sand? And Hsüeh-feng said, "I wash them both away together." Tung-shan asked what the samgha would eat, and Hsüeh-feng overturned the washing bowl. Tung-shan said, "You should go and study with someone else. Soon."

18. Dōgen makes a parallel point—with the same degree of ambiguity or contradiction—about the role of letters in general, especially poetic expression.

19. See Kawamura Kōdō, *Shōbōgenzō no seiritsu-shiteki no kenkyū* (Tokyo: Shunjūsha, 1986); and Steven Heine, *Dōgen and the Kōan Tradition* (Albany, N.Y.: SUNY Press, 1994).

20. Ishii Shūdō, *Chūgoku Zenshūshi wa: Mana Shōbōgenzō ni manabu* (Kyoto: Zen bunka kenkyūjō, 1988), p. 572.

21. Kagamishima Genryū, *Dōgen zenji to sono shūfū* (Tokyo: Shunjūsha, 1994), pp. 61–92.

22. Ishii Shūdō, *Chūgoku Zenshūshi wa*, pp. 532–545; and Ishii Seijun, "*Eihei kōroku*: Kenchō nenkan no jōdō ni tsuite," *Shūgaku kenkyū* 29 (1987): 91–94.

23. Ishii Seijun, "*Mana Shōbōgenzō* no seiritsu kansuru isshiken: 'Eihei juko,' 'Kōshōji goroku' to no naiyō taihi o chūshin toshite," *Sōtōshū shūgaku kenkyūjō kiyō* 8 (1994), pp. 61–62; and DZZ IV: 146–148.

24. Ishii Shūdō, *Chūgoku Zenshūshi wa*, pp. 572–576.

25. Ishii Seijun, "*Mana Shōbōgenzō* no seiritsu kansuru isshiken," pp. 65–67.

26. See Kenneth Kraft, *Eloquent Zen: Daitō* (Honolulu: University of Hawaii Press, 1993).

27. Hee-Jin Kim, " 'The Reason of Words and Letters': Dōgen and Kōan Language," in William R. LaFleur, ed., *Dōgen Studies* (Honolulu: University of Hawaii Press, 1985), p. 56.

28. DZZ I: 274–284, esp., pp. 282–284.

29. As was indicated in chapter 1, the *Ch'an-yüan ching-kuei* indicates that *jōdō* sermons should take place regularly (six times a month, on the first, fifth, tenth, fifteenth, twentieth and twenty-fifth, with *shōsan* taking place five times, on the third, eighth, thirteenth, eighteenth, and twenty-third). While Dōgen generally stuck to those days, he usually gave only three lectures a month (see Ishii Shūdō, "Saigo no Dōgen—*Jūnikanbon Shōbōgenzō* to *Hōkyōki*," in *Jūnikanbon Shōbōgenzō no shomondai*, pp. 319–374), and also included some other occasions. (See Table 3).

30. See Hee-Jin Kim, *Dōgen Kigen—Mystical Realist* (Tucson: University of Arizona Press, 1975), pp. 1–7.

31. Carl Bielefeldt, "Recarving the Dragon: History and Dogma in the Study of Dōgen," *Dōgen Studies*, pp. 38, 32, 43; Heinrich Dumoulin, *Zen Buddhism: A History II: Japan*, trans. James W. Heisig and Paul Knitter (New York: Macmillan, 1989), p. 62; and Yanagida Seizan, "Dōgen to Rinzai," *Risō* 513 (1976), pp. 81–83 (Bielefeldt, p. 35, refers to this as a "passing gibe").

32. Bielefeldt, "Recarving the Dragon," p. 28.

33. Dumoulin, *Zen: Japan*, p. 61.

34. Dumoulin, *Zen: Japan*, p. 62.

35. Bielefeldt, "Recarving the Dragon," pp. 34, 35.

36. Heine, *The Zen Poetry of Dōgen*, pp. 89–95.

37. DZZ IV: 74.

38. Dumoulin, *Zen: Japan*, p. 65.

39. Bielefeldt, "Recarving the Dragon," p. 35.

40. DZZ I: 471–488, esp. p. 477.

41. T. Griffith Foulk, "Myth, Ritual and Monastic Practice in Sung Ch'an Buddhism," in Patricia Buckley Ebrey and Peter N. Gregory, eds., *Religion and Society in T'ang and Sung China* (Honolulu: University of Hawaii Press, 1993).

42. DZZ I: 428.

43. DZZ I: 477.

CHAPTER 5

1. Note that the fact that there are no more letters in Dōgen's corpus may support the Decline Theory view of an indifference to laypersons, but the absence occurs even before Echizen. Ta-hui, on the other hand, specialized in composing letters to lay disciples in the context of Chinese society, where Confucianism was dominant and many of the lay followers of Ch'an were primarily Confucians who sought additional edification or literary cultivation.

2. Yoko Williams, *Tsumi: Offence and Retribution in Early Japan* (London: Routledge/Curzon, 2003), p. 154.

3. William M. Bodiford, *Sōtō Zen in Medieval Japan* (Honolulu: University of Hawaii Press, 1993), p. 28.

4. Bodiford, *Sōtō Zen in Medieval Japan*, p. 27.

5. DZZ III: 72–74.

6. See Martin Collcutt, *Five Mountains: The Rinzai Zen Monastic Institution in Medieval Japan* (Cambridge, Mass.: Harvard University Press, 1981), pp. 52–53. Onjōji was a rare temple that had two Buddhist bells. According to the legend, the first bell was stolen by Enryakuji warriors, so a second bell was constructed, since all temples were required to have such a ceremonial device, but eventually the original one was taken back.

7. Collcutt tends to support this argument; see *Five Mountains*, p. 53.

8. DZZ III: 60.

9. DZZ I: 197–198. Mount T'ien-t'ung had an exceptionally large Monks Hall, initially built by Hung-chih in 1132–1134; it was 200 feet in length and 16 zhang (160 feet) in width, with a statue of Manjusri in the center of the hall enshrined as the holy monk; see Yifa, trans., *The Origins of Buddhist Monastic Codes in China: An Annotated Translation and Study of the Chanyuan Qinggui* (Honolulu: University of Hawaii Press, 2002), pp. 70–71.

10. DZZ I: 198.

11. Hee-Jin Kim, *Dōgen Kigen—Mystical Realist* (Tucson: University of Arizona Press, 1975), p. 59.

12. In *Eihei kōroku* 7.498:

"The first thing to practice is to cut away all attachments and have no family ties, to abandon social obligations and enter the unconditioned. Without sojourning in towns, and without being familiar with rulers, enter the mountains and seek the way. From ancient times, noble people who yearn for the way all enter the deep mountains and calmly abide in quiet serenity." The last sentence echoes what *Hōkyōki* reports Ju-ching told Dōgen. Also "The patriarch Nagarjuna said, 'All meditators reside in the deep mountains.' You should know that for departing the troubling bustle and attaining quiet serenity, there is nothing like the deep mountains. Even if you are foolish, you should abide in the deep mountains, because the foolish abiding in towns will increase their mistakes. Even if you are wise, you should abide in the deep mountains, because the wise abiding in towns will damage their virtue. I [Eihei] in my vigorous years searched for the way west of the western ocean [in China], and now in my older years I abide north of the northern mountains. Although I am unworthy, I yearn for the paths of the elders. Without discussing our wisdom or unworthiness, and without discriminating between sharp or dull, we should all abide in the deep mountains and dark valleys."

13. DZZ VII: 14.

14. See Kawamura Kōdō, *Eihei kaizan Dōgen zenji gyōjō: Kenzeiki* (Tokyo: Taishū-kan shoten, 1975), pp. 27–30.

15. DZZ VII: 170.

16. Earl Miner, *An Introduction to Japanese Court Poetry* (Stanford, Calif.: Stanford University Press, 1968), p. 127.

17. DZZ IV: 290.

18. Kōsen Nishiyama and John Stevens, trans., *Dōgen Zenji's Shōbōgenzō (The Eye and Treasury of the True Law)* (Tokyo: Daihokkaikaku, 1975), p. xix. Nishiyama and Stevens also mention Ju-ching's injunction to stay free of worldly concerns and the role of Hatano in offering a parcel of land in Echizen.

19. However, since many of the former members of the controversial Daruma school, such as Gikai, who hailed from Echizen, came to Dōgen in 1241 while he was still at Kōshōji, it is possible that Dōgen was persecuted in Kyoto (if that is the case) because of this connection rather than that he turned to the newcomers' support out of desperation once he fled the capital. At the end of *Bendōwa*, Dōgen acknowledges that in his country all Buddhist sects are "subject to Imperial sanction" (DZZ II: 555).

20. Ultimately Tōfukuji would provide the main bridge in Kamakura-era Japan for the transmission of Chinese Ch'an, with numerous disciples of Enni trekking to Mount Ching for their training and returning to lead the development of Five Mountains literature (*gozan bungaku*), one of the main expressions of the heights of Zen cultural achievements during the medieval period. Dōgen's own *kanbun* verse is sometimes grouped into the category of *gozan bungaku* literature, which often included examples of poetry modeled on Chinese styles. However, especially following the evangelical role played by Keizan, the sect would be known primarily for assimilating esoteric Buddhist and local deities rather than following a Ch'an model. Although the

tradition of exegesis on Chinese texts was upheld in some of the subgenres, scholars of linguistics today study primarily late medieval *shōmono* commentaries done in vernacular because they represent a distinctive variation on medieval Japanese literary style. On the other hand, there was a brief revival of *kanbun* literature in the Tokugawa era composed by Sōtō scholastics such as Manzan and Menzan.

21. Imaeda Aishin, *Dōgen: Zazen hitosuji no shamon*, NHK Books, 255 (Tokyo: Nihon hōsō shuppan kyōkai, 1976), pp. 146–154.

22. Satō, "Hakusan shinkō to Sōtō-shū kyōdan shi"; Bodiford, *Sōtō Zen in Medieval Japan*, pp. 114–115; Bernard Faure, *The Rhetoric of Immediacy: A Cultural Critique of the Chan/Zen Buddhism* (Princeton, N.J.: Princeton University Press, 1991), p. 166n. 27; and Faure, *Visions of Power: Imagining Medieval Japanese Buddhism*, trans. Phyllis Brooks (Princeton, N.J.: Princeton University Press, 1996).

23. Yoshitani Hiroya, *Hakusan-Isurugi shūgen no shūkyō minzokugakuteki kenkyū* (Tokyo: Iwata shoin, 1994).

24. Bernard Faure, "The Daruma-shū, Dōgen, and Sōtō Zen," *Monumenta Nipponica* 42/1 (1987): p. 30.

25. DZZ I: 196–202.

26. For example, no 4.274 says, "On this day T'ien-t'ung [Ju-ching] mistakenly made a pilgrimage. He did not travel to Mount T'ien-t'ai or Mount Wu-t'ai. How sad that for ten thousand miles there is not an inch of grass. The old master Kuei-shan became a water buffalo and came here." The phrase "inch of grass" and the mention of Kuei-shan as water buffalo are obscure references to old Ch'an sayings that highlight Dōgen's veneration of Ju-ching.

27. In a *waka* verse composed on 9.25.1244, Dōgen writes, "Crimson leaves/ Whitened by the season's first snow—/Is there anyone/Who would not be moved/To celebrate this in song?" in DZZ VII: 154.

28. DZZ II: 71–72.

29. DZZ III: 122–124. "Walking like someone from Handan" refers to a story by Chuang-tzu in the chapter on "Autumn Water," in which someone from the countryside went to the city of Handan and imitated the fashionable walking of the townspeople, but before mastering this he lost his native ability and had to crawl home on hands and knees; see Burton Watson, trans., *The Complete Works of Chuang Tzu* (New York: Columbia University Press, 1968), p. 187. Memorial day for Ju-ching was 7.17; other memorial sermons are nos. 3.249, 4.274, 4.276 (out of sequence), 5.342, 5.384, and 7.515. (See Table 31.)

30. *Hōkyōki* nos. 16–17, in DZZ VII: 20–22.

31. For an interesting Western parallel, see Harold Bloom, *The Anxiety of Influence* (New York: Oxford University Press, 1973).

32. DZZ I: 457–470.

33. DZZ I: 467–468.

34. DZZ I: 144.

35. For example, in *Shōbōgenzō* "Butsudō" Ju-ching says, "In recent years the truth of the patriarchs has degenerated into bands of demons and animals" (DZZ I: 481).

36. Nakaseko Shōdō, *Dōgen zenji den kenkyū-sei* (Tokyo: Kokusho kankōkai, 1997).

37. DZZ I: 270–280.

38. However, this fascicle was composed on 4.20.1240, a few months before the Daruma school conversion.

39. For example, he *Hung-chih kuang-lu* (J. *Wanshi kōroku*, in *Taishō* 48:1–121) consists of nine volumes: (1) *jōdō* and *shōsan*; (2) *juko* and *nenko*; (3) *nenko*; (4) *jōdō* and *jishu*; (5) *shōsan*; (6) *hōgo*; (7–9) poetry; see Sakai Tokugen, "*Eihei kōroku*," in *Dōgen no chosaku*, 7 vols., eds. Kagamishima Genryū and Tamaki Koshirō (Tokyo: Shunjūsha, 1986), III: 75–118.

40. DZZ II: 113.

41. DZZ 1988, III: 70. A more flowery rendering, is "from the four directions gathered like clouds to practice with [Dōgen]."

42. This saying can be taken to mean that Pai-chang went on retreat to one of the main mountain peaks located behind the temple to practice *zazen*, or that he is characteristically identifying himself with the name of the mountain and thus saying, in effect, "I sit alone." In the kōan cited in *Pi-yen lu* no. 26, the disciple claims to understand the comment, and Pai-chang slaps him.

43. *Taishō* 51.250c–251b.

44. DZZ IV: 280.

45. Pai-chang was particularly known for carrying a ceremonial fly-whisk (*hossu*), which also figures prominently in the gestures and demonstrations Dōgen uses in his sermons.

46. DZZ III: 92–94.

47. DZZ VI: 19.

48. Kagamishima Genryū, *Dōgen zenji to sono shūfū* (Tokyo: Shunjūsha, 1994), p. 70.

49. DZZ III: 72–74.

50. In EK 4.290, for example, Dōgen says, "In recent years there have not been masters such as Lin-chi and Te-shan anywhere, however much we may look to find them."

51. DZZ III: 72.

CHAPTER 6

1. DZZ III: 116.

2. Suzuki Tetsuyū, "Sozanbon *Eihei kōroku* dai yonban jōdō go ni kansuru kenkyū," in *Dōgen zenji kenkyū ronshū*, Daihonzan Eiheiji, ed. (Tokyo: Taishūkan shoten, 2002) examines one particular *jōdō*, no. 1.4, and shows the extent of Dōgen's reliance on transmission of the lamp sources for this and other sermons. In this instance, the original ends with the put-down that those with foolish ideas should be "called someone who walks in front of an ass but behind a horse," to which Dōgen adds, "or someone with the head of a dragon but the tail of a snake," pp. 768–769.

3. Even today 95 percent of the temples of the Sōtō sect, which has the largest number of branch temples of any of the traditional Buddhist sects, are affiliated with Sōjiji and the rest with Eiheiji; yet both Sōjiji and Eiheiji are considered the *honzan* (head temples).

4. William M. Bodiford, *Sōtō Zen in Medieval Japan* (Honolulu: University of Hawaii Press, 1993), p. 32.

5. DZZ VII: 48.

6. DZZ II: 458; see Sugio Gen'yū, "Dōgen zenji no jiko-tōdatsu no go-shōgai to *Shōbōgenzō* no shinka: Jūnikanbon ni yotte 'Ippyaku-kan' o omou," *Shūgaku kenkyū* 27 (1985): 7–12.

7. According to Matsumoto Shirō, there are two levels of original enlightenment or Buddha-nature theory evident in Dōgen's early writings such as "Genjōkōan," including "immanence Buddha-nature" (*busshō naizairon*) and "phenomenalism Buddha-nature" (*busshō kenzairon*), in Matsumoto, *Dōgen shisōron* (Tokyo: Daizō shuppan, 2000), pp. 197, 222. Matsumoto argues that the former type of Buddha-nature is more deficient as a throwback to *atman* belief and that the latter type represents a more advanced understanding although not so well developed as in the 12-*Shōbōgenzō*.

8. For example, *Bendōwa* no. 18 alludes to the early Buddhist story of a prostitute whose karma is redeemed.

9. Carl Bielefeldt, *Dōgen's Manuals of Zen Meditation* (Berkeley: University of California Press, 1988), p. 53n. 20.

10. T. Griffith Foulk, "The Historical Context of Dōgen's Monastic Rules," in *Dōgen zenji kenkyū ronshū*, Daihonzan Eiheiji, ed. (Tokyo: Taishūkan shoten, 2002), pp. 962–1017.

11. Taigen Dan Leighton and Shohaku Okumura, trans., *Dōgen's Pure Standards for the Zen Community* (Albany, N.Y.; SUNY Press, 1996), p. 13.

12. DZZ VI: 140.

13. Other examples include *Eihei kōroku* 1.65, 1.66, 1.67, 1.71, 1.75, 1.76, 1.81, 1.83, 1.85, 1.86, 1.87, 1.95, 1.103, 1.104, 1.108, 1.109, and the entries from 1.112 through 1.122.

14. DZZ III: 26.

15. See Ishii Shūdō, "Saigo no Dōgen-Jūnikanbon *Shōbōgenzō* to *Hōkyōki*," in *Jūnikanbon Shōbōgenzō no shomondai*.

16. DZZ III: 80–82.

17. DZZ III: 158.

18. DZZ III: 98.

19. DZZ III: 140.

20. DZZ III: 118.

21. *Kamakura myōchō haku-e shajigi*, in DZZ VII: 274–281.

22. DZZ VII: 161.

23. DZZ IV: 280.

24. Tatematsu Wahei, *Dōgen no tsuki* (Tokyo: Shodensha, 2002). See also Satomi Ton, *Dōgen zenji no hanashi* (Tokyo: Iwanami bunko, 2000); and Kumamoto Hidehito, "Gekika sareta Dōgen," *Komazawa Daigaku bukkyōgakubu ronshū* 34 (2003): 187–192; and Rei Sakaguchi, "Zazen and the Art of Playwriting," *The Japan Times*, 20 March 2002; http://www.japantimes.co.jp/cgi-bin/getarticle.pl5?ft20020320a1.htm.

25. DZZ III: 206.

26. DZZ III: 260–262; and IV: 50. Pai-chang had suggested that Ch'an was a third way beyond the distinction of Greater Vehicle (Mahayana) and Lesser Vehicle (Hinayana), but Dōgen indicates that the authentic Zen approach should do away with the distinctions altogether.

27. Nakaseko Shōdō, *Dōgen zenji den kenkyū-sei* (Tokyo: Kokusho kankōkai, 1997), pp. 206–209.

28. See Kagamishima, *Tendō nyojō zenji no kenkyū* (Tokyo: Shunjūsha, 1983).

29. Takeuchi Michio, *Dōgen* (Tokyo: Yoshikawa kōbunkan, 1992), p. 136.

30. On how the notion of change in the late Dōgen is crucial to the theory of Critical Buddhism, see Steven Heine, "Critical Buddhism (*Hihan Bukkyō*) and the Debate Concerning the 75-fascicle and 12-fascicle *Shōbōgenzō* Texts," *Japanese Journal of Religious Studies* 21/1 (1994): 37–72 (rpt. "Critical Buddhism and Dōgen's *Shōbōgenzō*: The Debate Over the 75-Fascicle and 12-Fascicle Texts," in Jamie Hubbard and Paul L. Swanson, eds., *Pruning the Bodhi Tree: The Storm Over Critical Buddhism* (Honolulu: University of Hawaii Press, 1997), pp. 251–285.

31. DZZ III: 166–168.

32. DZZ IV: 26–28.

33. DZZ III: 216.

34. Some of the debate revolves around a cryptic colophon, mentioned earlier, to the *Hachidainingaku* fascicle written by Ejō and discovered in 1930 in a manuscript in Yōkōji temple. Ejō speaks of Dōgen's desire to create a 100-volume text (the only reference to such an idea) by rewriting all the fascicles, and he mentions the need to honor the "twelve fascicles" (or it could be read as the "twelfth fascicle") as being consistent with Sakyamuni's teachings.

35. See Steven Heine, *Shifting Shape, Shaping Text: Philosophy and Folklore in the Fox Kōan* (Honolulu: University of Hawaii Press, 1999).

36. According to the *Mumonkan* verse, in Shibayama Zenkei, *Zen Comments on the Mumonkan* (New York: Mentor, 1974), p. 34: "Not falling, not ignoring:/Odd and even are on one die./Not ignoring, not falling:/Hundreds and thousands of regrets!"

37. DZZ II: 187.

38. DZZ II: 390.

39. Ishii Shūdō, "Recent Trends in Dōgen Studies," trans. Albert Welter, *Komazawa Daigaku zen kenkyūjō nenpō* 7 (1990): p. 227.

40. DZZ II: 394.

41. Matsumoto Shirō, "Jinshin inga ni tsuite: Dōgen no shisō ni kansuru shaken," in Kagamishima Genryū and Suzuki Kakuzen, eds., *Jūnikanbon Shōbōgenzō no shomondai* (Tokyo: Daizō shuppan, 1991), p. 234.

42. Another way of framing the issue of Dōgen's relation to *nyoraizō* thought, suggested by Matsumoto in "Jinshin inga ni tsuite," is to distinguish Dōgen's later view from three perspectives: (1) all things have Buddha-nature, therefore one must practice but the goal appears unattainable; (2) Buddha-nature encompasses all things, therefore one need not practice, because the Buddha-nature is already present; (3) Buddha-nature is actualized by practice, therefore one must continue to practice. Dōgen's early standpoint is reflected in view (3) as a refutation of (1) and (2), but even this view does not sufficiently emphasize the retributive consequences of karmic conditioning (1991, pp. 209ff).

43. Kagamishima Genryū, "Jūnikanbon *Shōbōgenzō* no ichizuke," in *Jūnikanbon Shōbōgenzō no shomondai*, p. 7.

44. Kagamishima, "Jūnikanbon *Shōbōgenzō* no ichizuke," p. 13.

45. See the preface of Ishii Shūdō, *Sōdai Zenshūshi no kenkyū* (Tokyo: Daitō shuppansha, 1987). Hakamaya, *Hongaku shisō hihan* (Tokyo: Daizō shuppan, 1989), p. 347, responds to some aspects of the Ishii position and cites an influential article by Mizuno Yaoko, "*Hōkyōki* to Jūnikan *Shōbōgenzō*: toku ni 'Jinshin inga' kan ni tsuite," *Shūgaku kenkyū* 21 (1979): 27–30.

46. These issues include the matters of social discrimination, antifeminism, and nationalism/nativism/imperialism evident in some aspects of Zen rituals, and the question of whether these deficient trends are somehow traceable back to attitudes expressed in Dōgen and other classic texts, which must therefore be held to accept responsibility and accountability, retrospectively.

47. Ikeda Rōsan, "Shinsō Jūnikanbon *Shōbōgenzō* no kōsō to kadai," in *Jūnikanbon Shōbōgenzō no shomondai*, pp. 287–318.

48. Kuroda Toshio, *Nihon chūsei no shakai to shūkyō* (Tokyo: Iwanami shoten, 1990). For other interpretations in the complex issues involved in examining the changes in Buddhism during the Kamakura era, see Matsuo Kenji, *Shin Kamakura Bukkyō no tanjō* (Tokyo: Kōdansha gendai shinsho, 1995); and Matsuo, "What Is Kamakura New Buddhism? Official Monks and Reclusive Monks," *Japanese Journal of Religious Studies* 14/1–2 (1997): 179–189. Matsuo tends to support Ishii's approach but also broadens the context considerably by explaining Dōgen as an example of a "reclusive monk" (*tonseisō*), along with Hōnen, Shinran, Nichiren, and others, who established orders that catered to the needs of monks and laypersons alike, although, in contrast to Ishii, Matsuo also stresses the role of individual salvation in these movements.

49. DZZ III: 230.

50. DZZ III: 242.

51. DZZ IV: 30.

52. DZZ III: 162–164.

53. DZZ III: 206–208.

54. DZZ III: 274.

55. DZZ IV: 120–124. Another practice Dōgen helped introduce to Japan at Eiheiji based on the models in Sung China was the annual summer retreat, which was apparently not known in Japan, on Mount Hiei or anywhere else, prior to Eisai and Shunjō (who both set up Sung-style institutions in the early Kamakura period). In *Kōzen gokokuron* Eisai criticizes and mocks his fellow Japanese Buddhists for using "summers" (i.e., number of retreats spent since ordination) to reckon years of monastic seniority when in fact monks in Japan did not observe any retreats. Eisai gives details for the retreats (both summer for three months, from 4.15 to 7.15, and winter for three months, from 10.15 to 1.15) that were meant to inform his ignorant countrymen, so it is pretty clear that this was something "new" coming in from China at the time. See Yifa, trans., *The Origins of Buddhist Monastic Codes in China: An Annotated Translation and Study of the Chanyuan Qinggui* (Honolulu: University of Hawaii Press, 2002), pp. 38–43. Eisai did establish retreats at Kenninji on the Sung model. In the *Shōbōgenzō* "Ango" fascicle, Dōgen provides detailed instructions on many aspects of how the retreat should be conducted, frequently citing the *Ch'an-yüan ch'ing-kuei* as the main source. Dōgen pays particular attention to the issue of how the seniority of monks should be rated and cited, an issue that he was no doubt sensitive to because of his sense of having been mistreated while visiting China.

As far as the role of the retreats in China and the role Dōgen played there, it seems clear that the retreats involved the entire monastic community at places like Mount T'ien-t'ung and Mount A-yü-wang. Even the lay postulants were part of the retreat. Dōgen was able to be accepted into the retreat but what he could not do, apparently, was register for and get into the Monks Hall for communal training as a member of the main body of monks or fully ordained monks. Because he (probably) could not get into communal training in a Monks Hall at any time, Dōgen (probably) had to spend all of his retreats in China in some other facility, most likely the visiting Monks Hall. Even back at Mount T'ien-t'ung for his second stay, when he attained enlightenment, there is no evidence that he got into the Monks Hall. The fact that he sat *zazen* with a group and heard Ju-ching admonish the group when a practitioner was sleeping during meditation is not evidence to the contrary; that could have happened on the platforms in a visiting Monks Hall or postulants hall. Ju-ching as abbot could have allowed anyone he wished to become his disciple and enter his room, but he could not have contravened the rule that limited the Monks Hall to fully ordained monks. None of this is clear, however, because Dōgen himself was not eager for his disciples to know about the inferior status that he suffered throughout his stay in China, so he glossed it over. I thank T. Griffith Foulk in an e-mail exchange in April 2005 for clarification of some of these points.

56. It should be stressed that the laypersons that Dōgen dealt with at Eiheiji were a far different group than the literati in Sung China, where "The state had lost interest in all but the most illustrious monks and the greatest monasteries. All these factors caused elite Buddhism to focus its efforts on literati and local government officials in order to obtain needed financial and political support"; Morten Schlutter, "Silent Illumination, Kung-an Introspection, and the Competition for Lay Patronage in Sung Dynasty Ch'an," in Peter N. Gregory and Daniel A. Getz, eds., *Buddhism in the Sung* (Honolulu: University of Hawaii Press, 1998), p. 137.

Also one area Dōgen did not attend to was funerals; as Duncan Ryūken Williams points out, Dōgen "did not include funerary procedures in his ritual repertoire, so it was not until the third-generation monk Gikai's death in 1309 that the first Sōtō Zen funeral was conducted under Chinese Chan monastic regulations. The first Japanese Sōtō Zen monastic regulations, which included a section on how to perform funerals, was the *Keizan shingi*"; *The Other Side of Zen: A Social History of Sōtō Zen Buddhism in Tokugawa Japan* (Princeton, N.J.: Princeton University Press, 2005), p. 40.

57. The Rinzai Rinka temples were generally based in Kyoto with a network of countryside temples, such as Daitokuji and Myōshinji, with prominent intellectual/literary abbots such as Daitō, Ikkyū, and Bassui; and the Sōtō Rinka temples were generally in rural areas with popular preachers such as Gasan Jōseki, Tsūgen Jakurei, and Gennō Shinshō.

58. Ishikawa Rikizan, "Chūsei Sōtōshū ni okeru kirigami sōjō ni tsuite," *Indogaku Bukkyōgaku kenkyū* 30/2 (1982): 742–746. The tradition of using *kirigami* was widespread in diverse medieval apprenticeship programs. For the Sōtō approach see also Ishikawa, "Transmission of *Kirigami* (Secret Intiation Documents): A Sōtō Practice in Medieval Japan," trans. Kawahashi Seishū, in Steven Heine and Dale S. Wright, eds., *The Kōan: Texts and Contexts in Zen Buddhism* (New York: Oxford University Press, 2000), pp. 233–243; and Ishikawa, "Colloquial Transcriptions as Sources for Understanding Zen in Japan," trans. William M. Bodiford, *The Eastern Buddhist* 34/1 (2002): 120–142.

59. One of the main examples, as was indicated, is the 75-*Shōbōgenzō* "Keiseisanshoku," which begins with a celebration of naturalism and concludes with a plea for repentance, a topic not dealt with elsewhere in the 75-*Shōbōgenzō*, though prevalent in the 12-*Shōbōgenzō*, especially "Sanjigo."

60. DZZ VII: 36–40 and 42.
61. DZZ III: 258–260, and DZZ III: 242, respectively.
62. DZZ VII: 286–295.
63. DZZ III: 212–214.
64. DZZ IV: 250.
65. DZZ VII: 170.
66. DZZ III: 82.
67. DZZ III: 88–90.
68. DZZ III: 186.
69. DZZ III: 194.
70. DZZ IV: 304.
71. DZZ VII: 175.
72. DZZ VII: 306.
73. DZZ IV: 102.

Bibliography

COLLECTIONS AND REFERENCE WORKS

Buddhist Dictionary: Manual of Buddhist Terms and Doctrines, ed. Nyanatiloka Mahothera. Rpt. Colombo: Frewin, 1972.

Buddhist Hybrid Sanskrit Dictionary, ed. Franklin Edgerton. Delhi: Motilal Banarsidass, 1977.

Bukkyōgo daijiten, ed. Nakamura Hajime. Tokyo: Tokyo shoseki, 1981.

Dai Nihon Bukkyō zensho, ed. Takakusu Junjirō et al., 750 vols. Tokyo: Dai Nihon Bukkyō zensho kankōkai, 1931.

Daiyūzan: Daiyūzan Saijōji kaisō roppyakunen hōzan. Shinagawa-ken: Daiyūzan Saijōji kaisō roppyakunen hōzan jimuchō, 1994.

A Dictionary of Chinese Buddhist Terms, ed. William Edward Soothill and Lewis Hodous. Rpt. Taipei: Ch'eng wen, 1976.

Hsü tsang ching. [Rpt. of *Nihon zoku zōkyō*], ed. Nakano Tatsue, 150 vols. Taipei: Shin wen fang, n.d.

Japanese-English Buddhist Dictionary. Tokyo: Daitō shuppansha, 1965.

Kōjien, ed. Shinmura Izuru. Tokyo: Iwanami shoten, 1980.

Nihon koten bungaku taikei, ed. Yamada Yoshio et al., 100 vols. Tokyo: Iwanami shoten, 1961–1963.

The Pali Text Society's Pali-English Dictionary, ed. T. W. Rhys-Davids and William Stede. London: Luzac, 1966.

Sawaki Kōdō zenshū, 20 vols. Tokyo: Daihōrinkan, rpt. 1963.

Sōtōshū kankei bunken mokuroku. Tokyo: Sōtō shūmuchō, 1990.

Sōtōshū zensho, 20 vols. Tokyo: Sōtōshū shūmuchō, 1970–1973.

T'ai-p'ing kuang-chi, ed. Wang Meng'ou. 500 *chüan.* Beijing: Chuang-hua shuchū, 1981.

Taishō shinshū daizōkyō, ed. Takakusu Junjirō and Watanabe Kaigyoku, 100 vols. Tokyo: Taishō issaikyō kankōkai, 1921–1932.

Vinaya pitakam, ed. Hermann Oldenberg, 5 vols. London: Williams & Norgate, 1879.
Zengaku daijiten, ed. Zengaku daijiten hensanjo. Tokyo: Taishūkan, 1985.

DŌGEN'S WORKS

Cleary, Thomas, trans., *Record of Things Heard: The "Shōbōgenzō Zuimonki," Talks of Zen Master Dōgen as Recorded by Zen Master Ejō*. Boulder, Col.: Prajña Press, 1980.
———, ed. and trans., *Timeless Spring: A Sōtō Zen Anthology*. New York: Weatherhill, 1980.
———, *Shōbōgenzō: Zen Essays by Dōgen*. Honolulu: University of Hawaii Press, 1986.
———, *Rational Zen: The Mind of Dōgen Zenji*. Boston: Shambhala, 1993.
Cook, Francis, trans., *Sounds of Valley Streams: Enlightenment in Dōgen's Zen*. Albany: State University of New York Press, 1989.
———, *How to Raise an Ox: Zen Practice as Taught in Zen Master Dōgen's "Shōbō-genzō."* Boston: Wisdom Publications, 2002.
———, *The Record of Transmitting the Light: Zen Master Keizan's Denkōroku*. Boston: Wisdom Publications, 2003.
Dōgen, Zen Master, and Uchiyama Kōshō, *Refining Your Life: From Zen Kitchen to Enlightenment*, trans. Thomas Wright. New York: Weatherhill, 1983.
Dōgen zenji zenshū, ed. Kagamishima Genryū, Kawamura Kōdō, Suzuki Kakuzen, Kosaka Kiyū, et al., 7 vols. Tokyo: Shunjūsha, 1988–1993.
Dōgen zenji zenshū, ed. Ōkubo Dōshū. Tokyo: Chikuma shobō, 1969 and 1970.
Eihei Shōbōgenzō shūsho taisei, 25 vols. Tokyo: Taishūkan, 1974–1981.
Etō Sokuō, ed., *Shōbōgenzō*, 3 vols. Tokyo: Iwanami bunko, 1939–1943.
Funetsu Yoko, "Sanshōdōei no meishū, naritachi, seikaku," *Daisai Daigaku kokubun* 5 (1974): 24–44.
Hata Egyoku, "*Eihei kōroku*—sono sodoku to chūkai," *Sanshō* (1975–1977).
Hata Egyoku, et al., "Satori o utau: Dōgen zenji no uta," *Zen no kaze* 1 (1981): 22–37.
Ikeda Rōsan, *Gendaigoyaku Shōbōgenzō zuimonki*. Tokyo: Daizō shuppan, 1993.
Itō Shunkō, *Eihei kōroku chūkai zenshō*, 4 vols. Tokyo: Kōmeisha, 1962.
———, *Hōkyōki: Dōgen no nyūsō nōto*. Tokyo: Daitō shuppansha, 1997.
Kim, Hee-Jim, trans., *Flowers of Emptiness: Selections from Dōgen's Shōbōgenzō*. New York: Edwin Mellen Press, 1985.
Kishizawa Ian, *Zusuikaian zuihitsu*. Tokyo: Daibōinsatsu, 1960.
Leighton, Taigen Dan, and Shohaku Okumura, eds., *Dōgen's Pure Standards for the Zen Community*. New York: State University of New York Press, 1996.
———, trans., *Dōgen's Extensive Record: A Translation of the Eihei Kōroku*. Boston: Wisdom Publications, 2004.
Masunaga, Reihō, trans., *A Primer of Sōtō Zen: A Translation of Dōgen's Shōbōgenzō Zuimonki*. Honolulu: University of Hawaii Press, 1971.
Mizuno Yaoko, ed., *Shōbōgenzō zuimonki*. Tokyo: Chikuma shobō, 1963.
Nearman, Rev. Hubert, trans., *The Shōbōgenzō, or, The Treasure House of The Eye of The True Teachings*. Mt. Shasta, Calif.: Shasta Abbey Press, 1996.

Nishijima Gudo Wafu and Chodo Cross, *Master Dōgen's Shōbōgenzō*, 4 vols. Woods Hole, Mass.: Windbell Publications, 1994–1999.

Nishiyama Kōsen and John Stevens, trans., *Dōgen Zenji's Shōbōgenzō (The Eye and Treasury of the True Law)*, 4 vols. Sendai, Japan: Daihokkaikaku, 1975.

Ōba Nanboku, *Dōgen zenji Sanshōdōei no kenkyū*. Tokyo: Nakayama shobō, 1970.

Okumura, Shohaku, trans., *"Shōbōgenzō zuimonki," Sayings of Eihei Dōgen Zenji Recorded by Kōun Ejō*. Kyoto: Kyoto Sōtō Zen Center, 1987.

Okumura, Shohaku, and Taigen Dan Leighton, trans., *The Wholehearted Way*. Boston: Tuttle Publishing, 1997.

Ōtani Teppō, ed., *Manzan-bon Eihei kōroku sozanhon taikō*. Tokyo: Issuisha, 1994.

Ōyama Kōryū, *Kusa no ha: Dōgen zenji waka-shū*. Tokyo: Sōtōshū shūmuchō, 1971.

Takahashi, Masanobu, and Yuzuru Nobuoka, trans., *The Essence of Dōgen*. London: Kegan Paul International Limited, 1983.

Tanahashi, Kasuaki, ed. and trans., *Moon in a Dewdrop: Writings of Zen Master Dōgen*. San Francisco: North Point Press, 1985.

———, ed. and trans., *Enlightenment Unfolds: Life and Work of Zen Master Dōgen*. Boston: Shambhala, 1998.

———, ed., *Beyond Thinking: A Guide to Zen Meditation*. Boston: Shambhala, 2004.

Terada Tōru and Mizuno Yaoko, eds., *Shōbōgenzō*, 2 vols. Tokyo: Iwanami shoten, 1970.

Waddell, Norman, trans., "Being Time: Dōgen's *Shōbōgenzō Uji*," *The Eastern Buddhist* 12/1 (1979): 114–129.

Waddell, Norman, and Masao Abe, trans., "One Bright Pearl: Dōgen's *Shōbōgenzō Ikka Myōju*," *The Eastern Buddhist* 6/2 (1971): 108–117.

———, trans., "*Shōbōgenzō genjōkōan*," *The Eastern Buddhist* 5/2 (1972): 120–140.

———, trans., "Dōgen's *Fukanzazengi* and *Shōbōgenzō Zazengi*," *The Eastern Buddhist* 6/2 (1973): 115–128.

———, trans., "The King of Samādhis Samādhi: Dōgen's *Shōbōgenzō Sammai Ō Zammai*," *The Eastern Buddhist* 7/1 (1974): 118–121.

———, trans., "*Shōbōgenzō* Buddha-nature," *The Eastern Buddhist* 1/2 (1975): 94–112; 9/1 (1976): 87–105; 9/2 (1976): 71–87.

———, trans., "Dōgen's *Bendōwa*," *The Eastern Buddhist* 5/1 (1979): 124–157.

———, trans., *The Heart of Dōgen's Shōbōgenzō*. Albany, N.Y.: SUNY Press, 2002.

Warner, Jisho, Shohaku Okumura, John McRae, and Taigen Dan Leighton, eds., *Nothing Is Hidden: Essays on Zen Master Dōgen's Instructions for the Cook*. New York: Weatherhill, 2001.

Yasutani, Hakuun, *Flowers Fall: A Commentary on Zen Master Dōgen's Genjōkōan*. Boston: Shambhala, 1996.

Yokoi Yūhō, trans., *Eihei-genzenji-shingi: Regulation for a Monastic Life by Eihei Dōgen*. Tokyo: Sankibō, 1973.

Yokoi, Yūhō, and Daizen Victoria, trans., *Zen Master Dōgen: An Introduction with Selected Writings*. Tokyo: Weatherhill, 1976.

———, trans., *Shōbōgenzō*. Tokyo: Sankibō Buddhist Store, 1986.

———, trans., *The Eihei kōroku*. Tokyo: Sankibō Buddhist Store, 1987.

———, trans. *Zen Master Dōgen*. New York: Weatherhill, 1975.

OTHER SOURCES

Abe Chōichi, *Chūgoku Zenshūshi no kenkyū*. Tokyo: Seishin shobō, 1963.
———, *Zenshū shakai to shinkō: Zoku Chūgoku Zenshūshi no kenkyū*. Tokyo: Kindai bungeisha, 1993.
Abe, Masao, *A Study of Dōgen: His Philosophy and Religion*, ed. Steven Heine. Albany, N.Y.: SUNY Press, 1992.
Adolphson, Mikael, "Enryakuji—An Old Power in a New Era," in Jeffrey P. Mass, ed., *The Origins of Japan's Medieval World: Courtiers, Clerics, Warriors, and Peasants in the Fourteenth Century*. Stanford, Calif.: Stanford University Press, 1997, pp. 238–260.
Akizuki Ryōmin, *Kōan*. Tokyo: Chikuma shobō, 1987.
Andō Yoshinori, *Chūsei Zenshū bunseki no kenkyū*. Tokyo: Kokusho inkōkai, 2000.
Anonymous, http://www.zen-occidental.net/dogen/dogen-biographie1.html, 2004.
Aoyama Shundō, *Tenzokyōkun o yomu*. Tokyo: NHK shūkyō no jikan, 2003.
Arai, Paula, *Women Living Zen: Japanese Sōtō Buddhist Nuns*. New York: Oxford University Press, 1999.
Baroni, Helen J., *Ōbaku Zen: The Emergence of the Third Sect of Zen in Tokugawa Japan*. Honolulu: University of Hawaii Press, 2000.
Bielefeldt, Carl, "Recarving the Dragon: History and Dogma in the Study of Dōgen," in William R. LaFleur, ed., *Dōgen Studies*. Honolulu: University of Hawaii Press, 1985, pp. 21–53.
———, *Dōgen's Manuals of Zen Meditation*. Berkeley: University of California Press, 1988.
———, "No-Mind and Sudden Awakening: Thoughts on the Soteriology of a Kamakura Zen Text," in Robert E. Buswell, Jr., and Robert M. Gimello, eds., *Paths to Liberation: The Mārga and Its Transformations in Buddhist Thought*. Honolulu: University of Hawaii Press, 1992.
———, trans., "A Discussion of Seated Zen," in Donald S. Lopez, Jr., ed., *Buddhism in Practice*. Princeton, N.J.: Princeton University Press, 1995.
———, "Kokan Shiren and the Sectarian Uses of History," in Jeffrey P. Mass, ed., *The Origins of Japan's Medieval World: Courtiers, Clerics, Warriors, and Peasants in the Fourteenth Century*. Stanford, Calif.: Stanford University Press, 1997, pp. 295–320.
———, "Filling the Zen shū: Notes on the *Jisshū Yōdō Ki*," in Bernard Faure, ed., *Chan Buddhism in Ritual Context*. London: Routledge Curzon, 2003, pp. 179–210.
Bloom, Harold, *The Anxiety of Influence*. New York: Oxford University Press, 1973.
Bodiford, William M., "Dharma Transmission in Sōtō Zen: Manzan Dōhaku's Reform Movement," *Monumenta Nipponica* 46/4 (1991): 423–451.
———, "Zen in the Art of Funerals: Ritual Salvation in Japanese Buddhism," *History of Religions* 32/2 (1992): 146–164.
———, *Sōtō Zen in Medieval Japan*. Honolulu: University of Hawaii Press, 1993.
———, "The Enlightenment of Kami and Ghosts: Spirit Ordinations in Japanese Sōtō Zen," *Cahiers d'Extrême-Asie* 7 (1993–1994): 267–282.
———, "Zen and the Art of Religious Prejudice: Efforts to Reform a Tradition of Social Discrimination," *Japanese Journal of Religious Studies* 23 (1996): 1–28.

————, "Major Editions of the *Eihei Shōbōgenzō*," unpublished paper, 2000.

Chang, Chung-yüan, *Original Teachings of Ch'an Buddhism*. New York: Vintage, 1969.

Cleary, Thomas, trans., *Transmission of Light: Zen in the Art of Enlightenment* by Zen Master Keizan. San Francisco: North Point Press, 1990.

————, *The Five Houses of Zen*. Boston: Shambhala, 1997.

————, trans., *The Book of Serenity*. Hudson, N.Y.: Lindisfarne Press, 1990.

Cleary, Thomas, and J. C. Cleary, trans., *The Blue Cliff Record*, 3 vols. With a foreword by Maezumi Taizan Roshi. Boulder, Col.: Shambhala, 1977.

Collcutt, Martin, *Five Mountains: The Rinzai Zen Monastic Institution in Medieval Japan*. Cambridge, Mass.: Harvard University Press, 1981.

Dachuan Puji, ed., *Wu-teng hui yüan*. Taipei: Guang Wen Bookstore, 1971.

Dale, Peter N., *The Myth of Japanese Uniqueness*. Hampshire, England: Palgrave-MacMillan, 1986.

de Bary, Theodore, Donald Keene, George Tanabe, and Paul Varley, eds., *Sources of Japanese Tradition from Earliest Times to 1600*, vol. 1. New York: Columbia University Press, 2001.

Dumoulin, Heinrich, *Zen Enlightenment: Origins and Meaning*. New York: Weatherhill, 1979.

————, *Zen Buddhism: A History II: Japan*. New York: Macmillan, 1990.

Ebrey, Patricia Buckley, *The Cambridge Illustrated History of China*. Cambridge: Cambridge University Press, 1996.

Etō Sokuō, *Shūso toshite no Dōgen zenji*. Tokyo: Iwanami shoten, 1944.

Faure, Bernard, "Bodhidharma as Textual and Religious Paradigm," *History of Religions* 25/3 (1986): 187–198.

————, "The Daruma-shū, Dōgen, and Sōtō Zen," *Monumenta Nipponica* 42/1 (1987): 25–55.

————, "Space and Place in Chinese Religious Traditions," *Hisotry of Religions* 26/4 (1987): 337–356.

————, *The Rhetoric of Immediacy: A Cultural Critique of the Chan/Zen Buddhism*. Princeton, N.J.: Princeton University Press, 1991.

————, *Chan Insights and Oversights: An Epistemological Critique of the Chan Tradition*. Princeton, N.J.: Princeton University Press, 1993.

————, "The Kyoto School and Reverse Orienalism," in Charles Wei-hsun Fu and Steven Heine, eds., *Japanese in Traditional and Postmodern Perspectives*. Albany, N.Y.: SUNY Press, 1995, pp. 245–281.

————, *Visions of Power: Imagining Medieval Japanese Buddhism*, trans. Phyllis Brooks. Princeton, N.J.: Princeton University Press, 1996.

————, *The Will to Orthodoxy: A Critical Genealogy of Northern Chan Buddhism*, trans. Phyllis Brooks. Stanford, Calif.: Stanford University Press, 1997.

————, *Double Exposure: Cutting Across Buddhist and Western Discourses*, trans. Janet Lloyd. Stanford, Calif.: Stanford University Press, 2004.

Ferguson, Andy, *Zen's Chinese Heritage: The Masters and Their Teachings*. Boston: Wisdom Publications, 2000.

Foulk, T. Griffith, "The Ch'an School and Its Place in the Buddhist Monastic Tradition," Ph.D. Dissertation, University of Michigan, 1987.

————, "The Ch'an *Tsung* in Medieval China: School," *Pacific World* 8 (1992): 18–31.

————, "Myth, Ritual, and Monastic Practice in Sung Ch'an Buddhism," in Patricia

Buckley Ebrey and Peter N. Gregory, eds., *Religion and Society in T'ang and Sung China*. Honolulu: University of Hawaii Press, 1993, pp. 147–208.

———, "Sung Controversies Concerning the 'Separate Transmission' of Ch'an," in Peter N. Gregory and Daniel A. Getz, eds., *Buddhism in the Sung*. Honolulu: University of Hawaii Press, 1999, pp. 220–284.

———, "The Historical Context of Dōgen's Monastic Rules," in Daihonzan Eiheiji, ed. *Dōgen zenji kenkyū ronshū*. Tokyo: Taishūkan shoten, 2002, pp. 962–1017.

———, "The 'Rules of Purity' in Japanese Zen," in Steven Heine and Dale S. Wright, eds., *Zen Classics: Formative Texts in the History of Zen Buddhism*. New York: Oxford University Press, 2006, pp. 137–169.

Foulk, T. Griffith, and Robert H. Sharf, "On the Ritual Use of Ch'an Portraiture in Medieval China," *Bilingual Journal of the "Ecole Française d'Extrême-Orient"* 7 (1993–1994): 149–219.

Fu, Charles Wei-hsun, *Dōgen*. Taipei, Taiwan: Tungta, 1994.

———, "Mixed Precepts, the Bodhisattva Precepts, and the Preceptless Precept: A Critical Comparison of the Chinese and Japanese Buddhist Views of Śila/Vinaya," in Charles Wei-hsun Fu and Sandra A. Wawrytko, eds., *Buddhist Behavioral Codes and the Modern World*. Westport, Conn.: Greenwood Press, 1994, pp. 245–276.

Fu, Charles Wei-hsun, and Sandra A. Wawrytko, eds., *Buddhist Behavioral Codes and the Modern World: An International Symposium*. Westport, Conn.: Greenwood Press, 1994.

Furuta Shōkin, *Nihon Bukkyō shishō shi no shomondai*. Tokyo: Shunjūsha, 1964.

Geertz, Clifford, "Thick Description: Toward an Interpretative Theory of Culture," in *The Interpretation of Cultures*. New York: Basic Books, 1973, pp. 3–32.

Gernet, Jacques, *Buddhism in Chinese Society: An Economic History from the Fifth to the Tenth Centuries*, trans. Granciscus Verellen. New York: Columbia University Press, 1995.

Gregory, Peter N., "Is Critical Buddhism Really Critical?" in Jamie Hubbard and Paul L. Swanson, eds., *Pruning the Bodhi Tree: The Storm over Critical Buddhism*. Honolulu: University of Hawaii Press, 1997, pp. 286–297.

———, *Tsung-mi and the Sinification of Buddhism*. Honolulu: Kuroda Institute, University of Hawaii Press, 2002.

Gregory, Peter, and Daniel Getz, Jr., eds., *Buddhism in the Sung*. Honolulu: Kuroda Institute, University of Hawaii Press, 1999.

Groner, Paul. *Saichō: The Establishment of the Japanese Tendai School*. Berkeley, Calif.: Berkeley Buddhist Studies Series, 1984.

Hakamaya Noriaki, *Hongaku shisō hihan*. Tokyo: Daizō shuppan, 1989.

———, *Hihan Bukkyō*. Tokyo: Daizō shuppan, 1990.

———, "Nihonjin to animizumu," *Komazawa Daigaku Bukkyō gakubu ronshū* 23 (1992): 351–378.

———, *Dōgen to Bukkyō: Jūnikanbon Shōbōgenzō no Dōgen*. Tokyo: Daizō shuppan, 1992.

———, "Dōgen ni okeru jūnikanbon no igi," in Yasuaki Nara, ed., *Budda kara Dōgen e*, Tōkyō shoseki, 1992, pp. 238–250.

Hamill, Sam, and J. P. Seaton, trans., *The Essential Chuang Tzu*. Boston: Shambhala, 1999.

Harvey, Van, *The Historian and the Believer: The Morality of Historical Knowledge and Christian Belief*. New York: Macmillan, 1966.

He Yansheng, *Dōgen to Chūgoku Zen shisō*. Kyoto: Hōzōkan, 2000.

Heine, Steven, *Existential and Ontological Dimensions of Time in Heidegger and Dōgen*. Albany, N.Y.: SUNY Press, 1985.

————, "Dōgen Casts Off 'What'?: An Analysis of *Shinjin datsuraku*," *Journal of the International Association of Buddhist Studies* 9 (1986): 53–70.

————, *A Blade of Grass: Japanese Poetry and Aesthetics in Dōgen Zen*. New York: Peter Lang, 1989.

————, "Does the Kōan Have Buddha-Nature? The Zen Kōan as Religious Symbol," *Journal of the American Academy of Religion* 58/3 (1990): 357–387.

————, "The Flower Blossoms 'Without Why': Beyond the Heidegger-Kuki Dialogue on Contemplative Language," *Eastern Buddhist* 23/2 (1990): 60–86.

————, "From Rice Cultivation to Mind Contemplation: The Meaning of Impermanence in Japanese Religion," *History of Religions* 30/4 (1991): 374–403.

————, *Dōgen and the Kōan Tradition: A Tale of Two Shōbōgenzō Texts*. Albany, N.Y.: SUNY Press, 1994.

————, "Critical Buddhism (*Hihan Bukkyō*) and the Debate Concerning the 75-fascicle and 12-fascicle *Shōbōgenzō* Texts," *Japanese Journal of Religious Studies* 21/1 (1994): 37–72.

————, "Sōtō Zen and the Inari Cult: Symbiotic and Exorcistic Trends in Buddhist-Folk Religious Amalgamations," *Pacific World* 10 (1994): 71–95.

————, "Putting the 'Fox' back into the 'Wild Fox Kōan': The Intersection of Philosophical and Popular Religious Elements in the Ch'an/Zen Kōan Tradition," *Harvard Journal of Asiatic Studies* 56/2 (1996): 257–317.

————, "The Dōgen Canon: Dōgen's Pre-*Shōbōgenzō* Writings and the Question of Change in His Later Works," *Japanese Journal of Religious Studies* 24 (1997): 39–85.

————, *Shifting Shape, Shaping Text: Philosophy and Folklore in the Fox Kōan*. Honolulu: University of Hawaii Press, 1999.

————, "After the Storm: Matsumoto Shirō's Transition from 'Critical Buddhism' to 'Critical Theology,' " *Japanese Journal of Religious Studies* 28/1–2 (2001): 133–146.

————, *Opening a Mountain: Kōans of the Zen Masters*. New York: Oxford University Press, 2002.

————, "Ch'an Buddhist *Kung-ans* as Models for Interpersonal Behavior," *Journal of Chinese Philosophy* 30/3–4 (2003): 525–540.

————, "Abbreviation or Aberration: The Role of the *Shushōgi* in Modern Sōtō Zen Buddhism," in Steven Heine and Charles S. Prebish, eds., *Buddhism in the Modern World: Adaptations of an Ancient Tradition*. New York: Oxford University Press, 2003, pp. 169–192.

————, "Did Dōgen Go to China?: Problematizing Dōgen's Relation to Ju-ching and Chinese Ch'an," *Japanese Journal of Religious Studies* 30/1–2 (2003): 27–59.

————, "Kōans in the Dōgen Tradition: How and Why Dōgen Does What He Does with Kōans," in *Philosophy East and West* 54/1 (2004): 1–19.

————, "The *Eihei kōroku*: The Record of Dōgen's Later Period at Eihei-ji Temple," in Steven Heine and Dale S. Wright, eds., *The Zen Canon: Understanding the Classic Texts*. Oxford: Oxford University Press, 2003, pp. 245–273.

————, "Critical View of Discourses on the Relation Between Japanese Business and

Social Values," *The Journal of Language for International Business* 15/2 (2004): 35–48.

———, "Dōgen and the Precepts, Revisited," in Damien Keown and Mavis Fenn, eds., *From Ancient India to Modern America: Buddhist Studies in Honor of Charles S. Prebish.* New York: RoutledgeCurzon, 2005, pp. 11–31.

———, *The Zen Poetry of Dōgen: Verses from the Mountain of Eternal Peace.* Mt. Tremper, N.Y.: Dharma Communications, 2005.

———, "An Analysis of Dōgen's *Eihei goroku*: Distillation or Distortion?" in Steven Heine and Dale S. Wright, eds., *Zen Classics: Formative Texts in the History of Zen Buddhism.* New York: Oxford University Press, 2005, pp. 113–136.

———, "Is Eiheiji Temple 'Mount T'ien-t'ung East'? Geo-Ritual Perspectives on the Transition from Chinese Ch'an to Japanese Zen," in Steven Heine and Dale S. Wright, eds., *Zen Ritual.* New York: Oxford University Press, forthcoming.

Heine, Steven, and Charles S. Prebish, eds., *Buddhism in the Modern World: Adaptations of an Ancient Tradition.* New York: Oxford University Press, 2003.

Heine, Steven, and Dale S. Wright, eds., *The Kōan: Texts and Contexts in Zen Buddhism.* Oxford: Oxford University Press, 2000.

———, eds., *The Zen Canon: Understanding the Classic Texts.* Oxford: Oxford University Press, 2004.

———, eds., *Zen Classics: Formative Texts in the History of Zen Buddhism.* New York: Oxford University Press, 2006.

Heisig, James W., and John C. Maraldo, eds., *Rude Awakenings: Zen, the Kyoto School, and the Question of Nationalism.* Honolulu: University of Hawaii Press, 1995.

Hirakawa, Akira, *A History of Indian Buddhism: From Śākyamuni to Early Mahāyāna,* trans. Paul Groner. Honolulu: University of Hawaii Press, 1990.

Hirata Takashi, ed., *Mumonkan, Zen no goroku,* vol. 18. Tokyo: Chikuma shobō, 1969.

Hirose Ryōko, "Sōtō Zensō ni okeru shinjin kado-akurei chin'atsu," *Indogaku bukkyō-gaku kenkyū* 21/2 (1983): 233–236.

Hobsbawm, Eric, and Terence Ranger, eds., *The Invention Of Tradition.* Cambridge: Cambridge University Press, 1983.

Hori, Ichirō, *Folk Religion in Japan: Continuity and Change,* ed. Joseph M. Kitagawa and Alan L. Miller. Chicago: University of Chicago Press, 1968.

Hubbard, Jamie, "Introduction," in Jamie Hubbard and Paul L. Swanson, *Pruning The Bodhi Tree: The Storm over Critical Buddhism.* Honolulu: University of Hawaii Press, 1997, pp. vii–xxii.

Hubbard, Jamie, and Paul L. Swanson, eds., *Pruning the Bodhi Tree: The Storm over Critical Buddhism.* Honolulu: University of Hawaii Press, 1997.

Hung-chih, "Chianshi kuang-lo" (Extensive Record of Chan Master Hung-chih), in *Taishō shinshū daizōkyō,* vol. 48/2001: 73–78, 98–100. Tokyo: Taishō issaikyō kankokai, 1924–1933.

Ichikawa Hakugen, *Zen to gendai shisō.* Tokyo: Tokuma shoten, 1967.

———, *Bukkyōsha no sensō-sekinin.* Tokyo: Shunjūsha, 1970.

Ienaga Saburō, *Chusei Bukkyō shisō shi.* Rev. ed. Kyoto: Heirakuji shoten, first edition published 1947.

Ikeda Rōsan, *Dōgengaku no yōran.* Tokyo: Daizō shuppan, 1991.

———, "Shinsō Jūnikanbon *Shōbōgenzō* no kōsō to kadai," in Kagamishima Genryū and Suzuki Kakuzen, eds., *Jūnikanbon* Shōbōgenzō *no shomondai.* Tokyo: Daizō shuppan, 1991, pp. 287–318.

Imaeda Aishin, *Zenshū no rekishi.* Nihon rekishi shinsho. Tokyo: Shibundō, 1966.

———, *Dōgen: Zazen hitosuji no shamon.* NHK Books 255. Tokyo: Nihon hōsō shuppan kyōkai, 1976.

Imaeda Aishin et al., eds., *Sōtōshū.* Tokyo: Shōgakkan, 1986.

Iriya Yoshitaka, ed., *Baso goroku.* Kyoto: Zen bunka kenkyūjō, 1974.

———, ed., *Rinzai roku.* Tokyo: Iwanami shoten, 1991.

Iriya Yoshitaka et al., eds., *Hekiganroku,* 3 vols. Tokyo: Iwanami shoten, 1992–1996.

Ishii Seijun, "*Eihei kōroku:* Kenchō nenkan no jōdō ni tsuite," *Shūgaku kenkyū* 29 (1987): 91–94.

———, "*Jūnikanbon* Shōbōgenzō to *Eihei kōroku:* 'Hyakujō yako' no hanashi o chūshin toshite," *Shūgaku kenkyū* 30 (1988): 257–262.

———, "*Jūnikanbon* Shōbōgenzō honbun no seiritsu jigo ni tsuite," *Komazawa Daigaku bukkyōgakubu ronshū* 22 (1991): 236–260.

———, "*Mana* Shōbōgenzō *no seiritsu kansuru isshiken:* 'Eihei *juko,*' 'Kōshōji goroku' to no naiyō taihi o chūshin toshite," *Sōtōshū shūgakujō kiyō* 8 (1994): 53–67.

———, ed., "Shōbōgenzō zuimonki, Eihei kōroku to Dōgen Zen," in Ishii Shūdō et al., eds., *Dōgen shisō taikei,* vol. 10. Kyoto: Dōhōsha shuppan, 1995.

———, "Eiheiji senjutsu bunseki ni miru Dōgen zenji no sōdan un-ei," in Daihonzan Eiheiji, ed., *Dōgen zenji kenkyū ronshū.* Tokyo: Taishūkan shoten, 2002, pp. 409–440; and http://homepage1.nifty.com/seijun.

Ishii Shūdō, *Sōdai Zenshūshi no kenkyū.* Tokyo: Daitō shuppansha, 1987.

———, *Chūgoku Zenshūshi wa: Mana Shōbōgenzō ni manabu.* Kyoto: Zen bunka kenkyūjō, 1988.

———, "Recent Trends in Dōgen Studies," trans. Albert Welter, *Komazawa Daigaku Zen kenkyūjō nenpō* 7 (1990): 219–264.

———, *Zen no seiritsu-shiteki kenkyū.* Tokyo: Daizō shuppan, 1991.

———, *Dōgen Zen no seiritsu-shiteki kenkyū.* Tokyo: Daizō shuppan, 1991.

———, "Dainichi Nōnin, the Daruma Sect, and the Origins of Zen in Japan," trans. Florin Deleanu (1992) [Unpublished].

———, *Saikin no Dōgen zenji kenkyū ni omou.* Tokyo: Ishiken Sōtōshū seinenkai, 1994.

———, "Saigo no Dōgen zenji kenkyū ni omou," *Chōgoku Sōtōshū seinenkai isshiken dai-kai kōgi roku* 60 (1994): 1–130.

———, "Saigo no Dōgen-Jūnikanbon Shōbōgenzō to Hōkyōki," in Kagamishima Genryū and Suzuki Kakuzen, eds., *Jūnikanbon* Shōbōgenzō *no shomondai.* Tokyo: Daizō shuppan, 1991, pp. 319–374.

———, "*Hyakujō shingi no kenkyū:* 'Zenmon kishiki' to '*Hyakujō koshingi,*'" *Komazawa Daigaku Zen kenkyūjō nenpō* 6 (1995): 15–53.

———, "Nishimura eshin yakuchū 'Mumonkan,'" *Hanazono Daigaku bungakubu kenkyūjō kiyō* 28 (1996): 113–136.

———, "*Eihei ryaku roku* kangae: *Jūnikanbon* Shōbōgenzō to kanren shite," *Matsugaoka bunko kenkyū nempō* 11 (1997): 73–128.

———, "Shūgaku, Zenshūshi to 'shin shūgaku,'" parts 1–3, *Shūgaku to gendai* 2 (1998): 119–304.

Ishikawa Rikizan, "Chūsei Sōtōshū ni okeru kirigami sōjō ni tsuite," *Indogaku bukkyō-gaku kenkyū* 30/2 (1982): 742–746.

———, "Chūsei Zenshū to shinbutsu shūgō: Toku ni Sōtōshū no chihōteki tenkai to kirigami shiryō o chūshin ni shite," *Nihon Bukkyō* 60–61 (1984): 41–56.

———, "Chūsei Zenshūshi kenkyū to Zenseki shōmono shiryō," in Kawamura Kōdō and Ishikawa Rikizan, eds., *Dōgen zenji to Sōtōshū*. Tokyo: Yoshikawa kōbunkan, 1985.

———, "Transmission of *Kirigami* (Secret Initiation Documents): A Sōtō Practice in Medieval Japan," trans. Kawahashi Seishū, in Steven Heine and Dale S. Wright, eds., *The Kōan: Texts and Contexts in Zen Buddhism*. New York: Oxford University Press, 2000, pp. 233–243.

———, "Colloquial Transcriptions as Sources for Understanding Zen in Japan," trans. William M. Bodiford, *The Eastern Buddhist* 34/1 (2002): 120–142.

Itō Shūken, "Manabi jūnikanbon *Shōbōgenzō* ni tsuite," *Indogaku bukkyōgaku kenkyū* 36/1 (1987): 194–201.

———, "Jūnikanbon *Shōbōgenzō* no senjutsu to sono ito ni tsuite," in Kagamishima Genryū and Suzuki Kakuzen, eds., *Jūnikanbon* Shōbōgenzō *no shomondai*. Tokyo: Daizō shuppan, 1991, pp. 375–404.

———, *Dōgen Zen kenkyū*. Tokyo: Daizō shuppan, 1998.

Itō Takatoshi, *Chūgoku Bukkyō no hihanteki kenkyū*. Tokyo: Daizō shuppan, 1992.

———, "Zen to Bukkyō no honshitsu," in Yasuaki Nara. ed., *Budda kara Dōgen e*. Tokyo: Tōkyō shoseki, 1992, pp. 143–155.

Ives, Christopher, *Zen Awakening and Society*. Honolulu: University of Hawaii Press, 1992.

Jackson, Roger, "Buddhist Theology: Its Historical Context," in Roger Jackson and John Makransky, eds., *Buddhist Theology: Critical Reflections by Contemporary Buddhist Scholars*. Surrey: Curzon Press, 2000, pp. 1–13.

Jaffe, Richard M., *Neither Monk nor Layman: Clerical Marriage in Modern Japanese Buddhism*. Princeton, N.J.: Princeton University Press, 2001.

Kagamishima Genryū, *Dōgen zenji to sono monryū*. Tokyo: Seishin shobō, 1961.

———, *Dōgen zenji to in'yo kyōten-goroku no kenkyū*. Tokyo: Mokujisha, 1965.

———, *Tendō Nyojō zenji no kenkyū*. Tokyo: Shunjūsha, 1983.

———, "Zenkai no seiritsu to endonkai," in *Bukkyō ni okeru kai no mondai*. Kyoto: Heiraku, 1984.

———, *Dōgen zenji to sono shūhen*. Tokyo: Daitō shuppansha, 1985.

———, "Dōgen zenji no in'yō tōshi-goroku ni tsuite: Mana *Shōbōgenzō* o shiten toshite," *Komazawa Daigaku bukkyōgakubu kenkyū kiyō* 45 (1987): 1–14.

———, *Dōgen zenji goroku*. Tokyo: Kōdansha, 1990.

———, "Jūnikanbon *Shōbōgenzō* no ichizuke," in Kagamishima Genryū and Suzuki Kakuzen, eds., *Jūnikanbon* Shōbōgenzō *no shomondai*. Tokyo: Daizō shuppan, 1991, pp. 3–30.

———, *Dōgen zenji to sono shūfū*. Tokyo: Shunjūsha, 1994.

———, *Dōgen in'yō goroku no kenkyū*. Tokyo: Sōtō shūgaku kenkyūjō, 1995.

———, *Genbun-taishō gendaigoyaku Dōgen zenji zenshū*, vols. 10–13. Tokyo: Shunjū-sha, 1999.

Kagamishima Genryū and Suzuki Kakuzen, eds., *Jūnikanbon* Shōbōgenzō *no shomon-dai*. Tokyo: Daizō shuppan, 1991.

Kagamishima Genryū and Tamaki Koshirō, eds., *Dōgen no chosaku*, 7 vols. Tokyo: Shunjūsha, 1980.

Kagamishima Genryū, Satō Tatsugen, and Kosaka Kiyū, eds., *Yakuchū Zen'en shingi*. Tokyo: Sōtōshū shūmuchō, 1972.

Kalupahana, David J., *Causality: The Central Philosophy of Buddhism*. Honolulu: University of Hawaii Press, 1975.

Kasahara, Kazuo, ed., *A History of Japanese Religion*, trans. Paul McCarthy and Gaynor Sekimori. Tokyo: Kōsei, 2001.

Kasuga Yūhō, *Shinshaku Eihei kōroku*. Tokyo: Perikansha, 1998.

Kasulis, Thomas. P., *Zen Action, Zen Person*. Honolulu: University of Hawaii Press, 1981.

———, "Truth Words: The Basis of Kūkai's Theory of Interpretation," in Donald Lopez, ed., *Buddhist Hermeneutics*. Honolulu: University of Hawaii Press, 1988.

———, "The Zen Philosopher: A Review Article on Dōgen Scholarship in English," *Philosophy East and West* 28/3 (1978): 353–373.

Katz, Nathan, ed., *Buddhist and Western Philosophy*. New Delhi: Sterling, 1981.

———, ed., *Buddhist and Western Psychology*. Boulder, Col.: Shambhala, 1983.

Kawamura Kōdō, *Shohon taikō Eihei kaizan Dōgen zenji gyōjō: Kenzeki*. Tokyo: Taishūkan shoten, 1975.

———, "*Shōbōgenzō*," in Kagamishima Genryū and Tamaki Kōshirō, eds., *Dōgen no chosaku*, 7 vols. Tokyo: Shunjūsha, 1980, III: 1–74.

———, *Shōbōgenzō no seiritsu-shiteki no kenkyū*. Tokyo: Shunjūsha, 1986.

———, "Dōgen to *Shōbōgenzō*: Jūnikanbon to wa nanika," in Nara Yasuaki, ed., *Budda kara Dōgen e*. Tokyo: Tōkyō shoseki, 1992, pp.229–237.

Kawamura Kōdō and Rikizan Ishikawa, eds., *Dōgen*. Tokyo: Yoshikawa kōbunkan, 1985.

Kieschnick, John, *The Impact of Buddhism on Chinese Material Culture*. Princeton, N.J.: Princeton University Press, 2003.

Kim, Hee Jin, *Dōgen Kigen—Mystical Realist*. Tucson: University of Arizona Press, 1975.

———, " 'The Reason of Words and Letters': Dōgen and Kōan Language," in William R. LaFleur, ed., *Dōgen Studies*. Honolulu: Kuroda Institute, University of Hawaii Press, 1985, pp. 54–82.

———, "Review of Dōgen's *Manual of Zen Meditation* by Carl Bielefeldt," *Eastern Buddhist* 23/1 (1990): 141–146.

King, Sallie B., *Buddha Nature*. Albany, N.Y.: SUNY Press, 1991.

Kodera, Takashi James, "Ta hui Tsung-Kao (1089–1163) and His 'Introspecting the Kung-An Ch'an (Kōan Zen),' " *Ohio Journal of Religious Studies* 6/1 (1978).

———, "The Buddha Nature in Dōgen's *Shōbōgenzō*," *Japanese Journal of Religious Studies* 4/4 (1977): 267–298.

———, *Dogen's Formative Years in China*. Boulder, Col.: Prajña Press, 1980.

Kopf, Gereon, *Beyond Personal Identity: Dōgen, Nishida and a Phenomenlogy of No-Self*. Richmond, Surrey: Curzon Press, 2001.

Kosaka Kiyū, "*Eihei shingi*," in Kagamishima Genryū and Tamaki Kōshirō, eds., *Dōgen no chōsaku*, 7 vols. Tokyo: Shunjūsha, 1980, III: 119–166.

Kraft, Kenneth, ed., *Zen Tradition and Transition: A Sourcebook by Contemporary Zen Masters and Scholars*. New York: Grove Press, 1988.

———, *Eloquent Zen: Daitō*. Honolulu: University of Hawaii Press, 1993.

Kumamoto Hidehito, "Gekika sareta Dōgen," *Komazawa Daigaku bukkyōgakubu ron-shū* 34 (2003): 187–192.

————, "Shūgaku no ima: *Shōbōgenzō* no yomikata o megutte," *Shūgaku kenkyū* 38 (1996): 309–313.

Kurebayashi Kōdō, *Dōgen Zen no honryū*. Tokyo: Daihōrinkaku, 1978.

Kuroda Toshio, *Nihon chūsei no shakai to shūkyō*. Tokyo: Iwanami shoten, 1990.

LaFleur, William, *The Karma of Words: Buddhism and the Literary Arts in Medieval Japan*. Berkeley: University of California Press, 1983.

————, ed. *Dōgen Studies*. Honolulu: Kuroda Institute, University of Hawaii Press, 1985.

Little, Stephen, with Shawn Eichman, ed., *Taoism and the Arts of China*. Chicago: Art Institute of Chicago, 2000.

Los Angeles Times, "Zen and the Art of Modernity," May 21, 1993.

Maraldo, John, "Is There Historical Consciousness Within Ch'an?" *Japanese Journal of Religious Studies* 12/2–3 (1985): 141–172.

Masutani Fumio, *Rinzai to Dōgen*. Tokyo: Shunjūsha, 1971.

Matsumoto Shirō, *Engi to kū: Nyoraizō shisō hihan*. Tokyo: Daizō shuppan, 1989.

————, "Jinshin inga ni tsuite: Dōgen no shisō ni kansuru shaken," in Kagamishima Genryū and Suzuki Kakuzen, eds., *Jūnikanbon* Shōbōgenzō *no shomondai* Tokyo: Daizō shuppan, 1991, pp. 199–247.

————, *Zen shisō no hihanteki kenkyū*. Tokyo: Daizō shuppan, 1995.

————, *Chibetto Bukkyō tetsugaku*. Tokyo: Daizō shuppan, 1997.

————, *Dōgen shisōron*. Tokyo: Daizō shuppan, 2000.

————, *Hōnen Shinran shishō ron*. Tokyo: Daizō shuppan, 2001.

Matsunaga, Alicia, *The Buddhist Philosophy of Assimilation: The Historical Development of the* Honji-Suijaku *Theory*. Tokyo: Sophia University Press, 1969.

Matsunaga, Daigan, and Alicia Matsunaga, *Foundation of Japanese Buddhism*, 2 vols. Los Angeles: Buddhist Books International, 1976.

Matsuo Kenji. *Shin Kamakura Bukkyō no tanjō*. Tokyo: Kōdansha gendai shinsho, 1995.

————, "What Is Kamakura New Buddhism? Official Monks and Reclusive Monks," *Japanese Journal of Religious Studies* 14/1–2 (1997): 179–189.

Matsuoka Yukako, *Kobutsu Dōgen no shii*. Kyoto: Kokusai zengaku kenkyūjō, 1995.

————, *Shōbōgenzō* "Jūnikanbon no gendaiteki igi: Hakamya Noriaki *Dōgen to Bukkyō* hihan," *Zen bunka kenkyūjō kiyō* 22 (1996): 89–148.

McRae, John R., *The Northern School and the Formation of Early Ch'an Buddhism*. Honolulu: University of Hawaii Press, 1986.

————, "Shen-hui and the Teaching of Sudden Enlightenment in Early Ch'an Buddhism," in Peter N. Gregory, ed., *Sudden and Gradual: Approaches to Enlightenment in Chinese Thought*. Honolulu: University of Hawaii Press, 1987.

————, "Encounter Dialogue and the Transformation of the Spiritual Path in Chinese Ch'an," in Robert N. Buswell, Jr. and Robert M Gimello, eds., *Paths to Liberation: The Mārga and Its Transformations in Buddhist Thought*. Honolulu: University of Hawaii Press, 1991.

————, "Yanagida Seizan's Landmark Works on Chinese Ch'an," *Bilingual Journal of the Ecole Française d'Extrême-Orient* 7 (1993–1994): 51–103.

————, *Seeing Through Zen: Encounter, Transformation, and Genealogy in Chinese Chan Buddhism*. Berkeley, Calif.: University of California Press, 2003.

Miner, Earl, *An Introduction to Japanese Court Poetry*. Stanford, Calif.: Stanford University Press, 1968.

Mizuno Yaoko, "Kohon *Shōbōgenzō* no naiyō to sono sōgo kankei: Rokujūnikanbon *Shōbōgenzō* no seikaku o saguru tame ni," *Shūgaku kenkyū* 15 (1973): 68–73.

———, *Hōkyōki* to Jūnikan *Shōbōgenzō*: toku ni 'Jinshin inga' kan ni tsuite," *Shūgaku kenkyū* 21 (1979): 27–30.

———, "*Hōkyōki*," in Kagamishima Genryū and Tamaki Kōshirō, eds., *Dōgen no chosaku*, 7 vols. Tokyo: Shunjūsha, 1980, III: 217–240.

———, *Jūnikanbon Shōbōgenzō no sekai*. Tokyo: Daizō shuppan, 1994.

Miura, Isshū, and Ruth F. Sasaki, *The Zen Kōan*. New York: Harcourt Brace Jovanovich, 1965.

———, *Zen Dust: The History of the Kōan Study in Rinzai (Lin-chi) Zen*. New York: Houghton Mifflin, 1966.

Mizushima Hajime. *Shosetsu Dōgen*. Tokyo: Tōyō shuppan, 2002.

Momose Meiji and Sugita Hiroaki, *Dōgen zenji o aruku*. Tokyo: Tokyo Shinbunsha, 1999.

Morrell, Robert E., *Early Kamakura Buddhism: A Minority Report*. Berkeley, Calif.: Asian Humanities Press, 1987.

———, *Sand and Pebbles* (Shasekishū): *The Tales of Mujū Ichien, A Voice for Pluralism in Kamakura Buddhism*. Albany, N.Y.: SUNY Press, 1985.

Nakamura Hajime, *Shin Bukkyō jiten*. Tokyo: Seishin shobō, 1979.

Nakamura, Kyoko Motomochi, trans., *Miraculous Stories from the Japanese Buddhist Tradition: The Nihon Ryōiki of the Monk Kyōkai*. Cambridge, Mass.: Harvard University Press, 1973.

Nakano Tōzen, *Dōgen nyūmon: Makoto no buppō o motometa tamashii no kiseki*. Tokyo: Sanmāku shuppan, 2001.

Nakao Ryōshin, *Mumonkan zenseki zenbon kochū shūsei*. Tokyo: Meicho fukyūkai, 1983.

Nakaseko Shōdō, *Dōgen zenji den kenkyū*. Tokyo: Kokusho kankōkai, 1979.

———, *Dōgen zenji den kenkyū-sei*. Tokyo: Kokusho kankōkai, 1997.

———, "*Shōbōgenzō* 'Busshō' kan no rokushushōchi to Minamoto no Sanetomo no shari nōkotsu mondai ni tsuite." *Dōgen zenji kenkyū ronshū*. Daihonzan Eiheiji, ed. Tokyo: Taishūkan shoten, 2002, pp. 518–537.

Nara Yasuaki, ed., *Budda kara Dōgen e*. Tokyo: Tōkyō shoseki, 1992.

———, *Anata dake no Shūshōgi*. Tokyo: Shōgakkan, 2001.

Ogata, Sohaku, trans., *The Transmission of the Lamp: Early Masters*. Wolfeboro, N.H.: Longwood Academic, 1988.

Ōgawa Kōkan, *Chūgoku nyoraizō shisō kenkyū*. Tokyo: Nakayama shobō, 1976.

Ohnuki-Tierney, Emiko, *Monkey as Mirror: Symbolic Transformations in Japanese History and Ritual*. Princeton, N.J.: Princeton University Press, 1987.

Ōkubo Dōshū, *Dōgen zenji den no kenkyū*. Tokyo: Chikuma shobō, 1966.

Okumura, Shohaku, trans. and ed., *Dōgen Zen*. Kyoto: Kyoto Sōtō Zen Center, 1988.

———, "The Bodhisattva Precepts in Sōtō Zen Buddhism," *Dharma Eye* 13 (2004): 1–3.

Okumura, Shohaku, and Thomas Wright, trans., *Opening the Hand of Thought*. New York: Arkana, 1994.

O'Leary, Joseph S., "The Hermeneutics of Critical Buddhism," *The Eastern Buddhist* 38 (1998): 278–294.

Payne, Richard, ed., *Re-Visioning Kamakura Buddhism*. Honolulu: Kuroda Institute, University of Hawaii Press, 1986.

Polo, Marco, *The Travels*, trans. R.E. Latham. New York: Penguin, 1958.

Pollack, David, *Zen Poems of the Five Mountains*. New York: Crossroads, 1985.

————, *The Fracture of Meaning: Japan's Synthesis of China from the Eighth Through the Eighteenth Centuries*. Princeton, N.J.: Princeton University Press, 1986.

Prebish, Charles S., *Buddhist Monastic Discipline: The Sanskrit Prātimoksha Sūtras of the Mahāsāmghikas and Mūlasarvāstivādins*. University Park: Pennsylvania State University Press, 1975.

————, "Text and Tradition in the Study of Buddhist Ethics," *Pacific World* 9 (1993): 49–68.

————, "Varying the Vinaya: Creative Responses to Modernity," in Steven Heine and Charles S. Prebish, eds., *Buddhism in the Modern World: Adaptations of an Ancient Tradition*. New York: Oxford University Press, 2003, pp. 45–73.

Putney, David, "Some Problems in Interpretation: The Early and Late Writings of Dōgen," *Philosophy East and West* 46 (1996): 497–531.

Riggs, David. "The Rekindling of a Tradition: Menzan Zuihō and the Reform of Japanese Sōtō Zen in the Tokugawa Era." Ph.D. Dissertation, University of California at Los Angeles (2002).

————, "Life of Menzan," *Japan Review* 16 (2004): 67–100.

Said, Edward, *Orientalism*. New York: Vintage, 1978.

Sakaguchi Rei, "Zazen and the Art of Playwriting," *The Japan Times*, March 20, 2002; http://www.japantimes.co.jp/cgi-bin/getarticle.pl5?ft20020320a1.htm.

Sakai Ōtake, ed., *Dōgen zenji eden*. Tokyo: Yūgen gaisha Bukkyō kikaku, 1984.

Sakai Tokugen, "Eihei kōroku," in Kagamishima Genryū and Tamaki Kōshirō, eds., *Dōgen no chosaku*, 7 vols. Tokyo: Shunjūsha, 1980, III: 75–118.

Sasaki Kaoru, *Chūsei kokka no shūkyō kōzō: Taisei Bukkyō to taiseigai Bukkyō no sokoku*. Chūseishi kenkyū sensho. Tokyo: Yoshikawa kōbunkan, 1988.

Satō Shūkō, "Dōgen zaisōchū no sangaku kōtei ni kansuru shomondai (jō)," *Komazawa Daigaku Zen no kenkyūjō nenpō* 6 (1996): 93–121.

————, "Dōgen zaisōchū no sangaku kōtei ni kansuru shomondai (jō)," *Komazawa Daigaku Zen no kenkyūjō nenpō* 8 (1998): 73–97.

Satō Shunkō, "Hakusan shinkō to Sōtōshū kyōdan shi," 20 parts, *Sanshō* 556–575 (1990–1991).

Satō Tetsugen, *Chūgoku Bukkyō ni okeru karitsu no kenkyū*. Tokyo: Mokujisha, 1986.

Satomi Ton, *Dōgen zenji no hanashi*. Tokyo: Iwanami bunko, 2000.

Sawaki Kōdō, *Dōgen Zen sankyū*. Tokyo: Chikuma shobō, 1976.

Schlutter, Morten, "Silent Illumination, Kung-an Introspection, and the Competition for Lay Patronage in Sung Dynasty Ch'an," in Peter N. Gregory and Daniel A. Getz, eds., *Buddhism in the Sung*. Honolulu: University of Hawaii Press, 1999, pp. 109–147.

————, "Vinaya Monasteries, Public Abbacies, and State Control of Buddhism under the Song (960–1279)," in William M. Bodiford, ed., *Going Forth: Visions of Buddhist Vinaya*, Honolulu: University of Hawaii Press, 2005, pp. 136–160.

Schweitzer, Albert, *The Quest of the Historical Jesus*, ed. John Bowden. Minneapolis: Fortress Press, 1906, rpt. 2001.

Sekiryō Mokudo, ed., *Gendaigoyaku Kenzeiki zue*. Tokyo: Kokusho inkōkai, 2001.

Sheng, Yen. "On the Temporal and Spatial Adaptability of the Bodhisattva Precepts, with Reference to the Three Cumulative Pure Precepts," in Charles Wei-hsun Fu and Sandra A. Wawrytko, eds., *Buddhist Behavioral Codes and the Modern World*, Westport, Conn.: Greenwood Press, 1994, pp. 3–52.

Shibata Dōken, *Dōgen no kotoba*. Tokyo: Yuzankaku shuppan, 1978.

Shibayama, Zenkei, *Zen Comments on the Mumonkan*. New York: Mentor, 1973.

Spence, Jonathan, *The Chan's Great Continent: China in the Western Mind*. New York: Norton, 1998.

Steineck, Christian, *Leib und Herz bei Dōgen: Kommentierte Übersetzungen und theoretische Rekonstruktion*. Bonn: Academia Verlag, 2003.

Stambaugh, Joan, *Impermanence is Buddha-Nature: Dōgen's Understanding of Temporality*. Honolulu: University of Hawaii Press, 1990.

Steinhardt, Nancy Shatzman, *Chinese Imperial City Planning*. Honolulu: University of Hawaii Press, 1990.

———, ed., *Chinese Architecture*. New Haven, Conn.: Yale University Press, 2002.

Stone, Jacqueline I., "Some Reflections on Critical Buddhism" [Review Article on Hubbard and Swanson 1997], *Japanese Journal of Religious Studies* 26 (1999): 159–188.

———, *Original Enlightenment and the Transformation of Medieval Japanese Buddhism*. Honolulu: University of Hawaii Press, 1999.

Sueki, Fumihiko, *Nihon Bukkyō shisōshi ronkō*. Tokyo: Daizō shuppan, 1993.

———, "Two Seemingly Contradictory Aspects of the Teaching of Innate Enlightenment (*Hongaku*) in Medieval Japan," *Japan Journal of Religious Studies* 22/1–2 (1995): 3–16.

———, "A Reexamination of the *Kenmitsu Taisei* Theory," *Japanese Journal of Religious Studies* 23 (1996): 449–466.

Sugio Gen'yū, "Nanajūgokanbon *Shōbōgenzō* no kihonteki kōsatsu," in Kurebayashi Kōdō, ed., *Dōgen Zen no shisōteki kenkyū*. Tokyo: Shunjūsha, 1973, pp. 545–570.

———, "Dōgen zenji no jiko-tōdatsu no go-shōgai to *Shōbōgenzō* no shinka: Jūnikanbon ni yotte 'Iippyaku-kan' o omou," *Shūgaku kenkyū* 27 (1985): 7–12.

———, "Minamoto Sanetomo no nyōsō kikaku to Dōgen zenji," *Shūgaku kenkyū* 8 (1976): 41–46.

Suzuki Taizan, *Sōtōshū no chiikiteki tenkai*. Tokyo: Sōbunkan shuppan, 1993.

Suzuki Tetsuyū, "Sozanbon *Eihei kōroku* dai yonban jōdō go ni kansuru kenkyū," in Daihonzan Eiheiji, ed., *Dōgen zenji kenkyū ronshū*. Tokyo: Taishūkan shoten, 2002, pp. 768–769.

Swanson, Paul L., " 'Zen Is Not Buddhism'—Recent Japanese Critiques of Buddha-Nature," *Numen* 40 (1989): 115–149.

Taga Yoshiko. *Eisai*. Tokyo: Yoshikawa kōbunkan, 1965.

Ta-hui, *Daie sho*, ed. Araki Kengo. Tokyo: Chikuma shobō, 1969.

———, *Swampland Flowers, Letters and Lectures of Zen Master Ta-hui*, trans. Christopher Cleary. New York: Grove Press, 1977.

Taira Masayuki, *Nihon chūsei no shakai to Bukkyō*. Tokyo: Hanawa shobō, 1992.

Tajima Ikudō, "Sahen dōshi no hanasu—ibunka inyū no ippōbō toshite no *Shōbōgenzō* no hyōgen no ittokuchō," in Daihonzan Eiheiji, ed., *Dōgen zenji kenkyū ronshū*. Tokyo: Taishūkan shoten, 2002, pp. 807–830.

Takao Giken, *Sōdai Bukkyō shi no kenkyū*. Tokyo: Hyakugaen, 1973.

Takeuchi Michio, *Dōgen*. Tokyo: Yoshikawa kōbunkan, 1992.

Tamura Yoshirō, *Kamakura shin-Bukkyō shisō no kenkyū*. Kyoto: Heirakuji shoten, 1965.

———, "Critique of Original Awakening Thought in Shōshin and Dōgen," *Japanese Journal of Religious Studies* 11 (1984): 243–266.

Tanabe, George J., Jr., and Willa Tanabe, *The Lotus Sutra in Japanese Culture*. Honolulu: University of Hawaii Press, 1989.

Tao-yüan, ed., *Ching-te chuan-teng lu*, in *Taishō shinshū daizōkyō*, vol. 51, pp. 196–467.

Tatematsu Wahei, *Dōgen no tsuki*. Tokyo: Shodensha, 2002.

Taylor, Mark C., *Erring: A Postmodern A-Theology*. Chicago: Chicago University Press, 1984.

Terada Tōru, *Dōgen*, Nihon no Zen goroku, vol. 2. Tokyo: Kōdansha, 1981.

Tsunoda Tairyū, "Jūnikanbon *Shōbōgenzō* no kenkyū dōkō," in Kagamishima Genryū and Suzuki Kakuzen, eds., *Jūnikanbon Shōbōgenzō no shomondai*. Tokyo: Daizō shuppan, 1991, pp. 458–472.

———, "*Kana Shōbōgenzō* to *Mana Shōbōgenzō*," *Komazawa Daigaku bukkyōgakubu ronshū* 24 (1993): 143–60.

———, " 'Hihan shūgaku' hihan," *Komazawa Tanki Daigaku kenkyū kiyō* 26 (1998): 133–44.

———, "Shūgaku saikō," *Komazawa Tanki Daigaku kenkyū kiyō* 27 (1999): 73–102.

———, "Kai to so sō no genjō to taigen," in Tada Kōbun and Sueki Fumihiko, eds., *Gendai kaisō*. Tokyo: Bukkyō taimusu sha, 2004.

Ui Hakuju, *Zenshūshi kenkyū*. Tokyo: Iwanami shoten, 1935.

Victoria, Brian A., *Zen at War*. Tokyo: Weatherhill, 1998.

———, *Zen War Stories*. London: RoutledgeCurzon, 2002.

Waddell, Norman, and Masao Abe, trans., *The Heart of Dōgen's Shōbōgenzō*. Albany: State University of New York Press, 2002.

Watson, Burton, trans., *The Complete Works of Chuang Tzu*. New York: Columbia University Press, 1968.

Welter, Albert, *The Meaning of Myriad Good Deeds: A Study of Yung-ming Yen-shou and the Wan-shan t'ung-kuei chi*. New York: Peter Lang, 1993.

———, "Zanning and Chan: The Changing Nature of Buddhism in Early Song China," *Journal of Chinese Religions* 23 (1995): 105–140.

———, "Zen Buddhism as the Ideology of the Japanese State: Eisai and the *Kōzen Gokokuron*," in Steven Heine and Dale S. Wright, eds., *Zen Classics: Formative Texts in the History of Zen Buddhism*. New York: Oxford University Press, 2006, pp. 65–112.

Williams, Duncan Ryūken, *The Other Side of Zen: A Social History of Sōtō Zen Buddhism in Tokugawa Japan*. Princeton, N.J.: Princeton University Press, 2005.

Williams, Yoko, *Tsumi: Offence and Retribution in Early Japan*. London: Routledge-Curzon, 2003.

Wood, Frances, *Did Marco Polo Go to China?* Boulder, Col.: Westview, 1986.

Wright, Arthur F., *Buddhism in Chinese History*. Stanford, Calif.: Stanford University Press, 1959.

———, *Studies in Chinese Buddhism*, ed. Robert M. Somers. New Haven, Conn.: Yale University Press, 1990.

Yamaoka Takaaki, "Daiyūzan Saijōji ni okeru Bukkyōteki fukugō ni tsuite," *Shūgaku kenkyū* 25 (1983): 115–136.

Yamauchi Shun'yū, *Dōgen Zen to Tendai hongaku hōmon*. Tokyo: Daizō shuppan, 1986.

Yampolsky, Philip B., trans., *The Platform Sutra of the Sixth Patriarch: The Text of the Tun Huang Manuscript*. New York: Columbia University Press, 1967.

———, "The Development of Japanese Zen," in Kenneth L. Kraft, ed., *Zen Tradition and Transition: A Sourcebook by Contemporary Zen Masters and Scholars* (New York: Grove Press, 1988), pp. 140–156.

Yanagida Seizan, *Shoki zenshū shisho no kenkyū*. Kyoto: Hōzōkan, 1967.

———, "The Life of Lin-chi I-hsüan," *Eastern Buddhist* 5/2 (1972): 70–94.

———, *Zen no yuige*. Tokyo: Chōbunsha, 1973.

———, ed., *Sōdōshū*. Kyoto: Chūbun shuppansha, 1974.

———, *Zengaku goroku II*. Tokyo: Chikuma shobō, 1974.

———, "Dōgen to Rinzai," *Risō* 513 (1976): 74–89.

———, " 'The Recorded Sayings' Texts of Chinese Ch'an Buddhism," in Whalen Lai and Lewis R. Lancaster, eds., *Early Ch'an in China and Tibet*. Berkeley, Calif.: Berkeley Buddhist Studies Series, 1983.

———, "Dōgen to Chūgoku Bukkyō," *Zen bunka kenkyūjo kiyō* 13 (1984): 7–128.

———, "Goroku no rekishi: Zen bunken no seiritsu shiteki kenkyū," *Tōhō gakkō* 57 (1985): 211–663.

Yifa, *The Origins of Buddhist Monastic Codes in China: An Annotated Translation and Study of the Chanyuan Qinggui*. Honolulu: University of Hawaii Press, 2002.

Yokoi, Yūhō, *Gendaigoyaku Eihei kōroku*. Tokyo: Sankibō busshorin, 1978.

Yoshitani Hiroya, *Hakusan-Isurugi shūgen no shūkyō minzokugakuteki kenkyū*. Tokyo: Iwata shoin, 1994.

Yoshizu Yoshihide, *"En" no shakaigaku*. Tokyo: Bijitsu sensho, 1987.

———, "Hijiri no ningen-kan to mondō ni yoru satori," in Nara Yasuaki, ed., *Budda kara Dōgen e*. Tokyo: Tōkyō shoseki, 1992, pp. 131–142.

———, *Yasashisa no Bukkyō*. Tokyo: Shunjūsha, 1998.

———, "Shūshi no gaku o megutte," *Shūgaku to gendai* 3 (2000): 1–32.

———, "Dōgen no shisōshiteki ichizuke," *Shūgaku to gendai* 3 (2000): 33–60.

———, "Gendai Nihon Bukkyō no kiki to shūgaku," *Shūgaku to gendai* 3 (2000): 61–92.

Yuan Chi, ed., "Xu chuan deng lu" (Later Record of the Transmission of the Lamp). 14th century. In Taishō, vol. 51/2077: 579.

Index